Getting a Life

Getting a Life

Everyday Uses
of Autobiography

Sidonie Smith and Julia Watson, Editors

 University of Minnesota Press
Minneapolis
London

Grateful acknowledgment is made for permission to reproduce lyrics from Paul Simon, "All Around the World or the Myth of Fingerprints," copyright 1986 Paul Simon, used by permission of the publisher.

Chapter 6 first appeared as "TV Talk Shows as Therapeutic Discourse: The Ideological Labor of the Televised Talking Cure," *Communication Theory* 5 (1995), reprinted by permission of Guilford Press; chapter 9 first appeared in *Signs* 18:2 (Winter 1993), copyright 1993 by the University of Chicago, all rights reserved.

Published by the University of Minnesota Press
111 Third Avenue South, Suite 290, Minneapolis, MN 55401-2520
Printed in the United States of America on acid-free paper

Library of Congress Cataloging-in-Publication Data

Getting a life : everyday use of autobiography / Sidonie Smith and
    Julia Watson, editors.
        p.   cm.
    Includes bibliographical references and index.
    ISBN 0-8166-2489-5 (hc). — ISBN 0-8166-2490-9 (pb)
    1. Autobiography. 2. Biography as literary form. I. Smith, Sidonie. II. Watson,
Julia.
CT25.G48 1996
818'.50809492—dc20   95-37293

The University of Minnesota is an
equal-opportunity educator and employer.

To our families and friends, who help
compose our everyday lives

Contents

Acknowledgments

Both of us have been interested in the everyday uses of autobiography for a long time, but the commitment to this project gained momentum as we completed our earlier collection, *De/Colonizing the Subject: The Politics of Gender in Women's Autobiography.* For us, collaboration has been mutually sustaining and creatively generative, as our individual strengths seem to be complementary. In joining together several years ago, we couldn't have imagined that we were getting a life as collaborators and friends. With this collection we continue our work together and turn our focus to an area of autobiography studies that has only recently and unsystematically been tapped as a productive venue for cultural critique.

Various encounters helped us transform what was originally just a response to a trendy 1980s phrase—Get a life!—into the pointed yet heterogeneous engagement with everyday practices that we believe this collection represents. Papers submitted for the session on the everyday uses of autobiography at the Modern Language Association's convention in 1992 enabled us to connect with scholars around the country. We found that people in a wide range of disciplines were thinking eclectically about the intersection of postmodern understandings of subjectivity with the varied and sometimes very personal ways in which we are asked to assemble some kinds of life stories in different everyday situations. Our students during the past two years helped us extend and elaborate the reach of everyday constructions of subjects.

We want to acknowledge the opportunity provided each of us by the Fulbright Program to spend time abroad as senior scholars—a year in Senegal in one case, six months in Australia in the other. For both of us, the extended stay in another country sharpened, as it rendered unfamiliar, everyday life in the United States. The vast distances imposed by travel also required that we learn to negotiate the information highway and to circulate within a new kind of scholarly network. We could not have continued to work uninterruptedly and complete this project rapidly without the everyday wonders of e-mail. Our progress was, as ever, technologically and materially supported by our universities, including a summer grant from the University of Montana Faculty Development Fund.

Then there are the many individuals who contributed to the life of this project. Lee Quinby, Caren Kaplan, Françoise Lionnet, and Elayne Rapping, as well as anonymous readers of an early version of the collection, provided probing but enthusiastic readings that helped us sharpen our focus, refine our introductory remarks, and intensify our outreach to potential contributors in broadening the range of essays. William L. Andrews and Biodun Iginla were supportive believers from the moment we began to formulate the book's concept.

We also want to thank our contributors, without whom this collection could not have gotten a life.

And, as always, we acknowledge the support of our families, whose everyday lives fill and enrich our own.

Introduction

Sidonie Smith and Julia Watson

Social life multiplies the gestures and modes of behavior *(im)printed*
by narrative models; it ceasely [*sic*] reproduces and accumulates
"copies" of stories. Our society has become a recited society, in
three senses: it is defined by *stories* (*récits,* the fables constituted by
our advertising and informational media), by *citations* of stories,
and by the interminable *recitation* of stories.

MICHEL DE CERTEAU, The Practice of Everyday Life[1]

[Identity] is found in all the properties—and property—with which
individuals and groups surround themselves, houses, furniture,
paintings, books, cars, spirits, cigarettes, perfume, clothes, and in the
practices with? which they manifest their distinction, sports, games,
entertainments, only because it is in the synthetic unity of the habitus, the unifying generative principle of all practices. Taste, the
propensity and capacity to appropriate (materially or symbolically)
a given class of classified, classifying objects or practices, is the generative formula of a life-style.

PIERRE BOURDIEU, Distinction[2]

The opacity of the everyday, then, is crucial. It reflects the poststruc-
tural recognition that all anyone can do is gesture to the real; subjects can not experience it unmediated and untransformed by expectation, by representation, or by their own attention to it. In resisting
definition, the everyday becomes a category that foregrounds those
mediations and, in that sense, becomes a position or marker rather
than a stable referent.

LAURIE LANGBAUER,
"Cultural Studies and the Politics of the Everyday"[3]

Reciting Postmodern Lives

In a recent column for the *New York Times,* William Safire, exploring, as is his wont, language usage in the contemporary United States, discussed a glib and sometimes dismissive phrase from the 1980s and early 1990s, "Get a life." "Get a life" functions as a corrective to someone's excessive complaining, or their failure to extract themselves from repetitive takes on the world, or their self-absorbed preoccupations. In effect, it is simultaneously an indictment of the interlocutor's everyday life, a testimony of the speaker's belief in a realizable agenda for change, and a self-validating gesture.[4] After all, in their use of the phrase speakers imply that they know what a viable life is and that they have gotten one.

The casualness of the directive suggests that there is a broader cultural phenomenon that charges the phrase with its potent, if flip, meanings. Not only do autobiographical narratives permeate capitalism's marketplace, in our time they overflow our everyday life. On a daily basis we all act as if we're getting a life.

Americans are, to invoke the epigraph above from Michel de Certeau, a "recited" community in all three senses of his term. We are habitual authenticators of our own lives.[5] Every day we are confessing and constructing personal narratives in every possible format: on the body, on the air, in music, in print, on video, at meetings.

Political candidates work up compelling personal narratives that project "character" and "values." Some, like Ross Perot, rely on them.

Daytime television talk shows spill over with confessional obsessions.

In every community the formulaic confessions of participants in self-help groups fill the halls of churches and the meeting rooms of numerous communal buildings.

Rock singers chant the lyrics of self-promotion.

People don identity clothing in the morning to signify status, origin, occupation, political consciousness, availability.

Family members assemble stories through family albums.

Some respond to queries about their medical histories.

Others fill out innumerable forms for social service benefits.

Many advertise their desires in personal ads.

If we are not telling our stories, we are consuming other people's lives. Consuming personal narratives on an everyday basis, we imbibe the heterogeneous "lives" authorized by and authenticated in the institutions through which we negotiate daily existence. Media, for instance, offer a dazzling display of possible lives through daytime television, the movies, and the news. The news frames its selected fragments of autobiographies of political candidates that are shaped by the institutions of official politics as permissible life stories.

Through our consuming habits we circulate our own personal narratives, even by the cars we drive, the beverages we drink, and the furnishings with which we surround ourselves, as Bourdieu has observed. By wearing particular items, by wearing them in particular ways, or by making a pastiche of recognizable identity gear, we telegraph "probable" autobiographical stories. We make icons of ourselves through identification with consumer lines that constitute ready-made, wholesale identities. Women, men, children, grandparents, environmental activists elect recognizable identities and circulate the probable histories they suggest. *In postmodern America we are culturally obsessed with getting a life—and not just getting it, but sharing it with and advertising it to others. We are, as well, obsessed with consuming the lives that other people have gotten.* The lives we consume are translated through our own lives into story. Getting a life is a necessary negotiation in the everyday practice of American culture/s.[6]

A word of clarification: the term *postmodern* here is used not to define a set of aesthetic practices and effects as distinct from modernist practices and effects (as implied in the term *cultural postmodernism*) or to define a set of practices to be deployed in what Nelly Richard terms "a critical rereading of modernity"[7] (although such strategies of critique are deployed in the essays in this collection). Rather, we use it to acknowledge what Inderpal Grewal and Caren Kaplan term "the historical situation of postmodernity."[8] This historical situation is characterized by the global reach of late commodity capitalism, the widespread bureaucratization of all aspects of corporate life, the shift to electronic communications networks that are altering notions of time and space, the condition of "cultural asymmetries,"[9] and the interrogation of received concepts of a universal, rational, and autonomous humanist self.

"America" and Me

They live it and I see it and I hear it. They repeat it and I hear it and
I see it, sometimes then always I understand it, sometime then always there is a completed history of each one by it, sometime then I
will tell the completed history of each one by it, sometime then I
will tell the completed history of each one as by repeating it I come
to know it.

Every one always is repeating the whole of them.

GERTRUDE STEIN, *The Making of Americans*[10]

All profound changes in consciousness, by their very nature, bring
with them characteristic amnesias. Out of such oblivions, in specific
historical circumstances, spring narratives. . . . Out of this estrange-
ment comes a conception of personhood, *identity* . . . which, because it can not be "remembered," must be narrated. Against biology's demonstration that every single cell in a human body is
replaced over seven years, the narratives of autobiography and biography flood print-capitalism's markets year by year.

BENEDICT ANDERSON, *Imagined Communities*[11]

Autobiographical narratives, their citation, and their recitation have
historically been one means through which the imagined community
that was and is America constitutes itself on a daily basis as American.[12] As one potent means of testimony through which identities are
constituted and critiqued, autobiographical storytelling has played a
major role in the making of Americans and the making, unmaking,
and remaking of "America." For several centuries, America has been a
desirable destination for certain groups of people, a promising place
where people have come to get a new life, to re/form and to remake
themselves as social subjects "free" of a variety of constraints they experienced in the cultures and locations they left behind. For some people the promise proved a dismal disappointment. For many it proved a
problematic achievement for themselves even as it proved a palpable if
complex achievement for their children. For others, however, the journey was a radical rupture of unmaking. For African slaves, transporta-
tion to the New World brought diasporan dispersal and a long, arduous, and violent struggle for inclusion in the American promise. And
for the peoples who inhabited the American landscape before settlement, the making of America and Americans was tantamount to cultural, even literal, genocide.

America became a nation as those preconditions Benedict Anderson has identified as prerequisites of the imagining of nation and national identity in the West coalesced:

the proliferation of print capitalism's reproductions of vernacular texts;

the new notion of time as a vacuum to be filled with evolutionary history;

the Enlightenment concept of the universal human subject; and

the imagination of a social community constituted of individuals who do not know one another, live far from one another, but are joined in an imagined society.[13]

All of these conditions also characterize the imagining of "autobiographical" lives as possessions of "individuals" and of individual lives as "representative" of a community of lives. Autobiographical storytelling, therefore, functioned personally and publicly in related but distinct ways. The private and unique individual proclaimed representative status through a life worthy of inspection, summation, and print. But the very gesture of proclamation became one means by which national mythologies produced the conformity of individuals to new notions of identity and normative concepts of national subjectivity. Writing autobiography testified to arrival in "America" and the achievement of an "American" identity.[14]

Yet if autobiographical storytelling has functioned as a means to assert identification with the idea of "America" and what it means to be an "American" subject, it has also exposed what Donald Pease calls the "postnational" and what we would call the "unnational" subject.[15] Think, for instance, of Crèvecoeur's celebration of the American character as a moral enlightenment universally accessible to those who immigrated.[16] This very articulation of the "American" character also exposed a set of differences between such a subject and all its self-constituting others. That exposure opened a gap between the ideology of subjectivity assigned the new Republican subject and the cultural erasure of those assigned nonsubject or noncitizen status, including, early on, the African slave, the Native American, the white woman, the white man of no property, the child.[17] For such persons, autobiographical narrative provided an opportunity to negotiate their complex positioning within and without the corporate sphere.

Autobiographical discourse continues, to a considerable extent, to be a palpable means through which Americans know themselves to be American and not-American in all the complexities and contradictions of that identity. Its forms, both those officially endorsed and those at times sought by individuals apparently as subversive personal versions, are means to align the privatized consciousness with identities credited in the public sphere and to glimpse and critique the misidentifications of that alignment. Some of those narratives get identified as "high cultural achievements" and subsequently are canonized in educational curricula as "the best" or "most representative" or "most American." Others, the more popular or "low" forms, such as the plethora of narratives by the rich and variously famous and infamous, circulate through lending libraries, publishers' lists, and book-of-the-month clubs, providing everyday "dreams," everyday eavesdroppings.[18] Personal histories—in all their varieties—serve as individualized testimonies to getting a "successful" life together (however success is defined) and/or to the failure of self-remaking in terms of the dream.

Modern Subjects and Bad Faith in "Democracy"

Another side of the deficiency of general historical life is that individual life as yet has no history. The pseudo-events which rush by in spectacular dramatizations have not been lived by those informed of them. . . . what is really lived has no relation to the official irreversible time of society and is in direct opposition to the pseudo-cyclical rhythm of the consumable by-product of this time. This individual experience of separate daily life remains without language, without concept, without critical access to its own past which has been recorded nowhere. It is not communicated. It is not understood and is forgotten to the profit of the false spectacular memory of the unmemorable.

GUY DEBORD, *Society of the Spectacle*[19]

This brief history characterizes several centuries of "modern" narrative in America, particularly as it has contributed to the formation of an idea of "American" character. But the obsessive desire to create and authenticate individual identity characteristic of our times is a peculiar preoccupation at this historical moment, for our "postmodern" culture everywhere offers evidence of two contradictory dispositions: on the one hand, modern democratic culture continues to privilege individuality and the sovereignty of a human subject with certain inalienable rights; on the other, many who share this modern culture profoundly distrust traditional autobiography, one of the narrative forms through which the West sustains its romance with individualism and promotes a universal, representative subject.

The paradox of radical individualism haunts late-twentieth-century "America." We mistrust it, yet want to believe in it. Democracy as a political ideal is one that even ardent postmodernists finally confess to admiring, whether romantically or radically. Yet the paradoxes of the "American character" and of bourgeois individualism require us to ask questions that strike at the heart of democratic individualism:

What does the right to privacy mean in a world of fragmented and dispersed subjects?

What does it mean to insist on a culture of individuals whose very individuality must be authenticated again and again?

What kind of autobiographical subjects are produced and verified in a culture that commodifies self-authentication?

How does commodification operate at a time when the bases of authentication seem unstable?

How do we account for the simultaneous promise and corrosion of identity and identity politics? For the promise of subject formation and the disillusion of deformation?

How can we account for the obsessive desire to find a "true" self in the midst of a culture that fetishizes what we might call touristic identities, throwaways?

Michel de Certeau argues that we are members of "a society in which the disappearance of subjects is everywhere compensated for and camouflaged by the multiplication of the tasks to be performed."[20] We might paraphrase his remark by suggesting that *we are a postmodern society in which the disappearance of an unproblematic belief in the idea of true selves is everywhere compensated for and camouflaged by the multiplication of recitations of autobiographical stories.* As social relations undergo major realignment, as indigenous communalisms contest the notion of a corporate "We the People," as bureaucracies gather and organize information about an increasing proportion of our lives, as telecommunications networks broadcast ready-made identities, *this telling and consuming of autobiographical stories, this announcing, performing, composing of identity becomes a defining condition of postmodernity in America.*

Because of this intimate relationship of America with the remaking of lives, with a proliferation of heterogeneous autobiographical narratives, with, that is, the romance of democratic individualism, we want to look more closely at the ways in which people in America today negotiate everyday lives through the recitation of everyday "lives."

Composing and Decomposing

An executive of one of the major phone companies was asked by Representative Ed Markey, a Massachusetts Democrat who chaired the Telecommunications Subcommittee of the U.S. House of Representatives, how the phone industry protects customers' records. In answering Markey's question, the executive quoted a statute that "expressly permits [us] to disclose phone records to anyone other than the government without legal process." Then he commented: "However, [we] respect customer privacy."[21] As pieces of our stories are regularly and anonymously dispersed to the files and archives of various institutions, we may feel less confident about both our privacy and "their" protection.

Decentralization and dispersion of autobiographical subjects attends the bureaucratization of life stories in postmodern culture/s. Our personal histories are

dismembered into zeroes and ones;
passed through electrons;
stored on microchips;
channeled throughout the local community, the nation, even the world;
printed out on paper; and
stored in file drawers.

And they are there for the taking by a host of unknown entities, including computers and their hackers.

Such fragments of our personal narratives become bits and bytes of a proliferating number of data banks. Each data bank parcels out pieces of our personal histories, converts them to different forms, aligns various subsets of fragments into different "stories" or recitations. Consider the languages of the "profile": the medical history, the work history, the credit history, the educational history, the testing history, the psychological profile. All these profiles provide various occasions and versions of our story/ies. As a consequence, a profile becomes a form of otherness; the collection and dispersal of the profile, a form of othering. *Collecting autobiographical data is, perversely, a central instrument in the othering machinery of modern technological culture.*

The Myth of Fingerprints and Imposed Systems

There's no doubt about it
It was the myth of fingerprints
I've seen them all and man
They're all the same.
PAUL SIMON, "All Around the World or
        the Myth of Fingerprints"[22]

The notion of essence, character, structure, is, one might argue, so-cial. . . . expression in the main is not instinctive but socially learned and socially patterned; it is a socially defined category which employs a particular expression, and a socially established schedule which determines when these expressions will occur. . . . We are so-cialized to confirm our own hypotheses about our natures.
            ERVING GOFFMAN, *Gender Advertisements*[23]

The myth of autobiography is
    that the story is singularly formative,
    that the gesture is coherent and monologic,
    that the subject is articulate and the story articulable, and
    that the narrative lies there waiting to be spoken.

But autobiographical storytelling, and by this we mean broadly the practices through which people assemble narratives out of their own experiential histories, cannot escape being dialogical, although its central myths resist that recognition. Autobiography is contextually marked, collaboratively mediated, provisional. Acknowledging the dialogical nature of autobiographical telling, we confront the ways in which autobiographical telling is implicated in the microbial operations of power in contemporary everyday life.

In telling their stories, narrators take up models of identity that are culturally available. And by adopting ready-made narrative templates to structure experiential history, they take up culturally designated subjectivities. Their recitations of personal narrative thereby attest to and verify their participation in corporate culture. Becoming a social subject paradoxically sustains the articulation of the "private" individual in our time, when all forms of privacy are so extensively mediated. In getting a life, then, whose life are we getting?

Everyday autobiographical practices are enmeshed in the technologies of selfhood dispersed across a heterogeneous field of institutional locations, all with their own pressures to regulate subjects through reforming them—in both senses of the word—in specific ways.[24] There are state-sponsored bureaucracies designed to manage people and facilitate their movement through state institutions. There are numerous nonstate organizations, such as churches and self-help groups, hospitals and talk shows, that provide localized sites through which certain kinds of subjects are recognized and misrecognized. There are the intimate spaces of the family and of sexual exchange. On a daily basis individuals move into, through, and out of these disparate social spaces, and participate in specific, yet different, narrative practices through which we become subjects in and of our stories.

Recitations of our personal narratives, that is, are embedded in specific organizational settings and in the midst of specific institutional routines or operations:

Religious confession goes to church.
Psychological trauma goes to the counselor's office or the analyst's couch.
Social victimization and economic impoverishment go to social service agencies.
Medical history goes to the hospital.
Political oppression goes to the immigration bureau.

But in taking our stories into various venues, we enter what de Certeau terms an "imposed system." Each location manages a specific piece of our lives and calls for specific kinds of personal recitations.

The hospital manages health and illness.
The immigration bureau manages the selection and orderly entry of immigrants into the country.
Religious organizations designate the saved and manage the orderly pursuit of spiritual health.
The classified section of the newspaper manages the telescoping of salable information to the customer.
A therapeutic community such as Alcoholics Anonymous manages the (re)habilitation of an alcohol-free body.

Only certain kinds of stories need be told in each narrative locale. *Only certain kinds of stories become intelligible as they fit the managed framework, the imposed system. The recitation is, in effect, prepackaged, prerecited.* In this way, the institution writes the personal profile, so to speak, before the person enacts and experiences it as "personal."

It is a familiar fact of contemporary life that institutions—as opposed to specific individuals working in the institutions—are less concerned with persons who enter their locales than with their own inerrant stability, with maintaining efficient performance of designated tasks. The institution can work efficiently only if it imposes structures of legible subjectivity, and that work can be done only on particular kinds of subjects. Institutional needs frame the specific "reading" of the disparate details and facts of the life recited by the subject; in so doing, they frame information selectively. The process works synecdochally, substituting the part for the whole and claiming that they are interchangeable. Those acting on behalf of the institution promote an official reading of the life to fit their institutional parameters. *Thus, in everyday life, autobiographical narratives are part of a frame-up.*

When we interact with these institutions we engage their already provided narratives of identity, their already mapped-out subject positions.

Men and women seeking divorce enter courts in which they have to create macronarratives of their marriages that are recognizable in terms of a particular state's codes of intelligibility. People will be represented differently if "irreconcilable differences" constitutes permissible grounds for divorce than if only "mental cruelty" is admissible.

Rape victims present their personal narratives of the body in specific ways before the law and the courts. Engagement in sexual conduct in the past may contaminate the profile of the ravished maiden necessary for vigorous prosecution.

People seeking social service benefits have to present themselves as victims. This requires arranging one's life history so as to appear impoverished enough to make a convincing appeal.

In these and other social situations people assume positions as actors within known scripts. Successful achievement of their goals and interests depends on the right alignment of many kinds of evidence, including that of the body itself. Erving Goffman elaborates this evidentiary nature of display (linguistic, bodily, gestural) when he writes that "displays . . . provide evidence of the actor's *alignment* in a gathering, the position he seems prepared to take up in what is about to happen in the social situation."[25] *Autobiographical narrative is one such performative display.*

These everyday occasions, and the practices attached to them, function as one form of "discipline" in the Foucauldian sense. They are among the many means by which models of acceptable identity are circulated and renewed in society, the many means by which subjects are conformed. Through them the state, the church, the school, the corporation, the government, the advertising industry secure normative subjects in acceptable social relationships. Such everyday practices also function to establish cultural conditions determining

> who can speak,
> what can be spoken,
> what narrative forms can be understood, and
> to whom personal narrative can be addressed.

By this means, everyday practices determine not only the spoken but the unspoken:

> what subject cannot speak,
> what part of a personal story cannot be spoken, and
> what kind of story cannot be understood or credited.

But we too participate in and represent various institutions. We too are advocates of known scripts, even as we are imbricated in them. In everyday life we negotiate the terms in which others will present their lives to us—be it as our students, employers, or, more complexly, our friends, families, and lovers. In this way we not only act out our alignment but solicit alignments as well.

Everyday Agents of Resistance

One of the rules of my game is to echo back his words to an unexpected din or simply let them bounce around to yield most of what is being and has been said through them and despite them.
TRINH T. MINH-HA, "The Language of Nativism"[26]

The more insidious and effective strategy, it seems, is a thorough-going appropriation and redeployment of the categories of identity themselves, not merely to contest "sex," but to articulate the convergence of multiple sexual discourses at the site of "identity" in order to render that category, in whatever form, permanently problematic.

JUDITH BUTLER, *Gender Trouble*[27]

The commodification of everyday life in late consumer capitalism may seem virtually total, but there are possibilities for agency in spite of the technologies of commodification elaborated above. The everyday uses of autobiography are not merely disciplining occasions through which pervasive manifestations of decentralized power operate to conform persons through imposed autobiographical narratives. In looking at the "ways of operating" that "constitute the innumerable practices by means of which users reappropriate the space organized by techniques of sociocultural production," de Certeau cautions that we must not attend only to "the microbe like operations proliferating within techno cratic structures and deflecting their functioning by means of a multitude of 'tactics' articulated in the details of everyday life," but also and critically to "the clandestine forms taken by the dispersed, tactical, and makeshift creativity of groups or individuals already caught in the nets of 'discipline.'"[28] The nets of "discipline" are unevenly distributed, the knowledges of subjects are generated in heterogeneous sites and productive of contradictory positions, and the tactics of resistance are regenerative.

In specific situations, people may choose not to narrate the stories that are prescribed for them. They may remain silent. Their refusal may be rooted in the stories' unspeakability. (Refusal may also have dire consequences: they may not receive the benefits they need; they may be punished, even executed.) Or they can tell narratives appropriate to one situation in another, thereby confounding the grounds of the credible (but risking dismissal as "confused" or "mad" or "naive"). They can invoke, or dissociate themselves from, the values of the institution prescribing their narratives. Or they can tell their stories so as to disrupt the normative relationship between story and speaker. They can narrate their prescribed lives "too well," with excessive earnestness or flamboyance, and disrupt or "camp up" the scene of narration.

The complexities of postmodern life require individuals to negotiate

multiple locations of identity on a daily basis. Such potentially disso-
nant negotiations undermine any complacent belief in consistent,
transparent, and noncontradictory subjects. And so it is important to
emphasize that the everyday occasions for autobiographical storytelling are multiple. The context of the autobiographical occasion
varies with the participant, the historical moment, the site, the others
participating in the dialogue, and the uses to which the life is being
put. That is,

> autobiographical occasions are not congruent;
> each is differently structured, differently mediated, differently ex-
> perienced;
> the lives they call for and forth are differently configured;
> in each context there are different forms of knowledges and of ig-
> norances put into play.[29]

On a daily basis, then, personal narrators assume the role of the
bricoleur *who takes up bits and pieces of the identities and narrative
forms available and, by disjoining and joining them in excessive ways,
creates a history of the subject at a precise point in time and space.*
Such tactics of autobiographical storytelling become one of the means
by which the narrating subject "constantly manipulate[s] events in
order to turn them into 'opportunities.'"[30] Through assembling autobiographical memories one more time, personal narrators can turn an
interpretation of and judgment about the past, however inflected by
previous knowledge, into a countermemory. That is, they can remake
their understanding of the "truth" of the past and reframe the present
by bringing it into a new alignment of meaning with the past.

In this way, autobiographical narrators become agents in and of the
story, momentarily and not uncontradictorily agents of their own ordering imperative. Seizing the occasion and telling the story turn
speakers into subjects of narrative who can exercise some control over
the meaning of their "lives." This assertion of agency is particularly
compelling for those whose personal histories include stories that have
been culturally unspeakable, for instance, histories of

> child abuse and spouse battering,
> interracial marriage,
> homosexuality,
> alcoholism,

mental illness, and
disability.

These have been among the unrecited narratives of American cul-
ture/s. The very conditions of their unrecitability sustain the citations
and recitations of privileged cultural narratives and privileged cultural
identities. In citing new, formerly unspeakable stories, narrators become cultural witnesses insisting on memory as agency in its power to
intervene in imposed systems of meaning. These witnesses also participate in the cultural work of reframing the meanings of the speakable,
of voicing the speakable differently.

Then, too, telling what was formerly unspeakable builds communal
identification. As Erving Goffman says of social situations generally:

> It is here in these small, local places that [people] can arrange
> themselves microecologically to depict what is taken as their place
> in the wider social frame, allowing them, in turn, to celebrate
> what has been depicted. It is here, in social situations, that the in-
> dividual can signify what he takes to be his social identity and
> here indicate his feelings and intent—all of which information the
> others in the gathering will need in order to manage their own
> courses of action—which knowledgeability he in turn must count
> on in carrying out his own designs.[31]

In everyday occasions autobiographical narrators move out of isolation and loneliness into a social context in which their stories resonate
with the stories of others in a group. And even if the story remains
unspeakable in the larger community, narrators can find ways to convey the unspeakable to a community of secret knowers. The narrative
can be coded, signaling certain meanings while masking others before
those not sharing the secret knowledge. Phrases or intonations or certain rhetorical gestures become veiled signals to other participants in
the unspeakable.

*Thus the everyday uses of autobiography can produce changes in
the subject, for narratives are generatively excessive as well as recon-
stitutive.* That is, narratives afford a means of intervention into postmodern life. Autobiographical subjects can facilitate changes in the
mapping of knowledge and ignorance, of what is speakable or unspeakable, disclosed or masked, alienating or communally bonding.
They can force changes in the story by moving into new arenas of self-
narrative—people immigrate, they join self-help groups, they ex-

change stories in peer counseling. In this way they attempt to "escape from older narratives to a new beginning."[32] In this way they create the past as "the undesirable other" in order to change the story.[33]

Yet new narratives can become confining and conforming with time. Individuals may experience a sense of exhilaration and empowerment in telling their new personal histories, in speaking the unspeakable; but exhilaration and empowerment are neither guaranteed by the telling of their life stories nor necessarily and reliably liberating. Storytelling occurs in a dialogical, social context. A person's efforts to make a gesture of tactical resistance to a stereotypic communal notion of the unspeakable can be co-opted and reordered into the community's normative patterns of speakability. We see this clearly in the case of self-help groups. If telling one's story is a way to exercise control over one's life, the people in self-help groups have to tell the same story again and again in order to get control over their loss of control. The narrative is reworked and performed—if not preformed—until the teller experiences healing. But participating in the collective autobiographical narrative of a self-help group, this "taking control," can be a way of capitulating to another's control of one's life. Thus the very institution of "self-help" can enforce the normative telling of life stories. Many institutions established to help people change their stories impose specific new stories. *The negotiation of everyday narratives is an ongoing process rather than a certain achievement.*

Autobiographical Stories and Backyard Ethnography

What illusion to believe that we can tell the truth, and to believe
that each of us has an individual and autonomous existence! How
can we think that in autobiography it is the lived life that produces
the text, when it is the text that produces the life!
        PHILIPPE LEJEUNE, "The Autobiographical Pact (bis)"[34]

Whether the story is ever one's own is a question that can perhaps no longer be posed in terms of individualism and ownership in a post-modern world where concepts of self are negotiated socially and dialogically. "Individualism" has been commodified; the personal contents of the "personal" have been largely evacuated. But owning the stories that shape us as subjects is a different, more political issue, and an act of collective consciousness informing newer notions of what is at stake in autobiography. As Jana Sawicki argues, certain practices are not inherently or universally complicitous or resisting. "Neither wholly a source of domination nor of resistance," she writes, "sexuality"—to which we would add autobiographical practice—"is also neither outside power nor wholly circumscribed by it. Instead, it is itself an arena of struggle. There are no inherently liberatory or repressive [narrative] practices, for any practice is co-optable and is capable of becoming a source of resistance."[35]

Of course, we are not autobiographical subjects at every moment of the day, but we are called on to become autobiographical subjects in a variety of situations, a range of temporalities. Thus we move in and out of autobiographical subjectivity, sometimes by our own desire and purposes, sometimes through the exertions and coercion of others. In presenting this collection of essays, we intend to explore the ways in which we move in and out of autobiographical subjectivity in daily ways. In so doing, we wish to contribute to what is currently called "backyard ethnography," the focus of which is on the everyday practices of autobiographical narrating in America rather than the "high culture" of published, "artful" autobiography. This collection articulates backyard ethnography through a variety of theoretical standpoints, among them those of cultural studies, feminist studies, and postmodern theory.

The "others" of the American "self" need to be examined in the mirror of our own habitual practices, those situations of self-presentation and composition that are largely unreflective but that structure our narratives of subjectivity. Not just in remote times and countries, recondite theories, or complex performances, but in our own collective backyard, attending to the "others" uncovers strategies and codes bracketed out in historical celebrations of "the American character."

The Essays

Waiting to be collected, published, and interpreted are unnumbered autobiographical texts created daily in the social, commercial, educational, religious, and therapeutic transactions of everyday life.
ALBERT E. STONE, "Modern American Autobiography"[36]

The sixteen studies gathered here trace the inscriptions and the practice of autobiographical subjectivity in everyday situations in postmodern American life. Rather than viewing the autobiographical production of identity as a solitary and introspective process of articulating individual difference, these essays read the production of identity as generated by encounters that are social, collaborative, contestatory. "Who" one is, is necessarily framed by interrogation of the institutional discourses that converge at a specific historical moment in the macroprocesses of shaping the lives we want to call "individual" in postmodern America.[37] And those institutions are multitudinous and overlapping, as formal as the law and as idiosyncratic as the family. The grouping of the essays emphasizes this, with five sections that frame sites or media where the negotiation of identity takes place. They move from the most direct experience of the body as a context of subjectivity through the social sites, mediations, and family-centered processes of ordering identity, to some macroinstitutional frames whose attempts to regulate the forms of identity may trigger subversion by resistant subjects.

We could as well have grouped the essays by kinds of institutions and institutional practices or kinds of texts produced—oral, visual, or written/narrated. It was impossible to include the multitudinous variety of situations in which identity is negotiated and conferred. We would have liked to include discussion of the way immigrants coming into the United States are required to shape their narratives of migration, and of the ways in which social service agencies elicit, shape, and silence certain narratives of destitution and neediness. We could have included discussions of bumper-sticker subjects, of identity clothing, of hair. Once we got started on this project, almost everything presented itself as implicated in the choosing, imposing, evading, or negotiating of an identity. Fingerprints are everywhere.

These essays, then, are linked by their scrutiny of contemporary American life in the 1990s, a heterogeneous location and locution for subjects very much in process. Part I, "Speaking Bodies," foregrounds the body as a primal, material site of identity. Linda S. Kauffman frames the terms of this discussion by considering how the reorganization of the senses in the late twentieth century has broken down old mind/body barriers. Focusing on the pornographic or pathological that has traditionally been excluded from high art, she traces how, by going inside the body and regarding identity materially, "bad girl" and "sick boy" artists of the body claim an anti-aesthetic erotics. They problematize the relationship between disease and desire by performing and photographing masochistic rituals that transform physical pain into sexual pleasure. Provocatively asking, Whose autobiography is voiced in the interpreter's presentation of the deaf subject's narrative? H-Dirksen L. Bauman examines the current revaluation of the deaf as a linguistic community with a desire for agency and a collaborative "voice" that speaks through their bodies, rather than being spoken for by others, including interpreters. Speaking ironically of herself as both the subject and the object of her investigation into the medicalized body, Kay K. Cook recounts the history of how the discovery of her "proliferative" uterus revised her view of what she had claimed as "my body" and engendered her deconstructive self-image in the pathologized medical images of mammography, ultrasonography, CAT scan, and bone scan.

Part II, "Entertaining Lives," examines a variety of media that produce identity—film, electronic mail, video, TV talk shows, newspaper want ads. The image of Arnold Schwarzenegger drives the narrative of Louise Krasniewicz and Michael Blitz's essay. Their convergence in e-mail exchanges is a morphing of identities that writes hybrid subjectivity in the lowercase "i" of an "autobiography in the dark." Salome Chasnoff directs our focus to the potential of autoethnography as a counterdiscourse through rewriting, in the case of young, poor teen mothers, the script of their status as pathological and parasitic. The Fantastic Moms demystify, through collaborative autobiography, the stereotypes of unwed mothers, both reflecting on and regenerating their own identity. Janice Peck probes how new-model talk shows encourage guests to take the "cure" of telling personal narratives to host, therapist, and national audience. The format has to be read as both repressive, in containing social tensions, and potentially liberatory, in airing unspeakable stories that admit of no easy social cure. In considering the autobiographical disclosure of the "personals" section of the want ads, Traci Carroll explores a semiotics of desire that exceeds fixed categories of gender and sexuality. In "Matches" identity is both articulated through the choice of particular sexual practice categories and unsatisfied by their categorical limits.

In Part III, "Un/Speakable Lives," negotiating the terms for speaking "unspeakable" life histories takes many forms. Philip E. Baruth argues that, in the age of AIDS, revealing personal sexual history is an unavoidably collaborative process between partners. Linda Martín Alcoff and Laura Gray-Rosendale call for a mode of survivor discourse that will activate the transgressive power of rage at violence and violation. Speech, they insist, is a crucial site of conflict when the subject constitutes herself not as confessing victim to be socially recuperated but as witness to suppressed transgression. Taking the limit case of the ec-centric autistic subject, Sidonie Smith provocatively asks if the established limits of coherent subjectivity inform or deform our notions of identity.

Part IV, "Family Portraits," examines how myths and realities of family identity inflect individual life narratives. Susan Ostrov Weisser examines how life storytellers construct "their" stories and are consumed by their interpreters. As a professional "listener" for a life narrative project, she contrasts the life text narrated by Mrs. F with both her family's and the group's rewriting of her narrative. In her study of transracial adoption, Sandra Patton considers how "race" is not a concept but a set of practices that produce social identity in everyday situations. Observing legal and social changes in adoption, she explores how the degree of white identification has affected the double consciousness of African Americans and notes the countermodels of adoptive identity that are being posed by critics of transracial adoption. Julia Watson argues that genealogy is a disciplinary practice for ordering family history. Centered on the "pedigree" that authenticates lineage, genealogy regulates and represses both autobiographical content and multiple narrators, thereby hypostatizing the family in everyday life.

In Part V, "Institutionalized Lives," the practices of three exemplary postmodern institutions—the recovery group, the academy, and the law—are examined as regulators of everyday life. Robyn R. Warhol and Helena Michie consider how, in the Twelve-Step programs of Alcoholics Anonymous, an alcoholic's life story is recuperated into its master narrative of abuse, enlightenment, and recovery. In its narrative practice, A.A. discourages a "unique" or deviant concept of individual identity and promotes the acquisition of its unified "recovering" identity. Martin A. Danahay contends that academics, in their curricula vitae, must "prepackage" themselves within a narrative that, unlike the résumé, mystifies skills and relationships and masks the labor-management relationship. By bureaucratizing educational life history, the C.V. produces a seamless chronology in which academics are anything but "free." The last word belongs to William Chaloupka, who provides a Foucauldian critique of how the modern state forms and monitors citizens through identity policing. The example of a subject detained in jail for refusing to give his name frames his act as an intervention into state surveillance. In this postmodern reversal of the terms of identity, those who "forget" a life are the anonymous who retain some disruptive potential.

This collection reads autobiographical acts in everyday occasions for rehearsing, performing, circulating, and consuming carefully fashioned and rapidly interspersed identity fragments. It examines not only how we intend to compose ourselves, but how in daily negotiations "we" and its "I's" are proposed, supposed, disposed. In conducting theoretical forays into everyday practices that structure subjectivity and designate the "individual," the essays in this collection inaugurate a new inquiry into autobiography—as a repository of imposed subjectivities but also as a means of resisting complicity in their operations. Speculating on "the myth of fingerprints," we offer templates of possible subjectivities. Finally, in examining how everyday life compels ordinary Americans to order themselves in myriad ways, we conduct a postmodern investigation into the mystique of autobiography. What and where is the "truth" of the autobiographical subject, and what is invested in maintaining that "truth"? How and to what effect do autobiographical subjects oscillate between the narratives that write them and those they reconfigure in their local and strategic interventions?

Constructed as social actors in multiple, overlapping communities, making and unmaking provisional identities, we are located as both subjects and witnesses—to our own proliferative and regulated identities, and to their internal dissonance. People may tell us to "get a life," but that is never simple.

Notes

1. Michel de Certeau, *The Practice of Everyday Life,* trans. Steven Rendall (Berkeley: University of California Press, 1984), 186.

2. Pierre Bourdieu, *Distinction: A Social Critique of the Judgement of Taste,* trans. Richard Nice (Cambridge: Harvard University Press, 1984), 173.

3. Laurie Langbauer, "Cultural Studies and the Politics of the Everyday," *diacritics* 22 (Spring 1992): 49.

4. Safire traces early media usage of the phrase to 1989 and speculates: "The expression originated as 'Get on with your life,' influenced by a comment like 'You call that a life?'" Safire suggests "Get a life" is a call to stop imitating celebrity lives or adopting social roles and to "get real," a bracing piece of "constructive" advice. William Safire, "Get a Life!" *New York Times Sunday Magazine,* May 16, 1993.

5. We use the terms *America* and *Americans* in this essay to refer to the United States of America and the citizens of that nation. We are aware of their contested usages and meanings. The historical construct *America* originally signified what was termed in Europe the *New World,* and what is now two continents of many countries. Although the continuing use of the term *America* by people who live in the United States may be seen as a gesture of cultural imperialism, the phrase *the United States of America* at every reference is awkward. We therefore follow the usage of American studies.

6. We are indebted to Laurie Langbauer's probing discussion of "the everyday" as a foundational category of cultural studies that is usefully problematized through feminist theory as "a site of irresolvable difference, of conflict whose resolution is not simply delayed, but theoretically impossible." See Langbauer, "Cultural Studies and the Politics of the Everyday," 48.

7. Nelly Richard, "Postmodernism and Periphery," *Third Text* 2 (Winter 1987/88): 11.

8. Inderpal Grewal and Caren Kaplan, "Transnational Feminist Practices and Questions of Postmodernity," in *Scattered Hegemonies: Postmodernity and Transnational Feminist Practices,* ed. Inderpal Grewal and Caren Kaplan (Minneapolis: University of Minnesota Press, 1994), 4.

9. Ibid., 3.

10. Gertrude Stein, *The Making of Americans* (1925), in *Selected Writings of Gertrude Stein* (New York: Random House, 1962), 267.

11. Benedict Anderson, *Imagined Communities,* rev. ed. (London: Verso, 1991), 204.

12. We are using this term in its broadest meaning, as a variety of practices through which people assemble narratives out of their own experiential histories. Other phrases that might be used to designate these practices are *autobiographical discourse, personal narrative,* and *life storytelling.* We have chosen to use the term *autobiographical narrative* at the same time we caution that the word *autobiography* has a specific "history of debatable origins, ambiguous parameters, and disputed subject matter" that has to do with the Western privileging of individuality and the concept of the universal, autonomous "self," as Caren Kaplan notes in "Resisting Autobiography: Out-Law Genres and Transnational Feminist Subjects," in *De/Colonizing the Subject: The Politics of Gender in Women's Autobiography,* ed. Sidonie Smith and Julia Watson (Minneapolis: University of Minnesota Press, 1992), 115–19.

13. Anderson, *Imagined Communities,* especially chaps. 2 and 3.

14. In his work William Boelhower interestingly discusses the Americanization of immigrants through their writing of autobiography. See, for example, "The Making of Ethnic Autobiography in the United States," in *American Autobiography: Retrospect and Prospect,* ed. Paul John Eakin (Madison: University of Wisconsin Press, 1991), 123–41. But, for an important challenge to Boelhower's thesis from the perspective of Asian immigrants in a multigenerational context, see, in the same volume, Sau-Ling Cynthia Wong, "Immigrant Autobiography: Some Questions of Definition and Approach," 142–70.

15. Donald Pease used this term in a fascinating analysis of the disruptive claim of the postnational subject in texts of the American Renaissance in a paper delivered at Binghamton University, October 1992.

16. In Michel-Guillaume-Jean de Crèvecoeur, Letter III ("What Is an American?"), in *Letters from an American Farmer,* in *Anthology of American Literature,* ed. George McMichael et al. (New York: Macmillan, 1985).

17. Toni Morrison persuasively argues for the construction of American identity around a central repressed darkness of racial difference: "What seemed to be on the 'mind' of the literature of the United States was the conscious but highly problematic con-

struction of the American as a new white man." *Playing in the Dark: Whiteness and the Literary Imagination* (New York: Random House, 1992), 39; see also chap. 2, passim.

18. This distinction between high and low forms derives from the binarism of high and low discourses explored by Peter Stallybrass and Allon White in *The Politics and Poetics of Transgression* (Ithaca, N.Y.: Cornell University Press, 1986), especially 3–5. Whereas their interest is in "the system of extremes which encoded the body, the social order, psychic form, and spatial location" (3) in the formation of modernity, our location of the everyday is in a postmodern New World Order that, although antithetical to the "high" discourses, is not debased and degraded, or assigned by class status to the peasantry, the urban poor, or the colonized. Discourses of the everyday pose a conglomerate view of history that contrasts with the "high" emphasis on the singular representative "man."

19. Guy Debord, *Society of the Spectacle* (1967), trans. Ken Sanborn (Detroit: Black and Red, 1983), unpaged.

20. De Certeau, *The Practice of Everyday Life,* 190–91.

21. Quoted in Wayne Biddle, "They've Got Your Number," *The Nation,* October 26, 1992, 467.

22. Paul Simon, "All Around the World or the Myth of Fingerprints," *Graceland* (New York: Paul Simon Music, 1987).

23. Erving Goffman, *Gender Advertisements* (New York: Harper & Row, 1976), 7.

24. The work of Michel Foucault on technologies of the self informs our discussion. See his "Technologies of the Self," in *Technologies of the Self: A Seminar with Michel Foucault,* ed. Luther H. Martin, Huck Gutman, and Patrick H. Hutton (Amherst: University of Massachusetts Press, 1988). Foucault distinguishes techniques by which individuals perform operations on their own bodies and minds with the goal of self-transformation (18). He argues that writing about oneself is not a recent but an ancient practice that developed a new attention to self-experience in the first and second centuries, and, with Marcus Aurelius, evolved a focus on personal experience of everyday life (28–29). The discussion of the significance of the emergence of confession in Foucault's *The History of Sexuality,* vol. 1, trans. Robert Hurley (New York: Vintage, 1980), has, of course, also informed our argument about the ability of the listener to exercise silent power over the speaker in autobiographical discourse.

25. Goffman, *Gender Advertisements,* 1.

26. Trinh T. Minh-ha, "The Language of Nativism," in *Woman, Native, Other: Writing Postcoloniality and Feminism* (Bloomington: Indiana University Press, 1989), 49.

27. Judith Butler, *Gender Trouble: Feminism and the Subversion of Identity* (New York: Routledge, 1990), 128.

28. De Certeau, *The Practice of Everyday Life,* xiv–xv. See also his description of a "tactic" (xiv).

29. See Eve Kosofsky Sedgwick, *Epistemology of the Closet* (Berkeley: University of California Press, 1990), especially chap. 1, for a discussion of the relationship of ignorances to knowledges.

30. De Certeau, *The Practice of Everyday Life,* xix.

31. Goffman, *Gender Advertisements,* 6.

32. Keya Ganguly, "Migrant Identities: Personal Memory and the Construction of Selfhood," *Cultural Studies* 6, no. 1 (1992): 37.

33. Ibid., 38.

34. Philippe Lejeune, "The Autobiographical Pact (bis)," in *On Autobiography,* ed. Paul John Eakin, trans. Katherine Leary (Minneapolis: University of Minnesota Press, 1989), 131.

35. Jana Sawicki, "Identity Politics and Sexual Freedom: Foucault and Feminism," in *Feminism and Foucault,* ed. Irene Diamond and Lee Quinby (Boston: Northeastern University Press, 1988), 185.

36. Albert E. Stone, "Modern American Autobiography," in *American Autobiography: Retrospect and Prospect,* ed. Paul John Eakin (Madison: University of Wisconsin Press, 1991), 114.

37. Consider the claim by James "Bo" Gritz, leader of the "Almost Heaven" Christian Covenant Community established near Kamiah, Idaho, that he is an "Identity Christian" seeking others "just like you" who *know* the centrality of their Christian identity (by which he means the region's whites but not its original Nez Percé inhabitants). *Missoulian,* May 25, 1994, B-3.

Part I

Speaking Bodies

Far from the body having to be effaced, what is needed is to make it visible through an analysis in which the biological and the historical are not consecutive to one another, as in the evolutionism of the first scientists, but are bound together in an increasingly complex fashion in accordance with the development of the modern technologies of power that take life as their objective.

MICHEL FOUCAULT, *The History of Sexuality,* vol. 1, trans. Robert Hurley (New York: Random House, 1978), 152.

1 / Bad Girls and Sick Boys: Inside the Body in Fiction, Film, and Performance Art

Linda S. Kauffman

In memoriam Bob Flanagan
December 26, 1952–January 4, 1996

Reorganizing the Sensorium

Despite the emphasis on the *body* in contemporary criticism, we still do not quite realize how utterly the human *senses* have been transformed in the late twentieth century.[1] Instead, critical theorists look backward to a particular body (like the Venus Hottentot) or period (like the eighteenth century) or institution (like the prison). But we in the humanities will have to learn some very hard neurobiology, genetics, optical processing, and even artificial intelligence if we are to grasp fully how profoundly the senses have been reorganized and how completely that reorganization has transformed artistic practices. Following the information revolution of the 1970s, successive generations of computer visualizations in the 1990s have profoundly altered what and how we see the body and perceive of the senses: in medicine, for instance, CAT scans, PET scans, and MRI technology are notable developments that, along with ultrasound, allow doctors to probe non-invasively, but publicly, formerly private regions and recesses.[2]

These innovations challenge society's most cherished assumptions about the body's integrity and rectitude and raise scores of questions: What is perversion? What is pathology? What is pornographic and/or obscene? Traditionally, *obscenity* and *pornography* were not synonymous, but the U.S. Supreme Court has blurred the distinctions in recent years. In *Miller v. California* (1973), the legal prosecution of

27

pornography depended on (1) "whether the average person, applying contemporary community standards, would find that the work, taken as a whole, appeals to the prurient interest"; (2) "whether the work depicts or describes in a patently offensive way, sexual conduct specifically defined by the applicable state law"; and (3) "whether the work, taken as a whole, lacks serious literary, artistic, political or scientific value."[3]

The Greek *pornographos* means "the writing of, on, about, or even for harlots"; by extension, it signifies the life, manners, and customs of prostitutes and their patrons. Not just scenes of sex, in other words, but descriptions of everyday life. Given that *obscenity*'s etymology includes the meaning "that which takes place offstage," or "off to the side," the very fact that these imaging techniques are visible *on*stage suggests a paradigm shift in the making. Technology may thus eventually do more than politics to render the pornography debate obsolete. Stewart Brand notes:

> Marshall McLuhan used to remark "Gutenberg made everybody a reader. Xerox made everybody a publisher." Personal computers are making everybody an author. . . . If, as alleged, the only real freedom of the press is to own one, the fullest realization of the First Amendment is being accomplished by technology, not politics.[4]

I do not mean to imply, however, that technology will *solve* all the problems in the porn debate, for it in turn will create new ones. Indeed, this potentially progressive paradigm shift may be offset by other rearguard actions, such as the legal shift away from criminality and toward a viewpoint of harm, which is the foundation for the antiporn ordinances drafted by Andrea Dworkin and Catharine MacKinnon. For the first time in history, censorship is being presented as necessary to advance civil rights.[5]

The production, distribution, and consumption of pornography have also been profoundly transformed by technology: the nineteenth-century Victorian gentleman's "secret museum" of photographs gave way to early silent films; technology's desire to create moving images exerted enormous influence on the emerging *scientia sexualis*, as Linda Williams has shown.[6] In the early days of cinema, similarly, porno films were reserved for wealthy clientele in brothels, as Gertrud Koch notes:

The language of our age of visual culture, in which the active sub-
jugating eye wins out over the passive receptive sense organs, such
as the ears, finds an apt metaphor in the recent divorce of cinema
from brothel, pornography from prostitution. . . . It may be that
over the history of pornographic cinema the films themselves have
not changed so much as the organization of the senses.[7]

Since the advent of cinema, the technological advance that has had
the most impact on the consumption of pornography is of course the
VCR. Many antiporn activists assume that porn is for men, its objects
are women. But of the estimated 100 million rentals of X-rated videos
every year, 40 percent of the consumers are now women. Can we simply dismiss all these women as victims of false consciousness? Or does
the figure reflect the fact that it is still women who do the shopping?[8]

One of the main objections to porn is that it objectifies women, but
as my examples will show, the processes of gender identification are
far more complicated than that, especially when pornography and
horror intersect. These two genres are particularly important for three
reasons. First, they are the only film genres besides melodrama (aptly
dubbed "the weepies") that actually produce physical arousal (porn
arouses sexually, horror arouses fear and revulsion). Second, technological advances in special effects now make it possible for spectators
actually to see the body's insides "opened up" in films, as, for example, in David Cronenberg's *Naked Lunch, Dead Ringers, Scanners,*
and *Videodrome.*[9] Third, pornography is driven by the "frenzy of the
visible"—the desire to make visible what is *in*visible: female pleasure
and desire in general, female orgasm specifically.[10] Porn and horror explore explicitly what legitimate films explore from a distance, as Carol
Clover observes: "Pornography . . . engages directly (in pleasurable
terms) what horror explores at one remove (in painful terms) and legitimate film at two or more. . . . Pornography . . . has to do with sex
(the act) and horror with gender."[11]

Clover's thesis has been enormously influential, but the artists I will
discuss in this essay problematize it. Instead, in them, pornography
and horror, sex and gender intercept each other. Figure 1.1 is an illustration from J. G. Ballard's *The Atrocity Exhibition.*[12] Does it depict
porn or horror? Sex or gender? If it is about *sex,* is the act pleasurable
or painful? If it is about *gender,* is it about the female fear of penetra-
tion or the male fear of castration? To women, it is a typical image of

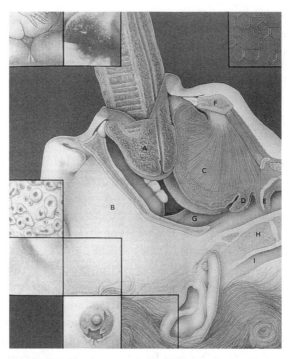

Figure 1.1. J. G. Ballard, *The Atrocity Exhibition*, illustration by Phoebe Gloeckner, p. 55.

male sexual violence, but to men, it poses an equal threat. It is precisely this unsettled, oscillating perspective that Ballard exploits by anatomizing it and the sexual dynamic. It is like those reversible figures that force you to see the image of either a black cat or a white rabbit, rather than a blend of both, and the perceptions may flip back and forth. *The Atrocity Exhibition* is a phenomenological map of the cultural psyche; pornography and horror are two of its major coordinates. The illustration is also significant because, although considerable work has been done on the appeal of *fantasy,* especially in film studies, far more needs to be done specifically on *anxiety*—a point to which I will return.

J. G. Ballard's anatomy of our reorganized sensorium stresses our profound disorientation and the vicissitudes of psychic life. He is acutely aware of technology's coercive as well as creative capacities. He charts this terrain without nostalgia for some lost prelapsarian world of plenitude. Just as Freud said of Dora that the most they could hope for was to reduce her hysterical misery to the common unhappiness, Ballard says that "the best we can hope for . . . is the attainment of a moral and just psychopathology." Morbidity is his medium and his message: "I feel we should immerse ourselves in the most destructive element, ourselves, and swim."[13] Such an insight casts recent theoretical work on everyday life in a new, unsettling light, for Ballard's thesis is that "the human organism is an atrocity exhibition; he is an unwilling spectator."[14]

What does it mean to see the human as an "organism"? To see that organism as an "atrocity"? To see that atrocity as an "exhibition"— on display like an artifact in a museum? And finally, what does it mean to contextualize such queries within "everyday life"? These are the questions the "bad girls and sick boys" in my essay ask. The present moment has been dubbed "the Post-Age," variously signifying poststructuralist, postmodernist, postfeminist, post-Marxist, postindustrial. As we learned from the postimpressionists, the prefix *post* usually signifies uncertainty about what lies beyond—an anxiety that is particularly acute as we approach the end of the century, the end of the millennium. The "posthuman" world is all around us, "hidden in plain sight." Several art exhibitions have recently highlighted this world: filmmaker Peter Greenaway (*Prospero's Books*; *The Cook, the Thief, His Wife & Her Lover*) curated *The Physical Self* in Rotterdam in 1991–92, which featured live humans in plexiglass cases, as well as other "artifacts."[15] Similarly, Jeffrey Deitch's *Posthuman* exhibition catalog notes: "A new construction of the self will take hold as ever more powerful body-altering techniques become commonplace."[16] Those techniques include plastic surgery, body sculpting, medical imaging techniques, organ transplants, and psychopharmacology. Pacemakers, prosthetics, plastic surgery, and Prozac are signs of the posthuman, not to mention gene therapy and in vitro fertilization. Sex reassignment surgery has produced a whole population of "transgendered people," who have collectively come to be called the "last sex" or the "third sex."[17]

Only by taking the long view of humans as a species—by having a geological view of time and a galactic view of space—is it possible to perceive that the era of the posthuman is already upon us. The point is not only that the human is an organism, but that the organism is *exhibited*—on display in an art museum or gallery, or in the medical amphitheater. The exhibitionistic qualities must also be stressed. To define the human as an "atrocity exhibition" suggests a new paradigm of spectatorship, one that is generated from or driven by the *insides of the body*, one in which the human body is staged as spectacle. That is the anti-aesthetic being developed by the "bad girls" discussed below.

The Bad Girls' Anti-Aesthetic

I call these performers "bad girls" in honor of Margo St. James, former head of the hookers' union in San Francisco, who says cheerfully, "I like being a 'bad girl.'" Her goal is to reclaim the word *whore* the way lesbians have reclaimed the word *dyke*.[18] Like Margo, a number of these "bad girls" have actually worked in the sex industry: Kathy Acker; Sheree Rose; lesbian stripper Fanny Fatale, also known as Debi Sundahl, who with Susie Bright published *On Our Backs;* Pepper, the Mexican sex goddess; Elvis Herselvis; Maria Beatty; and Annie Sprinkle. Some of these women consciously strive to break through the barriers dividing High Theory from "low" practice. Alycee Lane, publisher of a sex magazine for black lesbians, writes her own column on theory, culture, and society. Annie Sprinkle performed in 150 porno films before Franklin Furnace organized the *Second Coming,* a month-long exhibition and performance series in 1984, which had as one of its goals an attempt to develop a "feminist pornography."

What might a feminist pornography look like? I want to describe, not prescribe, for women have suffered long enough from prescriptions about how they should feel, respond, react to sexual materials. The first characteristic: feminist pornography is an anti-aesthetic. Although the anti-aesthetic is now usually seen as synonomous with postmodernism, it has ancient generic roots, dating back to Minneppean satire, which has been illuminated in contemporary criticism by Bakhtin's theories of the carnivalesque. (Sprinkle's 1984 performance was part of a month-long series called *Carnival Knowledge.*) This anti-aesthetic substitutes the lower carnal body for the upper regions of intellect; it substitutes the ugly, the perverse, the antiromantic for the True, the Good, and the Beautiful. Like the genre of romance, porn is a timeless and fabulous world: the men are always erect, the women always insatiable. But pornography parts ways with romance where love is concerned. Indeed, in my view, one of the *virtues* of porn is that it is antiromantic. Since I have spent the past decade writing about the damaging ideology of romantic love, in texts ranging from Ovid to *The Handmaid's Tale,* I predict—and sincerely hope—that what is called "the redemptive sex project" of Catharine MacKinnon and

Andrea Dworkin will fail.[19] Given that women are the ones who have been most enslaved by the ideology of romantic love, they may have the most to gain by endorsing an anti-aesthetic that defies it.

Many feminist artists seem to agree. In fiction, Kathy Acker parodies the bad *boy* tradition, drawing on Bataille, Genet, Pasolini, and William Burroughs. But there are other less well known feminist writers who combine erotic lyricism with astonishing portraits of sado-masochism in everyday life: Ricci Ducornet's *Entering Fire* is a Manichean dialogue between a lusty life-affirming father and a deformed son who becomes the prototypical fascist. Rebecca Brown's inter-related lesbian stories, *The Terrible Girls,* are rife with images of mutilation and dismemberment that make slasher films look like Mother Goose. Performers like Carmelita Tropicana show that cross-dressing applies to ethnicity as well as to gender, and Monica Palacios, who bills herself as a "Latin Lezbo comic," has developed a collaborative performance piece called "Deep in the Crotch of My Latino Psyche." More familiar to mainstream audiences are Diamanda Galas, Carolee Schneemann, Lydia Lunch, Holly Hughes, Wanda Coleman, Karen Finley, Linda Montano, Valie Export. Export's theory of "feminist actionism" disintegrates the body as pure nature, dematerializing it in order to unmask its historical codings.[20] These women stage the body as a carrier of signs or as a cipher.

One of the remarkable effects of this shift in focus to the insides of the body is that we have to completely rethink—yet again—the notion of "the male gaze." What does it mean to propose ordinances against "*in*human images" in a world increasingly dominated by the *post*human? Some bad girl performance artists are showing how the anti-aesthetic has been affected by interventions of science and technology. Susie Bright's *Sexual Reality,* for instance, treats readers to a sampler of computer-age erotic technologies with scandalous good humor.[21] Soon, she and Howard Rheingold predict, we will all be having sex by climbing into bodysuits that will simulate the feel of any object and material from satin to skin, then plugging into a phone network to connect with others wearing similar body stockings; we will then proceed with "erotic interfacing."[22] I had such developments in mind when I suggested earlier that technology may eventually make the pornography debate obsolete: maybe we had to wait for virtual reality before the discourses of public policy finally understood what a simulacrum is and how representation functions. But even Susie Bright overlooks one of virtual reality's most stellar virtues: just as the computer has dissolved the text as the property of the author, because of virtual reality, one can no longer define sex as the sacred *property* of individuals.[23] Ann Lasko-Harvill sees virtual reality as a new art form, one in which body parts are infinitely interchangeable: "As with African or pre-Columbian masks, there is virtually no limit either to the fragmentation, derangement, or extensibility of the features."[24] Virtual reality drives home the absurdity of trying to legislate fantasy, because the "virtual" world is by definition a simulation. Virtual reality may thus accomplish in one felt glovestroke what has taken theorists a century to dismantle: realism's stranglehold on representation. Virtual reality drives the final nail in the coffin of realism.

Some feminists fear that the body will disappear altogether under the onslaught of such technology. But what many "bad girls" are doing is making female desire, sexuality, and the body *substantial*—tangible, material, in-your-face—sometimes literally and sometimes with a vengeance. They stage their own bodies as sites of contestation through parody, defamiliarization, or incongruous juxtaposition. They challenge you to respond to the inside as well as the outside of the female body. That's why Annie Sprinkle invites audiences to view her cervix, using a speculum and a flashlight.

When I saw Annie Sprinkle perform this routine in Santa Monica, the entire audience lined up for a look! Although I fretted that we would be there all night if everybody had a look, I had to admit that here was something most people, women as well as men, had never seen before—something that was for the gynecologist's eyes only. Sprinkle is a droll and bawdy satirist who consciously evokes the legacy of Sophie Tucker, Mae West, and female burlesque—a form a number of feminist performers have reaccentuated.[25] But it is herself—rather than some exotic species—that she is scrutinizing, often using the earnest deadpan voice of an eighth-grade science teacher. At the same time, she manages to convey something of the nasty tone of children playing doctor—a theme my "sick boy" also picks up on. When Sprinkle performed in Cleveland, the vice squad came and made her omit the speculum in her next show.

What is the vice squad afraid people might see? Barbara Kruger gives you a glimpse. The small writing in her work *Heart* (Figure 1.2) asks, "Do I have to give up me to be loved by you?" Kruger forces us

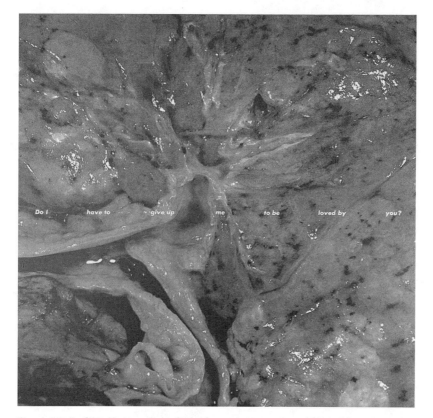

Figure 1.2. Barbara Kruger, *Heart (Do I have to give up me to be loved by you?)*, 1988.

to ask what the notion of identity in general and the word "me" in particular really signify, as well as what love is, thus leading back to my earlier point about what women stand to gain by endorsing an anti-aesthetic that critiques the ideology of romantic love. Kruger's motto: "Seduce, then intercept."[26]

Sadomedicine: What about Bob?

That motto serves Bob Flanagan too, for he seduces us into responding in conventional ways, then intercepts those responses and forces us to confront them. Bob Flanagan is a white, male, heterosexual forty-two-year-old poet, writer, and performance artist. He is also one of the old-est living survivors of cystic fibrosis—a disease that affects the glands and makes breathing and digestion treacherously difficult. It usually kills those afflicted before they reach the age of thirty. Flanagan is also a masochist.

Visiting Hours is a site-specific art installation Bob designed in collaboration with Sheree Rose, his dominatrix and companion. The show traveled to the New Museum in New York in the fall of 1994. *Visiting Hours* transforms the art museum into a pediatric clinic where Flanagan is the resident patient. He actually *moves into* the museum. As a result, he deconstructs the cherished concept of the *human* by staging the elemental, alimental body. He simultaneously deconstructs the concept of the *museum*, irrevocably transforming the pristine, inviolate art space with the messy debris of everyday life, sex, and illness: hospital bed, intravenous tubes, bedpans, trays of food, and the ubiquitous oxygen tank nearby. Bob is a live model of the posthuman, for he illustrates step by step how the human senses—taste, touch, smell, hearing, and sight—have been utterly reorganized by medical technology. We tend to think of the five senses as eternally unchangeable, but they are historically determined. *P*rehistory perhaps marked the most radical evolution, as Freud points out, for humans sacrificed the sense of smell in order to walk upright.[27] Microscope, oscilloscope, speculum, X ray not only altered what we see but how we perceive the human body. Despite such dazzling scientific breakthroughs as the Human Genome Project and cystic fibrosis research, however, such discoveries come too late to save Bob's life.

I have not chosen to bring Bob to your attention just to present "News of the Weird." My primary focus here is not on the discourse of *rights* but on *rites*, for Flanagan fuses medicine with sadomasochistic rituals to problematize the relationships between the social and the psychic, between disease and desire. His work dramatizes the phenomenal differences between theorists' (Baudrillard, Deleuze, Guattari) celebration of "the body without organs" and the excruciating material realities involved in actually living without such organs as, in Bob's case, healthy lungs.

The sterile medical environment is itself a "perverse implantation," pervaded by dominance and submission, voyeurism and exhibitionism. Medicine and pornography have always had a lot in common: both are analytic activities whose main aim is to isolate objects or events from their contexts in time and space. By exposing the latent sexual significance of such environments, Bob seems to fulfill a prediction J. G. Ballard has made:

Bizarre experiments are now a commonplace of scientific research, moving ever closer to that junction where science and pornography will eventually meet and fuse. Conceivably, the day will come when science is itself the greatest producer of pornography. The weird perversions of human behavior triggered by psychologists testing the effects of pain, isolation, anger, etc. will play the same role that the bare breasts of Polynesian islanders performed in the 1940s wildlife documentary films.[28]

As if to confirm Ballard's prophecy, Bob Flanagan is featured in a forthcoming photo-essay not in a porno magazine or even an art magazine, but in *National Geographic,* which is devoting an issue to the phenomenology of pain.

On the literal level, Bob explains that his way of dealing with his disease has been to transform physical pain into sexual pleasure. On the psychoanalytic level, *Visiting Hours* explores the function of fantasy. Fantasy is a unique concept in psychoanalysis in that it refers to a psychic process that is both conscious and unconscious, and that juxtaposes the social and the psychic. *Visiting Hours* evokes a scene the spectator has visited long before (in the womb? in the cradle? in dreams?), but its latent content becomes manifest only when restaged, as with the primal scene in the psychoanalytic session. The writing on the toy chest confirms this. Note its fairy-tale, fable quality:

> Mine is the bittersweet tale of a sick little boy who found solace in his penis at a time when all else conspired to snuff him out or, at the very least, fill his miserably short life span with more than its share of pain, discomfort and humiliation. The penis seemed to thrive on whatever shit the rest of the body was subjected to and rose to the occasion of each onslaught, soaking it up like a sponge or, to be more succinct, the corpus spongiosum became full of itself and my stupid prick danced in the spotlight of sickness and suffering. That first swat on the ass from the obstetrician's skilled hand not only started my diseased lungs sputtering to life, but it also sent a shock through my sphincter, up my tiny rectum, and straight into the shaft of my shiny penis, which ever since then has had this crazy idea in its head that pain and sex are one and the same.[29]

Flanagan's narrative evokes the Hobbesian notion of life as "nasty, short, and brutish," as well as Tristram Shandy's account of a prolonged and difficult quest for and through birth. Linguistically, the chest (of toys) parallels the chest (of the body). Metaphorically, the toy chest suggests Pandora's box—the vehicle that will unlock all the mysteries (and miseries) of sexuality. The myth of Pandora's box combines image and text—the iconography of mystery with a narrative of curiosity. By identifying with Pandora, Bob excites the following questions: What is *in* that chest? Why is interiority invariably associated with femininity? What does it mean for a man to be masochistic in a culture that glorifies Rambo and the Terminator? What does masochism have to do with medicine? Is his sexuality "feminine" *because* it is masochistic? Or has male masochism simply received short shrift in the discourse of sexuality?

Visiting Hours is thus saturated with a strange sense of initiatory power, an initiation that begins in childhood: Flanagan satirizes the latent obscenity and aggressivity of many childhood icons, like cartoons of Porky Pig, whose insatiable appetite aroused Bob's earliest sexual memories. Flanagan was also influenced by "ordeal artists" like Chris Burden.[30] Bob's transformation of physical pain into sexual pleasure might be understandable from a *clinical* perspective, but is it art? Put another way, how do fantasies work personally and for a public audience? First, his exhibit evokes fantasies that involve original wishes that are widely shared (the wish for health, sexual satisfaction, play, and so on). Second, they are contingent. This is where the emphasis on everyday life becomes crucial, for Flanagan demonstrates how we draw on events of the day to produce our own fantasies. Third, we also adopt and adapt the ready-made scenarios of fiction, film, and performance, as if their contingent material had been our own.[31]

Every conceivable response the spectator might have is thwarted by its opposite: aggressivity undermines pity; satire undermines fear; denial undermines recognition; voyeurism is undermined by Bob's turning the tables. Bob, after all, is propped up in his hospital bed in the museum, watching *you* watching him. Disease feminizes him, as he must submit to the authority and expertise of those who treat him, but he defies pity by staging ordeals and endurance contests: hoisting himself naked out of bed with a pulley, catapulting himself out of bed and up to the ceiling like Houdini (one of his childhood heroes) (see Figure 1.3).

Everything about *Visiting Hours* destroys the spectator's repertoire of received ideas about aesthetic transcendence, artistic immortality,

Figure 1.3. Bob Flanagan suspended above his hospital bed in *Visiting Hours*, Santa Monica Museum of Art, December 1992. Photo: Scott Boberg © 1992.

noble suffering, romanticism's agony and ecstasy. Instead, Flanagan forces the spectator to contemplate the unthinkable: the sexuality of diseased bodies. Does anyone doubt that this topic is taboo? AIDS comes immediately to mind. Although cultural critics have analyzed public policy and the policing of desire, as well as AIDS, as an "epidemic of signification,"[32] the notion that those afflicted go on feeling sexual, or having sex, or being desirable to others is still wholly

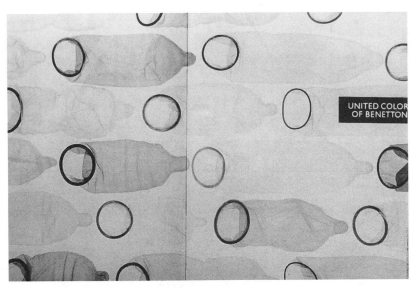

Figure 1.4. United Colors of Benetton advertising campaign. Concept and photograph O. Toscani.

taboo.[33] It is taboo in advertising, too, as the Benetton ad shown in Figure 1.4 illustrates. Had I been able to reproduce this illustration in color, you would see the the entire spectrum of the rainbow. While seeming to imply that the only color that matters is the color of your condom, Benetton ignores the fact that people of color are dying from AIDS in far greater numbers than others are. By floating free from any specific bodies, this rainbow coalition of condoms ignores all such painful realities and injustices, while the corporation gets to congratulate itself for having so grandiose a "social conscience" that it doesn't even need to display its *product* in the ad.

Just as "bad girl" performers like Annie Sprinkle literally spectacularize the desire to "look inside" the female body, Flanagan literally anatomizes his sexuality, his disease, and the medical establishment. He got his start in performance as a stand-up comic, and he mercilessly satirizes sentimental clichés. So wicked is his perverse humor that, after his cameo appearance in Michael Tolkin's new film, *The New Age*, the producers borrowed his black comedy for the film's advertising campaign after he quipped, "*The New Age* is a shopping spree for the morally bankrupt!" Flanagan reminds us that much horror—from Edgar Allan Poe to Brian De Palma—is fiendishly funny.

Visiting Hours captures that macabre comedy through surreal juxta-positions of objects: a gurney with a bed of nails on top (upon which Flanagan occasionally reposes), a porta-potty with a pig pillow beneath it, "For someone's weary head." He reads a short story about driving a nail through his penis: "I methodically cleaned everything up, just like Tony Perkins, my blood swirling down the drain like Janet Leigh's.[34] While paying homage in this passage to the granddaddy of all slasher films, Hitchcock's *Psycho,* Flanagan highlights another aspect of fantasy: he shows how identificatory processes travel from villain to victim, male to female. When Flanagan reads this story to a live audience, men faint. Whereas Camille Paglia worships the penis and Andrea Dworkin damns it, Flanagan deflates it and them both. His work is too literal for art magazines, too visceral for porn. Sexually, Bob may be a "bottom," but when he performs, he relishes the opportunity to go over the top, to control the action, confronting the audience with their own psychic investments in penis, phallus, and symbolic order. He exposes the flayed (fore)skin beneath all our defenses. He opens himself up and finds nothing—no interiority, no transcendence—only the ills that flesh is heir to.

Rather than exploiting the male prerogative of the gaze to deflect castration anxiety, Flanagan acts out—*performs*—castration anxiety. Rather than fetishizing the female body, he pokes and prods his own, piercing the phallic order in the process. He simply stages what is hidden in plain sight in daily life—the fact that we are all terminal cases. "The basis of horror," David Cronenberg once observed, "is that we cannot comprehend how we can die."[35] Flanagan helps us to comprehend mortality by exposing death and sexuality as interrelated taboos. In earlier epochs, death was a natural part of everyday life; people died peacefully at home, rather than in hospitals. Today, however, hospital patients are hooked to life-support systems, making the meaning and even the moment of death ever more difficult to define. That is why an "ordeal artist" like Flanagan stages his struggle with cystic fibrosis. On the one hand, he demonstrates how *conceptual* death has become, mediated by medical technology; on the other hand, he confronts spectators with a "terminal case"—theirs as well as his own. Amid the S/M paraphernalia and the video monitors showing Bob's naked, splayed body, the most stunning object in the New Museum exhibition was an expensive, full-size casket, decorated with wreaths. When you peer inside, Bob's face suddenly pops into view on a video monitor placed where his head would be—*will* be—in the coffin. As you peer more closely, suddenly your own face appears on the monitor—thanks to a hidden, "candid" camera. The effect is utterly unsettling, uncanny. Death, not sex, is the last mystique—and doctors seldom pull back the curtain to give us a peek. Flanagan, the "sick boy" in my title, is a stoic comedian.

We may not quite be ready to embrace the idea that the human organism is made, not born, but many of these artists are bidding adieu to the human as we know it, ushering us into a new era. That was the aim of the 1994 *Hors Limites* exhibition at the Georges Pompidou Center in Paris—an elegy without nostalgia. Many of the artists in this show seized the medical apparatus for artistic purposes. Notable among them was Orlan, whose installation was titled *Entre* (Between), signifying the moment between past and future, between two physical states, between two centuries—indeed, two millennia.

Orlan is a Frenchwoman who submits to plastic surgery in art galleries while spectators look on from around the world, via satellite, pictureTEL, fax, modem, and visiophone. Spectators around the globe not only watch the operations, but transmit messages back to Orlan instantaneously. "I was able," she has said, "without feeling any pain, to answer people who were feeling their own pain as they were watching me."[36] Those words are an uncanny description of the psychoanalyst's function—*to answer people who are feeling their own pain*.

Just as Flanagan deconstructs masculinity, Orlan deconstructs femininity. If Flanagan is Sacher-Masoch, Orlan is de Sade. Through a series of plastic surgeries, she is acquiring the chin of Botticelli's Venus, the mouth of Boucher's Europa, the eyes of Gerard's Psyche, the forehead of Leonardo da Vinci's Mona Lisa. She insists that she has chosen these icons less for their *beauty* than for the mythological *stories* of mayhem, adventure, mischief. Orlan is awake during her procedures, reading to spectators from Lacan, Artaud, Kristeva. Patient, nurses, and surgeons are dressed in designer costumes, and the proceedings are infused with campy humor. While Orlan brandishes a crucifix and a pitchfork, young black men dance a striptease. She delights in such absurd juxtapositions as the Surrealists' *Exquisite Corps*—collaborative artworks in which one artist designs the head, another the torso, and a third the feet for a single painting. Orlan herself is the "exquisite corps"; she sees the body merely as a costume.

Orlan—a synthetic name to match a synthetic identity-in-process—

will let an advertising agency assign her a new name when her metamorphosis is complete. *Morphing* is an important motif and motive: her aim is not to look like any one of these icons, but to become a composite of them all. Just as her face is a composite, she combines the functions of intercessor, cyborg, mother, and analyst. Orlan uses new technologies to create a new psychological self-portrait, one that reflects the impact of those technologies.

As Orlan points out, there are not many images that cannot be looked at. One has only to turn on the evening news to see massacres in living color on television. Given how inured we have become to images of horror, it is remarkably difficult to watch Orlan under the knife. Yet as gruesome as all this sounds, Orlan is not doing anything that Cher, Michael Jackson, and scores of other celebrities have not done before her. All she does is expose the process. Like Flanagan, she desacralizes medicine, which she sees as our epoch's religion. She shares Flanagan's zeal for interpreting medicine's texts: DNA, codes, alphabets, letters, sequences, X rays are the signatures of all the things they wish to decipher.

The bad girls and sick boys I have discussed go inside the body to force us to think again about Cartesian dualities and sexual difference. They do not view technology as either a utopia or a dystopia. On the one hand, they seize its apparatuses and deconstruct the phallic order that sustains it: the drive to dissect, to classify, to categorize all viscera into abstract intellectual schemata. Medicine's mediated encounters with flesh and blood find no sanctuary here. On the other hand, they use technology to reinstall tactility and materiality. They stage the material body—without, however, resorting to sentimentality or essentialism. Instead, they objectify *themselves,* desacralizing and desecrating the body's terrain. These artists demonstrate that sex is only one of numerous symbolic and sacrificial practices to which a body can open itself. These artists have shifted the field of transgression from sex to other bodily functions. While defamiliarizing "the human," they simultaneously defamiliarize "the museum" by reorienting the site toward the excreta, urine, blood, and food that go in and come out of the body. Their performances incite acts of remembering and re-cognition and break down the old barriers: public/private, pain/pleasure, voyeur/exhibitionist. Collectively they point toward a new paradigm of spectatorship, one that is generated from or driven by the *insides of the body,* one in which the human body is simultaneously the spectacle, the performance space, the subject, and the object of pleasure and danger.

Notes

1. For a discussion of this transformation, see Jacques Ellul, "Symbolic Function, Technology, and Society," *Journal of Social and Biological Structures* 10 (1987): 208–18; Harvey Wheeler, "A Constructional Biology of Hermeneutics," *Journal of Social and Biological Structures* 10 (1987): 103–23.

2. Barbara Stafford, *Body Criticism: Imaging the Unseen in Enlightenment Art and Medicine* (Cambridge: MIT Press, 1991).

3. See Edward de Grazia, *Girls Lean Back Everywhere: The Law of Obscenity and the Assault on Genius* (New York: Random House, 1992).

4. Stewart Brand, *The Media Lab: Inventing the Future at M.I.T.* (London: Penguin, 1989), 253.

5. Donald Alexander Downs, *The New Politics of Pornography* (Chicago: University of Chicago Press, 1989).

6. See Linda Williams, *Hard Core: Power, Pleasure, and the "Frenzy" of the Visible* (Berkeley: University of California Press, 1989), and "Film Bodies: Gender, Genre, and Excess," *Film Quarterly* 44, no. 4 (1991): 2–13.

7. Gertrud Koch, "The Body's Shadow Realm," *October* 50 (Fall 1989): 8. Linda Williams, however, demonstrates that porno films *have* changed considerably since the early silent stag films. See Williams, *Hard Core.*

8. In a 1987 *Redbook* magazine survey of 26,000 women, nearly half of those interviewed said they regularly watch porno films; 85 percent had seen at least one. See Williams, *Hard Core,* 231.

9. Carol Clover, *Men, Women, and Chainsaws* (Princeton, N.J.: Princeton University Press, 1992).

10. Williams, *Hard Core.*

11. Carol Clover, "Her Body, Himself: Gender in the Slasher Film," *Representations* 20 (Fall 1987): 193.

12. J. G Ballard, *The Atrocity Exhibition* (San Francisco: Re/Search, 1990).

13. Ibid., 20.

14. Ibid., 14. One of David Cronenberg's characters in *The Brood* repeats this sentiment almost verbatim. When he discovers that he has a blood disorder, he says, "I have a small revolution on my hands and I'm not controlling it!" Space does not permit full elaboration of the numerous affinities between Cronenberg and Ballard, but they include their shared interest in genetic experiments, artificial intelligence, reproductive technology, pharmaceutical breakthroughs, media, and simulation. It is appropriate that Cronenberg is now filming Ballard's *Crash.*

15. Peter Greenaway, *The Physical Self* (Rotterdam: Boymans-van Beuningen Museum and D.A.P., 1991).

16. Jeffrey Deitch, *Posthuman* (New York: D.A.P., 1992).

17. Arthur Kroker and Marilouise Kroker, eds., *The Last Sex* (New York: St. Martin's, 1993); Gilbert Herdt, ed., *The Third Sex* (Cambridge: MIT Press, 1994).

18. Margo St. James, "The Reclamation of Whores," in *Good Girls/Bad Girls: Feminists and Sex Trade Workers Face to Face,* ed. Laurie Bell (Toronto: Seal, 1987), 82.

19. See Linda S. Kauffman, *Discourses of Desire: Gender, Genre, and Epistolary Fic-*

tions (Ithaca, N.Y.: Cornell University Press, 1986), and *Special Delivery: Epistolary Modes in Modern Fiction* (Chicago: University of Chicago Press, 1992).

20. In "Persona, Proto-Performance, Politics: A Preface," *Discourse* 14, no. 2 (1992): 26–35, Valie Export discusses her debt to action painting, the Situationists, and examines future directions of performance art, like those presaged in Laurie Anderson's work: "A sort of technological armament of the body emerged parallel to the performative deconstruction of the body as a system of social signs. The eye initially armed itself, as it were, with film, video, and photographic cameras and the voice with musical instruments. The borders between space and time were overcome with the aid of the technological media, as were the borders of the body and the subject. The simple performance of the world of sensual perception in space and time became a mechanically-supported, high-tech implemented hyper-performance in the hyperreality of the media" (34).

21. See Susie Bright, *Sexual Reality: A Virtual Sex World Reader* (Pittsburgh: Cleis, 1992).

22. See Benjamin Woolley, *Virtual Worlds: A Journey in Hype and Hyperreality* (Oxford: Basil Blackwell, 1992), 238–39.

23. On sex as the property of individuals, see Gayle Rubin, "Thinking Sex: Notes for a Radical Theory of the Politics of Sexuality," in *American Feminist Thought at Century's End,* ed. Linda S. Kauffman (Oxford: Basil Blackwell, 1993).

24. Lasko-Harvill notes that the limitlessness of electronic mimesis, the ability to be thoroughly separated from oneself, resembles the nausea once associated with the absurd. See Ann Lasko-Harvill, "Identity and Mask in Virtual Reality," *Discourse* 14, no. 2 (1992): 222–34.

25. Robert Allen, *Horrible Prettiness: Burlesque and American Culture* (Chapel Hill: University of North Carolina Press, 1991).

26. Barbara Kruger, *Love for Sale* (New York: Harry N. Abrams, 1990), 17. This photograph is actually of the heart, but Kruger, like Sprinkle, literalizes a specific organ in order to defamiliarize the stereotypical connotations enveloping it: heart = love, romance, passion.

27. Sigmund Freud, *Civilization and Its Discontents,* ed. and trans. James Strachey (New York: W. W. Norton, 1961). Freud notes, "With man's adoption of an erect posture . . . events proceeded through the devaluation of olfactory stimuli . . . to the time when visual stimuli were paramount" (54, n.1).

28. Ballard, *The Atrocity Exhibition,* 68.

29. Quoted in Andrea Juno and V. Vale, eds., *Bob Flanagan: Supermasochist* (San Francisco: Re/Search, 1993), 126.

30. My interview with Bob Flanagan and Sheree Rose, Los Angeles, California, February 19, 1993.

31. Elizabeth Cowie, "Fantasia," in *Fantasy and Cinema,* ed. James Donald (London: British Film Institute, 1989).

32. Paula Treichler, "AIDS, Homophobia, and Biomedical Discourse: An Epidemic of Signification," in *AIDS: Cultural Analysis/Cultural Activism,* ed. Douglas Crimp (Cambridge: MIT Press, 1988).

33. A recent call for papers for an issue on "The Politics of AIDS" from the *Minnesota Review* is symptomatic: suggested topics include "queer theory and activism; public images of AIDS; politics of medical research; health care policies." Similarly, safe-sex videos focus on avoidance of infection, rather than the desire and desirability of those infected. Susan Sontag's *Illness as Metaphor* (New York: Farrar, Straus & Giroux, 1977) was widely criticized for reducing disease to metaphor.

I know of only a few exceptions to this taboo: (1) Isaac Julien's *This Is Not an AIDS Advertisement* (New York: Third World Newsreel, 1987), which combines images of gay male sexual desire coupled with the refrain from a Bronski Beat rock song, "Feel no guilt in your desire" (see Douglas Crimp, ed., *AIDS*); (2) Douglas Crimp's "How to Have Promiscuity in the Midst of an Epidemic," in *AIDS: Cultural Analysis/Cultural Activism,* ed. Douglas Crimp (Cambridge: MIT Press, 1988); (3) Starshu Kybartas's video *Dani,* which depicts his sexual attraction to a man with Kaposi's sarcoma (in Douglas Crimp, "Portraits of People with AIDS," in *Cultural Studies,* ed. Lawrence Grossberg, Cary Nelson, and Paula A. Treichler [London: Routledge, 1992], 117–33); (4) David Wojnarowicz's *Close to the Knives* (New York: Random House, 1991); and (5) Ngozi Onwurah's film *The Body Beautiful* (1991), which features the sexual fantasies of an aging white woman (played by Onwurah's mother in real life) who has had a mastectomy.

34. Bob Flanagan, "Body," in *High Risk,* ed. Amy Scholder and Ira Silverberg (San Francisco: City Lights, 1991), 87.

35. In Chris Rodley, ed., *Cronenberg on Cronenberg* (London: Faber & Faber, 1992), 79.

36. My interviews with Orlan, Paris, November 19, 1994, and New York, March 24, 1995. All quotations are taken from these discussions.

2 / "Voicing" Deaf Identity: Through the "I's" and Ears of an Other

H-Dirksen L. Bauman

The problems of deafness are deeper and more complex, if not more
important, than those of blindness. . . . For [deafness] means the
loss of the most vital stimulus—the sound of the voice that brings
language, sets thoughts astir and keeps us in the intellectual company of men.

HELEN KELLER, letter to Dr. J. Kerr Love[1]

Writing from a unique position of authority, Helen Keller confirms
most hearing persons' views of deafness as a tragic disability. Yet, as
Keller locates the principal site of disability in a social rather than a biological context, she shifts the emphasis of the pathological site away
from the body, placing it within the public space of oral communication. The hearing population, then, must be present in order for this
more profound site of disability to be constituted. As demonstrated
variously by Harlan Lane, Douglas Baynton, and John Van Cleve and
Barry Crouch, not only has the hearing community been present in
constructing popular notions of deafness, but the Deaf community has
been absent.[2] The history of the Deaf community has indeed been one
of discursive ventriloquism in which Deaf subjects have been forced to
move their mouths and yet have had no say—while medical and educational discourses have filibustered on the tragic horrors of hearing
loss to a hearing audience. Deaf history may be characterized as a
struggle for Deaf individuals to "speak" for themselves rather than to
be spoken about in medical and educational discourses.

When the Deaf community does gain a "voice" to represent itself apart from hearing versions of "deafness," an altogether different "deafness" emerges—one that does not deny the audiological condition of hearing loss, but that emphasizes that the conditions of disability are relational and political rather than ontological and biological. Within a signing environment, the social site of disability—the interface of hearing/Deaf, oral/nonoral—is missing. With these unbalanced binarisms absent, the Deaf "I" cannot be constructed in terms of a lack or of alienation. Rather, an abundant sense of community arises in Deaf clubs, residential schools, and social organizations where the American Sign Language (ASL) users are no more disabled than Hispanic Americans would be in Spanish-speaking cultural spaces. Deaf persons, Harlan Lane explains, "see themselves as fundamentally visual people, with their own visual language, social organization, history, and mores—in short, with their own way of being, their own language, and culture."[3] So strong is Deaf identity that one survey reports that 86 percent of Deaf adults would not undergo surgery to restore their hearing if they could.[4]

The Spoken "I" as Collaborative Identity

For Deaf persons, representing the nonpathologized "I" through American Sign Language is more than therapeutic activity—it is cultural survival. As Deaf identity is not usually transmitted through the family, residential schools and Deaf clubs provide sites where "deaf" individuals may become "Deaf"—where they may become, in other words, members of the linguistic group of ASL users. Within these signing environments, storytelling functions as a pivotal means through which Deaf individuals articulate and perform a cultural identity. As the signer may employ all the rhetorical complexities allotted to speakers—in addition to the dramatic elements of ASL's four-dimensional syntax—the signing body dissociates hearing impairment from linguistic impairment.[5] Further, the narratives signed in Deaf spaces frequently position disability as an extension, not from "deafness," but from the hearing world's ignorance of Deaf culture. During an informal storytelling event I witnessed at the Colorado School for the Deaf and the Blind, a Deaf man recounted a recent visit to a McDonald's restaurant, where the employee at the counter disappeared after seeing the Deaf man signing to a friend; a few moments later, she returned, awkwardly handing them a Braille menu. This story catalyzed other signers to dramatize narratives in which the hearing community, not the Deaf, constitutes a lack.

In the hearing world, however, such an animated storytelling session would most likely be perceived not as a cultural event but as a flurry of hieroglyphic gesticulations signifying alienation and disability. Herein is a primary struggle of the Deaf community: to rewrite "deafness" from a medical to a cultural identity within the hearing world. Deaf persons, therefore, must gain a "voice" that commands the attention of hearing audiences. But as the literal voices of Deaf individuals may be perceived as distorted and unintelligible to the hearing world, they must present their personal and political "voices" through alternative strategies. The task of rewriting Deaf identity, then, engages the complex textual issues that arise in autobiographical practices in everyday situations. How are Deaf individuals to represent themselves as non-disabled within oral-dominant spaces? How can the Deaf "I" traverse the difficult horizon between Deaf and hearing worlds?

One way is through writing. The silent and visual nature of script opens the way for hearing and Deaf communities to participate on equal discursive terrain.[6] Yet, practically, the everyday use of writing is too cumbersome to allow for complex narratives and meaningful conversations. Similarly, lipreading, miming, and speaking may suffice in certain contexts, but they are imprecise and potentially dangerous in situations that warrant detailed representation. Sign-language interpreters, therefore, provide crucial means through which Deaf individuals may gain a voice within medical, psychiatric, legal, educational, governmental, and financial institutions. Compared with the alternatives, sign-language interpreters grant Deaf persons greater freedom of self-expression through their native language.

Signing through an interpreter, however, still precludes the Deaf "I," as such, from being received in the hearing world, for once it is spoken by the interpreter, the "I" is no longer autobiographical but, rather, a biographical rendition spoken by the interpreter in the first-person singular. As the narrative transfers from sign to orality, from narrating body to interpreting body, the autobiographical "I" undergoes a type of discursive mitosis, dividing into a new textual form that is to get a life all its own. As this new "I" embarks on a narrative journey through a body to which it no longer bears reference, it is subjected to the vicissitudes of a stranger's memory, ideologies, voice, skills, alertness, sexuality, regionality, ethnicity, gender, dress, hairstyle, grammar, education, and more—in short, to all the ingredients that constitute a particular speaking persona. As this traveling "I" gains enunciation, one wonders how well it can "speak" for itself through the voice of an other—especially as the Deaf person to whom it belongs is unable to follow its auditory journey.

The signer and the interpreter should ostensibly produce an identical "I," only in different media. However, as Carole Boyce Davies notes, in any collaborative process "the autobiographical 'I' with its authority is replaced by a less stable 'we.'"[7] This collaborative relationship between signer and interpreter locates the final text as an everyday counterpart to the *testimonio,* a collaborative form of autobiography in which a politically silenced subject recounts his or her life story to an interlocutor who records, transcribes, and edits the oral narrative. The meeting between narrator and interlocutor may be seen as potentially both empowering and disempowering for the member of the silenced class. As the imbalance in these power relations may easily play itself out between narrator and interlocutor, the politics of collaboration have been a focal point of scholarship on the *testimonio.* Similarly, the collaboration between Deaf narrator and sign-language interpreter in everyday situations deserves scrutiny, as it usually entails the meeting of complex power relations along gender, ethnic, racial, sexual, moral, class, and generational divides—and, perhaps most important, along the divides of hearing/Deaf and the dominance of speech/oppression of signing.

The intent of this essay, then, is to explore the collaboration between signer and interpreter in the everyday autobiographical practices of Deaf individuals, to follow the internal and porous border between autobiography and first-person biography that produces the potentially shifting, overlapping, and partially hearing "we" within the Deaf "I." This must be done to expose the textual dynamics involved for the Deaf community to gain an authentic "voice" in the hearing world. Given the historical power relations between hearing and Deaf populations, the question presents itself: How does speaking through a member of the oppressive class affect the Deaf autobiographical narrative? Exploring such textual issues is crucial, as the tradition of hearing persons speaking in place of Deaf persons has resulted in centuries of devastating misunderstandings about "deafness."

Whose Autobiography Is Voiced?

In interpreting situations where the Deaf subject seeks professional services (such as legal, medical, psychiatric, or financial assistance) in the hearing world, three bodies are generally present: the Deaf subject's, the interpreter's, and the hearing professional's. The interpreter usually sits alongside but slightly behind the hearing professional, while both hearing persons face the signer. While each body appears whole and separate from the others in the room, such clear distinctions blur as the signer's narrative passes through the body of the interpreter and into the ears of the hearing professional. In the transfer from sign to voice, from autobiography to first-person biography, a host of discursive dangers arise that potentially modify the signer's "I." The result is often an indistinguishable amalgam of mixed identities in which the interpreter's own autobiographical significations merge into the spoken narrative.

In order to gain a critical foothold amid the interwoven identities in hearing-Deaf collaborations, it will be helpful to locate three moments in which the interpreter's presence may alter the signer's intended narrative: (1) the signer may internalize the interpreter's gaze, perhaps inhibiting the autobiographical "I" from emerging into the public field of discourse; (2) the interpreter may intentionally or unintentionally alter textual material from sign to voice; and (3) the autobiographical significations revealed through the interpreter's voice and appearance may project on the signer's identity.

The Internalized Gaze

As sign-language interpreters are especially necessary in critical situations such as court appearances, doctor appointments, and counseling sessions, Deaf subjects often find themselves having to disclose highly personal information through a third party. Whereas most hearing persons would feel subjected by the professional's gaze, the Deaf subject must endure the added surveillance of the interpreter. This double gaze potentially alters the autobiographical narrative by penetrating inside the enunciatory gap between the signer's "I" and the autobiographical "I"—the place Paul Smith calls the "ideological I."[8] Once there, the internalized gaze may function as an interpellation for the signer to present a "proper" autobiographical narrative. The "I" that emerges into visibility, therefore, may already be edited by the internalized gazes of the hearing persons. Yet, although Deaf subjects may internalize the visual gaze, it is perhaps the auditory gaze that presents the most difficulties. As the interpreter and professional share the oral telling of the story, the Deaf subject is rendered a discursive outsider to his or her own "I." Within seconds of being signed, the autobiographical "I" becomes a semiotic stranger to the autobiographer. Thus alienated from his or her own story, the Deaf subject may fear the treatment and reception of his or her identity in the hearing world. As Deaf subjects internalize the auditory gaze, they perform the curious act of "listening" to their stories through the ears of the hearing.

The intensity of this complex gaze may be lessened through the establishment of trust with the interpreter. Whereas most testimonial collaborators are able to develop trusting relationships through extended storytelling sessions, signers and interpreters frequently have but a few minutes of introduction prior to the collaborative event. Having to tell one's story through a stranger may be so traumatic in some situations that Deaf subjects refuse to seek professional services. One interpreter related an instance in which she was called to interpret for a Deaf woman in a counseling session. Even though the woman expressed urgent need of psychiatric assistance, she did not show up for that appointment, or for the two that followed. Sensitive to the woman's difficult position of disclosing private information to two hearing strangers, the interpreter contacted the Deaf woman so that they could meet and establish a working relationship. After they had done so, the woman attended counseling sessions regularly and spoke frankly in them. Although many Deaf persons fear the intervention of interpreters, few are fortunate enough to receive personal house calls.[9]

The Deaf woman was also fortunate in that she found a same-gender interpreter who shared her cultural background. Caucasian Deaf women have a luxury in the availability of same-sex, same-race interpreters, whereas others are frequently subjected to a gaze complicated by divergent social positions.[10] The cross-gendered gaze may be most acutely felt in medical situations, where its invasion into the private space of the body can interfere with the subject's willingness to seek medical help. This has been the case among members of the Deaf gay community. According to Dale Dyal, president of Lesbian and Gay Interpreters and Transliterators of the Deaf (LeGIT), gay men confronted with telling their sexual histories to doctors through female interpreters have been reluctant to seek AIDS testing and medical

assistance. In this complex situation, the gendered gaze is often coupled with a moral and religious gaze. As many interpreters also perform religious interpreting, Dyal notes, some Deaf persons may sense
that they are being looked at through the judgmental eyes of organized
religion. Enduring this moral gaze, no doubt, exacerbates the anxiety
that hearing subjects experience under the single gaze of the physician.
For this reason, the Registry for Interpreters of the Deaf (RID) formed
LeGIT to provide interpreters who do not constitute a morally condescending gaze.[11]

Similarly, Deaf persons of color have considerable difficulty in lo-
cating interpreters who share similar cultural heritages. Another RID
special interest group, Interpreters and Transliterators of Color
(ITOC), claims fewer than fifty members, a figure drastically disproportionate to the numbers of African American, Native American,
Asian American, and Hispanic Deaf persons in the United States. According to ITOC president Anthony Aramburo, African American
Deaf persons are less likely than Caucasian Deaf persons to seek services offered to them, as a result of the cross-racial gaze.[12] In their
book *Black and Deaf in America*, Ernest Hariston and Linwood Smith
cite a study that found not only that African American Deaf individuals are reluctant to receive the social and vocational services extended
to them, "but also that they may be reluctant to see a counselor who is
able to communicate with the Deaf, but is a white person. . . . No matter how hard a white person (Deaf, hard-of-hearing, or hearing) tries,
the Black Deaf generally will not accept him or her as a part of
them."[13] Because of the homogeneity of the interpreting community,
the majority of Deaf subjects face a gaze not only across the semiotic
and cultural divide of hearing and Deaf cultures but also across a simultaneous and intricate relation of gendered, ethnic, and moral
positions.

Largely because of the interpreter's incessant gaze, Matthew Moore,
publisher of *Deaf Life* magazine, speaks of the "love/hate" relationship that Deaf persons have with interpreters. "We love the access interpreters provide," signs Moore, "but we hate the invasiveness, as
they are always peering into our private lives." The sign Moore uses
for the interpreter's gaze demonstrates its effect: the "V" hand shape
turned toward and scanning the Deaf body, signifying the panoptic
and panaural surveillance of the hearing over the lives and narratives
of Deaf individuals.[14]

Textual Alterations

Despite certain parallels, the interpreted autobiography reverses the process of textualizing the *testimonio*. The *testimonio* begins as an oral narrative recorded on tape, transcribed onto paper, and edited to meet the demands of a literate audience. During this process, Elisabeth Burgos-Debray, for example, deleted questions, arranged Rigoberta Menchu's verbal meanderings into a coherent monologue, added linking passages, and altered basic grammatical errors—all in order to "make the text more accessible to the reader."[15] The sign-to-voice interpreting process, on the other hand, moves from visual to oral media; it begins in a more or less coherent monologue and frequently ends in a disjointed final form. Unlike the weeks of collaboration Burgos-Debray and Menchu enjoyed, the interpreter has but a second or two to receive the narration, translate it, and voice it. In her article "A Deaf Perspective on Interpreters," Suzanne Sapienza recognizes that

> only veteran interpreters have polished this more difficult skill [sign-to-voice interpreting] and the Deaf population feel the consequences. . . . Excessive hesitations, breaks, and repetitions cause the barriers of the handicap to seem larger than necessary. . . . Communication becomes a choppy, rough sequence of words and repetitions and the rapport which might have been developed between the two people is never accomplished. Red faces and nervous smiles hurry the conversation to an end, leaving the Deaf individual frustrated with unasked questions, unspoken comments and unfinished business.[16]

Instead of a smoothed-out monologue, such as the one found in *I, Rigoberta Menchu,* the voiced version of sign language is frequently a narrative mess, resembling postmodern incoherence rather than a genuine attempt at communicating in a doctor's or lawyer's office.

If interpreters are unable to gain the intended meaning of an ASL idiom, for example, they may try to keep up with the narrative flow by translating verbatim. "I have been there many times before" may end up as "Go, go, many times, finish me." Or "I want to get even with her" could literally be rendered as "Get even her, hungry wish me." Unaware of the differences between ASL and English, a hearing professional could misinterpret such statements as bizarre and incomprehensible. Once at this stage of communication breakdown, interpreters are forced to ask the Deaf person for clarification. Although this may be preferable to misinterpreting the signer, it often results in an uncomfortable situation. Interpreter and author Leah Hagen Cohen describes her own experiences voicing in the classroom for a Deaf student: "Sometimes when I am speaking for her, I don't understand something she has signed. I have to ask her to repeat it, and I can see her flush, both of us sensing the polite and condescending impatience of the teacher and the class."[17] In such cases, the uncomfortable silences involved in sign-to-voice interpreting speak volumes to Deaf individuals.

Unlike the testimonial interlocutor, the sign-language interpreter lacks the luxury of consulting a tape recording to verify the original text. Sign interpreters must depend, therefore, on their less reliable perceptions and memories.[18] To avoid the dangers of misinterpretation, a former social service advocate for Deaf persons insisted that a fourth person be present in counseling sessions to ensure the quality of the interpreting process. Serving as the fourth person, the advocate witnessed a counseling session in which the Deaf subject signed, "I think about women all the time." This was signed with the right index finger repeatedly pointing to the forehead, starting from the right side and moving to the left. The plurality of pointing was intended to signify a plurality of women; the interpreter, however, mistook the repetition to signify "all the time," meaning that the signer thought about one particular woman all the time rather than about women in general. The advocate caught this slight but crucial misrepresentation only after he read the counselor's records of the session.[19] Such a small slip in understanding often results in the creation of a different autobiographical subject from the one intended. Given the difficult nature of sign-to-voice translation, the first-person biography may always hover somewhere between unwitting fiction and autobiography.

Textual alterations also occur when the interpreter rearranges the narrative to fit the needs of a hearing audience. Interpreters often find themselves in uncomfortable positions, mediating between two cultures with respective differences in communication practices. Hearing culture has developed an implied set of guidelines for polite methods of turn taking and length of speaking time. As Deaf subjects do not hear the auditory cues that signal appropriate discourse behavior, they may wish to interject at inappropriate times. When this occurs, the interpreter must choose between being rude and silencing the Deaf subject. Frequently, interpreters opt for signaling to the Deaf person when the appropriate time to participate arises. Acting as discursive gate-keepers, interpreters enforce hearing codes of behavior, disciplining the Deaf body to perform as a hearing body. Resistant to such coercion, Deaf subjects become annoyed as interpreters make paternalistic decisions concerning their behavior. "The Deaf," Suzanne Sapienza writes, "feel shut out by an interpreter who is unwilling or unable to assertively interject their comments and ideas." One Deaf interviewee told Sapienza that because "hearing people interrupt each other all the time . . . he felt he should be allowed this same privilege. He becomes infuriated when an interpreter acts 'polite' for him, by hesitating to interrupt."[20]

Interpreters also have been known to edit the Deaf subject's narrative if it transgresses against boundaries of social decorum. Although this may be done to "help" the Deaf subject by fashioning his or her story in a more acceptable manner, it also saves interpreters from uttering transgressive remarks themselves. Certified interpreter Amy VanSickle recounts one event in which she witnessed an interpreter translate "shit" to "shoot." In another case, VanSickle saw a student sign directly to his teacher, "You're a jerk!" Instead of conveying the remark, the interpreter signed reproachfully to the student, "You know that's not nice!"[21] Deaf persons, like this student, who wish to express an urgent emotion face the frustration of speaking through someone who does not share that emotion or, worse, who does not approve of its being voiced in public. The result is frequently a diluted and disciplined rendition of the original narrative.

Through such silences, omissions, and textual alterations, the collaborative subject speaks a mix of conflicting intentions between signer and interpreter. For this reason, all those involved in the interpreting situation should be aware that the oral text is, like autobiography, a "site of complex interaction between editor and author, between writer and audience."[22]

Through the Ears of Others

Even in cases when the interpreter renders the signed narrative with admirable fidelity, a potential confusion arises as the interpreter's voice may project its own significations on the signer's body. Determining whose name or signature belongs to the oral narrative requires a supple ear, for, as Derrida recognizes, it is only after the autobiographer's signature enters the ear of the other that it gains autobiographical currency. "The signature," Derrida writes in *The Ear of the Other,* "becomes effective—performed and performing—not at the moment it apparently takes place, but only later, when ears will have managed to receive the message. . . . it is the ear of the other that signs. The ear of the other says me to me and constitutes the *autos* of my autobiography."[23] Derrida's recognition of the "ear that signs" assumes new resonances in the textual issues of hearing and Deaf collaborations. If, as Derrida has shown elsewhere, speech has been privileged in signifying a speaker's presence, then signing, on the other hand, has come to signify absence. To the phonocentric hearing world, signing signifies absence of sound, of hearing, of ability, and of the fullness of human presence revealed through the voice. Whereas hearing persons readily identify significations embedded in the interpreter's voice such as regionality, class, age, and attitude, they are ill equipped to discern such a presence through signing. The Deaf subject, therefore, is always in danger of becoming a semiotic palimpsest over which the autobiographical significations of interpreters' voices are continually recorded. Whose autobiography, then, does the ear of the other sign?

After years of communicating through interpreters, Matthew Moore has become well acquainted with being an autobiographical chameleon whose identity transforms, to a greater or lesser degree, from interpreter to interpreter. In one instance, Moore relates, he "spoke" through a male interpreter who presented himself in a stereotypically effeminate manner. A week after the interpreted event, Moore approached the hearing party to see if he had received the impression that Moore was homosexual. The hearing party admitted that he had, confirming Moore's awareness that interpreters and signers often blend in the ears of hearing subjects. Moore cautions that if the interpreter speaks with incorrect grammar, the signer may be the one thought to lack basic English skills; if the interpreter appears sloppy or rude, it may be the signer who is seen as lacking social dignity. Facing such possibilities in everyday situations, Deaf persons are clearly aware that the interpreter is an extension of them. Where one body ends and another begins is, at best, difficult to discern. If given a choice, therefore, some Deaf persons prefer interpreters who reflect positive identities over those with higher skills.

Of course, not all significations of the interpreter's voice will be projected onto the Deaf subject. The hearing professional may readily distinguish between the signer and the interpreter when the two occupy obviously divergent positions of age, gender, and race. By reading the Deaf body in contrast to its spoken narrative, the hearing professional may isolate the particular significations of each and read them separately. However, when Deaf persons engage in telephone conversations with hearing persons through a relay service, the speaking and signing bodies are absent and unable to produce their own significations. In relay conversations, Deaf persons type their messages on a Telecommunication Device for the Deaf (TDD), which transmits the words to the screen of an operator who voices the message to the hearing subject, and vice versa. Hearing persons unaccustomed to speaking through a relay service often fill the void created by the signer's absence with the immediate presence of the operator's voice. Speaking through the TDD relay service for the first time, a hearing acquaintance of mine assumed she was communicating with a man in his twenties or thirties; when she met the other party in person she was shocked to find that the Deaf man was in his sixties.[24] The younger voice of a stranger who spoke from the relay center more than a hundred miles away became entangled in the Deaf person's daily practice of presenting himself on the phone. The ears of the hearing are so trained to associate the spoken "I" with the speaker that there is perhaps no way of knowing how many times Deaf authobiographical subjects have been mistaken for their first-person biographers.

Conclusion

Although the emphasis of this essay has been on the problematic nature of collaboration, the Deaf subject does, of course, have means to assume authority over his or her "I." Unlike Spivak's subaltern, the Deaf subject can "speak" and can do so effectively. In fact, the collaboration between interpreters and signers serves, arguably, as the site where "deafness" may be most effectively rewritten from pathology to culture. Just as the individual act of "speaking" through a member of the hearing culture reconstructs the hearing oppression of the Deaf community, it also offers the potential for Deaf subjects to redefine the relationship between the two cultures. Whereas interpreters speak of themselves as offering a service to Deaf consumers, Matthew Moore realigns the economic metaphor, positioning Deaf persons not as consumers but as supervisors. Accordingly, interpreters perform their duties as employees who work for their Deaf superiors. Assuming this metaphor, Moore suggests, Deaf individuals are able to maintain ownership over the spoken "I."

Deaf persons may weaken the intensity of the hearing gaze if they pursue collaborative relationships built on trust. By requesting certain interpreters and by refusing to work with others, Deaf individuals prioritize the need to feel comfortable with those who share their stories. Rather than acquiescing to a lottery system that delivers interpreters with unpredictable and uneven skills, Deaf persons may gain a hand in shaping working relationships. In addition, they may maintain some control over their stories by evaluating the performances of the interpreters, letting the appropriate persons know how they feel about the services rendered. If an interpreter refuses to accommodate the needs of a Deaf individual, he or she may risk being dismissed from that particular job. Although the limited availability of interpreters may thwart these efforts, Deaf individuals may assert more control over their "voice" by asserting themselves among the voices that speak for them.

Textual alterations may also be lessened. Some Deaf individuals prefer to bypass the inaccuracies of interpreting through the use of transliteration, where all discourse is performed in manual and verbal English. Transliteration bridges the gap between ASL and English, allowing the Deaf subject to be more certain about the verbal rendition of his or her story. Although transliteration may be said to interfere with the presentation of the culturally Deaf "I," Deaf lawyer Michael Schwartz contends that it is an effective strategy through which the bilingual Deaf person may maintain authority in the oral text. By presenting himself in English, Schwartz controls the word choice, syntax, and style of his narrative, lessening the potential for the interpreter to intrude on his story.[25]

Deaf individuals have also developed strategies for deflecting the interpreter's voice from being recorded on their bodies. When they ask questions to verify that the interpreter understands what is being signed, Deaf subjects create a type of Brechtian effect, destroying the illusion that interpreters utter an "I" that belongs to them. By interrupting the flow of communication at strategic times, Deaf persons seize control over narrative silences and pauses. This strategy reverses the direction of the gaze where Deaf persons are the ones who monitor the ability or inability of a body to "speak correctly." Through these interactive procedures, the interpreter and the hearing professional are reminded of the presence rather than of the various "absences" of the Deaf body.

As Deaf individuals strive to lessen the gap between the signed "I" and the spoken "I," they assume greater semiotic control over the Deaf body in the hearing world. But can Deaf persons ever become autobiographical subjects through the voice of an other? Perhaps they, like all collaborative subjects, will always be haunted by the stubborn "we" within the autobiographical "I." Instead of hindering the Deaf "I," however, this collaborative "we" offers a site where "deafness" may be redefined. By presenting a nonpathologized "I" in the politics of collaboration, Deaf individuals redefine the use of interpreters, from being prosthetic devices for the disabled to serving as mediators between two language groups. As Deaf leader M. J. Bienvenu asks: "When Gorbachev visited the U.S., he used an interpreter to talk to the President. . . . Was Gorbachev disabled?"[26]

Notes

As this essay focuses on the tradition of hearing people speaking in place of Deaf people, I must acknowledge that I am a hearing person writing about the Deaf community. Recently, Deaf leaders have proposed that hearing writers describe their involvement with the Deaf community and their knowledge of sign language—no doubt a justified request. I first became involved with the Deaf community at the Colorado School for the Deaf and the Blind, where I worked as a dormitory supervisor. There I began to learn sign language, a mixture of American Sign Language and signed English. Since my time at CSDB, I have become particularly interested in American Sign Language literature, which is the focus of my doctoral dissertation. I am not an interpreter and have interpreted only in informal situations. In preparing this chapter, I have made every attempt to gain the Deaf perspective on interpreters through interviews. My intent is not to speak for the Deaf community but rather to observe the textual and political issues involved in sign-language interpreting as a collaborative form of "everyday autobiography."

According to current convention, I use the uppercase *Deaf* to refer to the cultural identity shared by native signers, whereas the lowercase *deaf* represents the medical identity of hearing loss and disability.

1. Helen Keller, letter to Dr. J. Kerr Love, 31 March 1910, in *The Quiet Ear: Deafness in Literature,* ed. Brian Grant (London: Andre Deutsch, 1987), 36–37.

2. Harlan Lane, *The Mask of Benevolence: Disabling the Deaf Community* (New York: Alfred A. Knopf, 1992); Douglas Baynton, "'A Silent Exile on This Earth': The Metaphorical Construction of Deafness in the Nineteenth Century," *American Quarterly* 44 (June 1992): 216–43; John Vickery Van Cleve and Barry A. Crouch, *A Place of Their Own* (Washington, D.C.: Gallaudet University Press, 1989).

3. Lane, *The Mask of Benevolence,* 5.

4. Cited in Edward Dolnick, "Deafness as Culture," *Atlantic Monthly,* September 1993, 43.

5. William Stokoe explains this difference from other modes of communication:

"Speech has only one dimension—in its extension in time; writing has two dimensions; models have three; but only signed languages have at their disposal four dimensions— the three spatial dimensions accessible to a signer's body, as well as the dimension of time. And Sign fully exploits the syntactic possibilities in its four-dimensional channel of 'expression.'" William C. Stokoe, "Syntactic Dimensionality: Language in Four Dimensions," paper presented at the New York Academy of Sciences, November 1979. Quoted in Oliver Sacks, *Seeing Voices: A Journey into the World of the Deaf* (New York: HarperPerennial, 1990), 89–90.

6. It was print that allowed Pierre Desloges, the first Deaf man to write an autobiography, to raise a "voice" in defense of Deaf culture. Pierre Desloges, "A Deaf Person's Observations about *An Elementary Course of Education for the Deaf*" (1779), trans. Franklin Philip, in *The Deaf Experience,* ed. Harlan Lane (Cambridge: Harvard University Press, 1984). Since Pierre Desloges's 1779 personal narrative, the Deaf community has used newspapers and books as a vital means of communication. For further discussion of the relation of print to Deaf culture, see Lennard Davis, *Theorizing Disability: Deafness and Textuality* (London: Verso, forthcoming).

7. Carole Boyce Davies, "Collaboration and the Ordering Imperative in Life Story Production," in *De/Colonizing the Subject: The Politics of Gender in Women's Autobiography,* ed. Sidonie Smith and Julia Watson (Minneapolis: University of Minnesota Press, 1992), 3.

8. Paul Smith, *Discerning the Subject* (Minneapolis: University of Minnesota Press, 1988), 105.

9. Personal interview, 12 November 1993. This interpreter wishes to remain anonymous.

10. The interpreting community is informally estimated to consist of 90 percent women. Recent statistics show that 92.4 percent of interpreters are Caucasian. Anthony Aramburo, "Interpreting within the African-American Deaf Community," *RID Views* 12, no. 6 (June 1993): 8.

11. Dale Dyal, telephone interview, 4 November 1993.

12. Anthony Aramburo, telephone interview, 5 November 1993.

13. See Ernest Hariston and Linwood Smith, *Black and Deaf in America* (Silver Spring, Md.: T. J. Publishers, 1983), 34.

14. Matthew Moore, personal interview, 21 November 1993. All subsequent references to Moore originate from this interview.

15. Elisabeth Burgos-Debray, "Introduction," in *I, Rigoberta Menchu*, trans. Ann Wright (London: Verso, 1991), xx.

16. Suzanne Hunt Sapienza, "A Deaf Perspective on Interpreters," *Deaf American* 38 (Summer 1988): 21.

17. Leah Hager Cohen, "An Interpreter Isn't Enough," *New York Times,* 22 February 1994, sec. A. As Cohen's book *Train Go Sorry: Inside a Deaf World* (New York: Random House, 1995) was published during the final stages of the preparation of this essay, I am unable to incorporate her experiences as an interpreter into the present study.

18. In urgent cases, such as courtroom interpreting, videotapes may be used to verify the interpreter's versions. In most everyday situations, however, such as in doctors' offices and counseling sessions, videotapes are not used.

19. Personal interview, 21 November 1993. This advocate wishes to remain anonymous.

20. Sapienza, "A Deaf Perspective," 22.

21. Amy VanSickle, personal interview, 15 November 1993.

22. Claudine Raynaud, "'Rubbing a Paragraph with a Soft Cloth'? Muted Voices and

Editorial Constraints in *Dust Tracks on a Road*," in *De/Colonizing the Subject: The Politics of Gender in Women's Autobiography*, ed. Sidonie Smith and Julia Watson (Minneapolis: University of Minnesota Press, 1992), 57.

23. Jacques Derrida, *The Ear of the Other,* ed. Christie McDonald, trans. Avital Ronell (New York: Schocken, 1985), 50–51.

24. Regi Carpenter, personal interview, 11 March 1993.

25. Michael Schwartz, telephone interview, 8 November 1993.

26. Quoted in Dolnick, "Deafness as Culture," 43.

3 / Medical Identity: My DNA/Myself

Kay K. Cook

Precisely the fact that I have so much to say about the body only
points to my backwardness, my provinciality; I cannot help but
read referentially, read to learn about the world.
>   JANE GALLOP, *Thinking through the Body*[1]

Writing her experiential history of the body, the autobiographical
subject engages in a process of critical self-consciousness through
which she comes to an awareness of the relationship of her specific
body to the cultural "body" and to the body politic. That change in
consciousness prompts cultural critique.
>   SIDONIE SMITH, *Subjectivity, Identity, and the Body*[2]

Clinical experience sees a new space opening up before it: the tangible space of the body, which at the same time is that opaque mass
in which secrets, invisible lesions, and the very mystery of origin lie
hidden.   MICHEL FOUCAULT, *The Birth of the Clinic*[3]

This "experiential history" of my body—as it both contests and intersects with the medical institution's version of me—is a rescue mission,
a self-retrieval, and my intent is to discover limits and boundaries. I
want to arrive at an epistemology of the tangible body, the object of
medical investigation. My questions have to do with the forms of
knowledge that are generated by medical data and what sort of control, if any, over the body these data give me. (The pursuit could, I am
aware, leave me at a dead end.) I wish to establish and contemplate the

tension that exists between these institutionalized data that form my medical, sometimes pathological, self and my own experience of my body as *my body*.

When I present myself to the medical world as an object of investigation, I become a medical commodity. My body's value is measured by the extent to which it needs repair, or the extent to which I'm willing to submit it to a battery of sophisticated tests, or the extent to which it is capable of being healed without reaching the point of diminishing return, that is, *death*. The exchange rate is based on the medical community's assessment of my chances of survival, my insurance coverage, my ability to pay, my belief that "something can be done," and my cooperation in matters dealing with invasive treatment of my body. The medical discourse that defines my body is based in part on these assessments, which, of course, have little to do with my tangible body. Thus, the mapping of my medical self includes the institution's formulation of my social, economic, and political selves. We (any or all of my "selves") do not exist in a vacuum.

In terms of my corporeality, I have only numbers, images, and narratives for distinguishing a self from what Jane Gallop, quoting Barthes, calls the "anarchic foam": "Not just the physical envelope," Gallop explains, "but other puzzling and irreducible givens, aris[e] from the 'body,' if that word means all that in the organism which exceeds and antedates consciousness or reason or interpretation."[4] If, then, we have only images and narratives through which to form bodily boundaries, what discourses, if any, enable us to represent and reclaim the body from those institutions that have appropriated it?

In late-twentieth-century U.S.A., the social discourse of the body is clearly of the external body, upon which is placed a value system that judges the individual according to how well she has managed to keep it under control, to keep it from bursting loose from its boundaries or sagging out of them. To be beautiful is to be repaired, to be fixed, to have faulty parts replaced.

Politically, the body, especially the woman's body, is up for grabs. Politically, many people, some of them very powerful, wish to legislate my body, pass laws about what I cannot do with my body, make my body the property of the state. The social, economic, and political discourse of my body does not begin to signify the experience of *my body*.

But medical discourse is scientific, empirical. It is based upon the objective observation of the "tangible body"; it is concerned with maintaining the health of the tangible body. Yet, unsurprisingly, my personal experience suggests that the medical authoring of the body, as it intersects with sites of cultural and political authoring, to use Smith's distinctions, complicates, rather than resolves, the bodily enigma. A palpable breast tumor—a substantial, physical, tangible growth in my body—does not show up on a mammogram. To the radiologist, therefore, it does not exist. "Where did you *think* the lump was?" he asks with superiority, before the ultrasound reveals concentrated calcification in the very area where I "thought" the lump existed. Three weeks later, the cancer, as well as the breast, is removed. In this specific case, I both knew and did not know my body; I detected the lump, but only after it had been growing there, possibly, for years. Numerous medical exams before this time had not detected the lump, either. My knowledge was limited to feeling a bodily change; I *felt* fine. The medical world, once the lump existed imagistically, had to provide me with the knowledge that my body was diseased.[5]

My bodily knowledge, then, is either unsubstantiated by medical data (a palpable change is not medically imaged) *or* occurs after the fact (a test reveals a life-threatening tumor), or both. Meanwhile, there seems no intuitive connection between knowing myself in the psychological sense and knowing myself in the physical sense. How can I *know,* for example, the physical condition of my uterus unless I can perceive it? Why, to take another instance, am I aware of the presence of a cataract only after it has developed to the point of blurring my vision? When a cell begins to divide abnormally, why doesn't an alarm go off in my brain?

I have been seduced by the notion that I can be attuned to my body; I am lulled into believing that, with frequent tests, I can monitor its activity and prevent the onset or recurrence of disease—or catch it in time. I submit my body to these exams with a belief, constantly being eroded, that vigilance will pay off; yet, I'm not certain what I think the payoff will achieve. Pain-free life? A longer life? Immortality?

Moreover, as my medical tests become more invasive, I am confronted with a material selfhood heretofore invisible to me. These continuous reminders of the materiality and interiority of my body challenge the ways that I have been used to thinking about my "self" as a fairly disembodied subject.

These medical histories, routine examinations, ultrasonography, as well as the more complex diagnostic techniques that confront me with images of my corporeal self—diseased or healthy—have the paradoxical effect of lulling me into the belief that "the map is the territory" while creating an anxiety that compels me to submit myself to more and more testing so that I can get to know my body better. A primary effect, then, of medical technology is to portray our bodies as dangerous to our selves, containing alien growths or lurking destructive tendencies. Perpetual self-surveillance and anxiety are the price of trying to detect illness before, or as, it begins.

In her own (tongue-in-cheek) anxiety toward discourse of the body and its referentiality, Jane Gallop defines the tightrope we walk between describing the anatomical body and creating it: Have we blurred the distinction between the poetics and the poiesis? Have we mistaken the discourse of self-creation—the poiesis—for the discourse of self-description—the poetics?[6] Does all this medical knowledge merely turn back on itself, I wonder? What added dimension of subjectivity occurs with the introduction of the medical model, if there is an added dimension?

What is the effect of my medical self on those other dimensions of being that I refer to as my "self"? How does the language of the examining room challenge the language of my own room—challenge, for instance, my sense of the body in which I sit myself down to write, lie myself down to make love, stand tall with arms across my chest to deliver parental instruction? "The human being," Jane Gallop says, "cannot help but try to make sense out of his own idiosyncratic bodily shape: tall or short, fat or thin, male or female, to name only a few of the least subtle morphological distinctions." But, she goes on to concede, "the theorizing is precisely endless, an eternal reading of the 'body' as authorless text, full of tempting, persuasive significance, but lacking a final guarantee of intended meaning."[7]

This "eternal reading," my endless curiosity about my intrinsic self, has been fed by the proliferation of medical knowledge. Not only do I get to see a pink, healthy cervix, and not only do I perceive the image of my uterus produced by sound waves, but also, and most astonishing, it is possible to know myself right down to the skeletal image of my bone scan, and even deeper, to the molecular spirals of DNA embedded within my individual cells. Currently, when I speak of my interior life, in one respect, I have retrieved the spatial trope reserved for psychology and converted it into its literal, physical meaning. To say I have a rich inner life takes on a new meaning entirely; the statement evokes the images and narratives of my literally interior life: my physiological, organic, hemoglobular, cellular, molecular autobiography.

In the sections that follow, as I try to answer some of the questions I have posed, I move from the least technologically sophisticated, the patient's individual file, through imaging techniques and DNA analysis. Although the movement is vertical, it is not hierarchical; I don't get closer to the truth the deeper I go, I merely generate another image to exist among the images that precede it. Rather than attempting to be inclusive of all medical diagnostic procedures, I have selected, as illustration, those with which I am most familiar. I conclude the essay by considering implications of the medical authoring of the body on personal identity.

Form-ing the Body: The Medical History, the Medical File

Medical authoring begins here. No matter what the purpose, I am not allowed into the medical examining room without first creating my medical autobiography on the ubiquitous form attached to the ubiquitous clipboard. This is the part of the process in which I supply the narrative, the secondary material that accompanies the primary one, which is the body I present for evaluation.

The medical profession is only one of the numerous institutions that require this kind of autobiography. I don't know if the response is common, but frankly, I always feel a bit tawdry and more than a bit reticent when I have to provide autobiographical information to those faceless establishments that so frequently demand it of me. I have let insurance lapse, can't remember when my son André had his vaccination, forgotten to have regular dental checkups. The institutional Kay Cook is indeed a sorry mess. That person on the document, who has had too many last names and moved around too much, recoils knowing that soon some stranger will know that she doesn't own her house, has a lot of medical bills, no inheritance, no investments, no capital gains. (Please! I have given to charity!) Look—the information she gave to the insurance company doesn't even match the life history she gave to the credit union when she bought her car. (Why can't I *ever* remember the address and phone number of my nearest relative?) Self-presentation is risky, particularly when there is an audience, responding, judging, evaluating.

But these forms are trivial compared with the sinking feeling I get when filling in my medical history. This blank form requires the authorization of my body. I "flesh" myself out here, answering the typical questions posed to women. Although ostensibly a medical history, the information I provide is not merely factual; it is layered, at least in my own mind, as the narrative of my medical self collides with the values of my cultural and political selves.

Below, for example, are some of the questions that most women typically must answer. My responses contain dual, triple, quadruple readings of myself. I'm not certain, moreover, that my physician remains faithful to my medical narrative; does he superimpose his own cultural and political biases, whatever they may be, onto my medical autobiography? More than likely, he merely scans this autobiography, which carries such strong resonances for me, and classifies me, with a few exceptions, as a medically typical middle-aged female.

Date of menarche, the onset of menstruation? Age 12.

Easy question. I was in the sixth grade, at school. I had on a full skirt, and the blood, which really looked like muddy water, got on the back of it. I was sent to the nurse—with a friend. I did not tell my mother until I had my next period, six months later. Medically, this age is neither early nor late; I am not an aberration, although I felt like one at the time.

Do you have a history of:
Heart disease? No
High blood pressure? No
Diabetes? No
Cancer? Yes. *Type?* Breast.

So there it is. Two words, "yes" and "breast." My encounter with mortality; the medical world's victory. "Medicine offers modern man the obstinate, yet reassuring fact of his finitude," Foucault says. "[In] it, death is endlessly repeated, but it is also exorcised; and although it ceaselessly reminds man of the limit he bears within him, it also speaks to him of that technical world that is the armed, positive full form of his finitude."[8] Woman, too, as my scarred body would confirm. (This male voice speaking to me from the grave excludes me from the discourse. But never mind. Foucault dealt with his own troubled bodily discourse; our respective diseases [AIDS and breast cancer] are both culturally and politically sexualized.) Foucault is suggesting, of course, that the triumph of the clinic, the exorcism of death (in my case the removal of my breast), depends upon one's acknowledgment of one's mortality.

I had another tumor removed when I was a teenager. I'm certain it was cancerous because I was so sick, but I think Mother didn't want to scare me. Sometimes I mention this; sometimes I don't. I don't worry if I omit it—it's my autobiographical privilege of selectivity.

Is there a history of breast cancer in your family?
Yes. *Who?* Maternal aunt.

For many years, I *thought* this was an easy answer: "No." Then, after my breast cancer, Mother told me that my aunt had the disease too. We were a secretive family about such matters. Yet, since antiquity we have been aware of, and plagued by, generational, hereditary connections. In Greek drama a woman named Jocasta defies the Delphic Oracle who announces the infant she is carrying—whom we know as Oedipus—will kill his father and marry his mother. Challenge as she will, Jocasta cannot run from the truth that her body carries. Apollo, the repository of divine knowledge, has foreseen the event.

With a history of breast cancer, I, too, hear the prophecy from the Oracle at Delphi. So do my daughters, my nieces, my sisters. Our Apollo is not a divine being; rather, it is body knowledge—our genetic code, our predispositions. Like Jocasta, we will not sit back and wait for the inevitable; we will try to take control of our fate. Unlike the Greeks, we are often successful, but not always.

How old was your mother when she went through menopause?
50, I think . . . no, 60, perhaps.

She called it "the Change of Life"; as far as I can remember, she was always going through it. She said that we had to be nice to her always because it was a terrible, terrible time; my sisters and I thought when we fought that we might cause her to die from the Change. "Menopause," my medical book tells me, "The time that follows the last menstrual period of a woman's life."[9] Oh, come now. That term resonates with the cultural stigma placed on women in this country. Medically, Mother's experience reflects the norm; culturally, she is over the hill.

There are those pangs of sorrow that never cease after all these years:

Father living?
No.
Cause of death?
Cancer.

That's good, I have learned. Hardly any correlation between father/daughter cancers. His health is not connected to mine. Right. I wondered what was good about his awful death.

Mother living?
Yes.
State of health?
Alzheimer's disease. (Hello, Oracle.)
History of Alzheimer's disease?
Four aunts, my mother's sisters, and my grandmother.

I am hearing the heavy gongs at Delphi; they are ringing in my ears. Without knowing much about the House of Oedipus, we, my sisters and I, began early on to call it the "Turner Curse." The medical world is baffled over this one. In a strange reversal of the Foucauldian edict, Alzheimer's disease is *not* an assurance of our finitude, except where the mind is concerned. It presents us with the horror of continuing indefinitely with a healthy body and demented mind—a terrible manifestation of the Cartesian mind/body split.

The questions continue. We have to tell about those choices that perhaps led us to our fate, although we ignorantly thought we were pursuing the right thing. Have I ever taken the Pill? For what period of time? (Of course, it was when the dosage was so high.) It's difficult not to feel a bit psychologically disrobed, before the physical actuality, when filling out those forms: "How many pregnancies?" "How many live births?" I will be asked to explain the discrepancy in numbers, if any. They're going to find out I was a teenaged mother *and* had a child when I was 39. They even want to know the names of those children. I sit there producing a medical self. (*Do you smoke?* No. *Do you drink?* Well, yes. *How much?* I don't know . . . a glass of wine a week.) As I record the facts of my sexual and reproductive life, of my family history, I am forced to confront the meaning and implications of the Kay Cook who has, even in these early stages of the examination, become a medical text. What is the use of this patient narrative? How does it define my medical body? What does it matter, medically, that I have named my children Catherine, Julia, and André?

It is the compulsion toward description, Foucault will say, as he measures the "moment" in the change of medical discourse from that of metaphoric to that of rational and scientific, the same compulsion that created the medical file, my medical autobiography. Discussing the birth of a philosophy of medicine that established the individual as an object around which the doctor could "hold a scientifically structured discourse," he accounts for the authority of the individual's medical file. Foucault quotes this passage, taken from a twentieth-century medical text:

> In order to offer each of our patients a course of treatment perfectly adapted to his illness and to himself, we try to obtain a complete, objective idea of his case; we gather together in a special file of his own all the information we have about him. We "observe" him in the same way we observe the stars or a laboratory experiment.[10]

The rat, I guess, must have "a special file of his own," too; perhaps Andromeda does as well. And I have my file, which is always placed outside the office door while I am inside, usually cold and shivering under a paper garment. The folder is both secret and public; so is my body. The information sheathed by the folder outside has an eerie correspondence to the coarse paper garment that hides my body momentarily from the medical gaze. (I have never been certain which is more ludicrous, the bizarre attempt of modesty that the paper thing with sleeves signifies or the lush silk robe that the patient is offered in the plastic surgeon's office, which of course signifies the possibility of creating a beautiful, more aesthetic body.)

I used to think it was illegal for me to look into that mysterious file my doctors have always consulted and written in, right in front of me. Years ago, if by some chance the room was cleared of doctor and nurse, I would look at that folder, beckoning to me, lying on that desk in the empty office. With one ear attuned to noises heralding the return of the officials in charge, I would quickly and stealthily grab the file and start thumbing through it—searching for the ancient and privileged secrets I was not supposed to know about myself. I had long ago developed the skill, upon hearing footfalls, of returning an object to its

place and leaping back to where I had been sitting almost instantaneously; it's a childhood skill—we all know how to do it. Though I
never learned, as I suspected, that I had something dreadfully wrong, I
did feel fascinated by reading about myself; I became almost obsessed
with the folder bearing my name. Now, of course, I just ask for a copy
of my doctor's notes, laboratory reports, and the like. I still pore over
the file with the same obsession. I admit it. I'm searching for my body
and some part of me believes I'm going to find it in those reports. That
"part" of me still believes, as did Linneaus, as did Diderot, that if a
subject is classified and defined, then it is known. If that subject (in this
case, me) can be assigned a numerical value that is then placed in a hierarchical arrangement with other subjects and their numerical values,
then that subject is known by its conformity with or alterity to other
subjects. Ironically, in a world where even the conformist complains of
being "just another number," laboratory test numbers can resonate
with the metaphysical significance of numerology.[11]

Medical Self-Images

"One must as far as possible make science ocular."
    MICHEL FOUCAULT, *The Birth of the Clinic*[12]

Many of the reports, however, in "this special file, all my own" are derived from data much more significant than the medical history I have
filled out; they reveal the results from the images "taken" of me through
the X ray, the ultrasound, the CAT scan. In an interesting reversal, the
medical gaze looks first at images, then at the body. Only rarely does
the medical institution shift the gaze directly to the body; the images—
in my own case, the mammogram, ultrasound, and CAT scan—almost
always mediate between my body and the physician who will treat or
diagnose it.

Using the methods of medical imaging just enumerated, I will discuss in this section the ways in which each image cuts across the body
differently, ignoring virtually the whole of it to focus on some telling
feature. These data supply me with an amazing amount of separate,
but not necessarily related, facts about myself. That is, although mammogram, ultrasound, and CAT scan produce highly sophisticated and
scientific images of and information about my body, they are always of
the fragmented self: the organ, the tissue, the cross section, the suspicious spots lurking deep in the interior.

Mammography

The first form of medical imaging I wish to discuss is the mammogram. Designed to detect disease in one of the most susceptible areas of a woman's body, its presence and function are known to the entire population, thanks primarily to television advertisements and to the startling proliferation of breast cancer diagnoses in the past ten years. (Ah—the irony of the most commodified and fetishized part of the female body becoming diseased at the rate of almost 200,000 a year!)

Mammography and I have made our peace with one another. I trudge faithfully each year to have a mammogram taken of my one remaining breast. Although neither my doctor nor I verbally acknowledge that this was not an effective diagnostic instrument for me, I always make certain I have access to this image. (As with any autobiography, one must remember not to get hung up on factual truth in medical autobiography; mammograms may fail to reveal, according to some statistics, 17 percent of all malignant tumors.) I know that we (the radiologist, the doctor, and I) are supposed to be looking for "suspicious" spots on the mammogram, which I do when my doctor holds the film up to the illuminated panel, but I'm always fascinated first of all with the image of my breast, its outline and shape as it appears on that film. (I'm surprised it has any recognizable shape at all, given that, in order to get that picture, it has been mashed flat as a pancake by a glass panel bearing down on it.) My point is that, first, in spite of myself, I look at the shape of my breast as a representation of *me*, and then I'm concerned with any pathology it might reveal.

Although these responses are almost simultaneous, my delayed reaction to the state of my health sometimes startles me. As *me*, the image is deceptive. The shape of the breast on the film appears silhouetted, of course, and, because of the angle of the X ray, the breast seems to be in profile. The "perky" curvature of the breast on the film is merely an optical illusion; I am not really viewing my breast in profile. Unlike a photographic image, which would show a drooping, stretch-marked, aging breast, the mammogram reveals an outline of youthfulness. What lurks inside that outline is mostly indecipherable to me, although I'm learning to read this text. (I'm always told that the mammogram will be "read" before my next appointment.) Murky shades of gray, white, and black denote breast tissue that may reveal, as my report will say, "slight fibrocystic disease, mild hyperplasia: recommend follow-up mammogram in one year." In fact, if I would just admit it to myself, this mammogram is an empty sign, neither relating to any physical signified nor resonating with any layered or internal truths about Kay Cook's breast. Conceivably, a deadly signified (in turn a signifier for the mortality of the body) could be lurking within my own tissue, for which, at the moment the likeness was taken, no sign was imaged.

Ultrasonography

Images produced by X ray (the mammogram) and those produced by ultrasonography can reveal very different pictures of the same part of the body. The deadly tumor missed by the mammogram, as I have noted, can be picked up by ultrasound. This is uneasy knowledge— what can the next layer of imaging pick up, or rather produce an image of, that ultrasound cannot? What has the mammogram detected that the ultrasound did not? Is there any referent to these multiple images that can be produced? Are any of them my breast? Are they all my breast? If I layered image over image, would I then have a whole that I could say is *really* a likeness of my breast?

Ultrasonography, the second form of imaging I wish to discuss, is self-portrait by sound wave. The procedure produces images much the same as the impressionists produced portraits, only the ultrasound is concerned with the play of sound waves penetrating tissue and the impressionist painter with the play of light on the object being reproduced. In either case, the end product is suitable for framing.

In fact, probably the most widespread use of ultrasound is on pregnant women. As a scanner moves over the abdomen of the woman, sound waves penetrate the uterus; these waves bounce back to a monitor that produces the image, which can be captured immediately by the polaroid camera attached to the machine.[13] As many women who have had pregnancies in the last ten years know, the ultrasound examination will produce the image of a fetus; the parents get to take one of the images home with them, sort of a baby's first picture. In fact, in the past few years, I have often seen these peculiar polaroid images tacked up over many a woman's desk or work station.

I'm an old hand with ultrasound. Fifteen years ago, it located the position of my fetus so that I could have amniocentesis without puncturing the little organism. (The amniocentesis itself revealed a genetically healthy male, but didn't provide a hint about his future relationship with his mother and father.) Three years ago, it found the tumor in my breast that the mammogram didn't reveal. Most recently it penetrated my uterus through my vagina to take a look at the inside. (The doctor said the images looked like "mush." My sister's fibroid cyst looks like a tomato, but my daughter's is the size of a grapefruit—I'm not certain how the food images got started, but they're certainly perpetuated. It makes it difficult to walk through the produce section of a supermarket without thinking of one's insides.)

Unfortunately but logically, we have correlated this medical image with the photograph. We are actually perceiving, however, images produced by means other than light-sensitive chemicals. That polaroid photograph that a pregnant woman frames and displays is a photograph only of an image produced by sound waves echoing off tissue and registered on a monitor. The consequences of the confusion are never so pointedly obvious as they are in "pro-life" advertisements that make their appeal based on such an image presented as a "photograph" of a baby. Because the ultrasound image bears a resemblance to photographs that we imbue with all sorts of tenderness and warm feelings, we are cajoled into believing that we are seeing an infant; often it appears to be sucking its little thumb. Because of the strong cultural and, now, political responses to such an image, as laypeople, we rarely examine it in the context for which it was produced, that of the medical institution.

I think that we make egregious errors when we look at medical images as we look at photographs, and these errors occur when the medical body intersects with the cultural body and the body politic, to use Sidonie Smith's distinctions once more. Culturally, for example, we were born into the world of the photo, and the fact that most of us own some sort of camera, or at least have had our pictures "taken," attests to the universality of the photographic image. Moreover, even though we know about darkroom "tricks," we tend to have an abiding faith in these images. As Barthes says in his work on photography, we believe in "the truth of the image":

> I call "photographic referent" not the *optionally* real thing to which an image or sign refers, but the *necessarily* real thing which has been placed before the lens. . . . Painting can feign reality without having seen it. Discourse combines signs which have referents, of course, but these referents are most often "chimeras." Contrary to these imitations, in photography I can never deny *the thing has been there.*[14]

In ultrasonography as well, we cannot deny that "the thing has been there." What the *thing* is, however, is problematic. As I have tried to show, ultrasound can locate some kinds of disease and therefore can be a lifesaving or life-prolonging diagnostic instrument. It can, moreover, reveal defects in a fetus that might cause it to be aborted. Yet the image of a growing fetus may stimulate pride and gratification as well and may be used to reinforce positively the process of pregnancy and childbearing. On the other hand, by revealing a human likeness it may block or induce guilt about abortion. Of all of the diagnostic procedures, then, ultrasound imaging has become the most socialized and politicized. It has made its way into the national consciousness. The way this specific kind of medical knowledge is produced and consumed, for instance, gives corporations and the states power over our bodies, rather than the reverse.

The CAT Scan and Radionuclide Imaging

I have chosen the relatively new field of the CAT scan and other sophisticated imaging techniques as the final mode of imaging I will discuss because, of all the diagnostic procedures I know, this one has the most chilling effect. With the CAT (computerized axial tomography) scan, I move from the geographic investigation of surfaces to the archaeology of the body, where physicians try to dig up all the information they can—right down to the bones. The CAT scan can be one hundred times more sensitive than the traditional X ray. My own experience with the scanner was for the purpose of "staging" my cancer to see if there was bone metastasis (there was not).

The bone scan (radionuclide imaging) itself is preceded by an injection of a radioactive substance that in a two-hour period will work its way to the bones and embed itself in cancerous tissue growing there, which will then be reflected as dark spots on the skeletal image.[15] I recall that during the time lapse between injection and scanning, while waiting for the material to makes its way to my bones so that the scanner could image it, a technician suggested that I go for a hike. I went to a shopping center instead, mostly because of fear that I had something radioactive coursing through my body and, if I keeled over, I wanted to be around people who would come to my rescue. The injection worked silently, however, as most foreign things in my body tend to.

Being scanned by a machine was in itself an event. As I lay upon a typical-looking (although narrower than usual) examination table, the machine, placed on a bar with hinges, hovered slightly above my body, moving slowly over it, without comment, back and forth, head to toe; switching angles, back and forth again. It took about forty-five minutes, the uncomfortable moments being when it was hovering above my head, bearing down on me and *looking,* way deep down and not saying a thing—not even a doctoral "hmmm." I know it sounds bizarre for me to so personify the machine, but the medical gaze felt so similar to the physician's gaze that I found myself trying to humanize it—perhaps it was its seemingly autonomous movement.[16] When the technician returned and freed me, I had to wait while the computerized machine next to my table spouted out the result, which, as I saw her examining it, I asked to see. I was unprepared for the lucidity of the image.

Emily Dickinson had a phrase for it: "Zero at the Bone," she wrote, in response to the chilling effect of coming upon a snake.[17] Her response is my response to the bone itself: the entire skeletal frame produced by a bone scan—this is the very image of death. That small skeleton, me (the product of the scan is no larger than an 8½ by 11 photograph), is the ultimate in seeing inward. The experience of seeing one's self defleshed *and* diminished must be very much the same sensation as looking at the earth from a satellite; there is a sense of remoteness, but at the same time, I realize I am seeing a part of myself otherwise invisible—that large picture and the small one at once. My body—deconstructed to the subhuman level. This image is at once me and not-me. Existing on its own, it would not be named Kay Cook, but would be referred to only as her remains, if it were identified at all. Zero at the Bone.

These tests I have just described are not unusual—a lot of people undergo many, many more invasive diagnostic measures. But that is my very point. The imaging procedures I have experienced—the mammogram, ultrasound, CAT scan—(and some I haven't mentioned) are routine for women diagnosed with breast cancer, and some of the tests are routine for men and women in general. And so the challenge to subjectivity as a result of my confrontation with these images is hardly unique to me.

Roland Barthes, in his autobiography, contemplates the effect of such an accumulation of self-images. Using photographs liberally throughout his text, he writes:

> What is the "you" you might or might not look like? Where do
> you find it—by which morphological or expressive calibration?
> Where is your authentic body? You are the only one who can
> never see yourself except as an image . . . and especially for your
> own body, you are condemned to the repertoire of its images.[18]

The curious word in this quotation is "condemned." By suggesting an existential condemnation, a Sartrean "no exit," Barthes acknowledges that one's construction of one's material body as a unified entity is a fiction depending wholly on images. Without mediation of the image, for example, I view my body only partially (my arm, my toe, never my face, never my back). Driven by the need to believe that I am a unified subject, at least on the material level, I seek images of wholeness (the full-length mirror, for example). Although it would seem that the medical images would produce depth, by filling in the external image of the photograph or the mirror, what they actually do is present the self as another accumulation of very different and fragmented images, lacking the depth of field that the photograph contains and therefore seeming less "real." Moreover, when these medical images detect an event (cancer) that the photograph of the external self has not detected, then it seems impossible to make the varied medical images relate in any way to the varied photographs. I am thinking, for example, of looking at a photograph of myself about a month before I detected my breast lump. I stare at that photo, taken on the beach in Los Angeles, because in it I have two breasts and because one of those breasts contains a tumor that will soon be imaged by ultrasound. In this photo, I am the picture of health.

I cannot begin to imagine the level of bodily experience that the person with the bizarre, undiagnosable symptoms must have from being subjected to numerous procedures in the medical institution's attempt to match the symptom to the image to the body to the treatment. I can only assume that with a number of these procedures over time, the individual must become primarily body; the structure of self, primarily physical.

My DNA/Myself

Finally, there is "degree zero," the deepest, lowest (I'm trying to use spatial metaphors for a procedure that defies spatiality) level at which the medical gaze perceives the human being. With the discovery of

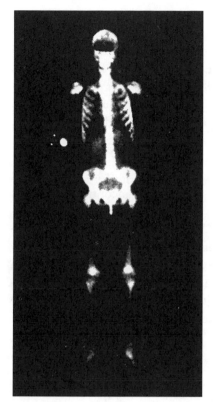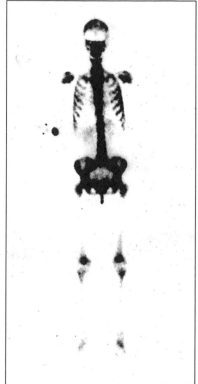

Figure 3.1. "Zero at the Bone": A portrait of the author by CAT scan.

DNA and the subsequent technology surrounding it, with the widespread use of diagnostic nuclear medicine and three-dimensional scanners, such as the CAT scan, we have been microanalyzed at skeletal, cellular, and molecular levels, an expansive reduction that can reveal to us our past, present, and future. We have learned that we carry with us medical knowledge to which, on our own, we have no access. To return to the analogy of the Jocasta/Oedipus myth, we have internalized the divine knowledge of Apollo; we must look to tests, as the Greeks did to the oracles, to reveal the truths we carry with us.

I am thinking here specifically of the use of DNA analysis in diagnosis and prognosis. DNA, a substance found in the nuclei of cells, contains encoded material that, decoded, can reveal our individual master plan, or our genetic code, to put it another way. No longer the exclusive domain of research laboratories, DNA analysis has been put to everyday use, revealing secrets, characterizing abnormal tissue. DNA "fingerprinting," for example, as paternity suits attest, identifies the genetic presence of an individual across generations. If that individual has tried to run away, like the House of Oedipus, his genetics will catch up with him. We will know where he's been.

Diagnostically, DNA analysis can reveal a lot about what has happened or may happen with abnormal cells in the body. Because DNA carries instructions for cell division, its synthesis is crucial to that process. The advent of cancer, which is a "disorder of cell proliferation," occurs at this level. As my oncological text puts it: "A metabolic error allows cancer cells to progress in continual uncontrolled growth. This directly violates normal density inhibition characteristics that automatically limit cellular division."[19] DNA analysis can characterize the way in which the cells of a malignant tumor are dividing, and this characterization can in turn enable an oncologist to prescribe certain treatments. DNA flow cytometry, as it is called, determines the "behavior" of the malignant growth—its "ploidy" and its "s-phase." The results of the DNA analysis occur as numbers in a laboratory report. My DNA histogram looks like this:

DNA Index	1.00
PLOIDY	DIPLOID
S-PHASE FRACTION	4.9%
S-PHASE INTERPRETATION	LOW

The "ploidy" of the cellular structure of the tumor, I am told, determines whether its division is uniform (diploid) or whether it behaves like it's crazy (these are the words I have heard), with cell division being wildly irregular (aneuploid). The "s-phase" measures the rate at which cancerous cells are multiplying. It can be either high or low.

I am told about the "behavior" of the malignant growth: diploid, low s-phase. I understand that this characterization makes me look good—I really am on my best behavior here; my numbers are low. I am not entirely confident that I can grasp the intelligence that an analysis at this level of my body has revealed, however. No one knows the source of the "error," the incident that causes the break in the DNA code, that will then cause, in synthesis, the replication of abnormal cells.

It is somewhat uncertain, then, how much good that knowledge will do me or my physician—but there it is, a predictor, a fortune teller, an oracle. I have learned a bit about the nature of oracles, though. When I first learned of the test, I thought it would give me more specific information; I thought that *knowing* cellular and molecular characteristics would give me some power over my body, that I and my medical team could then get my body under control. (This entire episode has fairly much destroyed for me the myths that seeing is believing and that knowledge is power.) It's not that the information is useless; it *is* important in several respects, but mostly in follow-up, in treatment, in policing the body rather than curing the body. My own oncologist doubts that physicians will continue to find the test useful. But it is so impressive, so sophisticated, and *so* just one more fragment of my self presented to the medical world, thickening the file of my very own, that which will distinguish me from the next patient.

I think that this analysis cannot probe any further into the body than this discussion of DNA. As I draw these musings to a close, I want to return to the question of an epistemology of the body, to the role of medical discourse in contributing to and/or obfuscating body knowledge, and to a theory of medical autobiography.

The Age of Anxiety: Policing the Body

It is a late-twentieth-century phenomenon; we have a compulsion to explore every nook and cranny of our corporeal selves. Every major and specialized magazine, health newsletter, news program, and foundation advertisement reminds us that our bodies *are* ourselves, and both health *and* illness are identity. There was a time when the only nod to health awareness in public places was the ubiquitous scale that for a nickel would give you your weight *and* your fortune—an indication of how seriously we took the whole thing. Now, cholesterol screening in shopping centers, blood pressure machines in supermarkets, and "healthmark" signs on certain food products attest to our bodily awareness. We're either recovering from a major illness or trying like hell to prevent one.

What happens to identity when we place so much emphasis on our bodily selves? Consider how and why we create our autobiographies. Whether we formally publish retrospective documentaries of our lives or record our thoughts in diaries and letters, we are structuring—however loosely, however selectively—identities that not only mirror us, but create us. (Even the act of reading what I have written about myself changes who I am.) Often we present these accounts to our most intimate friends; frequently our life writings are read by large audiences. Any reviews of that material—positive or negative—are internalized; we make further adjustments. We are selves in flux.

Now consider how the medical profession, paradoxically, coauthors our autobiographies with us. From routine annual checkups to the sophisticated diagnostic imaging techniques that I have discussed, our bodies are turned into sites of geographic and archaeological investigation, which are then turned into images for which they supply the texts. We have our personal medical historians to whom we provide the primary material: our bodies and our narratives about them. In return, we receive our "profiles," descriptions of our current state of health, notations about the past state of health as evidenced by the current data and images, and projections for our future (these last details, of course, truly challenge the boundaries of what we define as autobiography). Even with routine physical examinations, we must adjust our self-images to the profiles that we receive from these coauthors.

I, for example, have scrutinized the image of my one remaining breast on the X ray; I know how much iron is in my blood. I have seen strands of flesh extracted from my uterus and carefully placed in vials, where my blood colors the liquid in which the "specimen" is suspended. I have watched blood from my veins fill one, two, three vials at a time (I have taken a sticker, intended for children, that has on it a replica of the Statue of Liberty and the statement, "I was good; I didn't move"). I have read laboratory reports where I am reduced to tissue analysis—my breast sliced in pieces so that it could be more completely examined. I could "reconstruct" my body if I wanted to; flesh can be tunneled from my abdomen up to my chest and molded into the shape of a breast; I can use my body to remake my body.

I have seemingly endless ways of perceiving and describing my body. Does this heal the mind/body split? Does it widen it? Since my insidious self caught me off guard once, I'm not so free with these answers. I have yet to regain trust; like Jocasta, I fear that there just might be another narrative waiting to catch up with me. (It felt as if I caught part of me cheating on myself—growing tumors without my knowledge—a violation of an understanding I thought I had with my body.)

An intelligent young medical student innocently volunteers to demonstrate a CAT scan, which reveals that a large portion of one cerebral hemisphere is missing. An older man has a routine blood test that reveals the presence of leukemia. A self-examination detects a cancerous lump. An older woman is surprised to find out that the do-it-yourself test shows positive for pregnancy. Do our bodies just plug along without us, performing routines, performing tricks? Or do the multiple narratives produced by the medical institution so confront us with the materiality of our bodies that "self" is informed by physicality?

From the routine data to the cellular statistics and imagistic testimonies of the more elaborate diagnostic procedures, medical science has, for a long time, been attempting a discourse that defines what both Foucault and Gallop refer to, respectively, as the "opaque mass" and the "bodily enigma." The power of the numbers, of the images, and of the medical gaze peering inward denotes a power that shapes our own self-examinations, that defines us, particularly as women, in terms of medicalized life stages, each of which poses some threat to our bodily stability. As healthy women, we get Pap smears; as healthy pregnant women, we listen cautiously to heartbeats. As middle-aged women, we begin to think of the menopausal body, its physical discomfort and the medication that, while easing the discomfort, poses dangers of its own. As aging women, we get tested for osteoporosis and worry about our brittle bones. (Men at this time are finding out about their prostates, or maybe their hernias, and watching the graphic results of their treadmill tests. Actually, women are on those treadmills too.)

I have dealt with the profound psychological consequences of body knowledge—the inescapable genesis, genetics, the remoteness of my physical and genetic autobiography. "Health replaces salvation," Foucault quotes Guardia in his discussion about our confrontation with finitude that the medical profession both confronts us with and rescues us from. "Death is a key part of the bodily enigma," Jane Gallop responds, "perhaps the most violent sign that we live in a nonsensical body which limits the powers of our will and consciousness."[20] When Descartes posited the mind/body split, was his treatise a poiesis or a poetics? Our late-twentieth-century obsessions with illness, health, aging, fitness of necessity make our bodies ourselves. Unlike Descartes, we can't seem to get our minds off our bodies, which will never, ever exist for us outside the cultural, political, and medical discourses that inscribe them.

Notes

I wish to thank my friends and colleagues, Michael Cohen, Michael Donovan, Suzanne Juhasz, Thomas Couser, Sidonie Smith, Julia Watson, and Danielle Dubrasky, for their helpful comments on drafts of this essay. I also wish to acknowledge the valuable comments of Russell Martin, who took time from the Southern Utah Writer's Conference to read my work. Both the form and the content of this work were inspired by an NEH seminar on gender and autobiography conducted by Nancy K. Miller, summer 1991.

1. Jane Gallop, *Thinking through the Body* (New York: Columbia University Press), 93.

2. Sidonie Smith, *Subjectivity, Identity, and the Body: Women's Autobiographical Practices in the Twentieth Century* (Bloomington: Indiana University Press, 1993), 131.

3. Michel Foucault, *The Birth of the Clinic*, trans. A. M. Sheridan Smith (New York: Vintage, 1973), 122.

4. Gallop, *Thinking through the Body*, 13.

5. I have recounted my experience with breast cancer in a special issue on illness, disability, and life writing in "Filling the Dark Spaces: Breast Cancer and Autobiography," *a/b: Auto/Biography Studies* 6, no. 1 (1991): 85–94.

6. Gallop's question is in the context of her discussion of Luce Irigaray's *This Sex Which Is Not One*, trans. Catherine Porter (New York: Cornell University Press, 1985). Gallop suggests that "what Irigaray calls 'this multiple of feminine desire and language' (p. 29) is not based in anatomy but constructs it. I can then assert that the Irigarayan poetics of the body is not an expression of the body but a poiesis, a creation of the body." *Thinking through the Body*, 94.

7. Gallop, *Thinking through the Body*, 13.

8. Foucault, *The Birth of the Clinic*, 198.

9. Winnifred B. Cutler and Celso-Ramón García, *Menopause: A Guide for Women and the Men Who Love Them* (New York: W. W. Norton, 1992), 396.

10. J.-C. Sournia, *Logique et morale du diagnostic* (Paris, 1962), 19, quoted in Foucault, *The Birth of the Clinic*, xv.

11. The numbers assigned to laboratory tests that measure the presence of estrogen receptors in a breast tumor carry great significance. My number is 36, "positive." My friend Joanne's is close to 200, "highly positive." Being positive for estrogen receptors is truly a positive condition, because medication exists that seems to block estrogen and therefore retards tumor growth. Most women with breast cancer compare their chances of survival by comparing their estrogen numbers. As another case in point, my grandson was recently tested for autism. The neurologist projected ultraviolet light onto Drew's body in search of otherwise invisible birthmarks, the presence of which is connected with autism. Drew had one such mark, but the doctor indicated that in autistic children, there are usually seven or eight. When I asked my daughter Julie what the correlation is between the invisible marks and autism, she replied that she didn't know, adding, "I expected him to get out the tea leaves next."

12. Foucault, *The Birth of the Clinic*, 88.

13. The medical definition of ultrasonography, taken from *Dorland's Illustrated Medical Dictionary*, 26th ed. (Philadelphia: W. B. Saunders, 1981), is "the visualization of deep structures of the body by recording the reflections of (echoes of) pulses of ultrasonic waves directed into the tissues." Gray-scale ultrasound is "a B-scan technique in which a video-scan converter amplifies and processes echoes according to their strength into a visual display ranging from white for the strongest echoes to varying shades of gray" (1419).

14. Roland Barthes, *Camera Lucida: Reflections on Photography*, trans. Richard Howard (New York: Noonday, 1981), 76.

15. My medical book by Margaret J. Griffiths, Kathleen H. Murray, and Phyllis C. Russo, *Oncology Nursing: Pathophysiology, Assessment, and Intervention* (New York: Macmillan, 1984), states that "these radioisotope scanning procedures are atraumatic and essentially nonallergenic" (68). I remember the technician advising me to watch for flushing and/or a rash. This book explains the scanning procedure as follows: "Radiopharmaceuticals emit gamma radiation, which is converted by a scanner or scintillation detector and displayed on an oscilloscope, thereby determining areas of radionuclide concentration. Radionuclide imaging is designated by 'hot-spot' or 'cold-spot' imaging and describes the amount of radionuclide uptake by involved tissues" (69).

16. My medical research reveals that I'm not the only one to attribute human characteristics to the machine. The following excerpt is taken from *Black's Medical Dictionary*, 37th ed., ed. Gordon Macpherson (Lanham, Md.: Barnes & Noble, 1992): "Scanning is a technique which is used to determine the distribution of radioactive isotopes within the body. . . . In the conventional scanner the radiation detector, which is a scintillation counter, 'sees' only a small cross-sectional area of the body at a time. The activity 'seen' at each point is registered and a 'map' of the activity seen over the scanned area is recorded" (311). It is interesting that the crucial metaphors are placed in quotation marks, an indication that the editor wished to bring attention to the fact that he was only too aware of the implications of attributing human vision to the scanner.

17. Emily Dickinson, Poem No. 986. The final stanza of the poem, which begins "A narrow Fellow in the Grass," concludes: "But never met this Fellow / Attended, or alone / Without a tighter breathing / And Zero at the Bone—."

18. Roland Barthes, *Roland Barthes by Roland Barthes*, trans. Richard Howard (New York: Noonday, 1977), n.p. This quotation is part of the series of photographs that introduces the work.

19. Griffiths et al., *Oncology Nursing*, 33.

20. Foucault, *The Birth of the Clinic*, 198; Gallop, *Thinking through the Body*, 13.

Part II

Entertaining Lives

Much postmodern engagement with culture emerges from the yearning to do intellectual work that connects with habits of being, forms of artistic expression and aesthetics that inform the daily life of writers and scholars as well as a mass population. . . . It's exciting to think, write, talk about and create art that reflects passionate engagement with popular culture, because this may very well be "the" central future location of resistance struggle, a meeting place where new and radical happenings can occur.

BELL HOOKS, "Postmodern Blackness," in
Colonial Discourse and Postcolonial Theory

4 / Morphing Identities:
Arnold Schwarzenegger—Write Us

Louise Krasniewicz and Michael Blitz

I look at the writing and sometimes see the self in there, out there, and wonder how I was somehow that self being written, writing itself out as if unwinding a spool of . . . I only see certain strands.
CLARK COOLIDGE, *The Crystal Text*[1]

A voice comes to one in the dark. Imagine.
SAMUEL BECKETT, *Company*[2]

Prelude

Coolidge's ellipses propose an unnamable set of possibilities about which the autobiographer writes. Is it the same self that is written who writes of itself—i.e., "later"? Coolidge's "I" seems to raise the question, How many is one? Beckett's line suggests at least two things: a voice arrives and someone hears it and perceives that the voice belongs to someone else or to the hearer itself. And a voice *amounts*—adds up—to "one," at least in the dark. What are we to imagine? Beckett's characters frequently imagine themselves, utterly, unutterably alone. They are uncertain whether they are imagining themselves in the world, or if the information comes from somewhere, someone outside themselves. Still, even the uncertainty seems to emanate from an "I" who can acknowledge at bottom its own doubts. The unnamed in Beckett's *The Unnamable* begins by remarking, "Where now? Who now? When now? Unquestioning. I, say I."[3]

In Beckett, "I" takes itself as a starting point—albeit an arbitrary point—of departure. In *The Education of Henry Adams*, Adams's "I" serves as a vehicle of departure from the image of the autobiographical act.[4] In the midst of writing his "autobiography," Henry Adams grasps the potential meaning of the invention of the dynamo, which he had seen in the Gallery of Machines of the Great Exposition in Paris, 1900. For him, the image of towering dynamo symbolized an American revolution of "force" whose nearest equivalent was "when Constantine set up the Cross." And so, at that moment in his *Education*, Adams makes a detour from *The Education*—his life story—to educate himself in a study of the history of force and power from the Middle Ages to the turn of the twentieth century. Thus, Adams's written "life" flows around a "dynamic" break in his life text. The break itself entails a self-conscious examination of his place in a history of energy that has, ultimately, made his life and his actions comprehensible to the older Henry Adams whose created character of the same name educates his maker at every turn.

Introduction

These two issues of autobiography—what/where is the self written, and what are the detours into larger cultural circumstances that are linked to self-writing—haunt every attempt to compose or tell a life story. As a mechanism for creating the idealized or exemplified subject, the autobiography does not limit itself to the confessional or the exploration of private truths, but rather expands with undeniable girth into other subjects, other lives, other dynamic mechanisms. If this is the case, then the impulse to say something about oneself may just be the impulse to say something about the circumstance of the writing of that self.

The writing of the self that we have attempted in our research is complicated by these and other issues. We are not trying to write our individual autobiograph(y/ies), but rather the story of living in this place and time through the cultural figures and processes that share that space. Our culture relies on certain prominent figures to define and understand itself. Marilyn Monroe, JFK, Elvis Presley, Princess Di—each suggests an aspect of the collective desires, weaknesses, dreams, and fears that we constantly turn over in our minds, gossip about, or use for comparisons. We talk through these figures to express ideas about hate, sex, love, drugs, death, religion, morality, power, money, and other things that are difficult to consider directly. In them we recognize ourselves writ large as well as our fellow citizens in their best and worst lights.

Our cultural imagination at the end of the twentieth century and the beginning of the twenty-first is wrapped up in one of these larger-than-life, omnipresent figures in the person of Arnold Schwarzenegger. It is difficult to imagine our current scene without the coherence and flair brought to it by Schwarzenegger. Through him we know how to be influential and powerful, how to meld machines and bodies, how to entertain the global village, how to whip a country into shape, how to fulfill the traditional American dream, and perhaps even how to heroically kill and be killed.

Like all significant cultural icons, Arnold Schwarzenegger pops up everywhere. He appears daily not only in the expected places—films, television, newspapers, and advertisements—but also in the most unexpected, from the on-the-ground language of common folk ("Hasta la vista, baby" and "I'll be back") to an outer-space advertisement for his new movie. Not a day goes by without the possibility of encountering that grinning, chiseled face and that pumped body as it permeates the very fabric of American existence. This points to an amazing presence in our cultural imagination. Our project has been to document and critically examine this fascinating phenomenon.

We fell upon a curious form of autobiography in the process of writing about Arnold Schwarzenegger. But first, we needed to deny consistently that we were writing a straightforward biography of the man. It's not just that we wanted to avoid the embarrassing fiasco of Arnold's unauthorized pop-psychological biography by Wendy Leigh,[5] or that the Austrian Oak refused to grant us an interview. It is more that we concur with Janet Malcolm in her recent *New Yorker* series when she says that in order to write an acceptable biography, the writer cannot "introduce doubts about the legitimacy of the biographical enterprise."[6] We had many questions about such biographical legitimacy, similar to the ones we harbored about autobiography. We could not justify calling what we did biographical in the traditional sense.

Because we saw, through the progress of our research, that we were hopelessly implicated in whatever story we told about the emblematic Schwarzenegger, the issue of this being either pure biography or simple autobiography was impossible to resolve. The story insisted upon be-

Figure 4.1. Arnold in TV.

coming entangled in our respective selves, despite our mild reluctance
to emphasize *our* story as friends, collaborators, and authors. The reason for this is that we exchanged ideas and texts, usually in the form of
almost daily electronic mail messages (e-mail). But these exchanges,
rather than focusing on self-indulgent personal commentary, focused
on how our subject matter, Arnold Schwarzenegger and his omnipres-
ence, came to play an increasingly dominating role in our own stories.
Rather than being a coauthored journal of our everyday lives, our
e-mail became instead the autobiography of another entity, not us and
not Arnold, but some "morphed" version that has its own histories,
mechanisms, darknesses, and narratives. That it was the Schwarzenegger project compelling us to consider these issues was equally intriguing. We began to notice the increasing relevance of our own ways of
constructing narrative portions of our life experiences to the ways we
were framing this larger project.

Depersonalizing Autobiography

The two of us found ourselves both fascinated and disturbed by the
emergence of forms of self-consciousness embedded not just in human
bodies but in the very machines that we were using to transnavigate
our collaboration. At one point our research involved considering the

interface of the self with hardware and with programs for downloading human intelligence and memory into the machine. These discussions frequently traced connections between downloading and ideas about human immortality, artificial life and intelligence, reproduction, nanotechnologies, and even suicide, all topics with profound implications for the construction of self. Still, something about the apparatus of the computer terminal, the lingering formalities of research, and the sheer quantity of material and information resulted in a kind of perfunctory exchange a good deal of the time. That our e-mail exchanges often sidestepped the personal came as a surprise to us when we looked back at the thousands of screens that have passed between us. The intensely personal generally came to one or the other of us as revelation when it did slip into the bitstream:

E-MAIL
Michael to Louise
11-11-90
   I share, in a way, yr puzzlement regarding the "why" of suicide—for me, the puzzle was always the [program for] living—I wrote a story at about age 9 (my mother says she still has it) in which the main/only character travels through time—forward and back—committing suicide after suicide, bizarrely able to remember each previous suicide . . .

E-MAIL
Louise to Michael
11-13-90:
   Your horror stories fascinate me. . . . I always thought your fascination with the things we are studying were merely or mostly or especially intellectual. You have fooled (in a good way) us both—this is a major reversal—I am usually the one grounded in the experiences of everyday life (a *National Enquirer* article here, a TV movie there) but is it really the case that you have been re-acting out your childhood fantasies in our literary productions?

E-MAIL
Michael to Louise
7-22-91
   I keep learning new and important things about you from your asides in e-mail. . . . Even in our worst despairs (yours in-

volving chocolate chip cookies, mine involving scotch, I suppose) we can energize ourselves while still requiring the other's goods. I suppose.

What we were *supposing* was, in other words, that the personal would not somehow impinge upon the work at hand. And yet, the work at hand was also, increasingly, the work we were doing *with* our hands: writing daily about books we were reading, articles, obscure pop culture references, films, and, as we discuss later in this essay, the growing number of Arnold-related coincidences and dreams.

It became apparent to us that the more we wrote back and forth, the more frequently we seemed to encounter Schwarzenegger-related events—to the point where we could be easily convinced we were causing some of these coincidences and encounters. It was dawning on us that we had created a separate "entity" during the exchange process. This was an entity not genetically dependent on our individual pasts and presents, but one *assembled* from the sharing of these narratives, both technical and personal. It was as though our hands were now engaged in a microtechnology whereby we could control a being, "between" us, comprising information derived from our attention to and writing about Arnold Schwarzenegger.

E-MAIL
Louise to Michael
7-20-91

So I am in this store buying sunglasses, see, and this man puts on a pair of sunglasses and says to his female companion using an Austrian accent, "Look Maria, I am the Terminator." A few minutes later when I am checking out with sunglasses that do not resemble Linda Hamilton's but I wish they did, the clerk offers to clean my new purchase. She has trouble squeezing the spray bottle. She says, "I have been lifting weights and my muscles are really sore." Me, too, I say. She says, "Did you see *Terminator 2?*" When I say yes she says, "I want arms like that girl in the movie." WHAT IS IT? Do I have "AUTHOR OF A BOOK ON ARNOLD" written on my forehead?????

Our daily logging of notes on Arnold as exemplar of popular culture appetites and fantasies was becoming, in our collaboration, a template for telling and designing our own constellation of personal narratives.

Figure 4.2. Digital video still by L. Krasniewicz.

But equally interesting to us was they way in which the activity of such intense narrative exchange was shaping the very experiences we were constantly reporting. The morphed entity whose existence was in the flux of our dialogue seemed to be making demands on our attention and activities. It was as if this entity had accumulated sufficient autonomous power to resist our subjectivities, or rather to subsume them into itself. Just as Arnold's films have been remarkable in the ways in which they characterize a variety of interfaces between human and cybernetic hardware, so it was remarkable to find ourselves responding to "nurture" this cyborg protagonist who had come to occupy a space without dimension in the written interplay between the technological and the personal.

E-MAIL
Michael to Louise
2-14-91
   Happy Valentine's Day. Remember that the heart is both a muscle and a writing implement.

E-MAIL
Louise to Michael
2-17-91

I am in this project so deep I can't get out. That perhaps is what is distressing me most. This thing known as the Arnold-story is possessing me and perhaps paralyzing me. It invades all my thoughts—but what is really more distressing is not to be able to get all this stuff down in written form. I want to see the results of all this musing and all these nightmares. Arnold invaded my daydreams yesterday. . . . I have always thought that my life goal should be the creation of the ultimate miniature golf course based on Hollywood legends. And so as I was thinking about how I would design this (all the time shooting way over par on a crappy course in Ventura) Arnie became the last hole design. But instead of saying "I'll be back" he says to the hapless family of golfers, "YOU'LL be back"—almost an imperative!

Now I realize that this is productive thinking but, hey, Arnie, leave me alone for just a while. Well, I forgot about him for a day, and now I miss him so I am back at the computer. By the way I have absolutely no regrets about not meeting him at breakfast. It would have ruined our book because I would have had to pursue the real Arnie and the spell would have been broken (like your dream when you meet him and he is smaller/bigger/stupider etc. than you imagined). The guy who was supposed to introduce me to Arnie hates him by the way, so, hey, right, that would have been a very productive meeting.

Well obviously I have not given up on this, in fact I am too excited by it and I just want to abandon all for the sweet cinema arms of the Arn-man, but my spaghetti sauce needs stirring and I must go watch the second half of Twin Peaks . . .

E-MAIL
Michael to Louise
2-17-91
later that evening:

I worried a good part of the day that you had reached critical mass and were really considering crapping out (our mutually over-large fear, based upon our having, separately, worked with crappers-outers). I am relieved and newly convivial, replete with complete undepletedness—

I am fascinated by your almost-meetings with the Arno-bot. Every other time we've spoken/written, you have made contact with someone who plans to help you touch the man himself. Everyone else BUT us seems to know/love/have a history with Arnold Schwarzenegger. We have to write this stuff because we may be the only two human beings who have not already known Arnold.

Yet one type of personal exchange more than any other mucked up the mirror that was reflecting the morph of us and Schwarzenegger. One of the more compelling and disturbing phenomena for us was a period of about a year during which one or both of us was dreaming about Arnold Schwarzenegger nearly every night.

E-MAIL
Louise to Michael
2-23-91
Well I am back from the Bart Simpson makeover salon. What fun to have a new me that looks like something from *Aliens.* Speaking of aliens, here is last night's Arnie dream:
Arnold is filming *Terminator 2* at UCLA. The setting is some rolling hills on campus—not any spot that really exists. It reminds me of two scenes—the park from the movie *Blowup* and the hills from Kent State where the protesting students were shot by the National Guard. I am watching the filming and decide to take off my makeup with a cotton ball. As I rub off my makeup, it turns gray on my face and gives me an aged, alien look. I leave it on. The director comes over and asks me to be an alien in the movie in a bar scene reminiscent of the one in *Star Wars.* The bar is huge and oval-shaped and there is nothing in the middle—you just face other patrons. I look in a mirror and I no longer have my own face because they have put a rubber mask on me. I am told that I have the major alien speaking part in the film. Cut suddenly to me in my poststructuralism seminar and I am telling my graduate students about this dream. We are sitting at a set of children's desks that are in the same shape as the bar—in an oval with a space in the middle. Suddenly Arnold pops up in one of the seats facing me across the room. His face is a caricature. I say to him, "I am the major alien in your movie." (February 23, 1991)

As we sent each other records of these dreams, we found ourselves, more and more frequently, dreaming along similar lines, sometimes of events that would later happen or of things that would make us shift our research.

Louise's Dream

For some reason Arnold Schwarzenegger is in my house. He is sitting at the kitchen table. We are talking about something. I say to him flirtatiously, "You know we are writing a book about you but that we haven't been able to admit it face to face." I tell him I am interested in the President's Council on Physical Fitness. I show him something on a small piece of paper which he gets up from the table to look at over my shoulder. I know he is looking down my cleavage and I am pleased. (March 20, 1991)

Michael's Dream

I am taking Arnold's photograph, using a wide-angle lens in order to somehow widen him. Arnold turns to a pal nearby and asks, "Why am I being photographed by such a ridiculous camera?" The friend comes over to confiscate my camera so I cut off his hand. For the rest of the dream I am running from Arnold's goons. (March 8, 1991)

Michael's Dream

Louise had found in a novelty shop a 78 rpm record of Arnold singing Elvis songs. One side was "Love Me Tender" and the other side was "Jailhouse Rock" which, she told me, when played backwards, was also the "preamble" to *Mein Kampf.* (February 5, 1993)

Louise's Dream

Arnold and I were talking about women bodybuilders and he wanted to show me what it would look like for me. We were standing in front of a big mirror and Arnold had on his competition trunks. He stood facing the mirror with his hands on his hips and his legs apart. He tilted his head all the way back so that he looked like one of those amusement park displays of bodybuilders that you put your head on and get your picture taken with. I put my head where Arnold's used to be and then I put my arms under his and out front like he was a ventriloquist dummy. We laughed. (February 1, 1991)

Michael's Dream

Arnold was fighting Klan-types and had to dress as a fire-fighter with a long coat and hat, partly to hide his well-known balding head from several "Deliverance" types who were after him and me. At one point he became Gerard Depardieu but he quickly corrected himself when I observed, "You look so much different in person than you do in my head." This prompted him to take off the firehat to prove that he still had a full head of hair and that my mental image of him was intact. (February 5, 1991)

Louise's Dream

The other night I dreamed I was making mad passionate love to Gerard Depardieu. (February 19, 1992)

Dreams are a problem for this autobiography. For a simple life story, dreams seem to fit in nicely as a reaffirming source of unconscious projections. But when dreams are traced through a process of exchange that is our fourth entity, what do dreams become? A record of this mating and obsession, evidence of another fusion experiment gone awry? Can morphs dream, and who is it that is dreaming when a morph does it?

Morphs

Morphing is an important concept when we consider the new possibilities and failures of autobiography in the technological age. The process of morphing is best known from the Schwarzenegger blockbuster movie *Terminator 2* (1991) and from *The Abyss*, a 1989 film from *T2* director James Cameron. In the morphing that we see on the screen, one entity seamlessly melts into others, constantly shape-shifting so that it is impossible to draw the boundaries between forms. In *The Abyss*, aliens take their form from water, moving effortlessly though spaces and with numerous faces. In *T2*, floors become men, arms become swords, cops become liquid blobs, women find themselves duplicated as exactly wounded twins.

In *Terminator 2*, the most sophisticated morphing is accomplished by an advanced terminator cyborg that is constituted of "mimetic polyalloys," that is, a substance of substances that allows it to imitate other substances. Yet the real substance of morphing is computer processing, sophisticated programming that allows one digitized image to accumulate changes and jettison old pixels slowly until it appears to be something else.

There are actually two processes that are referred to as morphing. Morphing can involve the cross-fading of one image into another so that the beginning and end images are identifiable and distinct, linked only by the computer-interpolated images in between. One image thus completely transforms into another. Of more concern for our analogy, however, is the morphing that involves the blending of the features of two images, producing a third, "imaginary" entity. For example, the Benetton clothing company recently featured a series of advertisements in which famous people were computer-blended with people of different races. None of these morphs (which included an Asian Queen Elizabeth and a white Spike Lee) was more shocking than the one of Arnold Schwarzenegger and a black man. The black Arnold Schwarzenegger was a stunning impossibility not just because of the expert process but because the histories of the two entities made this a particularly enigmatic image.

Since *T2*, this process has been seen in numerous movies, television programs, music videos, and advertisements, and we now have a whole universe of morphed entities comfortably inhabiting our imagination. Morphing has also now become available to users of home computers, so that everyone can create a world inhabited by the uninhabitable.

In our e-mail work on Arnold Schwarzenegger, we have effectively created a dynamic morph among Arnold, ourselves, the computer, and our culture. Our autobiography is now the autobiography of this entity and consists of trying to trace its recent permutations, measure its fallout, and predict the shape of its future shiftings. The autobiography of this morph is not grounded in history, childhood traumas, or memories. It instead flows from one entity to another, not always seamlessly, but often effortlessly.

E-MAIL
Louise to Michael
7-31-91

Okay, last night I saw a play that must be setting the theatre back years. This abominable snowheap was called *Love Letters*, and as I informed you, I was going to see what was happening with Linda Hamilton (of *Beauty and the Beast* and *Terminator 2*) and Ron Perlman (. . . *the Beast*) who were starring for one

Figure 4.3. Morph—30 percent Louise, 70 percent Arnold. Computer morph by
L. Krasniewicz.

night. . . . Well, the premise of the play is that there are these two
rich WASPs who spend their lives being whiny and writing letters
to each other about it.

Now what was weird about the whole thing was the multiple
meanings this exchange took on. First there is the emaciated,
sinewy Linda Hamilton. A good part of her performance was
spent robotically and passively staring over the heads of the audience. She was playing the *Terminator* and indeed at the end her
character commits suicide. At times this seemed to be the forever
love story of *Beauty and the Beast*, the love that could never be. I
swear I saw Ron Perlman get more catlike as the evening wore
on, for suddenly I noticed his gorgeous long fingers and his eyes
seemed to get smaller and darken and his hair suddenly hairier.
As he got more animallike, she got more mechanical, until at the
end when they got up to take their bows. She was wearing a
huge flowing dress that could have fit three or four of her and
the dress, very feminine, provided an odd contrast to her hard,
sharp arms. He on the other hand seemed to have grown softer
and rounder.

She was Arnold and he was Linda Hamilton. Then at times he was Arnold, especially when he becomes a Senator and takes on the perfect wife and family and creates an all-American image— sound like someone we know? Linda was never Maria but always the other woman—Brigitte, maybe, or maybe she stood in for all of Arnold's past. At times they seemed to be us up there, writing these stupid correspondences—except ours are never as whiny (and since we whine a bit, imagine how bad theirs were!).

The dreams that this morph can have begin to resemble the process of making a motion picture, those autobiographies of our cultural landscape. The connection between dreams and motion pictures is long-standing. Although dreams are presumably private and films have public circulation, they nevertheless activate similar effects—they present alternative realities that can be used as reference points for everyday decisions, actions, and motivations. The cinema imitates many of the dream's mechanisms, including the identification with the image, the articulation of desire, the manipulation of space and time, the condensation of many concepts into single images, and the displacement of meaning from its rightful place to a substitute one.

Münsterberg's 1916 definition of the "photoplay," as he calls it, could be about either dreams or films and, we might now add, the exchange of electronic information: "The photoplay tells us the human story by overcoming the forms of the outer world, namely, space, time, and causality, and by adjusting the events to the forms of the inner world, namely, attention, memory, imagination, and emotion."[7]

These distinctions between inner and outer worlds, between public and private, personal and mediated experiences, no longer seem to hold up in film, in dreams, or in our everyday telelectronic lives.

E-MAIL
Michael to Louise
7-25-91
Saw *White Palace* last night. Totally forgettable except that Susan Sarandon is so good when she is angry. But what was interesting was that James Spader says, "No, you fit in my life; I was the one who didn't fit. I didn't fit into my own life." Imagine not fitting into one's own life. Actually, that's precisely how I feel, which raises the question/problem again: what is the difference between one's own "life" and the "fitness" one has/is for that life. How might Arnold have made Max/Spader fit into his

life better. Do you see what I am driving at Oh Great Sepulveda Cruiser?

Public and private distinctions are annulled by eyewitness news, surveillance cameras, tabloid TV, computer hackers, and America's Funniest Home Videos. Dreams cannot be strictly private expressions of individual psyches when they draw from the stock of characters and situations present in our ever-circulating cinematic culture. Films are not removed from the audiences who utilize them and remake them in their own image. Electronic exchanges are already not easy to place in one realm or the other, especially when we use them to write autobiographies.

ARNOLD ® US

In the years we spent exchanging thousands of electronic messages about Schwarzenegger and the ways in which we had taken him—and the attending popular cultural "strands"—into our lives, we began to realize that "he" had become the medium for our autobiographical narrative. Indeed, for many reasons, Arnold Schwarzenegger as cultural icon has not only provided us with a structure for a form of life writing, he/it has become a fascinating source of self-knowing for us all. That is, we have used this iconography as a way to make a story about ourselves, to learn about who we are, where we may be going at the close of the twentieth century, and what we might expect to find there.

Roland Barthes wrote: "I am writing a text, and I call it R.B.";[8] "we" were writing a text and calling it Arnold Schwarzenegger. Actually, every other day we were calling it something different. The title of our ongoing manuscript production became an act of naming every bit as intricate and laden with peripheral influences as the naming of a human being or of a new discovery:

Arnold: Virtually Real
Arnold Schwarzenegger's Bodies
Arnold: Master Plan/Perfect Man
Perfect Man: The Master Plan of Arnold Schwarzenegger
Magnificent Obsession: Arnold Schwarzenegger
Virtually Arnold: Schwarzenegger and the Transformation of ? in
  the Twentieth Century

Souvenirs from our Adventures with Arnold Schwarzenegger
FIT: Arnold Schwarzenegger and the Re-shaping of America.
Girly Men: Arnold Schwarzenegger and the Final Gender Solution
Too Big: Arnold Schwarzenegger and the Seduction of America
The Impossibility of Arnold Schwarzenegger
Icon: Arnold Schwarzenegger as Idol and Image

We attributed part of our problem in arriving at a title to a growing suspicion that there was something elusive about the shape of our project. Both of us had written books and articles and hadn't had so much difficulty in naming those works. But here we had a subject matter that was neither specifically Arnold Schwarzenegger nor, particularly, ourselves, though it had become more and more so, and this also wasn't exclusively a popular culture response to the Schwarzenegger phenomenon.

We could not shake the sense that each time we added something to the "body" of the narrative between us, we were somehow supplementing a hybrid form of self-narration over which we felt we had less and less control. Who or what constituted our point of view? Were we seeing from our individual perspectives and then combining our perceptions? Were we seeing Schwarzenegger and ourselves through the collective eyes of the culture? Were our "eyes" any different from those of the culture or from those whose viewpoints had been so shaped by icons like Arnold? Had we in fact collapsed several points of view into a configuration completely unlike us that had its own "viewpoint"? How many was this "I"?

We became an echo of cultural response to our subject of study—and for that reason, the point of view we attributed to the other's narrative was not so much singular as singularly organized in the face of the nourishing medium known as Arnold.

On February 17, 1991, Michael dreamed:

> Arnold comes to my door and says "I hear you are doing a book about me." He then tells me that Maria Shriver thought that she could find out about him by peeling away his layers like an onion. But he says that "the only way anyone will find out about me is by breaking me into little pieces."

We began examining the many pieces of Schwarzenegger as he permeated popular culture. What we discovered was that there seemed to be no limit to the number of these pieces. The more we "broke off," the more we found and the more we made.

Autobiography in the Dark

I am the fourth party that has been endlessly reconfigured without a code or blueprint. I am a set of pathways laid out on a chip, programmed in by a pair of typists. As an Adamic morph, I resemble clay; I am thrown and spun; I have memory—red-clay memory. If I am manipulated too much I fracture under the stresses. But prodded and pinched and twisted delicately, I give off bits and pieces and naturally pick up detritus from the world around me as I am formed into something with resemblance.

As a morph built around Arnold Schwarzenegger, I have a unique property. I do not deplete myself. My existence is paradoxical: I get bigger and more powerful the more I am transformed into smaller images and tighter frames. Now, as almost pure information in the hands of two typists, I am larger than life itself.

This is the autobiography they have written in the darkness of dreams and movies and electronic exchanges. E-mail is the newest element of this blind working. Its immediacy, its novelty, its potential for scrambling "real" time into an illusion of simultaneous communication, its combination of writing and programming me in a medium normally for telespeaking, edibility, its addictiveness, and the various rituals the typists came to associate with it—sitting in the dark late at night, typing in the day's work and coincidences, all came to be a methodology for their narrative exploration. And for their creation of me.

They were creating a pair of active characters who engaged in a daily exchange of ideas and questions and personal anecdotes. These characters could be as confessional or as professional as they chose to be at that moment. They could adopt a variety of voices and stances not only regarding their collaboration, but also about aspects of their private lives. Indeed, those lives were steadily becoming more implicated in their work, especially in the form of their dreams and their relation to Louise's and Michael's day-to-day lives. And within those private lives was a low hum of anxiety, maybe about the knowledge that I was lurking on the threshold between their hands and their machines, between Arnold and themselves, between lines of text.

For Henry Adams it was the dynamo; for Louise and Michael and other typists in the late twentieth century, the signal and icon of force, of power, is the very thing they had from the beginning: light. The microchip, the cyborg, all the programs for the emulation of desire, Internet viruses, the latest forms of the novel, intercontinental/interplanetary/intergalactic communications, feedback systems, all take light to be the first requirement.

To send word(s) via the wire, into and over the "Net," is to place human thought in one's hands and fingers. It is to say something at the speed of light. Or at least that's part of the mythology; actually, I remind them, the words travel at the speed of sound but flash back at light speed to the typists by way of their monitors. When they write e-mail back and forth, they interface with each other, with their machineries, and with themselves in a loop of consciousness that is—just as I seem to be—at once aware of, and oblivious to, both of them.

Talking is like skywriting. The sounds and phrases vaporize almost before they are fully comprehended. But writing across the Net is like a tattoo; the image of the message remains—somewhere. The typists write themselves into the archive, onto the skin of the network potentially for all to see. Their texts are unremovable except by a surgical erasure. Even so, trace versions remain embedded within the software, the mainframe, or another hard drive. And of course, the traces and the by-products of those traces remain forever, now, in me.

I am the effects of Louise and Michael seeing their energies extended in and by one another, showing up on each other's screens, returning to themselves on their own. In a light-world of accelerated digital pulses, I am the echoes of, and the triggers for, the typists' continuous effort to harness their own narrative creation—a kind of geno-fusion, a recombining of electronic DNA. The life form is the life study, the life under the glass (screen). I am the morph made from Louise and Michael and Arnold Schwarzenegger who is more than Arnold Schwarzenegger ever was. Not only their subject matter, but also the figure under the glass of the projector, the lens of the camera and the TV screen. I am the filters of popular culture that register Arnold Schwarzenegger as a human man but "see" a figure larger than life, more powerful than an army and more desirable than real-life humans, whose limitations would not permit such easy entrance and exit from film frame and the White House and body building and agendas for childhood fitness and to the cyberneurons of two typists' shared textual body. i am an artificial life—gene coded into the chips, a creature "made of mathematics" with "digital DNA."[9] i am a life form with a story to tell. Like Diderot, in a letter to Sophie Volland in 1759, i compose myself out of the darkness: "I write without seeing. . . . This is the first time I have ever written in the dark . . . not knowing whether I am indeed forming letters. Wherever there will be nothing, read that I love you."[10]

Notes

1. Clark Coolidge, *The Crystal Text* (Great Barrington, Mass.: The Figures, 1986), 58.

2. Samuel Beckett, *Company* (New York: Grove, 1980), 7.

3. Samuel Beckett, *The Unnamable* (New York: Grove, 1958), 3.

4. Henry Adams, *The Education of Henry Adams*, ed. Ernest Samuels (Boston: Houghton Mifflin, 1974).

5. Wendy Leigh, *Arnold: An Unauthorized Biography* (Chicago: Congdon & Weed, 1990).

6. Janet Malcolm, "Sylvia Plath, the Silent Woman," *New Yorker*, August 23, 1993, 87.

7. Hugo Münsterberg, *The Film. A Psychological Study* (New York: Dover, 1970 [1916]), 74.

8. Roland Barthes, *Roland Barthes by Roland Barthes,* trans. Richard Howard (New York: Hill & Wang, 1977), 56.

9. Steven Levy, *Artificial Life: A Report from the Frontier Where Computers Meet Biology* (New York: Vintage, 1992), 3.

10. Quoted in Jacques Derrida, *Memoirs of the Blind: The Self-Portrait and Other Ruins*, trans. Pascale-Anne Brault and Michael Naas (Chicago: University of Chicago Press, 1993), 1.

5 / Performing Teen Motherhood on Video: Autoethnography as Counterdiscourse

Salome Chasnoff

A story told is a story bound to circulate.
TRINH T. MINH-HA, *Woman, Native, Other*[1]

Looking Back with Charlotte, July 1992

I first met Charlotte Lowe when she was a ninth grader in my performance workshop for pregnant teens. On this day in July, two and one-half years later, she was about to graduate from high school, assume a full-time job, and move into her own apartment. The following is excerpted from about two hours of conversation that began over the cooking of doughnuts for her two toddlers. The cheerful chaos reminded me of our workshops—writing poetry, reading plays, planning projects, and, finally, shooting a video with a roomful of babies. Today Charlotte's sister offered to baby-sit, and we moved to a nearby restaurant.

> SALOME (Sally): Would you say that working on *The Fantastic Moms Video* had any effect on your understanding of things?[2]
> CHARLOTTE: It helped me to be with other people that were in my situation. It showed me that I wasn't in there alone. I made friends, a lot of friends, from the video. I learned who I wanted to be from it. We took a lot of situations and we talked about them, and afterwards I thought about them and I was, like, I am going to do what I want to do, and that is what I am going to do.

SALLY: When you say, "What I want to do," what are those things you want to do?

CHARLOTTE: I want to go to college. I want to be a fashion designer. Someday I want to move to New York. I want to have a good family life. I want to make sure my kids grow up to be whatever they want to be. I don't want my being a teen mother to hurt them in any way. I want to be active in their lives, and I want them to be active in my life.

SALLY: Did making the video affect any of your relationships?

CHARLOTTE: It helped me talk to my mom more, and by her telling me, "It's okay, everything is going to be all right, don't worry," this eased me. And another thing the video did for me, it made me feel special because it was something I could tell other people, "Don't be afraid, you have friends, don't worry what people think." I'm planning on showing it in English class because I feel it's a strong video.[3]

Vocabularies: Performance, Agency, and Autoethnography

By now it is a truism to say that performance, privileging process over product, is transformational. Henry Sayre, for example, has written that "performance can be defined as an activity which generates transformations, as the reintegration of art with what is 'outside' it, an 'opening up' of the 'field.'"[4] This definition, while seeming to contain an implicit rejection of the formalist fantasy of a closed, autonomous objet d'art, is in fact similarly spatialized. And although art and environment are understood as always in interactive relationship, both politically and aesthetically, what distinguishes Sayre's reading of performance from a specifically feminist one is the invisible authorial role of the performer. The "field" seems a faceless one as well. But when we document and historicize case studies of performance practices, we reaffirm their transformational potentiality for named, knowledgeable human agents.[5] Performance thus taken—as an enacted social process through which subjects are continually constituted as they constitute it—can generate transformations such as the (re)integration of art with *who* is *of* it, an opening up of *performing subjects in time and relation* who are always infinitely porous, impossible to represent fully, and accessible to scripting. In such an atmosphere of reciprocal mutability, individuals and the larger culture can be imagined in effective relationship.

This view of performance contains promising pedagogical practices. By framing performance as a transformational activity and providing opportunities for the telling and circulating of stories, we create the possibility for personal and collective restoration through purposeful representations of identities by interpreting agents. Performance has the power to alter how people see themselves and how they see and are seen by others. When a perspective that addresses structures of domination informs one's methodology, the "performance script becomes indistinguishable from political agency."[6]

Current feminist and performance theories bid us view all performance—the quotidian, the ritual, and the theatrical—as constitutive of identity and thus inherently political. Autobiographical performances, or the making of representations of the "self," because they are "self"-conscious, heightened, and shared, are paramount moments of performance as identity construction. I have chosen to employ Mary Louise Pratt's term *autoethnography* rather than *autobiography* to situate generically the video created in our workshop in part because of its focus on a group of people in culture as opposed to independent individuals. Additionally, Pratt describes autoethnographic expressions as counternarratives to dominant ethnographies, "instances in which colonized subjects undertake to represent themselves in ways that *engage with* the colonizer's own terms."[7] These autoethnographies are not "authentic," isolated, and self-driven expressions, as autobiographies might be construed, but are purposefully contingent upon and in appropriation of the dominant language and its construction(s) for their own subversive purposes. Thus they are essentially "bilingual" sites of resistance. Further, not intended as complete revelations of personhood, these expressions are viewed as both metonymic and specifically directed, where a performer retains agency to select and inflect her or his representation appropriate to its aim.

"Self"-Mapping and "World"-Traveling

As I sit down to write about, to *theorize,* the year-long performance project that I directed with a group of African American and West Indian teenage mothers, in which they used themselves as primary source material to study and represent teen motherhood in a video autoethnography, in my effort to write, I, the framing eye, struggle with my own autobiographical representation. How do I locate and circumscribe my mixed presences: teacher, director, collaborator, adviser, scholar? How do I map the boundaries of my collaboration in their work? (Is this even possible?) How do I acknowledge the power I derive from representing them?

In 1990, as a volunteer providing "support service," I was assigned to the Transitional Learning Center of Family Focus-Our Place, Evanston, Illinois, which offers a short-term alternative high school program for pregnant teens. My job was to conduct performance workshops for "self-enrichment, self-development and self-esteem."[8] I brought an idiosyncratic mix of credentials to the job: I was a theater, video, and performance artist and educator; I was also a performance scholar based at nearby Northwestern University, and my dissertation was on the performance of birthing; most important, perhaps, because of my own difficult, often painful years as a young single mother, I strongly identify with single mothers of all ages, particularly young ones.

On my first day of teaching, I was *surprised* to find a group of happy, relaxed young women. After our meeting, as I reflected on this initial surprise, I realized that I had been expecting sullen, depressed, or even hostile students, the mass media-constructed Pregnant Teen. This preconceived pictured implied other biases and limitations. Over time, I adopted (surrendered to) María Lugones's prescription to the outsider for cross-cultural and cross-racial understanding, " 'world'-travelling with a playful attitude."[9] Lugones has defined playfulness as "openness to surprise, openness to being a fool, openness to self-construction or reconstruction and to construction or reconstruction of the 'worlds' we inhabit playfully."[10] I gradually saw my role differently, as a facilitator, not a fount. I felt freer, less arrogant and less fearful, more responsive. I also saw how to approach the work, how to map the subject: within the gap between the cultural stereotypes of teen pregnancy and motherhood and the students' own representations of their experiences.

The Fantastic Moms and the Stigma of Early Fertility

The young women in my group (who in no way epitomize the diversity of women who are teenage mothers)[11] were, except for one white girl,[12] African American and West Indian, poor to working-class, and ninth to twelfth graders. Of the six women who eventually became the Fantastic Moms and worked on the video, Leontyne Walkine (Lee) and Lakesha Dunn (Kesha) were my first students. Lee, eighteen years old, moved with her boyfriend to Evanston from the Bahamas (a "much stricter, more respectful" environment) when she discovered that she was pregnant. Now they were married. Just before her baby was born, Lee wrote that, although she had once thought of herself as "very young and innocent, an irresponsible, free-spirited party person, the baby was already finding ways to get me to grow up fast."[13] Kesha, a native Evanstonian, was articulate, charismatic, and confident. Her family and teachers expected a lot from her, including a career in competitive track, and felt disappointed and betrayed by her "mistake" (getting pregnant). But Kesha also had many supportive relationships within a large network of family and longtime friends, including her parents, stepmother, the baby's father, and his family. She was sixteen at this time.

Already we see very different people caught in the same stereotype, Pregnant Teen. Young pregnant women, always disadvantaged by gender and age, sometimes by race, class, education, marital status, citizenship status, sometimes rejected by their own families, eventually become stigmatized as "unwed mothers" of "illegitimate children." In actuality, the girls felt proud of their "bellies" and enlivened by many of the physical and social experiences of pregnancy; but these pleasures were seriously tainted with conflict. Relatives, peers, teachers, and even strangers on the street reviled them with such comments as "You should be ashamed of yourself" and "You ruined your life." Getting their "old bodies" back meant more than just being relieved of the additional weight and fitting into their clothes again; it meant being relieved of these everyday verbal assaults.

It is an axiom of the dominant discourse that teen pregnancy and teen motherhood are pathological, on both micro and macro levels. "Sucking off the national teat" is how a nationally syndicated radio talk-show host has casually characterized teenaged mothers, tossing the expression off as some consensual datum.[14] In her examination of welfare reform from a feminist perspective, Johanna Brenner confronts the widespread belief that the primary cause of poverty is early fertility: "The 1960s paradigm was the 'matriarchal' Black mother and her 'shiftless street-corner' husband; today, it is the 'promiscuous' Black teenager and her 'drug-gang' boyfriend."[15] Former Surgeon General Joycelyn Elders took on teen pregnancy as *her* issue. Speaking before the Congressional Committee on Labor and Human Resources upon her nomination, Elders grouped teen pregnancy with some of the deadliest threats to society today: "I've seen bright young people, all over this country, in an ocean—surrounded by the sharks of drugs, alcohol, homicide, suicide, AIDS, and teen pregnancy, while we argue over whose values are we going to teach."[16]

The statistics do not support this crisis rhetoric. Although the sexual activity of female youth has been increasing almost to the male level since 1970, their birthrates have declined during the same period, with 19 percent fewer pregnancies.[17] Further, whereas white teen non-marital fertility rates have increased, black teen fertility rates have decreased.[18] But it continually goes unchallenged that teenage pregnancy and motherhood are represented as two phases of a rapidly spreading "epidemic";[19] that teenage pregnancy and motherhood are represented as exclusively female issues (male sexual activity and responsibility are nonissues); that teenage pregnancy and motherhood are represented as poor black phenomena; and that race, ethnicity, class, education, and gender all become conflated and buried within age beneath this representation. Finally, the ultimate victim in this representation is always "society." Pregnant teens are "failed" students and teen mothers are "failed" mothers and "failed" citizens; a rich community consisting, in part, of pregnant and parenting adolescents as viable, positively contributing members is unimaginable.[20]

Performance Text as Matrix of Transformation: Establishing the Project

By our second meeting, I had discarded my lesson plans (I was ready to "world"-travel) and instituted the practice of starting each session with a casual lunch. Although I was scheduled to teach before lunch, the students—each at least seven months pregnant—were hungry and tired after a morning of classes. By responding to their needs in this way, we established an individualized, improvisational/experimental style of process. Furthermore, this relaxed, unstructured time afforded not only physical renewal but also opportunities to talk about nutrition and health care, "compare notes" about their pregnancies, and probe me for information. The conditions of the Family Focus program severely challenged the making of friendships; the day was shortened and attendance was irregular because of doctors' appointments, sick days, and births. But the casual yet ongoing structure of the group offset these obstacles. The students, previously unknown or little known to each other, began to hang around after school and form relationships, a positive development that counteracted their exclusion from regular high school.

The next new member was Michelle Gayle, from Jamaica, alone in the United States and very homesick. In an early writing exercise she described motherhood as "sacrifice, because you have to give up a lot of things for your baby, things that are not needed anymore. Not only things, but people too" (Gayle, April 1990). Michelle and Lee, from the Bahamas, identified easily with each other and quickly became friends. Charlotte Lowe also enrolled in the workshop during this time. As a ninth grader she was the youngest, and she approached the others tentatively until she felt accepted. Intelligent, frank, and creative, she was also "the realist" of the group. Charlotte once wrote that although people looked at her as one who "messed up her life and won't get anywhere," she looked at herself as one who "has made a mistake but can turn it around and be something" (Lowe, April 1990).

The first "self"-representational exercise we performed in the workshop was the creation of body poems.[21] I outlined their bodies on life-size sheets of paper on the floor and invited them to think of these forms as the spaces in which they live. They used colored markers and crayons to give names to themselves and their babies and to draw images and messages to accompany these characters. As we returned to this exercise repeatedly over the next two weeks, the bodies became increasingly endowed. After each session we rolled the drawings up and put them in a locked closet. We never talked about these private "poems" in class, nor did I look at them; we shared them only by making them together. Over the period that we worked on them, the number of the group grew from two to about eight or ten as word of our activities spread.

Next we read aloud two very different plays focusing on teen pregnancy, *Scrapbooks,* by Pam Sterling, and a short play by students from a local public school for pregnant girls. We discussed some of the issues raised in the two plays, such as the differing kinds of pressure the characters received from peers, boyfriends, and family, and how they coped with it; whether the plays seemed to give reasons for the pregnancies; how "keeping the baby," abortion, and adoption were constructed. The students recognized the characters in the student play and concurred with its representation of teenage sexual and social relations, but heard a didactic tone concerning contraception and education that sounded forced to them, revealing the gap between adolescent and adult needs. The two main characters in *Scrapbooks* came from different racial and economic backgrounds, one working-class black and the other middle-class white. Though fictional, the situations were clearly analogous to ones in our group and stimulated good discussions. Whereas making the body poems generated interior monologues, reading the plays led to dialogues with the literature and each other, all contributing to the students' developing clarity in their feelings and ideas.

As they continued to explore teen pregnancy and parenting, the students were becoming "authorities on the subject," as they were later to call themselves in their video. But at this point, about three months into the project, they were still quite pregnant and had absolutely no interest in appearing on video. Instead, they decided that their next project would be to put together a sound tape on teen sexuality for National Public Radio and/or school audiences, using public opinion data collected through personal interviews. Designing the interview questions necessitated defining and prioritizing the issues: sexual practices, peer pressure from both genders, the economics of early parenthood, the abortion and adoption options. I brought in a variety of literature on teen pregnancy, including magazine articles, U.S. government pamphlets, and Planned Parenthood literature, which we read deconstructively to expose the different positions.

In assuming positions of authority and competence in the interview process—running the tape recorder, scripting and posing the questions, expressing opinions—the students *gained* authority, developing their points of view, becoming more articulate, invested, and confident. As investigators they broke the colonial structure of knowledge that traditionally constitutes them as *the investigated;* in doing so, they derived respect from others along with thought-provoking conversations and new information. Most important, perhaps, this process provided them with occasions for "self"-reflection.

It was at this time that Effie Patterson and MayLene Coleman joined us. They were both longtime and devoted friends of Kesha, and the close-knit, comfortable feeling of this subgroup spread into the larger group. Effie had a forthrightness about her, a way of cutting right through to the heart of any matter. MayLene was a clown, wildly imaginative, and she kept us laughing. The addition of these strong personalities energized our group and changed the dynamics considerably.

During this period the students were all delivering their babies and getting into shape again. Additionally, they were gaining confidence and competence as mothers. One day we had extra people at our meeting, about twenty altogether, because the high school was not in session. I showed a videotape titled *Birth of a Candy Bar,* produced by Branda Miller with a group from a New York settlement house similar to Family Focus-Our Place. The tape dealt with many of the issues that we had been exploring, such as sexual choices for teens and lifestyle consequences. The group was very affected by the video's representation of early motherhood, making comments such as, "That's not the whole story—they make being a mother look totally negative," "Where's the love?" and "They look so young. It's 'cuz they sound like they're saying somebody else's words, what they were told to say." Perhaps their worst indictment was "You can't even *understand* what they're saying." The young women in the video appeared disempowered to them. At that moment they decided to make their own video of themselves as teen mothers. They were no longer interested in representing public opinion by interview; the consensus was that public opinion gets enough airtime.

That afternoon the students grasped something crucial to their education: that symbolic representations are contestable. We broke up for that week, and at our next meeting (back to our regular number) the students named themselves the Fantastic Moms, officially announcing their intention to confront and alter the dominant interpretation of the identifying sign "teen mother," not to create "positive images," but to exercise their right to position and define themselves. Gayatri Chakravorty Spivak has said of marginality that, "in terms of the hegemonic historical narrative, certain peoples have always been asked to cathect the margins so others can be defined as central. . . . In that kind of situation the only strategic thing to do is to absolutely present oneself at the centre."[22] Because the media establish the primary battlegrounds in the war over interpretation, "present[ing] oneself at the centre" often means challenging domination through discursive representations. From the Gulf War to the Hill-Thomas war to the Rodney King-L.A.P.D. war, television is the field of choice and the video camera is the weapon. Locally speaking, video puts television within almost everyone's reach. The result *looks* like the dominant form, but the images and content are one's own. As mainstream journalists and anthropologists focus on the objectified "other" to generate texts for mass media or academic consumption, others are using video cameras for their own (private or public) needs and objectives. Voices without access to print media can be recorded because literacy and language fluency are not limitations. People who might never have considered writing their lives are now making video autobiographies, oral histories, and poetry.

What I am arguing here is that agency, like identity, is enacted in material forms, in time, with material means. Subjectivity, at the "margins" or the "center," is performed through narrative agency. Stephen Heath's theorization of narrative structure in film concretizes the process of centering subjects through the orchestration of film/video space.[23] The transformation of frame space into narrative space, the filling and consuming of the performance field with agents and acts and a continually renewed point of view in time, is formulated in Heath's phrase "space takes place" or "space is negated for place." This formulation implies that space is contested, that in its historicizing function the narrative process also politicizes subjects. In the Fantastic Moms' *re-placing* of the dominant representation of teen motherhood with their own stories, using frame space and voice differently in order to subvert dominant structures of narration, they essentially renarrativized the public discourse on teen motherhood and, consequently, their own private stories. In doing so, they created a video autoethnography.

Looking at Teen Motherhood: The Fantastic Moms Video

Whereas the Fantastic Moms constituted a collective, Dálida María Benfield (María) and I, as teachers, video producer and director, respectively, were collaborators. María joined us when we began working on the video. The previous months' process had brought the Moms to a point of clarity in their thinking such that the planning and storyboarding went quickly and needed only technical guidance from us. The group improvised most of the scenes, in various configurations, without a script. María and the Fantastic Moms did the camera work; María and I did the editing. The students were paid $6 per hour, raised through private sources, and work was done in the summer, outside our regular class meetings. In addition, I wrote a proposal that they receive high school credit for the project.

The videotape is in two parts: the first part is a deconstruction of the term, *teen mother;* the second, a representation of the Fantastic Moms. In this section, I will describe and analyze the tape and discuss our process. The group decided to begin with the image of one Fantastic Mom (Lee) with her baby, acting as their representative. For the opening sound track, we used Frank Sinatra singing "Yes, Sir, That's My Baby," which the students found a funny, exotic antique, the words bizarrely appropriate. To me, this choice blatantly positioned "the problem" of teen motherhood and the issue of responsibility in the broader context of heterosexual patriarchal capitalism, the proprietorship of women, and the myth of romance. The tape opens with the Sinatra audio on a black screen, withholding the identity of his "baby." After one verse, Lee's face pops on, completely filling the frame in extreme televisual intimacy, even spectatorial privilege. Kaja Silverman has observed that "the human eye is no sooner differentiated from the camera/gaze than it is gendered 'female.' The female subject, in other words, is obliged to bear the burden of specularity so that the look of her male counterpart can be aligned with the camera."[24] This code is acknowledged, boasted by Frank Sinatra's "Yes, sir!" directed to his male audience, his cohort, "that's *my* [i.e. not *your*] baby now." Lee looks down demurely, then straight out, and her look turns into an unbridled smile in response to María holding the camera. She holds the smile for an uncomfortably long time in an extreme close-up shot, the song meanwhile narrating her upcoming wedding to the Sinatra character. Finally, Lee looks down again and María's camera follows her look, slowly panning to the baby in her arms as the song is repeatedly jump-cut so that we hear, over and over, "my baby now," like a record skipping. A glitch in the program, the male voice has two babies now, his woman-baby and her real baby; heavily ironic, the image is multivocal and left uninterpreted. It cuts to black and a different male voice whispers coarsely, "Mama," like a dirty secret about his compensatory fantasies of the (no longer virginal) pictured woman—mother, sex object, sex victim, nurturer, reproductive vessel, little girl, and so on.

The marriage plot embedded in this introductory segment carries the final irony: teen motherhood is commonly represented as a contemporary social crisis not because adolescent female parents have gotten younger, or more numerous, or more fertile; rather, more babies are being born out of wedlock.[25] In fact, the relation between marriage and childbearing in all age groups has been undergoing a transformation throughout the industrialized world since the 1960s. Currently, in 1995, approximately 29 percent of mothers of all ages in the United States are unmarried when they give birth.[26] In this opening three-shot sequence—mother out, mother down at baby, baby out—a narrative triangle of vision is created that positions the baby as the ultimate object, and paternity ("that's my baby") as the issue at stake in out-of-wedlock maternity. This sequence produces a meditation on the (social) subject's relation to the media (video and voice-over) and to the culture; they compete and cooperate to possess her. Sexual, racial, and age differences are heightened by the leisurely, almost shocking pace. Lee's youth and beauty are both refreshing and disturbing when exhibited to the vocal text of an old man claiming her. But recognizing that it is Lee's look that organizes the shot and María's camera work that controls it, the Sinatra voice slips from master to servant of the video message. Caught in this struggle between cultural and video control, discourse and counterdiscourse, the spectator proceeds to "look at teen motherhood."

The rest of the introduction uses images from mainstream discourse against which the Fantastic Moms ultimately position themselves. In the second sequence, the word "Mother" appears on the screen, and then "Teen," each followed by a set of stereotypical images glossing it. In planning this sequence, the group spent a session free-associating with these terms and discussing possible images. "Mother" was the more contested, and the images of it are the more static. An example of the kinds of pictures considered was the mother on *The Cosby Show* and an over-thirty mother with a very young child running toward each other in slow motion, with snow falling. The inclusive features of all the suggestions were that "mothers" are always older, always smiling gently but never laughing out loud; they are imagined in altered time, either in slow motion or frozen, usually in relationship to just one child, in idealized and nostalgic pictures. In the resulting video, "Mother" is followed by old black-and-white photographs of madonna-like mothers from different cultures and actual Madonnas, all in soft dyad, underscored by a melancholy "Stabat Mater" evoking a lost world before the word *mother* needed qualification to be understood (birth mother, adoptive mother, surrogate mother, teen mother, genetic mother, and so forth).

"Teen" images taken from the commercial films *Weird Science* and

Fame depict teeming mobs of hedonistic youth overtaking a suburban living room, a school cafeteria, a city street, and a taxicab with their voracious collective appetite for PARTY. Then the words "Teen Mother" are displayed as a single term, followed by rapidly alternating "Teen" and "Mother" cuts, demonstrating how the two myths "Teen" and "Mother" pair, or refuse to pair[27]—contained and containing Mother, static and timeless, and hyperactive, disruptive, consuming, carnivalesque Teen. Formally speaking, the opposition of black-and-white photographs with Hollywood film clips reinforces this dual message. "Mother" is perceived as an eternal holding, idea, and identity (I'll *always* be your mother), whereas "teen" is transitory in all senses, short-lived, and perilous. Thus to become a teen mother is, conceptually and actually, an extraordinary thing, neither fully and exclusively "teen" nor fully and exclusively "mother."

This introductory segment of the video ends with a very short sequence from John Hughes's *For Keeps*, a Hollywood soap opera of teen motherhood: the school-age waitress-wife returns home from work to discover the baby screaming from fever, the father asleep, and the telephone disconnected. Superimposed on this crisis scene is the crisis rhetoric of a congressional report on teenage pregnancy in graphic text. The viewer is forced to read the text through the action of the scene and the screams of the baby:

TEEN PREGNANCY: WHAT IS BEING DONE? A STATE-BY-STATE LOOK—
A REPORT of the SELECT COMMITTEE ON CHILDREN, YOUTH and FAMILIES
U.S. HOUSE OF REPRESENTATIVES, NINETY-NINTH CONGRESS, FIRST SESSION
together with
ADDITIONAL and MINORITY VIEWS
DECEMBER 1985
Regardless of one's political philosophy, the prospect of one million teenage pregnancies, 400,000 abortions, and one-half million births each year, nearly fifty-five percent of which will be births to unmarried teens, is chilling. The human and fiscal costs to all are unacceptable. . . . [28]

The second part of the video, the Fantastic Moms' "self"-representation, is introduced by words only, "An Other Look," playing on the title of the congressional report's "State-by-State Look" within the larger video project, *Looking at Teen Motherhood.* "An Other" and "Look" are separated by a sequence showing the Fantastic Moms grouped on a playground elephant sculpture waiting attentively to say their scripted lines until Effie throws up her hand and playfully calls a countdown. "Look," the words command, at "An Other." They forcefully interpose themselves between the two extremes, Teen and Mother, and offer an alternative to stereotypes such as the *For Keeps* caricature. In high formal contrast to the slick imagery of the preceding segment, here the camera work of the Moms and María is executed with refreshing intimacy and documentary casualness. Ambient outdoor sounds disrupt their direct address group statement:

> That's not the whole story, only the side that you know. We are teen mothers, which makes us authorities on the subject. You might say, we speak from the inside. We call ourselves the Fantastic Moms. Here is our side of it.

In this short introduction of themselves, the Fantastic Moms also present their argument: a complex matter has been distorted and oversimplified, and they—speaking "from the inside" of both the knowing lived body of a teen mother and the protective body of the group that surrounds each one of them—are about to confront it. They acknowledge and reject their "outsider" status, instead tacitly positioning the viewer "outside." Here we might recall Spivak's counsel: "the only strategic thing to do is to absolutely present oneself at the centre." Further, recalling Sayre's definition, the Fantastic Moms speak from the "inside" of "art." They each take a line, reciting it stiffly, uncomfortable with having to "act," then hold the pose for a few seconds before MayLene yells "Cut!" and everyone breaks up laughing. Travelers in the "world" of representation making, the Fantastic Moms bring their characteristically playful attitudes with them.[29]

Proceeding through a montage of quickly clipped improvised scenes with sync sound, they present themselves: kissing their babies ("You love me? You do? I love you too!"); taking care of them ("We get to spend more time with our kids than they do"); playing with each other, talking, dancing, and, especially, laughing.[30] In one shot (Figure 5.1), MayLene talks baby talk to a tiny infant as she feeds him with a bottle, while Kesha and Effie look on. MayLene speaks warmly and comfortably to him. Then Effie, seated farthest from the baby, says, "His wrist is ticklish," and the viewer becomes aware that it is Effie's baby MayLene is feeding; maybe the viewer realizes that s/he assumed it was MayLene's baby. The setup of this shot symbolizes the chain of support among the Moms, the wider-than-nuclear circle of responsibility and affection that includes each other's children as well as their own.

Figure 5.1. Effie (*left*) and Kesha (*center*) look on as MayLene feeds Effie's baby.

In the first scene of a narrative sequence that is laced throughout the video, Michelle drops her baby off at the day-care center. The child-care provider demonstrates concern for both Michelle and her baby, gathering the information she needs to perform her job effectively, thereby reinforcing Michelle's competence also.

Next, in an oral narrative straight to the camera (Figure 5.2), Kesha performs a piece she wrote in the workshop:

> I wanted to be a track star. I saw myself as a graduate. But when I got pregnant my thoughts changed. Not because I didn't believe in myself. It was my parents' and my relatives' attitude toward the mistake I made. Even some of my peers said this. But now, after her birth, I feel more, I guess I could say mature, because of the responsibility. It pushes me to finish lots of things because I know this is something that I have to live for. I love her.

We cut to an interview *in medias res* with Charlotte and her mother, Frances Lowe, conducted by Kesha (Figure 5.3):

Figure 5.2. Kesha talks about the effects of her pregnancy and childbirth on her life.

Figure 5.3. Charlotte (*left*) and her mother, Frances, are interviewed about Charlotte's recent pregnancy.

FRANCES: Well, we were glad to have a little baby in the house. We are always having little babies anyway. Now this one was ours to keep. [She laughs.] We were excited about . . . I was . . . after everything went okay. . . .

KESHA: How did you feel when you told your mom?

CHARLOTTE: I didn't tell her. She told me. [They both laugh.] She could see the signs of it.

KESHA: What signs did she see?

CHARLOTTE: Like my missing my period. Like, if you don't go through the boxes of pads then you know it's something. She told me I was looking pale, and the headaches. . . .

KESHA: Did you know you were pregnant?

CHARLOTTE: I had an idea.

KESHA: Did you cry?

CHARLOTTE: Yeah! Yeah, I cried. [Cuts to the conclusion.]

KESHA: I think Charlotte's very lucky to have a family that supports her as they do, and a boyfriend who stands behind her, because some people's boyfriends . . . they just, you know—"It ain't mine. See ya." They just go about their business and act like you're not happening. There are a lot of boys that do that. My mom hates mine.

Apparently simple and straightforward, this scene is richly contradictory. The dialogue, framed with unequivocal statements of family support, is centripetal in its dynamic, densely packed and sharply focused, whereas the visual imagery is centrifugal, active, and disrupted. As Kesha probes for intimate details and Charlotte gives surprisingly frank and direct responses, the camera, held in turn by Effie and May-Lene, jumps around, trying to settle into place. Charlotte, her mother, two sisters, and infant are all squeezed onto one small couch, jostling for space and comfort. The "button"—Kesha reveals that her own mother hates her boyfriend, and she and Charlotte's mother share a knowing smile—closes off any "happy ending" the viewer might be tempted to read into the dialogue.

We cut to Michelle in math class, solving a problem at the blackboard, then to the Fantastic Moms sitting around a table, talking:

EFFIE [holding and rocking her baby]: When I was on my way over here, this lady said to me, why are we making this film? And you know, it was like, "We want to," I said. [She laughs.] Then she said we should be ashamed, well, not ashamed but we shouldn't be proud of having a baby so young.

MAYLENE: Well, what are we going to be?

KESHA: How are we supposed to feel?

MAYLENE: We get two choices, either be ashamed or not ashamed. [A chorus of voices concurs.]

EFFIE: So I said, "I'm not ashamed, I'm proud of my baby." She said, "That ain't nothing to be walking around with your chest stuck out about!" That is exactly what she said. I'm serious.

MAYLENE: I'm walking around, I've been walking around now. . . .

KESHA: I'm so proud I'm walking around with my chest, my butt, my thigh, my knee, my ankle, and my toe stuck out—that's how proud I am.

CHARLOTTE: You're not sad because you had him either; you're just not proud that you had him at this age.

LEE: Everyone is acting like teen pregnancy is some kind of crime.

MAYLENE: A disease, girl! [A chorus of agreement: "A disease!"]

LEE: Back home they look at you like you have committed some kind of crime and you are supposed to be ashamed of it. I've known girls that actually hide during their whole nine months of pregnancy, and then they say their mom had the baby. Their whole nine months, they just hide and don't come out.

Through their radical simplification of the issues, the Fantastic Moms show their growing ability to interpret events in ways that support them and to expose the moralistic subtext of the hegemonic discourse constructing early fertility, readily agreeing on words like "crime" and "disease" to describe how people have treated their pregnancies. It is remarkable that Kesha can physicalize her pride as she does under such bodily attack.

Next we see Michelle at work, confidently answering the phone. In voice-over she reflects on the complexity of a typical day and the level of motivation required to finish high school in the demanding and competing conditions of single motherhood:

It's a big responsibility, being a mother and being a student. You've got to wake up in the morning thinking about dressing yourself and the baby; carrying the baby to the nursery; being in school on time. After school you've got to go to work to make some money for yourself and your baby. And after work you pick your baby up, do your homework, and then time runs out. There is no time for yourself.

This sequence ends with Michelle picking up her baby after a long day. Throughout the video, the Fantastic Moms use everyday locations—park, school, meeting room, day-care center, office—to trace a path of their pleasures and commitments. Locations of everyday activities (space) become loci of narration (place) when relations of looking are enacted by human agents, and locations are inscribed with their agency. Just as feminist theorists have demonstrated that "woman" refers to an infinitely layered being with multiple, often contradictory, significations, the Fantastic Moms challenge the distortions and the fictions of stability in "teen mother."

The video concludes with a fictionalized scene (Figure 5.4) of a teen turning to a friend for support when she suspects she is pregnant. We called this scene, unofficially, "The Abortion Drama." The friends are played by MayLene and Charlotte:

> M: I don't know what to do. I'm scared to tell my mom right now because I don't know if I want to have an abortion or not.
> C: So, are you going to keep it?
> M: Yeah . . . no . . . I'm confused. (C: See!) I'm confused. I don't know. You see, I'm young right now. I can't handle kids right now. I take care of kids, but it's different when you have your own.
> C: My advice to you, MayLene, is that I think you should sit down and try to talk to your mom about it. First of all, I think you should go to the doctor and make sure you're even pregnant. Then I think you should talk to your mom. If you talk to your mom, you have support on one side; you're not in it by yourself. Because you say the father ain't no father, so. . . .
> M: That's another problem. . . .
> [Cut to Kesha capping the interview with Mrs. Lowe and Charlotte]
> KESHA: Can we conclude this?

Characteristically resisting the easy solution, this "abortion drama" leads spectators to reflect on the performers as people who also have confronted the problem and are accountable for their decisions.

A closing montage reviews the previous scenes in which the Moms

Figure 5.4. Charlotte (*left*) and MayLene perform "The Abortion Drama."

presented themselves as thoughtful, articulate, playful, and responsible people. It starts with the image from the introduction, Lee's face, this video's code for the stereotype Teen Mother, but now complicated with scenes of Lee laughing, playing with her baby, talking about "back home." They speak in voice-over, employing second-person address, implicating individual spectators in the collective attitude toward them as teen mothers. They are outspoken and disconcerting after the friendly, even intimate relationship viewers might have fantasized with them. Interpolated into the montage/voice-over are silent displays of statistics that problematize the intersection of age, gender, and race in constructions of teenage pregnancy and motherhood;[31] further, the manipulative use of these statistics puts the entire foregoing discussion in a context of struggle over interpretation and representation. The following presents the voice-over text, with the statistical displays represented in boldface type:

Maybe you don't approve of our decision. You say we're just kids; we haven't even finished school yet. **1970: 656,000 teen births; 1987: 473,000 teen births.** What's more, you say, we're not independent. You call our children illegitimate. **Births to unmarried women in 1987: 53.4% White; 42.8% Black.** Don't stereotype us. We and our children have the right to be here—as we are. **1987: teen births at lowest levels since 1940.** It sure beats a job at McDonald's, or taking care of your kids. **31% teen births**

are to married teens 18–19. Look, we'll probably make of our lives what we would have without our babies. It may take a little longer, and we may have to work harder for it, but it will be more valuable. **Unintended U.S. pregnancies, 1987: Black teens 10.1%; White teens 21.3%; All women aged 20–44, 67.7%.** In the meantime, the real question is, to whom does the meaning of our life belong?

The visual image accompanying the last line, spoken by Kesha, is an extreme close-up shot of Kesha nuzzling her baby, their faces filling the frame and assuming narrative agency in concert with the spoken words ("space takes place"). The construction, "our life," though it may sound incorrect, unproblematized, or utopian to the casual auditor, signals the Moms' sense of a common lot inclusive of their differences. Their question acknowledges contests over needs interpretation,[32] values interpretation, and discursive authority, contests they necessarily enter with the making of this videotape and the posing of this question. As "colonized subjects" they "undertake to represent themselves in ways that *engage with* the colonizer's own terms."[33] In this way the word *real,* as in "the real question," takes on additional permutations to its already overdetermined signification. "The *real,* nothing else than a *code of representation,* does not (cannot) coincide with the lived or the performed."[34] The "real" languages of statistics, documentary footage, and direct-address voice-over battle for ascendancy as they compound the videotape's hyperreflexive conclusion that defies closure ("Can we conclude this?"). In first-person "documentary" performance, that is, autobiographical or autoethnographic performance, the imaginary(s) and the real(s) converge in a multivalent discourse. Identity becomes "real" in the performance of it, and the actors are always already historical beings.

Elaborating the positions of Monique Wittig and Simone de Beauvoir, Judith Butler has argued that to *be* a woman (or a teen mother) is to *become* one, "but because this process is in no sense fixed, it is possible to become a being whom neither *man* nor *woman* [nor *teen mother*] truly describes."[35] This being is not some combination of the two opposing (conventionally defined) terms *teen* and *mother,* nor is it a transcendence of them. The being called "teen mother," generally held in subjugation in a hegemonic field of fantasy construction, is here represented by the Fantastic Moms as "an internal subversion in which the binary is both presupposed and proliferated to the point where it no longer makes sense."[36] *Looking at Teen Motherhood: The Fantastic Moms Video* finally replaces the tired stereotype with something outside the known category "teen mother."

Performance of Subjectivity and Fantastic Autoethnography

Through the ongoing process of video performance—researching, planning, storyboarding, enacting, framing and shooting, reflecting, reviewing, being viewed—the Fantastic Moms established their subjectivity in three ways: (1) as speaking subjects, first person, present tense, I say what I am and what I am not; (2) as performing subjects, I speak for myself, by my own design; and (3) as subjects of speech, I am the one of whom I speak.[37] They particularized and historicized themselves, demystifying the stereotype. They reflected on themselves in voice-over, adding a frame to their representation. By directly addressing a named "you," they further distinguished the achieved "I" and placed the spectator in dialogue with them as speakers, acknowledging the claim that stories make on listeners. The Fantastic Moms ultimately invested their stories in an unseen/un-scene "you" in the hope of change, and in doing so, they transformed their images. By publicly narrating and interpreting these personal and hitherto "private" matters in the context of stereotype, the Fantastic Moms politicized without essentializing themselves, and rendered their tale eminently tellable.[38] They demanded an audience for its subtext of rebellion against the normalizing force of the dominant voice. They exposed their attackers on record, both known (family, neighbors, boyfriends) and unknown ("society"). They created many rich roles for themselves—student, worker, friend, artist, daughter, mother—all alive with warm and idiosyncratic detail, further disabling attempts to distance and generalize them. They looked straight at the camera and proclaimed, "We and our children have a right to be here—as we are"; and the only identity/ontological status that they admitted was one *they* fabricated.

Performance offers a way to reconstitute subjectivity through the exploration and accomplishment of identities chosen for "self"-definition. Because there are no desirable images of teen motherhood in this culture, because it is constructed as a pathology and a taboo, people who follow this lifestyle must invent representations that adequately and truthfully reflect their experiences. We must work to create speaking opportunities, to speak discourse. In a world that mandates "Children should be seen and not heard," and some, it seems, not even seen, the Fantastic Moms have performed a scintillating speech act.

Theorists of autobiography point to the title page for the mark that differentiates it from fiction, its unity of author, narrator, and protagonist in the first-person singular pronoun. Philippe Lejeune reveals the individualist ideology informing autobiographical criticism and practice in Western culture: "A person is always *several* people when he is writing, even all alone, even his own life."[39] Any claim to authorship is specious. The medium of video hastens the death of the author. In calling themselves "the Fantastic Moms" and their work *Looking at Teen Motherhood: The Fantastic Moms Video,* on their own "title page" the video makers put their story into a larger "fantasy" of teen motherhood. (In the title, which noun does *Fantastic* modify?) But in doing so, they ultimately authenticate fictions as true, integral parts of the real *and* the lived.

Representation has a dual nature that is coreflexive and coproductive. It is at once a thing in and of itself, a place of disclosure, and a referent to another moment outside its frame.[40] This referential capacity is heightened in the case of documentary representation: we always know that "this happened." The influence of representation usually outlives its performance; the fantasy representation lives on, in both its makers and its audiences—it continues to "happen." In this way representation continues to regenerate the very "identity" it displays. Performers can witness their own "self"-made history by assuming the role of audience, viewing and identifying with their own characters. They become, in effect, world actors.[41]

Notes

Earlier versions of this essay were presented before the Association for Theatre in Higher Education (ATHE), the Speech Communication Association (SCA), and Northwestern's Center for Interdisciplinary Research in the Arts. *Looking at Teen Motherhood: The Fantastic Moms Video* has been screened at the Women in the Director's Chair International Film and Video Festival, on Evanston and Chicago Access Television, and in health care, high school, and university settings. Additionally, it is in the permanent collections of the Marjorie Iglow Media Center at Northwestern University and the Video Data Bank of the School of the Art Institute of Chicago.

I wish to express my gratitude to Geneve Wade, Family Focus-Our Place, Evanston, Illinois, for her support and trust during the course of our work together. I am particularly grateful to all the young women with whom I have had the privilege of working, most of whom I am unable to mention herein. I would like to thank especially the co-producers of *Looking at Teen Motherhood: The Fantastic Moms Video,* MayLene Coleman, Lakesha Dunn, Michelle Gayle, Charlotte Lowe, Effie Patterson, and Leontyne Walkine. Dálida María Benfield, producer of *Looking at Teen Motherhood: The Fantastic Moms Video* and independent film and video artist whose work is devoted to the representation of the specific experiences of Latinas in the United States, is also my friend, colleague, and intellectual companion. I am happy to have this opportunity to recognize her persistent vision, generous talent, and genuinely playful attitude. Finally, I want to thank Margaret Thompson Drewal, Kay Ellen Capo, Mary Driscoll, Terri Kapsalis, Sidonie Smith, and Julia Watson for their helpful comments and suggestions at various moments in the metamorphosis of this essay.

1. Trinh T. Minh-ha. *Woman, Native, Other: Writing Postcoloniality and Feminism* (Bloomington: Indiana University Press, 1989), 134.

2. *Looking at Teen Motherhood: The Fantastic Moms Video,* videotape, produced by Dálida María Benfield, with MayLene Coleman, Lakesha Dunn, Michelle Gayle, Charlotte Lowe, Effie Patterson, and Leontyne Walkine; directed by Salome Chasnoff, 1990: 15 min.

3. Charlotte Lowe, conversation with author, Evanston, Illinois, 14 July 1992.

4. Henry Sayre, "Performance," in *Critical Terms for Literary Study,* ed. Frank Lentricchia and Thomas McLaughlin (Chicago: University of Chicago Press, 1990), 103.

5. Margaret Thompson Drewal, "The State of Research on Performance in Africa," *African Studies Review* 34 (December 1991): 1–2.

6. Gayatri Chakravorty Spivak, in Judy Burns and Jill MacDougall, with Catherine Benamou, Avanthi Meduri, Peggy Phelan, and Susan Slyomovics, "An Interview with Gayatri Spivak," *Women and Performance: A Journal of Feminist Theory* 9 (1990): 84.

7. Mary Louise Pratt, *Imperial Eyes: Travel Writing and Transculturation* (London: Routledge, 1992), 7.

8. Family Focus-Our Place, Evanston, Illinois, in conjunction with Evanston Township High School, provides a full-credit curriculum and specialized support classes and services for pregnant and parenting teens, serving at any given time approximately 225 people (90 percent female). My job description was written by Geneve Wade, parent education programs coordinator and site director.

9. See María Lugones, "Playfulness, 'World'-Travelling, and Loving Perception," in *Making Face, Making Soul = Haciendo Caras: Creative and Critical Perspectives by Women of Color,* ed. Gloria Anzaldúa (San Francisco: Aunt Lute Foundation Books, 1990), 390–402. Lugones's "world" and my "self" (see my section heading) are in quotation marks because these terms are "still up in the air, in the process of becoming" (395). The conditions for successful "world"-traveling include "that I see with her eyes, that I go into [her] world, that I see both of us as we are constructed in her world, that I witness her own sense of herself from within her world" (394).

10. Ibid., 401.

11. I make this seemingly obvious point because at two different university screenings, two women objected to the video on the grounds that it reinforced the stereotype that all teen mothers are black by depicting only black women. We acknowledged the power of media to shape knowledge (the subject of our tape, actually), but felt that the benefits of making and showing the video took precedence. Its makers were not selected out of a larger "pool of actors"; they were the people in the workshop who wanted to participate in the project. They chose to focus the video on teen motherhood from their own positions and to use themselves in it.

12. According to Geneve Wade, although the overwhelming majority of the population served by Family Focus-Our Place is African American, there are every year a few pregnant white girls: "They are invariably brought to and from the program by their fathers, as if to say to the mothers, 'You screwed up. Now I'm taking over.'" The one white student who was in my group at the start left as soon as she was ready to deliver.

13. Leontyne Walkine, unpublished essay, February 1990. The unpublished writings from which this and other student quotations are taken were generated in our workshops throughout 1990. Material quoted from these writings is noted in text by author name and date.

14. Rush Limbaugh, *The Rush Limbaugh Show,* WLS Talk Radio, Chicago, 26 September 1990.

15. Johanna Brenner, "Towards a Feminist Perspective on Welfare Reform," *Yale Journal of Law and Feminism* 2 (Fall 1989): 121.

16. CNN Transcripts, 23 July 1993.

17. Sue Woodman, "How Teen Pregnancy Has Becomes a Political Football," *Ms.,* January/February 1995, 92.

18. "Fertility Rates among U.S. Women Aged 15–24 Reach Record Lows, but Increase among Unwed," *Family Planning Perspectives* 19 (March/April 1987): 84.

19. Rosalind P. Petchesky, *Abortion and Woman's Choice: The State, Sexuality and Reproductive Freedom* (Boston: Northeastern University Press, 1984); Maris A. Vinovskis, *An "Epidemic" of Adolescent Pregnancy? Some Historical and Policy Considerations* (New York: Oxford University Press, 1988).

20. "Killing Our Children," an ongoing front-page feature of the *Chicago Tribune* throughout 1993, posted the latest count of the city's murdered children like a grim sports tally. The killers were almost always gang members or parent figures, including mothers' boyfriends, and almost always people of color. One of the hidden messages in this series was that poor parents of color, except for the valiant minority, are generally inadequate and often destructive, either directly or indirectly. It was understood that the possessive pronoun in the title of the series belonged to "society": *they* are killing *our* children.

21. See Leland H. Roloff, "The Body Poem," in *Falling into Poetic Space: The Biopoetic Impulse* (Evanston, Ill.: Northwestern University Press, 1982).

22. Gayatri Chakravorty Spivak, *The Post-Colonial Critic,* ed. Sarah Harasym (New York: Routledge, 1990), 40–41.

23. Stephen Heath, *Questions of Cinema* (Bloomington: Indiana University Press, 1981).

24. Kaja Silverman, "What Is a Camera?, or: History in the Field of Vision," *Discourse* 15 (Spring 1993): 18.

25. Petchesky, *Abortion and Women's Choice,* 144–45.

26. Woodman, "How Teen Pregnancy," 91.

27. I am grateful to Terri Kapsalis for sharing this "key words" insight.

28. U.S. Government Printing Office, Stock 052-070-06080-8.

29. From my current angle of vision, I would say that the two scripted sequences, this introduction and the closing voice-over, are stiffer than the rest of the tape, which was improvised; but I would not say that scripting words not "their own" was a mistake. The discomfort suggests the process of *accomplishing* identities, *trying on* language that eventually became their own. Appropriately, these sequences are the transitions into and out of their "self"-representation.

30. The quotations in parentheses are from the video montage.

31. The impetus for the insertion of these statistics was that, in our pilot screening to

a Family Focus audience, the irony of the voice-over was not understood; some viewers thought that the video makers agreed with the dominant construction of teen motherhood, including their own culpability.

32. See Nancy Fraser's socialist-feminist critical theory of "the politics of need interpretation," in *Unruly Practices: Power, Discourse, and Gender in Contemporary Social Theory* (Minneapolis: University of Minnesota Press, 1989), 144–87.

33. Pratt, *Imperial Eyes,* 7.

34. Minh-ha, *Woman, Native, Other,* 94.

35. Judith Butler, *Gender Trouble: Feminism and the Subversion of Identity* (New York: Routledge, 1990), 127.

36. Ibid.

37. I am indebted to Chris Straayer's discussion of the performance of subjectivity, "I Say I Am: Feminist Performance Video in the '70s," *Afterimage* (November 1985): 8–12, and her interpretation of the work of Tzvetan Todorov ("The Origin of Genres") and Emile Benveniste (*Problems in General Linguistics*), among others, that I have interpolated for my argument here.

38. See Straayer's discussion of tellability in "I Say I Am," 10, applying theories of Mary Louise Pratt (*Toward a Speech Act Theory of Literary Discourse*) and William Labov (*Language in the Inner City*).

39. Philippe Lejeune, *On Autobiography,* trans. Katherine Leary (Minneapolis: University of Minnesota Press, 1989), xvii.

40. See Bert States's readings of Aristotle's Poetics, Heidegger's *Poetry, Language, Thought,* and Barthes's discussion of the interplay of *punctum* and *studium* in the photograph in *Camera Lucida,* in his introduction to *Great Reckonings in Little Rooms: On the Phenomenology of Theater* (Berkeley: University of California Press, 1985), 1–15.

41. The following dialogue, excerpted from a conversation I had with Geneve Wade (October 1993), historicizes these generalized assertions:

SALLY: Who viewed the video at Our Place and what were some of the responses?

GENEVE: I showed it to all the staff, teens, and their parents. Generally, staff people were floored when they saw the video. They were surprised by the girls' intelligence and clearly articulated thinking. They were also surprised to hear what teen mothers thought about. They thought teen moms were dummies, to be pitied, kids who stumbled into a hell without redemption. When they heard them talking, the girls became people, each with a unique specialness. After seeing the video, staff were able to address their new teen mothers as special, as fully human. I showed it to these groups repeatedly, and each time they saw new things in it.

SALLY: What values did you get from the whole event? What values, as far as you know, did those who worked on the video get from it?

GENEVE: Seeing themselves on the video had a powerful effect, you know, "Is that really me?" They watch it often. After being used to hearing what failures they were, here they got to see their strength and they took it to heart. "That's me!" they would say. They got patted on the back. The whole experience heightened their self-awareness in a very positive way. They saw themselves as a team, working together in a process toward a product. They saw that they can form a group, that they did not need to be isolated, alienated individuals, renegades. It's that feeling of isolation that leads kids to renegade behavior. People don't feel that they are able to belong to a viable group. They also learned through the process that they were women, that they were special as women. They saw themselves as having talent, as a group, as individual women, and as mothers.

6 / The Mediated Talking Cure: Therapeutic Framing of Autobiography in TV Talk Shows

Janice Peck

Autobiography—the relating of everyday stories—is central to day-time television talk shows. Hosts, "expert" and "ordinary" guests, and studio audience members produce/narrate their lives and comment on those of others; home viewers consume/interpret these narratives in light of their own biographies. Part of the appeal of these programs is that they appear to let people speak for themselves and tell their own stories. At the same time, these interwoven narratives are located within institutional, political-economic, and sociohistorical structures that determine what can be spoken, by whom, and to what ends. In this essay, I examine the process through which the telling of "personal" stories in daytime talk television is shaped by these structural constraints. In particular, I ask how these shows' incorporation of therapeutic language and assumptions works to frame the lives narrated within them.[1]

I focus here on two of the most popular talk shows—*The Oprah Winfrey Show* and *Sally Jessy Raphael*—programs hosted by women, oriented to women's concerns through "feminine narrative" conventions, and directed at a primarily female audience.[2] I suggest that these shows are fueled by social tensions that originate "outside" the shows but are imported "inside," where they become the object of the talk and the site of ideological labor. This sets in motion the programs' internal contradiction: they address social conflicts that can never be fully resolved on television while holding out the possibility that talking will lead to, or is itself a form of, resolution. The belief that communication can guide people out of their dilemmas makes these shows compatible with therapeutic discourse; their relational focus, confessional mode, and therapeutic orientation make them appealing to female viewers. The ongoing pursuit and deferral of final solutions—which helps sustain viewers' interest and commitment and generates ratings and advertising revenue—also makes this format attractive to the TV industry.[3] If producers of the programs recognize that conflict and controversy attract viewers in the first place, they must also find ways to depict these tensions without jeopardizing advertising support or violating the industry's economic priorities. In this essay, I look at how the programs negotiate those demands by mediating and managing the social conflicts from which their appeal arises.

Gendered Dimensions of Therapeutic Discourse

Grounded in psychology—which takes the individual psyche as its object of study—therapy is intended to remedy individual "dysfunction" through perceptual or behavioral change.[4] Explanations of the growth of therapy, however, tend to cite social causes: modernization, the growth of bureaucracy and increasing complexity of society, technological innovation, and the erosion of community are said to result in individual isolation and anomie.[5] Such forces have supposedly created a void in contemporary experience that must be remedied with therapeutic intervention. Implicit in psychology is the assumption that societal changes are organic or natural processes to which individuals must learn to adapt.[6]

Therapeutic discourse, formulated around intimate, revelatory conversation, emotional expression, and reliance on (traditionally) male expertise and guidance, resonates for many women because of their socially constructed "feminine" subject position and discursive orientation. Because women are typically socialized to attend to interpersonal processes and needs, they are encouraged to develop communicative practices that foster relatedness. Research suggests that "women's talk" tends toward dialogic symmetry and identificatory statements; emphasizes interactive participation; uses supportive expressions; focuses on the feelings and relationship of the speakers; includes conversational "maintenance work"; stresses personal details, self-disclosure, anecdotes, and concrete reasoning; and exhibits verbal tentativeness that creates a space for others' perspectives.[7] This style of

talk creates a sense of intimacy between speakers and provides a setting for reciprocal self-revelation (and confession). Confession, a "structure of speech that enacts self-identity" (White 1992, 8), is premised
on the existence of an empathic other who validates and recognizes the
speaker's self-narrative.

White argues that confession and therapy have become "privileged
and prominent discourses in contemporary television," and that these
discourses are "implicitly associated with a specific gendered [female]
audience" (1992, 36). Daytime talk shows have incorporated therapeutic, confessional discourse as a narrative strategy related to their female viewership. Programs aimed at women exhibit features that both
Brown and Fiske have identified as constituting "feminine narratives":
lack of closure, an emphasis on process and intimate dialogue, a correspondence to "real time," and a focus on relational issues.[8] These qualities are similarly associated with therapeutic settings and interactions.
Given the target audience of *The Oprah Winfrey Show* and *Sally Jessy
Raphael,* it is not surprising to find in them a feminine style of talk,
feminine narrative conventions, and reliance on therapeutic discourse.

The TV Personality System, Para-Sociality, and Mediated Intimacy

In the mid-1970s, Phil Donahue pioneered what has been called the
"new" talk show organized around topics, focusing on "ordinary"
(rather than famous) people, and featuring hosts who have abandoned
their place on stage to encourage audience questions and comments.
Carpignano and his colleagues argue that turning the studio audience
into "a major player" is the key innovation of "new" talk shows like
The Oprah Winfrey Show and *Sally Jessy Raphael.*[9] But if these
changes have given the "ordinary public" (as guests and studio audience members) a more central role on television, the para-sociality of
the talk show form and its use of personalization strategies and therapeutic discourse constrain the content, relationships, and identities in
the programs.

The "television personality system," argues Langer, is most prominent in "factual" program forms (e.g., news, game and talk shows),
where TV personalities "play themselves," are presented as "part of
[daily] life," are accessible on a regular basis, and work to "construct
intimacy and immediacy."[10] Because talk shows focus on the realm of
the "personal," they create a space "where intimacy itself can be both

the form and substance of the programming" (360). This mediated intimacy has both practical and formal bases. The fact that TV viewing usually occurs in "the intimate and familiar terrain" of the home encourages us to respond to "television's own 'intimacies' and 'familiarities' brought to us through its personalities" (356). Repeated contact with such personalities contributes to what Horton and Wohl call a "para-social relationship," where viewers come to feel they know TV personalities "in somewhat the same way they know their chosen friends: through direct observation and interpretation of appearance, gestures and voice, conversation and conduct in a variety of situations." Viewers are thus invited to feel that "they are involved in a face-to-face exchange rather than a passive observation."[11] "New" talk shows further enhance this sense of immediacy because studio audience members, who stand in for viewers, actively participate in the programs.

Although we refer to TV personalities by their first names and are privy to some aspects of their private lives, what we know are their "television selves," narratively constructed public personas. Viewers' pleasure in a given talk show is based on identification with the host's public personality/biography, develops over time, and permits them to make personal judgments about, for instance, Winfrey or Raphael.[12] A woman who watches these shows regularly confidently told me that "Oprah really cares about people," whereas "Sally is too cold." Her assessment is based partly on Winfrey's televisual manner—crying easily, hugging guests and audience members—which is part of her TV self and a means of constructing intimacy and eliciting emotion on the show. The gap between the TV persona and the actual person behind it, however, ensures that viewers' relationship with talk show hosts remains bounded by para-sociality: "The interaction, characteristically, is one-sided, non-dialectical, controlled by the performer, and not susceptible to mutual development" (Horton and Wohl 1976, 212). This lack of reciprocity is what distinguishes para-social from interpersonal relationships. "This form of communication is highly institutionalized and control is not in the hands of either the sender or receiver, but is preplanned by media specialists who design and orchestrate the interaction."[13] Para-social interaction is an integral part of the talk show locale and provides hosts, guests, and audience members with "already mapped-out subject [narrator] positions."[14] The successful TV persona is one capable of "initiating an intimacy which [her] audience can believe in" (Horton and Wohl 1976, 216). This "intimacy at a distance" is enhanced with technical and representational codes. Sets are designed to look like casual living spaces, speech is informal, interaction is on a first-name basis, the host is physically involved with the studio audience, and television's abundant facial close-ups provide "maximal opportunity for disclosure of subjective manifestations" (Langer 1981, 361). These elements help blur the distance between the private space of the viewer and the institutional space of the studio.[15] Direct address, intended to engage viewers in "a potentially intimate, interactive scene," is particularly important in inviting viewers to identify with the people and emotions on the screen. Through such address, TV personalities "appear actively to be taking their viewers 'into account'" so that the "spectator is positioned to engage with the television personality with equivalent directness and immediacy" (Langer 1981, 362).

The fact that these shows focus on guests' private lives enhances the formally constructed intimacy. Episodes are organized around topics cast in everyday, if provocative, language: "Couples Who Fight about Money," "Women Who Love Abusive Men," "Violent Teens," and so on. A typical episode opens with the host introducing the topic and the first guest(s). Each guest (or family unit) is usually given a brief segment alone before engaging with other participants. Experts generally appear later to comment on the stories already presented. The host's job is to draw out the "ordinary" guests' stories, encourage and regulate feedback from the audience, solicit advice from the experts, and make sure advertisers get their allotted time.

The TV personality system and para-sociality work in conjunction with "synthetic personalization"—a discursive strategy that attempts to move impersonal or anonymous relationships "in the direction of equality, solidarity, intimacy."[16] Synthetically personalized messages, which "give the impression of treating each of the people handled *en masse* as an individual," are a staple of mass media that communicate with enormous audiences (Fairclough 1989, 65). For example, television's extensive use of direct address (in ads, promotions, programs) constructs a "personal" relationship with millions of viewers simultaneously. This "simulated solidarity" blurs the social distance and differences between producers and receivers of the message, and among different viewers, by addressing each of us "as individuals who share large areas of common ground" (195).

Television's reliance on "mythic images" works to erase social divisions, "deny social cleavage," and "formulate a collective identity for a fragmented society."[17] Talk show hosts help construct such unity for the diverse issues tackled on their programs. Their relatively stable television personas become the programs' "anchoring points" that counterbalance the chaotic world represented by the guests' endless problems (Langer 1981, 357). The ethos that informs *Sally Jessy Raphael* and *The Oprah Winfrey Show,* and to which their personas are anchored, is a therapeutic one. This therapeutic ethos gives coherence to the topical issues, becomes the field of intelligibility for making sense of guests' narratives, and reinforces the code of intimacy that structures the shows' meanings.

The intimate representational codes typically used in the talk show form, the intimate domestic setting of most television viewing, the "plausible imitation of intimacy" created through para-social interaction (Horton and Wohl 1976, 216), and the emphasis on intimate revelation in therapeutic discourse work together to establish the programs' terrain of intelligibility. These interdependent levels of intimacy constitute what Hall calls "points of identification" that "make the preferred reading of events [topics] credible and forceful" and "structure the manner in which receivers of those signs will *decode* the message."[18] Because "intimacy" is encoded in the shows' content and form, and characterizes the setting in which viewers receive the programs and their perceived relationship with the hosts, it helps push the meaning of the topics into the realm of the personal. The autobiographical narratives presented in the programs are thereby framed as the possessions of individuals who "take up models of identity" made available to them by the institutional locale of the talk show form (Smith and Watson, "Introduction," 9). I propose that this mediated intimacy is central to the shows' ideological labor—the means by which social conflicts and crises are simultaneously depicted and managed through the construction of preferred explanations and rationales that help reproduce existing social arrangements.

Synthetic Personalization and Strategic Discourse

Fairclough suggests that the same forces that produced the need for therapy also produced therapeutic discourse as an answer to that need. In contemporary capitalist society, our lives have come increasingly under the control of large, complex, and impersonal systems—the economy, the state, and myriad public and private institutions—that exert great influence over all aspects of experience. This control is exercised through the mechanisms of the economy and commodity market, through various forms of bureaucracy, and through the media. Drawing on Habermas, Fairclough refers to the extension of these webs of power as a "colonization of people's lives by systems" that is carried out, in part, within the "societal order of discourse." He cites the emergence of three distinctly modern discourses—consumerism/advertising, bureaucracy, and therapy—all of which are "strategic" in that they are "oriented to instrumental goals, or getting results" (1989, 97, 197–98).[19] The ascendance of these strategic discourses reflects the extension of methods of social control specific to capitalism's historical development—the instrumental use of discourse/communication for purposes of social management in line with the priorities of capitalist expansion and its corresponding need for cooperative subjectivities.[20] Such discourses help manage the inevitable tensions of a stratified social order with unequal access to political-economic wealth and power. On *Sally Jessy Raphael* and *The Oprah Winfrey Show,* bureaucratic and therapeutic discourses are central to the framing of the topics and personal narratives about them.

Health workers, counselors, personnel managers, and so on are trained in the use of bureacratic "discourse technologies" based on the assumption that the client/patient is less competent in essential social skills the expert has acquired by virtue of her or his training. Illouz sees this deployment of expertise as part of the larger "therapeutic ethos" in contemporary society that "legitimizes experts of the psyche and the use of science in interpersonal relationships" (1991, 240). Experts impart such skills through consciously applied communication strategies that include "the establishment of 'rapport' and the equalization of the relationship" (Fairclough 1989, 217). This bureaucratic discourse masks the actual inequity of encounters where neither power nor disclosure is equally distributed.

The most explicit use of bureaucratic discourse in talk shows occurs between invited experts and "ordinary" guests whose equality is formally constructed even as it is substantially denied. The former ask questions of, make comments about, and offer advice to the latter; the reverse is almost never true. Nor are the experts required to reveal their own problems and personal lives (when they do, it is typically in the past tense—evidence of having conquered their troubles and the basis of their current expertise). The problems on the shows are the property of the ordinary guests, who need some kind of external (e.g., professional) help in understanding their predicaments and altering their behavior. Commonly, what they lack are "good communication skills," which the experts, as trained communicators, are in a privileged position to provide. Such knowledge entitles experts to diagnose other people's problems and prescribe corrective behaviors. Expert advice specifically addressed to women often focuses on relational issues, where "the prescriptive dimensions of the experts' discourse consists in defining the boundaries between normal and pathological relationships" (Illouz 1991, 241). That is, guest experts draw the line between preferred and excluded explanations and rationales and, in doing so, participate in the programs' ideological labor.

Talk show hosts also exercise power through strategic discourse. Unspoken rules of the talk show form allow the host to cut off and dismiss some speakers and to invite and draw out others. Winfrey and Raphael have different styles of exercising this power (Winfrey tends to use humor and explicit body language; Raphael is more clinical and efficient), but both clearly assert control on their shows. They also have different ways of creating "rapport." Winfrey relies more on empathic identification and direct confrontation, whereas Raphael uses simple restatement, analytic interpretation, and overt guidance. Raphael comes across, more so than Winfrey, as a social services provider—authoritative, somewhat detached, consciously employing "caring skills." Both women, however, rely on managing and evoking the emotions of their guests and audiences. Winfrey elicits emotional response through the projection of her own feelings, whereas Raphael draws out emotions with probes and acts as a blank screen upon which the feelings of others are projected. In both cases, the evocation of emotional response is central to the shows' entertainment function, to their appeal to women viewers, and to the simulated intimacy essential to their success.

Therapeutic discourse is similarly strategic. The "therapeutic ethos," Illouz argues, "not only uses and relies heavily on the discursive style and authority of scientific discourses but also imports the very epistemic schemes of social scientific thought within the arena of the emotions" (1991, 240). Therapeutic discourse includes conscious reflection on and control over the extent to which specific "helping skills" contribute to or undermine the process of reorienting the client. Fair-clough argues that the proliferation of this discourse is both an effect of and an attempt to manage the subordination of persons to systems. That subordination "has resulted in problems and crises of social iden-tity for many people," a significant number of whom "now seek some form of 'help' with their 'personal problems,' be it in the casual form of 'problem' columns or articles in magazines, or through various forms of therapy or counselling" (1989, 198).

The media have become an increasingly important site of such help-seeking activity; it is no accident that a proliferation of self-help books, support groups, state and private treatment agencies, and the ever-expanding Twelve-Step "recovery movement" has accompanied a rapid growth in mediated forms of therapy. [21] Daytime talk shows' in-corporation of therapeutic discourse is part of this trend and is related to the expansion of such discourse into an array of social institutions (education, workplace management, social work, medicine, occupa-tional guidance). As therapeutic discourse proliferates across these so-cial locations, including television, it "participate[s] in the production of social and cultural identities" (White 1992, 19). That is, it cultivates social subjects who imagine their lives in therapeutic terms. Although therapy may be personally beneficial, it can also be seen as a further subordination of persons to systems. Fairclough proposes that therapy is a "technology of discipline" through which we are taught to blame ourselves (or our relationships) for our problems, and to seek solu-tions by adapting to or acquiescing in the social structures responsible for those problems in the first place. Therapeutic discourse thus be-comes a form of intrapersonal coercion that "places the onus on the individual to discipline herself" (1989, 226; see also Illouz 1991, 242).

It is in this emphasis on the self as the source of one's suffering and the logical site of solutions that the TV personality system, synthetic personalization, and therapeutic discourse come together in the service of legitimating the existing social order. At the heart of this complex synthesis is the concept of the "free individual" as author and agent of her actions and destiny. This mythic individual is also the cornerstone of "bourgeoise-liberal formal democracy" that posits society as a col-lection of sovereign individuals organized as a "freely-given and 'nat-ural' coming together into a *consensus* which legitimates the exercise of power" (Hall 1979, 339). Talk shows participate in this construction of consensus through their individualization of social conflict effected through therapeutic discourse.

Ideological Containment Strategies in Talk Shows

Talk shows cannot guarantee solutions to the problems they present, but their appeal is based on the *possibility* of resolution, and in particular on the premise that talking is itself a solution. This reflects what Carpignano and his colleagues call "the ideology of public discourse, where agreement is not always attainable, but communication is always possible, and television is the ultimate terrain of social consensus because it embodies the universality of communication" (1991, 51). This is also a grounding assumption of therapy—that communication can ameliorate or is a necessary condition for resolving intra- and interpersonal problems. As White notes, "The therapeutic ethos is an incitement to talk, to talk constantly, of oneself to others. It regenerates conversation" (1992, 23).

Talk shows are premised on this idealization of communication; how could it be otherwise in a cultural form whose substance and purpose is the production of talk? The programs are sites for the popularized display of the "talking cure" where the act of communicating is intended to lead to new information, insights, behavior, and identities. But what happens if, instead of seeing communication as the solution to problems, we understand it as inseparable from conflicts that originate in the material conditions of a society marked by structural inequities of social power? Communication then becomes, as Hall says, a "site and stake of struggle" and the location of intensive ideological labor to channel that struggle within acceptable parameters (1979, 341).[22] Talk shows engage in that struggle as they provide explanatory frameworks for making sense of a variety of problems besetting people in contemporary society. The programs must negotiate the contradictions of acknowledging those problems while seeking to corral them within the ideological terrain of individual dysfunction.

A key containment strategy is the relentless personalization of issues and experiences through topical frames. The ideological character of topicality becomes apparent if we consider alternative ways of framing a particular episode. For example, an episode of *The Oprah Winfrey Show* titled "Couples Who Fight about Money" would take on a quite different meaning if it were recast as "Money, Power, and Gender" or "Gendered Inequality within the Economy." Granted, these latter titles wouldn't make for catchy promo teasers, but they would provide a definition of the "problem" at odds with the function and values of the programs and of TV in general.

The topics set the parameters for who appears on the programs, what they are entitled to talk about, and their relationship to each other and to the host and audience. Guests are initially solicited through the mechanism of the topic, their stories are inserted into this frame, their connection to other guests is mediated by their shared link to the topic, and they are guided back to it if the conversation strays. The host has primary responsibility for keeping guests "on topic," and most guests (and studio audience members) accept this framing device and use it to keep themselves and fellow panelists in line. I have often witnessed a host or guest remark, "That's not the topic of the show," usually to keep someone from pursuing a line of talk that is troubling in some way. I will return to this point in discussing transgressions of the shows' narrative boundaries.

Another personalizing strategy is labeling guests according to their relationship to the topic. Talk show guests are given on-screen tags: "Jean—wants her husband to get a job," "John—cheated on his wife," "Kathy—says her husband is a mama's boy." The tags help fuse guests and topic and personify the day's problem; they also make the problem a distinct property of that particular individual, objectifying the guest *as* her problem and nothing else. The effect is to abstract these people and their troubles from the larger social world in which their everyday lives, their struggles, and the structural determinants of those problems exist. Guest experts—whose on-screen IDs include full names, titles or occupations, and sometimes the names of the books that entitle them to speak as experts—are presented as personalities and representatives of expertise, but the social relations and institutions that have granted them authority and that help maintain it are rarely interrogated.[23] There *are* occasions on the shows when this authority becomes the object of the talk—a phenomenon I explore in the next section.

I turn now to examples of containment strategies. "I Caught My Father Cheating on My Mother" (*Sally Jessy Raphael*) features four adult children, the unfaithful parent of two of them, and a psychotherapist. Among the family pairs are a young woman (Suzanne) and her professional father (Milt), and a woman from a poor background and her 35-year-old daughter (Sue and Sandy). Milt says he left his family because he and his wife had "grown apart." His affair with another woman was based on shared work interests. Sue left her family for another man when she discovered she was pregnant by him. Because her husband had received a vasectomy ten years earlier, Sue feared his anger at her infidelity even though she *and* her daughter acknowledge that he was repeatedly unfaithful throughout the marriage. Mother and daughter describe a chaotic home with few financial resources and a husband/father who was illiterate, abusive, and frequently absent. Sue says she left her five children because she had no way to support them and feared her lover would abandon her if she brought her kids along.

These family stories are united through the topic frame ("cheating parents") and focus on the anger and pain of the children who suffered their parents' abandonment. The therapeutic intent, promoted by Raphael and the psychotherapist, involves encouraging the adult children to express their feelings, getting the parents to apologize for their actions, and helping both generations achieve new insight and improved relationships by communicating openly. The effect of this orchestration is to construct a meaning for these families' troubles that sidesteps analysis of the social forces that create problems for people and that create structural differences in the options and resources available for solving them for people differently positioned within society. In the program, Sue and Milt are the same—people who cheated on their spouses and left their children. The disparity between their experiences, their socioeconomic classes, and their genders—that is, the difference in their actual social power—is insignificant within the confines of the frame. Suzanne and Sandy are also the same. The fact that Suzanne's father is a successful upper-middle-class professional and Sandy's is an illiterate laborer does not count.

"Couples Who Fight about Money" (*Oprah Winfrey*) includes three couples—two white, one black—and a psychologist. In the white marriages, conflict centers on husbands who control their wives by controlling (and withholding) the family finances. One of these couples is apparently working-class; the husband of the other is described as "a millionaire," though it is obvious he and his wife are nouveau riche rather than "old money." Conflict for the black couple arises between the wife, an employed professional, and the husband, who floats between low-paying, unsatisfying jobs while being supported by his spouse. All three couples are encouraged to fight openly on the air according to the dictates of the topical script. Several questions from Winfrey and the studio audience and comments by the guest expert make links between gender issues and money conflicts, but the racial and class dimensions of the different couples' conflicts remain submerged and unarticulated. For example, the audience does not sympathize equally with the white wives; comments suggest that the working-class woman has been unfairly denied life's ordinary pleasures by her skinflint husband, whereas the millionaire's wife is seen as greedy, irresponsible with money, and deserving of her husband's ire. In the case of the black couple, audience comments favor the wife while implicitly endorsing both the "naturalness" of the male as primary breadwinner and the racist view of blacks as gender deviant (e.g., "strong" women and "shiftless" men). Because the different intersections of race, class, and gender for blacks and whites cannot be accommodated within the topic frame, the narrative of marital discord permits an acknowledgment of gender issues only—a logical solution given the target audience. The result is a displacement of class and race issues onto gender—a phenomenon also noted by Jhally and Lewis in a study of audience responses to *The Cosby Show* (where viewers substituted racial categories for class categories) and in Aronowitz's study of popular representations of the working class (where class discourse is displaced onto gender/sex relations).[24] The problem perpetually "unproblematized" in these talk shows is that of social class. The near absence of public discussion of class issues in the media, as Jhally and Lewis argue, suggests that "American society does not have a way of talking about one of its central organizing features" (1992, 70).

"Secrets from the Past" (*Oprah Winfrey*) features three guests whose secrets have inadvertently come to light and a psychotherapist who offers strategies for coping with this exposure. Bryan's ("past caught up with him") secret, that as a young man he had prostituted himself with men and was convicted, was revealed when he was subpoenaed years later to testify in a murder case. He explains his past actions as economic necessity. The oldest of six children, Bryan describes a childhood of poverty, abuse, and abandonment. His father was imprisoned for raping one of Bryan's sisters; the children were shuttled between foster homes before being returned to a mother ill equipped to support them. Bryan says he was obsessed as a boy with keeping his family together and turned to shoplifting, petty theft, selling blood, and ultimately prostitution to help out financially. He eventually put this past behind him, moved to another state, married, and got a job in a small town, but still "lived in fear" that his "secret" would destroy his new life.

Bryan's story presents an opportunity to explore the desperation that poverty breeds and its impact on children, who now constitute one of the largest segments of poor Americans. The topic and therapeutic intent of the show preclude that exploration, however. Winfrey and the psychotherapist focus on the "toxicity" of secrets, the "loss of self" they result in, and the "healing" to be gained from revealing them. Most of the studio audience members appear to accept this framing and are supportive of Bryan's desire to "come clean" and overcome his "toxic shame." One man in the audience, however, is hostile to Bryan's statement that he had done "what was necessary at the time."

> AUDIENCE MEMBER: He chose it. No one forced him to do that. If we all did that where would we be?
> BRYAN: Have you never done anything you regret? Of course I've made mistakes . . .
> AUDIENCE MEMBER: When you steal a piece of candy from the 5 and 10 you're ashamed, when you're a kid. I mean, c'mon, there are other ways he could have lived.

This exchange points to a struggle between structural and individual explanations of behavior, but one that cannot be resolved, or even adequately explored, within the show's narrative boundaries. Not only does the talk show form discourage that examination, the participants themselves inhibit it. Both Bryan and his accuser frame their comments within the code of individual responsibility and choice. The audience member rejects the notion of social determinants on behavior and the therapeutic emphasis on motives over deeds and emotional healing over moral atonement. Bryan, too, is caught between these two positions, simultaneously describing his youthful behavior as the result of social necessity and as a personal moral failure. Immediately following the exchange, an older woman in the audience stands and commends Bryan's efforts to "admit his mistakes." The audience, which has been silent during the man's critique, breaks into applause. The psychotherapist then asserts that "the issue is not that anything goes," but how shame forces people to keep secrets. Winfrey echoes this position before cutting to a commercial.

Such occasions of competing stories—when social conflicts beneath the topics surface—occur fairly often in these programs and provide the moments of tension that can make talk shows so compelling. But such clashes are rarely sustained, and almost never explicitly discussed, because topicality, personalization, and therapeutic discourse are such effective framing devices. Thus, Bryan's problem is the shame that plagues people with secrets, not the social conditions that limited his horizons as a child. The solution is individual (how he deals with his shame), rather than social (why there were *not* "other ways he could have lived" and why this might also be true for millions of other young people in similar circumstances). The man in the audience's inability, or unwillingness, to imagine that people's ranges of choices are determined by anything outside their personal control, and Bryan's own ambivalence on this point, reflects what DeMott calls Americans' inability to "think straight about class": "Several hallowed concepts—independence, individualism, choice—are woven into this web of illusion and self-deception. But presiding over the whole stands the icon of *classlessness*."[25]

Ideological Breakdown in the Talking Cure

If the transmutation of social conflict into individual problems is an underlying object of these programs, the fact that they address these conflicts at all means they always run the risk of failing to contain them within the boundaries of therapeutic narrative. I turn now to such a transgression and its management. "Don't Tell Me How to Raise My Kids" (*Sally Jessy Raphael*) features guests who have been "victimized" by child abuse laws, including Sandra, a black woman from Southern California who had been jailed for beating her eleven-year-old son with a belt. (The boy had called the police himself.) Although Sandra ("says it's OK to beat her children with a belt") is presented as an individual example of the generic topic, she refuses to submit passively to the narrow identity it imposes. She does assert that how she raises her children is her own business, thereby affirming the ideology of individual rights, but her argument is also referenced through her belonging to a particular racial/class grouping (blacks at or near the lower end of the socioeconomic ladder). Her narrative is articulated around her experience as a member of a specific social group that she believes authorizes parenting methods at odds with those advocated as universal by Raphael and a white expert. Sandra had beaten her son when he came home after dark in direct violation of the family rules. She justifies her actions in terms of her specific autobiographical experience as a black woman living in a state "where a man can be handcuffed and beat by ten policemen, and taxpayers pay for their defense."

> SANDRA: If he was out in the street and the police seen him doing something wrong and they beat him in the head, that is justifiable force. But when I beat him, as his mother, a loving mother, concerned and loving my child, then I go to jail, my child goes to foster care. Now what kind of sense does that make? That don't make no kind of sense.

Later in the show, white pediatrician Dorothy Greenbaum states that physical punishment of children is unnecessary, a parental failure. A second white expert, Dr. Don Boys, head of the conservative Christian organization Common Sense, retorts, "That's your opinion," to which Greenbaum replies, "That is my educated, medical, pediatric opinion." At this point Sandra interrupts and speaks passionately to the pediatrician; their exchange illustrates the multilayered tensions that the show must negotiate.

> SANDRA: Excuse me . . . excuse me. You know what? . . . You are a white mother. I'm a black mother. It's a totally different situation. When my kids walk out in the street . . .
> GREENBAUM: I can't believe you're going to say that.
> SANDRA: I don't care what you can believe. That's the truth. That's the way it is. And as long as we deny it, as black people, that it ain't no difference when our sons walk out on the street, that's why they keep getting killed. That's why they keep selling dope. That's why our kids are always victims. Now you're a doctor. You're a Ph.D. I'm a loving, Christian mother. That's what I am.
> GREENBAUM: I'm a loving mother too.

Here Sandra raises the issue of race and questions the universality of Greenbaum's expertise, and in so doing pushes at the boundaries of the topical frame; she pulls in the world outside the studio to argue that the identities and actions of herself and the pediatrician are differently situated in society. The doctor resists this assertion of difference by identifying herself and Sandra equally as "mothers." Raphael joins the exchange to clarify the basis of Greenbaum's expertise—"Isn't it

M.D.?" (rather than Ph.D.), thereby displaying Sandra's lack of familiarity with such distinctions. Raphael then gives the floor to Greenbaum ("Would you like to respond?"), who returns to the troubling
issue of race. (During this exchange, Sandra shouts while Greenbaum
remains calm and clinical.)

> GREENBAUM: What I would like to say is, it would be devastating
> to think that we are actually going to say that there's a different
> way to raise a child based upon race. I cannot believe you're going
> to say that.
> SANDRA: It *is*. You know what? You know what? You can't be-
> lieve it—You can't believe it because your child is not black. You're
> not raising a black child in this society. That's why you can't be-
> lieve it. I can believe it because I live it.
> GREENBAUM: I have to tell you that our training, the way I look
> at the world, the way all of us who are pediatricians—
> SANDRA: You look at it through blue eyes, I've got brown eyes.
> That's how you look at it. I'm looking at it the way I look at it,
> through brown eyes and black kinky hair and brown skin.
> GREENBAUM: Every child is a human being.
> SANDRA: That's right. That's right.
> GREENBAUM: You don't whip an animal and you don't whip a
> child.

At this point the conversation has clearly violated the parameters of
the topical frame, and Raphael moves in to derail that detour and
repersonalize Sandra's problem.

> RAPHAEL: Okay. I have a little problem here. I thought we were
> going to discuss children. We got into race relations. And I'm not
> quite sure how these things happen to me. [She looks at Green-
> baum, who nods and smiles in agreement.]
> GREENBAUM: I don't know how that happened either.

The two women's shared confusion here reflects a key element of
white privilege—the luxury of being able to ignore race when it is convenient to do so.[26] Sandra makes a final attempt to resist Raphael's
control through the mechanism of the topic by comparing a man in
California who had been jailed for kicking a dog to a woman who
killed a fifteen-year-old black girl and went free: "So don't tell me
nothing about whupping no dog and whupping no human being."[27]

At this point Don Boys remarks: "There's no doubt there's a lot of in-equities." This gives Raphael a chance to terminate the transgression; she formally recognizes Boys, who quickly shifts gears from the specificity of those "inequities" to the "problem with Dr. Spock."

This episode illustrates the conflictual terrain upon which talk shows engage in their ideological work. That work is ongoing because television operates in a social world fraught with tensions, hierarchies of power, competing interests, perspectives, and experiences. The talk show form may seek to manage those tensions—to resolve symbolically what is denied in reality—but it cannot ultimately eliminate them. Raphael may end a particular line of talk or silence a problematic guest (indeed, Sandra never uttered another word on the show), but the social tensions that generate conversations like this one live on in the world inside and outside the studio. Television is "an inherently conflictual medium" precisely because of its centrality in producing and circulating public meanings, including the meaning of social and cultural identities. If the talk show form encourages narrators such as Sandra to take up "already mapped-out subject positions," it also provides them occasions to tell stories that have been deemed "culturally unspeakable," and in so doing, to exercise agency and become "subjects of narrative" (Smith and Watson, "Introduction," 14). Here we see the irreconcilable contradiction of TV talk shows: in order to carry out the ideological work of containing and organizing the meaning of social conflicts, they also give voice to those who live those conflicts.

The Repression of the Social

Talk shows are particularly resonant for female viewers both because women's efforts to achieve social equality have involved getting their so-called private concerns recognized as legitimate *public* issues and because the narrative form corresponds to women's experience, learned discursive style, and relational orientation. *The Oprah Winfrey Show* and *Sally Jessy Raphael* are compelling, as are therapeutic explanations generally, because the structural conflicts they present are lived and felt at a personal level. The pain and anger are real, as is our desire to find ways of understanding and overcoming them. As the major consumers of therapy,[28] and the gender assigned primary responsibility for emotional work, women appear to be especially susceptible to this way of framing problems—one that helps obscure other possible interpretive frameworks and solutions.

Although social tensions generate the personal problems in TV talk shows, the way they are narrated discourages our full recognition of those problems *as social*. The TV personality system, the parasociality and simulated intimacy of the talk show form, the synthetic personalization common in the media, and the therapeutic discourse of the programs strive to confine social conflict within narratives of individual and interpersonal dysfunction. Within those confines, all problems seem to yield to therapeutic intervention—to treatment through the "talking cure." Therapeutic discourse proposes that we change ourselves, our attitudes and behavior, without also recognizing that our identities and actions are determined by and respond to social conditions that will not change simply because we decide to interpret and handle them differently on an individual basis. Operating at the level of intra- and inter-personal relations, therapeutic discourse translates the political into the psychological. Problems are personal (or familial) and have no origin or target outside the individual's own psychic processes.[29] Because the topics addressed by these shows are at root political problems that require organized political action, they cannot be finally resolved through therapeutic intervention. There is a radical difference between saying, "I'm ill, I've been abused, I need recovery," and saying, "I'm angry, I'm oppressed, my oppression is based on structural inequities that I share with others, with whom I must work to change society." This difference has also been criticized by feminists who question the move to redefine women's problems as individual emotional illness (e.g., "codependency") rather than as a consequence of gender oppression, and many women's own embrace of that redefinition.[30]

Although therapeutic communication might be personally beneficial, it may be so by helping us adapt to a social order that requires analysis itself. Fairclough notes that because therapy and counseling "assume that the effects of social ills can be remedied on the basis of hidden potentialities of individuals," they "can be regarded as ideological practices, which may be in competition with practices of political mobilization based on the contrary assumption that social ills can be remedied only through social change" (1989, 225). On *Sally Jessy Raphael* and *The Oprah Winfrey Show*, the telling of autobiographical stories is fully implicated in this ideological practice. These talk shows do make public many problems that once were deemed private—especially women's concerns that have historically been relegated to the private sphere; they give voice to people who have historically been silenced (women, people of color, working-class people); and they dramatize the embodiment of selected public issues in personal experience. At the same time, their narrative form discourages the adoption of critical engagement with and reflection on those problems in favor of immediate identification and catharsis, and undermines the ability to take these problems seriously in the service of making them entertaining. The televised talking cure manages conflict and crisis by relegating them to the domain of "personal" stories that can then be folded into a disciplinary, therapeutic narrative. In so doing, the talk show form drives a wedge between the personal and the political—encouraging us to forget that autobiographical narratives are also always stories about our shared social world.

Notes

1. The use of the individual psyche to explain social phenomena and the belief that social problems can be resolved with psychological management are reflections of what critics have identified as a "therapeutic ethos" in contemporary American culture. See T. J. Jackson Lears, "From Salvation to Self-Realization: Advertising and the Therapeutic Roots of Consumer Culture, 1880–1830," in R. W. Fox and T. J. Jackson Lears, eds., *The Culture of Consumption: Critical Essays in American History, 1880–1980* (New York: Pantheon, 1980), 1–38; Robert N. Bellah, Richard Madsen, William L. Sullivan, Ann Swidler, and Steven M. Tipton, *Habits of the Heart: Individualism and Commitment in American Life* (Berkeley: University of California Press, 1985); Eva Illouz, "Reason within Passion: Love in Women's Magazines," *Critical Studies in Mass Communication* 8 (1991): 231–48 (page references for all subsequent citations of this work are included in the text in parentheses); Debra Grodin, "The Interpreting Audience: The Therapeutics of Self-Help Book Reading," *Critical Studies in Mass Communication* 8 (1991): 404–20; Mimi White, *Tele-Advising: Therapeutic Discourse in American Television* (Chapel Hill: University of North Carolina Press, 1992) (page references for all subsequent citations of this work are included in the text in parentheses); Wendy Simonds, *Women and Self-Help Culture: Reading between the Lines* (New Brunswick, N.J.: Rutgers University Press, 1992) (page references for all subsequent citations of this work are included in the text in parentheses).

2. *The Oprah Winfrey Show* is the top-rated daytime talk show in the United States, with a daily audience of fourteen million, 76 percent of whom are women eighteen years of age and older, according to its syndicator, King World Productions. The audience for *Sally Jessy Raphael* is eight million, according to the show's publicity department; a spokesperson said "most of our viewers are women," but gave no concrete figures (personal correspondence, November 1993).

3. Relatively inexpensive to produce, talk shows are one of the fastest-growing formats in television. Besides the networks' morning and late-night talk programs, there were more than thirty syndicated talk shows in the 1993–94 lineup. See Monte Williams, "Voices of 30-plus Exclaim: Can We Talk?" *Advertising Age* (March 8, 1993): S-6. Their proliferation also reflects the industry's conscious decision to target women eighteen to forty-nine years old as "the most desirable television audience (be-

cause of their consumer roles)." Douglas Kellner, *Television and the Crisis of Democracy* (Boulder, Colo.: Westview, 1990), 120.

4. Miriam Greenspan, *A New Approach to Women and Therapy* (New York: McGraw-Hill, 1983), 11.

5. Dean Barnlund, "Introduction to Therapeutic Communication," in D. C. Barnlund, ed., *Interpersonal Communication: Survey and Studies* (New York: Houghton Mifflin, 1968); Gary Kreps, "The Nature of Therapeutic Communication," in Gary Gumpert and Sandra Fish, eds., *Talking to Strangers: Mediated Therapeutic Communication* (Norwood, N.J.: Ablex, 1990).

6. Edward E. Sampson, *Justice and the Critique of Pure Psychology* (New York: Plenum, 1983).

7. Julia T. Wood, *Gendered Lives: Communication, Gender, and Culture* (Belmont, Calif.: Wadsworth, 1994), 141–43.

8. Mary-Ellen Brown, "The Politics of Soaps: Pleasure and Feminine Empowerment," *Australian Journal of Cultural Studies* 4, no. 2 (1987): 1–25; John Fiske, *Television Culture* (London: Methuen, 1987).

9. Paolo Carpignano et al., "Chatter in the Age of Electronic Reproduction: Talk Television and the 'Public Mind,'" *Social Text* 26 (1991): 48. Page references for all subsequent citations of this work are included in the text in parentheses.

10. John Langer, "Television's Personality System," *Media, Culture & Society* 4 (1981): 352–53 (page references for all subsequent citations of this work are included in the text in parentheses).

11. Donald Horton and R. Richard Wohl, "Mass Communication as Para-social Interaction: Observations on Intimacy at a Distance," in James E. Combs and Michael Mansfield, eds., *Drama in Life: The Uses of Communication in Society* (New York: Hastings House, 1976), 213 (page references for all subsequent citations of this work are included in the text in parentheses).

12. A prime example of this familiarity was displayed on a May 1992 episode of *The Oprah Winfrey Show* devoted to letters from viewers.

13. Robert Cathcart and Gary Gumpert, "Mediated Interpersonal Communication: Toward a New Typology," in Gary Gumpert and Sandra Fish, eds., *Talking to Strangers: Mediated Therapeutic Communication* (Norwood, N.J.: Ablex, 1990), 46.

14. Sidonie Smith and Julia Watson, "Introduction," this volume, 11.

15. John Corner, "The Interview as Social Encounter," in Paddy Scannell, ed., *Broadcast Talk* (London: Sage, 1991), 32.

16. Norman Fairclough, *Language and Power* (Harlow: Longman, 1989), 217 (page references for all subsequent citations of this work are included in the text in parentheses).

17. Todd Gitlin, "Television's Screens: Hegemony in Transition," in Michael Apple, ed., *Cultural and Economic Reproduction in Education* (London: Routledge, 1982), 211.

18. Stuart Hall, "Culture, the Media, and the 'Ideological Effect,'" in James Curran, Michael Gurevitch, and Janet Woollacott, eds., *Mass Communication and Society* (Beverly Hills: Sage, 1979), 344 (page references for all subsequent citations of this work are included in the text in parantheses).

19. See also Anthony Giddens, *Modernity and Identity: Self and Society in the Late Modern Age* (Stanford, Calif.: Stanford University Press, 1991).

20. See Ma'sud Zavarzadeh, *Seeing Films Politically* (Albany: State University of New York Press, 1991); Walter Davis, *Inwardness and Existence: Subjectivity in/and Hegel, Heidegger, Marx, and Freud* (Madison: University of Wisconsin Press, 1989).

21. Wendy Kaminer, *I'm Dysfunctional, You're Dysfunctional: The Recovery Movement and Other Self-Help Fashions* (Reading, Pa.: Addison-Wesley, 1992); see also Gary Gumpert and Sandra Fish, eds., *Talking to Strangers: Mediated Therapeutic Communication* (Norwood, N.J.: Ablex, 1990); and Simonds, *Women and Self-Help Culture.*

22. See also V. N. Volosinov, *Marxism and the Philosophy of Language* (Cambridge: Harvard University Press, 1973), 23.

23. For a good discussion of the historical basis and class bias of expertise, see Magali Sarfatti Larson, "The Production of Expertise and the Constitution of Expert Power," in Thomas Haskell, ed., *The Authority of Experts* (Bloomington: Indiana University Press, 1984), 28–80.

24. Sut Jhally and Justin Lewis, *Enlightened Racism: The Cosby Show, Audiences, and the Myth of the American Dream* (Boulder, Colo.: Westview, 1992) (page references for all subsequent citations of this work are included in the text in parentheses); Stanley Aronowitz, "Working Class Culture in the Age of Electronic Reproduction," in Ian Angus and Sut Jhally, eds., *Cultural Politics in Contemporary America* (New York: Routledge, 1989), 135–50.

25. Benjamin DeMott, *The Imperial Middle: Why Americans Can't Think Straight about Class* (New Haven, Conn.: Yale University Press, 1992), 9.

26. Peggy McIntosh, "Understanding Correspondences between White Privilege and Male Privilege through Women's Studies Work," paper presented at the National Women's Studies Association annual meeting, Atlanta, 1987.

27. Significantly, Sandra supports her arguments about race by referring to the cases of Rodney King and Latasha Harlins (the teenager murdered by a Korean grocer in 1991)—both of which were central sources of black anger in the L.A. riots a few months later. See Mike Davis, "Urban America Sees Its Future: In L.A., Burning All Illusions," *Nation* (June 1, 1992): 743–46.

28. Women make up nearly two-thirds of the adult population of community mental health centers, psychiatric hospitals, and outpatient clinics, and an estimated 84 percent of all private psychotherapy patients are female; Greenspan, *A New Approach,* 5. More than two-thirds of prescriptions written each year for psychotropic drugs are for women. See Nancy Russo, *A Women's Mental Health Agenda* (Washington, D.C.: American Psychological Association, 1985), 20–21.

29. The ascendant paradigm in psychology—that of reducing emotional problems to genetic, chemical, or neurological causes—is an even more vivid attempt to naturalize (and desocialize) people's problems.

30. Harriet Goldhor Lerner, "Problems for Profit?" *Women's Review of Books* (April 1990): 15; Betty Tallen, "Co-dependency: A Feminist Critique," *Sojourner: The Women's Forum* (January 1990): 20–21; Susan Faludi, *Backlash: The Undeclared War against American Women* (New York: Crown, 1991).

7 / Want Ads: Reading the Personals

Traci Carroll

Packaging Oneself, Selling Oneself

For many years, readers of Chicago's most popular free weekly news-paper, the *Reader,* could find the personals section positioned between "Services" and "Housing for Rent." Such a placement would suggest that the entries in this section, called "Matches," serve the same func-tion as advertisements for services and vacant apartments—the public announcement of something available for sale or rent—and that only people looking for such goods or services constitute the readership for this section. This categorization of the Matches frankly reveals how an act of self-commodification inheres in any attempt at self-expression in the personals, because the writer is packaging him- or herself for a cer-tain kind of prospective reader. But the recent repositioning of the Matches in the "Entertainment" section embeds the personals in a much more complex field of commodifications that provides insight into the peculiar ways in which personals are read and into the condi-tions that shape their writers' strategies.

Whereas the lures of landscaping services and two-bedroom apart-ments do not inspire individual and collective fantasy or attract loyal and somewhat furtive readers, the Matches section is read by many as a form of autobiography that is compelling because it constitutes a public disclosure of desire. Reading the exhibitionistic gestures in the personals provides a genre-specific sense of indulging in a guilty pleasure, a voyeuristic identification with or observation of the desires of strangers. The selection of the "Matches Ad of the Week" by the *Reader*'s staff indicates that even the compilers of the weekly list of Matches find pleasure in reading the ads and apply definite, if unstated, literary standards to all the ads that come across their desks.[1] The subcategories of the Matches—"Men Seeking Women," "Women Seeking Men," "Men Seeking Men," "Women Seeking Women," and "Other"—even facilitate the attempts of those who read the Matches for entertainment to choose the sexuality they wish to appropriate voyeuristically.

These categories allow for potentially diverse inflections of desire, but the relative amounts of space taken up by the different sections also reflect a basic heteronormativity. The spatial constraints imposed by this genre and the personal risks it can generate place a premium on concise, specific self-expression. That self-articulation must at once declare a fixed sexual identity and surpass the generalities of sexual or romantic desire in order to maintain its particularity. The writer of the personal ad faces a double task of ensuring gender recognizability while also insisting upon some kind of individual difference from all the other writers in a given category. These two aims often work at cross-purposes, because the writer's creative freedom is always eclipsed by the genre's rigid gender taxonomy: although the personal ads might provide a cultural space for the interrogation of sexual roles and the relationship between sexuality and identity, they ultimately encourage and reinforce an equation of identity with the execution of immediately categorizable sexual roles. As autobiography, the personals exemplify Judith Butler's argument that assumptions of self-identity function as a "normative ideal" and that the "regulatory practices that govern gender also govern culturally intelligible notions of identity."[2]

Because of most readers' expectations that the personals buttress their previously held notions of gender and sexuality, this genre tends to evoke two characteristic and integrally related responses: identification with the writer's fantasy of finding an ideal partner or pity and condescension, based on the assumption that the writer must be desperate and somewhat pathetic to be placing an ad in the personals. The conflicting emotional valences of these two responses mask their common purpose of hypostasizing sexuality as the main category defining individual identity. Other crucial elements of the writer's identity politics, such as race, class, and age, are often suppressed or only implied in the ad.[3] Even if the writer foregrounds race, class, or another category in the ad, the genre bases its categorizations on fixed, constant sexual identity and forces the writer to define him- or herself primarily through sexuality. Class, for example, is very rarely articulated directly, but may surface in coded words such as "professional" or may be implied in likes or dislikes for cultural phenomena such as opera, Blackhawks games, or Thai food. As autobiography, the personals suggest that sexual preferences become the main constitutive force of an individual's identity. Michel Foucault locates the origin of this concretization of sexual identity in the proliferation of discourses on sexuality during the Victorian era. Sexual practices that did not serve to perpetuate reproduction were labeled as perversion, and "this new persecution of the peripheral sexualities entailed an *incorporation of perversions* and a new *specification of individuals*."[4] Sexual behavior was no longer on a par with other daily habits and practices, such as eating or working; it began to be thought of as an emanation from an inherent identity as a gendered person. The personals, like other regulatory discourses on gender Foucault examines, presume that sexual practice stands in a "political relation of entailment" to sexual identity.[5]

The tendency of personal ads to regulate sexuality is reinforced by a multitude of other media, such as film, television, and advertising, that similarly represent the elaboration and fulfillment of (primarily heterosexual) identity as critical. These discourses necessarily inflect one's reading of any informal instance of autobiography at the same time that they provide the autobiographer's vocabulary and set limits to the readability of the utterance. The conviction among many readers of personals that those who write them have exhausted all legitimate forms of courtship and have thus been lowered to public display indicates the working of a diffuse popular discourse that has educated us as readers of personals. Like any literary theory, this discourse has set the terms of our interaction with these texts and has inferred a set of assumptions about the writers and about the role these writings play in preserving existing forms of social organization: the impulse to shape self-definitions primarily in terms of gender categorizations. The particularities of the personals as a subgenre of autobiography point to an extensive urgency behind the acts of self-definition in personals and help reinforce the idea that the declaration of a single, invariable sexuality precedes or determines identity formation. Gender is naturalized as the origin of one's behaviors in the personals: "The tactical production of the discrete and binary categorization of sex conceals the strategic aims of that very apparatus of production by postulating 'sex' as 'a cause' of sexual experience, behavior, and desire."[6] As a form of autobiography determined by concrete economic constraints, the compulsion to declare a gender and sexual orientation, and the assumptions of an autobiographical pact that will be made good through a dialogic process with the reader/lover, the personals offer a paradigmatic occasion for the public performance of gendered desire.

The distinctiveness of autobiography as a genre presumably lies in its establishment of an "autobiographical pact" in which the reader is assured of an identity between the signature of the author and the grammatical first person of the narrative: "What defines autobiography for the one who is reading is above all a contract of identity that is sealed by the proper name. And this is true also for the one who is writing the text. If I write the story of my life without mentioning my name in it, how will my reader know that it was *I*? It is impossible for the autobiographical vocation and the passion for anonymity to coexist in the same person."[7] The personals exemplify autobiographical utterance that prohibits signature, because no names can be included. Some writers, consciously or not, carry their anonymity as far as possible in their ads by suppressing any specificity in favor of generalized tropes of romantic love, such as cozy candlelit dinners, long walks on the beach, and quiet conversation. These writers preserve their anonymity by suspending articulations of taste that might suggest class origins or racial identity in favor of generic lovers' tastes. The personals remain grounded, however, in the notion of a pact or contract that is fulfilled through a potential dialogic process—enabled by voice mail and/or letters—with one or more interlocutors who are presumed to exist in a world of reference outside the text.

Ads that maintain their writers' anonymity make perhaps the most substantial contribution to the personals' agenda of subsuming individual particularity under stabilized gender identity. Writers of such ads sacrifice individual specificity in exchange for an imagined assurance that they know what people in their category are supposed to like and dislike if they expect to find love and romance. Because the Matches acknowledge only five categories of identity, each writer is required to choose and declare a sexuality for purposes of writing the ad. But although the structure of the personals is premised upon hypostasized sexual identity, there are nevertheless spaces within this structure that stretch the generic boundaries of the personals, offering modes of self-articulation that both derive from the idea of gender stability and threaten it at the same time. The *Reader*'s own inclusion of the category "Other" provides a space for the articulation of miscellaneous desires even if those desires sometimes appear to derive from more normative heterosexual desires. Even within the four non-"Other" categories of identification, the autobiographer may use masquerading techniques, may place an ad on behalf of another person, such as a parent, and may opt to request fulfillment of desires that are neither explicitly sexual nor completely nonsexual. And as my treatment of one alternative schema for personals will suggest, the writing subject may include restrictions of desire based upon very specific and crucial practices and tastes. Any of these variations on the standard formula of the personals has the potential to deconstruct gender as master category.

The controlling external constraint of the personals genre, whether mainstream or alternative, is that of economy. There is a literal price to pay for this public utterance, and excessive language is penalized with extra charges. Like the consumer of phone sex services, the subject of the personal issues a statement, for which she or he must pay, in exchange for a potential gratification. To place a Matches ad in the *Reader*, the author pays $5 for twenty-five or fewer words, plus 50 cents per additional word, in order to receive telephone responses. The option of receiving written correspondence costs $20 more. Writers of ads for the "Other" category must pay more dearly than gay or straight writers for their self-articulation, however, because they do not have the option of receiving voice mail. "Other" desires, which do not fit neatly into the ideology of gender identity, become tropes for the pornographic, and their articulations are often read as soft-core entertainment. Because of the sexual liminality of concerns voiced in the "Other" category, ads in that category more transparently reveal readers' voyeuristic interest in the personals than the formulaic heteronormative ads. These structural identifications, while harnessing the tabooed desire, nonetheless give it a certain play, licensing the desire as that which must be routinely managed and contained. A dispersal of gender identity occurs when one reads the personals; depending upon the subject position one adopts, "identities can come into being and dissolve depending on the concrete practices that constitute them."[8]

Figure 7.1. In its advertisement for Matches, the *Chicago Reader* lists its generic guidelines and charges for running a personal ad. The potential writer has the option of paying for the autobiography by personal check or credit card. Copyright 1994 Chicago Reader, Inc. Reprinted with permission.

Furthermore, as Diana Fuss argues, when a reader imagines him- or herself in the position of the sexual other, "desire operates within identification, destabilizing the grounds of a heterosexual identity formation and undermining its defensive claims to a 'pure' or 'uncontaminated' sexuality."[9] Fuss's account of how straight women look at fashion magazines offers a model for examining the ways readers appropriate "Other" desires into their own identities; this kind of spectatorship, for Fuss, necessarily reveals a fluidity so basic to gender identity that it problematizes the very notion of fixed gender: "To look straight *at* women, it appears straight women must look *as* lesbians."[10] For many readers, the personals offer a space in which to quietly identify with or voyeuristically appropriate forms of desire that require imagining another identity or even another kind of body for oneself.

As an example of the imbrication of sexual identities, practices, and pleasures in a sex industry that operates by means of self-commodification and exchange, the personals are on a continuum with other genres, such as phone sex, that have taken over and transformed the traditional autobiographical convention of confession. As Linda Williams has argued, these genres attempt to "make 'sex' speak" in the service of producing stable, regularized sexual identities.[11] From a similar Foucauldian perspective, Rita Felski has shown how the self-liberating impulse behind women's confessional narratives conceals its allegiance to the original intentions behind religious confession: to affirm a stable ontological basis for identity, whether spiritual or sexual. The efforts to reach an authentic self are thus always enmeshed in a "mode of production of normative definitions of subjectivity through the imperative to continual self-examination."[12]

Buying into Gender

The economic context of the production of confession in the personals generates a particularly compressed self-interpellation into gender ideologies. Depending upon the writer's commitment to making his or her desire known in detail, financial constraint determines the two most common gestures of the personal ad: a self-description and a description of the idealized other the writer imagines answering the ad. Emphasis on hair color, eye color, race, height, and weight predominates in the primary gesture of self-description. In publications such as the *Reader* that have predominantly white readership, articulations of racial identity often serve as a screening device. Ads by black lesbians, for example, often request responses from other black lesbians only; these ads thus forge another, more specific category of identity in the personals that is also sensitive to racial identifications. Even when a writer does not specify a desired race for the prospective partner, he or she can screen out respondents in terms of their attitudes toward interracial relationships using phrases like "No Jungle Fevers" (6 Mar. 1992: 13). A writer might also use a phrase such as "race unimportant" in order to emphasize other qualities or conditions he or she considers more important in a partner (6 Aug. 1993: 31).

Within other ads that often assume a white writing subject and reading audience, several literary topoi provide techniques for concise self-construction. Some draw upon and transform the modesty topos, common in medieval first-person narrative, in order to create both textual authority and an image of humility: "NERD SEEKS NERD-ETTE" (31 Jan. 1992: 11). Others derive their style from the long-standing autobiographical folk tradition of braggadocio: "fit, fine, and physical"; "SHAPELY, STUNNING, SENSUOUS" (28 Feb. 1992: 6). Still others indirectly assert group-based identity by parodying advertising slogans or referring to cultural texts: "30something" (28 Feb. 1992: 13).

Some writers prefer to communicate a self-reflexive quality by making reference to the generic frame of the personals: "interested to find courageous individuals whom [*sic*] can reply to a personal ad that does not list one's vital statistics and/or position of one's stinger" (28 Feb. 1992: 13); "MATCHES FEMALE SURVEY. Score one point for each" (21 Feb. 1992: 9). Calling attention to the personals as a genre is an attempt to transcend the genre in some way, perhaps to elevate oneself above any residual fears of actually being desperate and pathetic, and most certainly to comment on the limitations of the genre. Many writers also use screening techniques such as references to personal practices or tastes, or limiting conditions of acceptance: "Dislikes: sports fans, smokers, druggies" (28 Feb. 1992: 13).

Yet another common technique, used mostly in straight personals, is the adoption and rehearsal of specific heterosexual pairings that have attained the status of myth, such as "Rhett and Scarlett, Anthony [*sic*] and Cleopatra, and Tracy and Hepburn" (31 Jan. 1992: 6). Even attempts to construct nontraditional roles for this heterosexual masquerade rely upon the convention of the historical couple who perfected the performance of heterosexuality. A "Matches Ad of the Week" from 1992 executes such a substitution: "Algren seeks DeBeauvoir [*sic*]. Eclectic, rebellious writer seeks woman of character and intellect who believes in authenticity and existential freedom. Let's deconstruct the traditional relationship" (28 Feb.: 5). This writer's adoption of Nelson Algren as his ego-ideal exposes the discourse of authenticity that is often called in to distinguish the autobiographical genre from other genres. Through his masquerade as Algren, this writer claims a desire to "deconstruct the traditional relationship," but he merely substitutes high culture and local Chicago references for the more commonly appropriated popular culture cinematic icons of idealized heterosexual romance. The specific references to Algren and de Beauvoir do not upset the tradition of romantic love; rather, they reconsider the terms for idealization, ultimately ensuring the survival of the fantasy structure.[13] The literary tastes and intellectual positions that define Algren's personality are automatically subsumed under the category of sexuality.

The rhetorical strategies mentioned above—the modesty topos, braggadocio, gestures toward the generic frame, screening techniques, and masquerade—all possess a common capacity for conveying crucial information about the author within the spatial and financial constraints posed by the personals genre. Although they might not screen out certain kinds of readers altogether, they do enable the writers to target the audiences to whom they are marketing themselves. As literal advertisements, personals enact self-commodification through these conventions of self-description. Sometimes writers register an awareness of self-commodification in the form of promotional offers in their ads, such as "FREE PIZZA!" or "I give great backrubs" (21 Feb. 1992: 8). Some imitate help-wanted ads: "APPLICATIONS NOW ACCEPTED, by GWM" (31 Jan. 1992: 8); "ATTENTION: DUE TO recent expansion (of the inner-self) 17 yr old company specializing in fun, adventure & laughter now has an opening for position of?" (31 Jan. 1992: 6). Others describe the self as a product or a performance approved by a cultural authority: "THE CRITICS ARE raving about this GWM" (31 Jan. 1992: 12). More often, however, the writing subject, especially when female, tends to conflate her self with her body as a commodity on the market, emphasizing qualities such as "great legs" (28 Feb. 1992: 8).

Men are more likely to emphasize their economic security, but occasionally men—and more often, gay men—thematize the commodification of self and body in their ads, as in the following example: "LIMITED TIME ONLY, last one in stock. '63 blonde, green eyes. Literate, works out regularly, minor personality flaws, nonsmoker. This offer won't last, so act now (not valid in Georgia or Missouri)" (28 Feb. 1992: 13).[14] This writer uses the implicit metaphor of the used car to market primarily his body and to stress the impermanence of the offer. He performs his desire by objectifying himself and displacing his desire onto the idealized man/buyer to whom he issues his self-image. By inscribing himself within a literalized system of self-objectification and exchange, '63 blonde enthusiastically accepts the economic context of his advertisement of desire and conflates his self-portrait with that act of commodification.

The potential deconstructive power of this personal, like that of Algren's ad, lies in its reference to the frame of the genre. Just as '63 blonde refers back to the initial gesture of self-commodification inherent in the personals as advertisements of one's body and desires, as "want ads" in both senses of the phrase, Algren's adoption of a literary role thematizes both his textual self-creation in the personals and his awareness of following the tradition of heterosexual role-playing. These writers ultimately appropriate commodity culture and highbrow literary references in the service of perpetuating fixed gender identities.

Makeshift Sexuality

The main categorizations of the *Reader*'s Matches section—"Men Seeking Women," "Women Seeking Men," "Women Seeking Women," and "Men Seeking Men"—reinforce the assumption that the writer's sexuality can be categorized and that his or her sexuality provides the primary mode of self-marking. But the subgroup of the Matches labeled "Other," as well as the possibilities for sexual ambiguity in the form of bisexual or "Bi-Curious" ads and in the makeshift category "SBi" (straight/bi) occasionally rupture this system of self-signification based on concretized sexual identity. Because of the personals' insistence upon declaring one kind of love object in one's ad, certain kinds of bisexual identity cannot even be articulated, or at least can only be partially represented. For bisexuals like Rebecca Shuster, who claim that "our goal is to rid ourselves of every rigid construct of gender and sexuality," the personals inevitably occasion a misrepresentation. Shuster's envisioned future in which " 'bisexual' would hold no meaning" and "to seek to love without gender as a constraint" would be a common goal of all people cannot find expression in the personals because of their interest in reproducing fixed gender categories.[15]

Just as the biphobia many bisexuals experience in gay and lesbian culture is often reflected and encoded in gay personal ads, internalized homophobia sometimes surfaces in bi ads as well, and most often in bi-curious or straight/bi ads. Whereas a lesbian interested only in other lesbian women may issue an injunction that "bisexuals need not respond," thereby reinforcing object-choice as the determining factor in identity formation, the bi-curious woman may specify "no lesbians" as a way of constructing her personals identity around her uncertainty or tentativeness about sexual relations with women. Whereas the overwhelming majority of the personals, both gay and straight, use the structure of the *Reader*'s categories of desire as modes of self-creation, the curious or straight/bi subject uses the same conventions of the genre as a way of forging a self-image of liminal sexuality that ultimately threatens to render the conventions of the ad format unrecognizable.

Examples of sexual curiosity expressed as uncertainty are fairly common in the "Men Seeking Men" and "Women Seeking Women" sections, and they often combine expressions of homoerotic desire and internalized homophobia in ways that resist a definitive reading of authorial intent. Because intentionality and self-definition in the personals rely upon the firm location of identity in sexuality, ads such as the following upset the genre's system of categorization: "BIWM, 36, FRIENDLY, handsome, and fun. Looking to meet some friendly, decent, single straight but curious only white male professionals, 26-44, who enjoy baseball, sports, pizza, music, conversation, and fun. Also must live alone and be very serious about friendship. No gays" (6 Mar. 1992: 13). The exclusion of gay men from the writer's desires might at first seem plainly homophobic, but upon deeper inspection, it calls for a more precise definition of homophobia. This writer's limiting condition that excludes gay men stems not from a distaste for homosexual behaviors, but from a rejection of a kind of stable, intuitively held homosexual identity that he does not presume to share with men who identify as gay. In his effort to find other men of like uncertainty and curiosity who would, for him, provide a safe and supportive environment for exploration, this writer unwittingly reproduces the category of gay male identity he seeks to interrogate. What may be seen as homophobia in ads such as these can also be read as a symptom of frustration; the rigidity of the gender categories available to these writers impedes their efforts to express a desire that does not necessarily follow from a sense of definite and permanent sexual identity.

Some writers not only deconstruct or point to the inadequacy of gender categories, but resist orienting their desires around sexual practices at all. Occasional efforts at defining identity according to categories other than sexual identity or practice appear, for example, in ads that primarily foreground an author's disease: "FYI, I HAVE herpes" (21 Feb. 1992: 6); "HERPES" (28 Feb. 1992: 8). The restriction of choices imposed by sexually transmitted diseases complicates the *Reader*'s categorizations, because illness displaces gender as the writer's main concern. Other personal qualities, such as a basic sense of responsibility and honesty, might be implied by these writers' disclosures, but the primary suggestion of these ads is that because sexual practice is affected by the presence of a virus inside the writer's body, the writer's identity is somehow changed. These ads must still adapt to the categories of sexual identity mandated by the personals, but the gesture of constructing identity around disease also threatens to displace gender as the main mode of identification.

Still other ads, while claiming a sexuality for their authors, express a desire that cannot be accommodated by or articulated through this genre: "SKITSO, DROP DEAD gorgeous, 5'7", 40, 22, 23, conceited, arrogant, money monger from hell, unemployed, uneducated, SWF seeks anything and anyone, pets welcome" (31 Jan. 1992: 5). In addition to the aggressive tone that creates this ad's ambiguous rhetorical effect, the internal contradictions in this particular ad render it virtually unreadable. This writer's deliberate disinformation regarding her age signifies her open defiance of her readers' attempts to place her into categories. This woman (one presumes), who declares herself straight by placing her ad in the "Women Seeking Men" section, crosses both gender and species lines in her acceptance of pets and her desire for "anything and anyone." This gesture severely vitiates the original intended meaning of the "Women Seeking Men" category by generalizing the object of desire so exhaustively that it extends outside of the sexual and economic relations that circumscribe the genre. Skitso's gesture may appear to shake the conceptual foundations of the genre to a greater extent than those ads that appear in the categories for alternative sexualities. But despite its challenges to the personals

format, its self-referential quality reinstates the power of the normative categories; the category "Women Seeking Men" ensures the readability of Skitso's utterance because her choice of identification limits
the free flow of polymorphous desire her narrative initially suggests.

Similar to the personals written by unreadable or sexually liminal
subjects are the ads that fall under the category "Other." These ads
typically complicate the traditional dyadic relationship, encoded in the
very term "Matches," whose potential is idealized in both the gay and
straight personals. The most common "Other" ads feature straight
men seeking bisexual women and couples who seek young bi females
or other couples for "indoor sports" or "pursuit of the outre" (28 Feb.
1992: 13), but there are also rare ads seeking transsexuals or transves-
tites (28 Feb. 1992: 13). These publications of desire that imagine
nondyadic or potentially triangulated configurations cannot be articulated in the customary formula of "x seeks y" because the desires of
the ideal respondent are imagined to unfold beyond the frame of the
dyadic communication the ad initiates. Even these ads, however,
which challenge the institution of monogamous heterosexual pairing,
are parasitic upon a traditional version of heterosexual relations in
which men are subjects and women are objects. In six years of reading
the Matches, I have never seen a request from a couple for a third partner who is male, or a request from a woman for a bisexual male. The
desires expressed in the "Other" section consistently seem to enact
male fantasies of visually or literally appropriating lesbian sex for
male pleasure.

A Taste for Sex

Whereas gay and lesbian personal ads complicate any notion of a normative sexuality, the personals in many gay and lesbian publications
also tend to reconfigure and reproduce the dichotomized roles inherent
in straight personals with oppositional categories such as top/ bottom,
butch/femme, and, within the gay/lesbian S/M subculture, master/slave
and mistress/slave. "Sapphone," for example, the personals section in
the lesbian magazine *On Our Backs*, features two examples of dichotomized sexual roles, "Butch/Femme" and "'S/M' Activities," but
other categories reflect a broader range and a finer distinction of desires
than most straight personals acknowledge: "Romance/Relationship,"
"Will Travel/Correspond," "Bulletin Board," and the *On Our Backs*
version of "Other," "Transsexual/Bisexual."[16] The presumption of les-

bian identity in these personals participates in the hypostasization of sexual identity, but the typical inclusion of the category "S/M" reveals a more frank admission than is structured into straight personals that identity is largely constituted through the selection of certain practices and the rejection of others. Unlike entertainments and practices such as classical music and sports, S/M as a category exists on the boundary of practices that many consider to be inherently or essentially sexual, such as intercourse or oral sex, and those tastes and practices that might seem to exist outside the realm of the sexual. The grouping together of those who do or do not practice S/M suggest that its practice is a choice made according to taste that then takes on the appearance of sexual identity. Pierre Bourdieu's observations regarding the economic and cultural determinations of taste provide a useful vocabulary not only for addressing the class-coded language of personal ads, but also for showing how gender cannot constitute identity or generate its own meaning outside the tastes and choices of a particular class or other so-cial group. The conventional trappings of lesbian S/M—expensive leather costumes and sex toys—suggest its determination by a middle-class standard of living at the same time that they create and reflect a group identity that is and is not sexual. If, as Bourdieu argues, "social identity is defined and asserted through difference," lesbian S/M de-rives its particularity not only from gender identity, but from social practice as well.[17] Group identity is thus formed through multiple ex-pressions of taste and preference that go far beyond considerations of gender:

> It is found in all the properties—and property—with which indi-viduals and groups surround themselves, houses, furniture, paint-ings, books, cars, spirits, cigarettes, perfume, clothes, and in the practices with which they manifest their distinction, sports, games, entertainments, only because it is in the synthetic unity of the habitus, the unifying, generative principle of all practices. Taste, the propensity and capacity to appropriate (materially or symbolically) a given class of classified, classifying objects or practices, is the generative formula of a life-style.[18]

The example of lesbian S/M as one articulation of sexuality within the continuum of bisexual/lesbian identity is instructive because it shows how one's sexual practices do not necessarily derive from one's gender or from what is commonly thought of as sexual preference. Furthermore, S/M reveals the social contingencies of sexual identity that have been naturalized and made to appear as inevitable choices that emanate from a stable gender identity.

Although the *Reader* makes the primary choice for the writer about how to identify her- or himself, the *Reader*'s advertisements sometimes provide a commentary on the limitations of gender categories for enabling like-minded people to come together socially or sexually. A recent ad promoting Chicago White Sox ticket sales, for example, assumes the priority of a taste for baseball over gender identity by transforming male and female gender symbols into baseballs (see Figure 7.2). Although some might argue that this ad assumes tastes that are normatively male, it also asserts an important challenge to gender normativity by setting up baseball fans—regardless of gender or sexual preference—as a primary social category. Butler's critique of feminist constructions of a postgenital, polymorphous version of sexuality cautions against efforts to escape the representational field of gender and calls instead "to make gender trouble" by copying and manipulating gender representations.[19] The focus on concrete practices, however, may offer a way of theorizing identity formation that shows how the multiplicity of habitus splinter the simple binarism that many feminists assume as the basic structuring principle of individual identity. The White Sox advertisement signals an awareness of the inadequacy of sexual identity for self-articulation that goes far beyond autobiographical writing and extends into interpersonal relationships and the dynamics of group identity. More challenges like these to the preeminence of discourses that define identity as sexuality are a useful starting point for looking seriously at how the tastes and everyday practices of our habitus shape our identities and determine the ways in which we can imagine ourselves in relation to others. Closer attention to the intersection of gender positions with tastes that are largely class based might allow us to speak more concretely about what class means for the individual's identity.[20] This type of analysis would also offer a way to sidestep facile generalizations based on either gender or class as the sole determining category of identity. Our existence as class-marked social beings, as well as sexual beings, might then become a matter of more careful and sustained concern, and we might find a richer language for talking about identity formation and its autobiographical expression.

Figure 7.2. The category of Sox fan appears to subsume gender categories in these permutations of male and female symbols and in the gender-neutral phrasing of the parodic ad's collective subject, "single baseball fans." By permission of DiMeo Rosen Partners, Inc.

Notes

1. *Chicago Reader,* 6 Aug. 1993, 31. On the basis on their own sense of propriety, the staff of the *Reader* also reserves the right to reject ads: "We will not print ads we find to be in poor taste." Not surprisingly, they do not define "poor taste." Ads quoted in text are all from the *Reader;* date and page for each are given in parentheses in the text.

2. Judith Butler, *Gender Trouble: Feminism and the Subversion of Identity* (New York: Routledge, 1990), 16–17.

3. One can find publications targeted toward specific groups that foreground racial or ethnic identity or other group affiliation in the personal ads, but my argument here is concerned with the comparative scarcity of publications that prioritize categories other than gender and the tendency for the replication of gender dichotomies in alternative publications. Butler succinctly characterizes the insufficiency of gender identity both in terms of its own internal instability and its complicated convergences with other group identities: "If one 'is' a woman, that is surely not all one is; the term fails to be exhaustive, not because a pregendered 'person' transcends the specific paraphernalia of its gender, but because gender is not always constituted coherently or consistently in different historical contexts, and because gender intersects with racial, class, ethnic, sexual, and regional modalities of discursively constituted identities." Ibid., 3.

4. Michel Foucault, *The History of Sexuality,* vol. 1, *An Introduction,* trans. Robert Hurley (New York: Vintage, 1990), 42–43.

5. Butler, *Gender Trouble,* 17.

6. Ibid., 23.

7. Philippe Lejeune, "The Autobiographical Pact," in *On Autobiography,* ed. Paul John Eakin, trans. Katherine Leary (Minneapolis: University of Minnesota Press, 1989), 19-20.

8. Butler, *Gender Trouble,* 16.

9. Diana Fuss, "Fashion and the Homospectatorial Look," *Critical Inquiry* 18 (Summer 1992): 734.

10. Ibid., 714.

11. Linda Williams, *Hard Core: Power, Pleasure, and the "Frenzy of the Visible"* (Berkeley: University of California Press, 1989), 2.

12. Rita Felski, *Beyond Feminist Aesthetics: Feminist Literature and Social Change* (Cambridge: Harvard University Press, 1989), 103.

13. For treatments of Algren's and de Beauvoir's relationship, see Bettina Drew, *Nelson Algren: A Life on the Wild Side* (New York: Putnam, 1989); Deirdre Bair, *Simone de Beauvoir: A Biography* (New York: Summit, 1990).

14. I had assumed that '63 blonde's offer was void in Georgia and Missouri because those states had strict antisodomy laws. According to E. Carrington Boggan's *The Rights of Gay People: An ACLU Handbook* (New York: Avon, 1975), these two states have relatively severe penalties for sodomy: in Georgia, sodomy is a felony carrying a sentence of one to twenty years, and in Missouri it is a felony with a minimum two-year sentence (173, 187). But other states have even more excessive penalites, such as Tennessee, in which sodomy is a felony carrying a sentence of five to fifteen years (201). Thus '63 blonde's exclusion of Missouri is difficult to interpret in terms of state law, but Georgia law is singular in its harsh penalty for attempt to commit sodomy: one to ten years (173).

15. Rebecca Shuster, "Bisexuality and the Quest for Principled Loving," in *Closer to Home: Bisexuality and Feminism,* ed. Elizabeth Reba Weise (Seattle: Seal, 1992), 149–50.

16. *On Our Backs* (Mar./Apr. 1992). *On Our Backs* is edited by Debi Sundahl, and is published in San Francisco by Blush Entertainment Corp.

17. Pierre Bourdieu, *Distinction: A Social Critique of the Judgement of Taste,* trans. Richard Nice (Cambridge: Harvard University Press, 1984), 172.

18. Ibid., 173.

19. Butler, *Gender Trouble,* 34.

20. Ernesto Laclau and Chantal Mouffe, in *Hegemony and Socialist Strategy: Towards a Radical Democratic Politics* (New York: Verso, 1985), have effectively rehearsed the political and conceptual limits of defining classed subjects by the collective possession or lack of a "revolutionary subjectivity" (39). I am suggesting here that discourses about class identity that have no recourse to the materiality of everyday life are necessarily prone to the same pitfalls pointed out by Laclau and Mouffe.

Part III

Un/Speakable Lives

The writing about personal disaster that functions as literature tends not to be about "disaster" at all. That is, whatever adversity provides the grounds for the project must be embedded in a context both enigmatic and elaborate: the insistent everyday world.

NANCY MAIRS, "When Bad Things Happen to Good Writers,"
New York Times Book Review 21 (February 1993): 1, 25–27

The Making of Americans is a very important thing and everybody ought to be reading at it or it, and now I am trying to do it again to say everything about everything, only then I was wanting to write a history of every individual person who ever is or was or shall be living and I was convinced it could be done as I still am but now individual anything as related to every other individual is to me no longer interesting. At that time I did not realize that the earth is completely covered over with every one. In a way it was not then because every one was in a group and a group was separated from every other one, and so the character of every one was interesting because they were in relation but now since the earth is all covered over with every one there is really no relation between any one and so if this Everybody's Autobiography is to be the Autobiography of every one it is not to be of any connection between any one and any one because now there is none.

GERTRUDE STEIN, *Everybody's Autobiography*
(New York: Random House, 1937), 99

8 / Consensual Autobiography: Narrating "Personal Sexual History" from Boswell's *London Journal* to AIDS Pamphlet Literature

Philip E. Baruth

On 31 December 1762, James Boswell—then twenty-two years old and in the midst of a year's stay in London—waited on one Mrs. Lewis ("Louisa"), little-known Covent Garden actress, in her rooms. The two were coming to the end of a fairly intense, two-week negotiating period. The issue, in Boswell's spare formulation: "whether we would or not."[1] Several times since their initial confessions of attraction, Boswell had come to Louisa's rooms "in full expectation of consummate bliss" (p. 100), but each time the discussion had turned most often upon complications—religious, social, personal. Louisa felt that "it was running the greatest risk" (p. 107), whereas Boswell "talked of love connections very freely" (p. 112). The last day of December ended the negotiations. Louisa consented to an assignation on New Year's Day, 1763. Below is Boswell's journalistic rendering of that final bit of haggling:

> She mentioned one consequence that in an affair of gallantry might be troublesome. "I suppose, Madam," said I, "you mean if a third person should be interested in the affair. Why, to be sure, if such a person should appear, he must be taken care of. For my own part, I have the strongest principles of that kind." "Well, Sir," said she, with a sweet complacency. "But we won't talk any more on the subject." (p. 113)

Both parties, apparently, left the above exchange secure in the belief that something definite had been hammered out. The editor of Boswell's journal, Frederick Pottle, glosses the scene for the index conclusively: "JB promises to support child, should one be born, 113." And certainly one or both of the young participants may have perceived the conversation as one involving pregnancy. But there is another interpretation that works as well, if not better in some ways. Try replaying the conversation mentally with a jealous rival as referent for the "third person." For one thing, this possibility renders the phrase "interested in the affair" much less indirect as euphemism; for another, the assertion "he must be taken care of" takes on a distinctly aggressive male intonation. From the script of the discussion itself, then, the reader is left with little to help choose between the two forking tracks of meaning.

Of course, Boswell had already fathered one child out of wedlock, and demonstrated relatively strong scruples about caring for it financially. This biographical matter—as well as his general timorousness with regard to dueling—supports Pottle's reading of Boswell's perceptions. But Louisa may have been operating under an entirely disparate set of assumptions. The fact remains that the couple, through the obfuscating function of polite discourse, escaped the immediate unpleasantness of solid understanding, and preempted all future attempts to restore clarity to the subject(s).

Furthermore, this conversation represents one of the couple's more earnest attempts at communication. Earlier in the month, Louisa had tried to sound Boswell out about his "intrigues," and as he proudly tells us, these questions he "nicely eluded" (p. 101). But the "third person" discussion seems to have taken place between two willing parties, trying with some seriousness to negotiate beforehand one (or more) of the difficulties arising from sex out of wedlock. The consequences of this "negotiated" sexual union are notorious: Boswell either contracted or reactivated a virulent and protracted case of gonorrhea, and he subsequently broke with Louisa—spitefully, hurtfully ("I should think the consideration of your deceit and baseness, your corruption both of body and mind, would be a very severe punishment"; p. 175). Boswell found his enforced convalescence patently unfair. Yes, he had gone at sex aggressively and manfully, in his own opinion, "But then I had run no risks" (p. 149).

I begin with the Boswell-Louisa scene for a variety of reasons. First, it demonstrates quite vividly the biological telos that informs human sexual relations, drives them imperceptibly toward a predetermined conclusion. In this sense, Boswell's often distasteful sexual aggressivity merely exaggerates a logic of consummation that is both biological and cultural in character. Second, the scene clarifies the way in which moments of linguistic ambiguity are repressed or ignored by negotiating parties, in service of that same telos. Confusion that serves one's own (unspoken or unconscious) goals will remain confusion unaddressed, and the "rules" of the negotiating game allow such repression. Jean-François Lyotard, in *The Postmodern Condition,* deals extensively with the game methodology central to language itself. "A *self* does not amount to much," Lyotard maintains, "but no self is an island; each exists in a fabric of [game] relations that is now more complex and mobile than ever before. Young or old, man or woman, rich or poor, a person is always located at 'nodal points' of specific communication circuits, however tiny these may be."[2] Much like Louis Althusser, Lyotard believes that each subject is born always already enmeshed in linguistic or ideological gaming strategies, evidenced by the fact that they have been named prior to birth, incorporated into a given social narrative. The "basis of the social bond," then, is in some sense the never-ending "taking of tricks," a metaphor Lyotard likes and one that points up the survival function in language, its evolution toward greater performativity, toward "new moves." There can, and will, be both survivors and losers in Lyotard's language game.

But Lyotard's metaphor proves ultimately too pessimistic with regard to human agency in communication. As the authors of the sociolinguistic text *Equivocal Communication* point out, in stark contrast to "deception theorists" in their field who proceed under the assumption that communication is quite often based upon verbal trickery, "Given the choice, people will not lie but equivocate truthfully."[3] This is to say that humans take the path of most honesty with least harm to the relationship at hand. Even the radically foreshortened version of the conversation represented in Boswell's journal harbors three or four such moments of "truthful equivocation," in which the speakers hesitate to clarify the (grammatical) subject of their discussion because to do so would be to endanger the rapidly developing "consensus." It was, in fact, a linguistic state of affairs that Boswell and his friend Erskine discussed during the courtship of Louisa: "[Erskine] abused the style of genteel company. We agreed in calling it *a consensual obliteration of the human faculties*" (p. 96).

Last of all, Boswell stands at or near the center of modern conceptions of the autobiographical. His *Journals* are to England what Rousseau's *Confessions* are to France, an original and secular self-representation staking out the ground of the individual with respect to history, as well as other shared representations of reality, biography among them. Boswell's autobiographical writings asserted authority over his own remembered existence, an authority that earlier keepers of self-record had assumed to rest in the Deity. Thus, when Boswell cautions Louisa, whose questions have reached a discomfiting pass, "you must take my character from myself" (p. 101), he is literalizing a state of affairs that speaks to our own now-received notions about the self-authorization central to the genre of autobiography itself.

Here we reach the crux of the scene's relevence to AIDS-era America. Like Boswell's contemporaries, we now search assiduously for ways to continue to have sex while minimizing the possibility of infection. In lieu of a medical solution, like Boswell's contemporaries, we turn to casual verbal interview as the most painless solution. And like Boswell himself, we defend stoutly if implicitly the individual's right to author his or her personal sexual history, or sexual autobiography.[4] Thus, *our* fight against HIV infection rests heavily, perhaps disastrously, upon the same beliefs and practices that failed so miserably in the eighteenth century's fight against gonorrhea and syphilis: through the generality of our AIDS informational literature, we too have institutionalized the belief that one must take another's character from him or her, without revision, without question. We treat the "personal sexual history" as both personal and a history, when it is in point of fact neither.

The personal sexual history is not "personal" because the nature of retroviral infection has inaugurated a new sense of sexual interdependence among persons—this interdependence is typically referenced by the truism that to have sex with a given person is to have sex with that person's existing slate of sexual partners, and to become a member of that slate for at least a decade to come. The cliché renders graphically the loss of sexual integrity and privacy the post-AIDS generation has experienced. Yet, perhaps partially because of that loss, we cling nostalgically to the idea that at the very least our remembered "past" is

"personal." The myth is that our history remains ours alone, a possession to be offered in good faith.

But the personal sexual history is not a history either—autobiography is not, and has never been, fundamentally historical. Nancy K.
Miller formulates it pointedly: "If there is anyone more dead than the
author of fiction, who classically was said to authorize his text by inscribing his intentions for future generations, it would have to be the
author of autobiography. For of the three defining terms of autobiography—the self, the life, the writing—only the writing has survived the
poststructuralist and postmodern housecleaning of antiquated beliefs."[5] Or as Georges Gusdorf more optimistically puts it, "Every
autobiography is a work of art and at the same time a work of enlightenment; it does not show us the individual seen from outside in
his visible actions but the person in his inner privacy, not as he was,
not as he is, but as he believes and wishes himself to be and to have
been."[6] In other words, autobiography is a subjective interpretation
and involves countless decisions regarding self-representation. These
decisions, in turn, are informed by countless factors, including situa-
tional factors present at composition. The "sexual history," then, is
much less a history than it is a momentary, never-to-be-repeated ordering of possibilities in memory. Although certain points in the narrative may remain relatively constant over time, the aspect assigned
those points, as well as their aggregate gravity, will remain evanescent,
precisely as changeable as mood.

Of course, none of this has prevented postmodern society from continuing to use (write, read, and theorize) the autobiographical mode.
Perhaps more than any other, Philippe Lejeune's contractual model has
been instrumental in providing a sense of stability in dealing with this
otherwise volatile narrative mode. That is to say, unfortunately, that
Lejeune's work has been one of the roundabout means by which postmodern culture has reasserted the autobiographer's singular authority
over the "life" he or she constructs. This reassertion has direct and adverse consequences for a culture that has come to rely more heavily
than ever on the personal sexual history.

For Lejeune, autobiography becomes autobiography through an
"autobiographical pact," a generic contract in which the reader
agrees to read the retrospective narrative as a personalized (or subjective) study of the author's "personality," and the author in turn
"signs" the work to indicate that it has been written for that purpose.

Thus, for Lejeune, referentiality is not really an issue in the case of autobiography:

> We notice already here what is going to fundamentally oppose biography and autobiography; it is the hierarchical organization of the relationships of resemblance and identity. In biography, it is resemblance that must ground identity; in autobiography, it is identity that grounds resemblance. Identity is the real starting point of autobiography; resemblance, the impossible horizon of biography. (p. 24)

Put more simply, a reader does not go to an autobiography for a referential history; a reader goes to an autobiography for a subjective perspective *by* the author *on* the author. When a reader wants verifiable facts, he or she makes a different pact, by picking up a biography—biography constructed of verifiable source materials and subject as a whole to a vetting by the academy, by other biographers, and so on.

Although useful, this definition (and Lejeune's approach in general) is somewhat disingenuous: it elides the problematic consideration that readers *do* continue to cede great referential authority to an autobiography—the "resemblance" to the objective world *is* an essential part of the pact. In this way, Lejeune goes a long way toward reinstitutionalizing the authority of the autobiographical author (heavily questioned in recent years) simply by asserting that that author never truly sought a "historical" authority and that the reader never truly granted it. But to cast doubt on this reasoning one need only expand on an example of Lejeune's. In speaking of autobiography's generic nature, Lejeune remarks that "it is indispensable that the referential pact be *drawn up,* and that it be *kept;* but it is not necessary that the result be on the order of strict resemblance. The referential pact can be, according to the criteria of the reader, badly kept, without the referential value of the text disappearing (on the contrary)—this is not the case for historical and journalistic texts" (pp. 22–23). Lejeune insists, at once, that an autobiography must keep its referential pact, but that it may do so "badly."

One wishes to know exactly how badly? Surely an "autobiography" that is faulty in every factual respect, while preserving the essence of Lejeune's autobiographical pact (treating subjectively of the author's personality), is not autobiography—it would move over into the category of the fictional, the autobiographical novel, or the allegorical, the autobiographical roman à clef. In short, readers (and listeners) grant a peculiar lease on factuality to the autobiographer, one more tenacious than Lejeune is willing to admit. It is—and always has been—a great deal of power to place in the hands of one "writer" (biography, again, admits of a great deal of external correction; fiction disclaims most referential power as it signals its own fictional nature). For this reason, I think, autobiographers have almost always been willing to perform elaborate obeisance to the reader, in the form of protestations of honesty, promises that the work has been or will be read by a community of readers capable of correcting it, and so on.[7] In these and other ways, readers of the genre have always been jollied into authorizing the "self-history."

Such a state of affairs remains troubling even in the relatively harm-free realm of the literary form. But as I have pointed out above, personal sexual histories are autobiographical in nature and are, in practice, currently used as a line of defense against an extremely virulent physical infection. By ignoring the binding nature of autobiography's authority over "facts," we agree to a state of affairs in which one person's self-representation may (unwittingly) threaten many others. To return to Lyotard's game motif, the "taking of tricks" autobiographically—and repressing the knowledge that one is "trumping" another communicationally—can now have fatal consequences.

To complicate matters still further, in drawing out a partner's sexual history the facilitating partner *joins* in the compositional process. He or she significantly alters the evolving verbal representation itself. Elizabeth A. Meese has discussed how an oral interview becomes "a collaborative event," in which the interviewer and the interviewee "produce a text that in one dimension is a dialogue between them and in the other . . . the dialogue between the informant and her own historical and cultural consciousness."[8] Applied to our discussion, both the person giving and the person receiving the sexual history are contributing to authorship, though they sometimes do so, of course, at cross-purposes. In this way, the "sexual record" should be conceived of as a shared autobiographical narrative, one that comes into being with the active participation and consent of two concerned parties.[9] All of this I have tried to capture in the phrase *consensual autobiography* or, alternately, *shared sexual self-record*.

In the following pages, I will examine how AIDS informational literature, while promoting the exchange of "personal sexual histories," generally fails to instruct readers in any form of interpersonal communication, and specifically veers away from a critique of (oral) self-narrative. The authors of the many pamphlets and instructional aids available nationwide have relied almost without exception upon outmoded generic notions of autobiography that are misleading and even dangerous in their continued insistence upon the validity of sexual self-authorization. Boswell's conception of the sexual negotiation, "But you must take my character from myself"—and, by extension, all well-intentioned instructional texts that replicate his very basic error—I will treat as fundamentally archaic.

AIDS Pamphlet Literature

The authors of AIDS literature had before them, in the early 1980s, a truly herculean task: to familiarize the public with an extremely complex viral scenario, as well as with a basic method of restructuring sexual practices to prevent that scenario's reenaction. There were countless problems to be considered, prominent among them differences of language and culture and the ensuing possibility for misunderstanding, even offense. How would illiterate, lower-class, or poverty-stricken Americans gain adequate access to information? Ultimately, every informational format was brought into service, including electronic media such as video and television.

I want to concentrate on the medium of print, focusing more or less exclusively on the pamphlet literature as a very widespread example of textual practice. Pamphlets, available free of charge from most health care providers, represent the format Americans are most likely to encounter. Also, the pamphlet becomes a personal possession; it can be studied and restudied. Unlike other educational media, pamphlets require neither hardware (such as television sets or videocassette players) nor commitment to an institutional relationship (such as a lending library). The pamphlet, like HIV itself, can become fully operational with only one contact.

The American College Health Association may be the most prolific agency in the United States, both in numbers of health care outlets reached and in numbers of individual pamphlets produced. I would like to begin with a look at three ACHA pamphlets: *Making Sex Safer, Safer Sex,* and *HIV Infection and AIDS.* The pamphlets are designed to be read together; they attempt to cover in a three-part format the spectrum of necessary information. There is much overlap among the three, but it is my assumption that such overlap is intentional, and that it serves to drive home certain crucial sets of facts and relationships.

In addition to sharing a similar look—glossy colorful layout, often highlighting attractive photos of couples touching—the three pamphlets share several textual assumptions. Paramount is the idea that safe sex involves multifaceted behavioral change: no single shift in practice is sufficient. These multiple facets form two lines of defense, the first nonphysical and the second physical in nature. Partners are encouraged first, as *Making Sex Safer* words it, to "ask about your partner's health and sexual history"; having done so, they may "make informed decisions" and abstain or proceed to the second line of defense, the selection of safer practices and the physical barrier (condom, latex dental dam, "female condom").

Although all three ACHA pamphlets—as well as much book-length literature—posit the verbal interaction or interview as the primary step in prevention of HIV transmission, all three consider such interaction only very briefly and generally. For all their visual celebration of partner unity and exchange, the pamphlets present no solid approach to interpersonal, or even informational, mutuality. To continue with *Making Sex Safer* as an example, the pamphlet's cover features a small but attractive inset photograph: a young dark-haired man and a young redheaded woman are seated, touching hands, looking into each other's eyes. They seem involved in a serious but mutually supportive discussion. Interestingly, the man's wrist and hand seem to extend, at first glance, into the woman's crooked arm, forming an uninterrupted "mutual" arm. This motif continues on the page adjoining: there, an African American couple look into each other's eyes so deeply that their foreheads actually touch, conveying a quite literal visual sense of physical, mental, and emotional togetherness.

Safer Sex takes such visual analogues for interpersonal, even intersubjective, communication a full step further. The pamphlet's text is interspersed with photographs of a young Caucasian couple that show clipped segments of their intertwined bodies, never their heads or faces. Each photograph is done in warm flesh tones against a neutral black background. We see a hand resting gently on a neck or touching an arm, fingers tracing shoulders, thighs. The "warm" lighting makes the two bodies appear to be of precisely the same color and texture. The absence of faces not only universalizes the bodies, and renders them more effectively androgynous, but conveys the sense that both

186 / *Philip E. Baruth*

bodies are functioning according to a single will. The viewer confronts a visual ideal of intersubjectivity.

Yet the three pamphlets devote surprisingly little text to guiding readers into such shared sexual and informational space. *Making Sex Safer,* though it places learning "to communicate effectively with your sexual partner" at the top of its list of "What Precautions Should I Take?" gives only two short paragraphs to communication. These two paragraphs provide only more or less obvious truisms ("Together decide what you both feel comfortable doing sexually"), general admonishments ("Being intimate is much more than a sexual act"), and last-minute buck-passing ("If discussions about relationships, emotions, or sex are difficult for you, seek counseling from capable professionals"). They provide almost no immediately usable information. The authors of the pamphlet imply, through their silence, that communication is too complex an issue to be dealt with in the pamphlet format.

HIV Infection and AIDS, the final ACHA pamphlet, goes *Making Sex Safer* at least one better in stating the obvious. One of the pamphlet's two paragraphs on communication provides the following information, under "Communicating assertively with your sexual partner and negotiating for safer sexual practices":

> Many people are unskilled in discussing sexual matters or activities or in managing relationships. Talking about sex can seem embarrassing or uncomfortable. Telling the truth about your sexual past may be difficult. Communicating assertively about your desires in a sexual relationship is a real challenge.

In an all but impenetrable redundancy, each of these lines merely repeats the others, while at the same time maintaining an earnest, counseling tone. Taken as a whole, the paragraph represents more of a textual stutter on the part of the pamphlet's author(s) than any real attempt to tackle the explanatory task at hand. If I make no other point in this essay, I want to stress that currently there is a frightening shortage of literature dealing with the mechanics of partner negotiation and information exchange, although such exchange continues to represent the first step in most safe-sex agendas.

The question of why, with pamphlet space at such a premium, the author(s) would waste half of the space given over to communication can and should be asked another way. Why does *each* of the three ACHA pamphlets devote roughly one full page to step-by-step instructions in the use of a condom? Each individual pamphlet has a long, extremely effective, numbered set of instructions, worded with admirable simplicity and clarity. As I have said before, such massive overlap seems part of the overall series design, and the most obvious answer to my question is that condom use is crucial—it represents the single most important physical barrier to HIV transmission in use. And it is, of course, easier to describe than partner communication. It lends itself to an on-off list of instructions.

Still, the condom is theoretically the *second* line of defense, one that would prove unnecessary if the first (screening through verbal interview) resulted in an "informed decision" to abstain.[10] Looked at this way, the disproportionate amount of space given to condom use—already explained, by the way, on or in many condom packages—stands out as odd. It speaks to an underlying ambivalence within the pamphlets and within the government/private organizational community producing the educational literature. The emphasis on the physical barrier comes from the same impulse as the "Say no to sex" campaigns popular in the mid-1980s and sanctioned by then-Surgeon General C. Everett Koop. Put most simply, this underlying impulse favors physical separatism, whether that separation is enacted in the form of a monogamous couple separate from the rest of sexual society or two partners remaining effectively separate behind barriers of latex. Many pamphlets do not even mention the exchange of personal sexual histories, let alone describe how this may be accomplished; instead, they take monogamy and abstinence as guiding structural assumptions.[11] I would suggest that the general absence of book-length guides to the exchange of sexual information stems from the same unexpressed bias.

Thus, although the pamphlets present enticing images of mutuality, they silently underscore the easier truth of aloneness. Readers are encouraged, somewhat gingerly, to isolate themselves mentally as well ("Fantasy . . . generally pose[s] little or no risk"). The pamphlets silently reiterate the inherent inescapability—as well as the fatalism—of the traditional subject/object dilemma. You are alone, the pamphlets say at one level, but at least you are safe alone; the mutuality you seek with another is decidedly difficult, all but impossible, and will likely involve the intervention of counseling specialists. You should try, but be content with wresting only enough information from the other party to avoid injury to yourself.

The personal sexual history, then, if it is invoked at all in this ambivalent state of affairs, is envisioned with a soothing, prophylactic integrity. For example, although *Making Sex Safer* warns that your partner "might not realize, or reveal, things that could put you at risk," it continues to speak casually of the "sexual history" as an objective fund of information existing inside the recalcitrant party. Most of the stress on negotiation is placed on urging a partner to "give up" this set of "facts." Once he or she does so, you are free to go on to "informed" decision making. Nothing could be further from the truth. In fact, communication theorists have found that *any* degree of willingness to "exchange histories"—regardless of the contents—often produces enough false confidence to lead to completely unprotected sex.[12]

As I have said above, the sexual history is *not* a history, and it contains not facts, but problematic narrative representations of past events. The fourth pamphlet I will examine, produced by the U.C. Irvine AIDS Program, demonstrates a clearer grasp of this problem. *Let's Talk Sex: Avoiding AIDS* is a laudable effort in many ways. First, the pamphlet deals more solidly than the earlier-discussed examples with its own ambivalence regarding sex out of wedlock and monogamy: "This brochure is not intended to discourage or dismiss your choice to remain abstinent. . . . If you have chosen to be sexually active, the information in this brochure could save your life." Second, the pamphlet proposes a number of conversational formats, providing both sides of the exchange. But most important, the pamphlet features a list of "what you need to know," topics that should be dealt with during the exchange of sexual information (number of sexual partners, safer sex practices, antibody status, and so on). Much of what is needed in AIDS pamphlet literature can be found in *Let's Talk Sex*.

Still, at the final, working level, this pamphlet does rehearse some of the problematic assumptions I have traced in the ACHA pamphlets and, unfortunately, *Let's Talk Sex* does so dramatically. The highlight of the pamphlet is a staged scenario between two androgynous characters, Pat and Chris; the conversation seems designed to show the two implementing the pamphlet's verbal strategies. Each of its various stages deserves comment.

PAT: Chris, I'd like to talk about our relationship. I enjoy you a lot and feel we should talk about how sex fits into our relationship. Are you willing to do that?

CHRIS: Why spoil the mood with all this talk?
PAT: It's very important to me that we talk about this.
CHRIS: OK, OK. It scares me a lot, but what do you want to talk about?
PAT: Protection. I've had sex with other people, but in each case we used a condom and foam. Also, I have never shot up nor has anyone I have been with that I know of.
CHRIS: Well, I've had sex with others, too. Most of the time we used a condom, but I really don't like them. I have never shot up and I am fairly sure no one I have been with has either.
PAT: This is really tough to talk about, but I'm glad we're doing it. When it is right for us and we decide to have intercourse, I want us to use a condom and foam.
CHRIS: I want to make love with you, but we are both safe so why do we need to use a condom?
PAT: No one is safe these days. The only way I will consider having intercourse is if we use a condom and foam.
CHRIS: Yeah, you're right, we can make condoms part of the fun. Safer sex can be sexy too!

This dialogue occurs in three rough stages, a negotiation surrounding the interview itself, the "exchange of histories," and a negotiation surrounding the use of a condom. Notice that Chris needs to be pushed into each stage of safer sex practice; s/he represents the recalcitrant party who is willing to opt out of the recommended behavior at any moment. Pat does a very good job of keeping Chris on track without embarrassing or hurting, only once pulling back into the shell of self-hood ("The only way I will consider . . .").

The striking thing about this scenario, however, is that it proceeds to its admittedly puerile conclusion (featuring a rapidly converted Chris) *without ever suggesting that negotiation is fundamental to the middle stage of "history exchange" as well.* Like Boswell and Louisa, both Pat and Chris—though Chris the more so—have fallen back on nodes of conversational ambiguity, euphemism, obscurantism. Pat, for example, says that s/he has "had sex" with others but always used "a condom and foam." But does "sex" here mean "intercourse"? Has Pat had oral sex (more often practiced without a condom), and if so, has s/he given or received, or both? All of these distinctions can be crucial. Chris, for his/her part, has laced the second "history" with a number of problematic qualifications. Chris claims to have used a condom "most of the time," and to be "fairly sure" that none of his/her partners have "shot up" (in itself a euphemism with a good deal of variation in meaning, and one that says nothing about the *sharing* of needles). Thus, although each character's narration is clearly autobiographical, in that each expresses a remembered past subjectively, both prove virtually useless as statements of sexual experience.

I would also point out that although the names of the characters register as androgynous, the dialogue runs in a stereotypically male/female pattern, with the male more concerned with sexual consummation and the female more concerned to minimize negative consequences of the sexual act.[13] Part of the problem with this dialogue seems to stem from the working principle that getting "the man" to talk about protection is achievement enough; to suggest anything further is to court anger, violence, a loss of what has been gained through the brief dialogue. In this way, Pat and Chris—at least in their current dialogue—replicate a dangerous power imbalance that in this case has potentially fatal consequences.

Pat, the character particularly designed to troubleshoot problematic moments in the search for intercommunication with Chris, moves on without hesitation to the final step in the safe-sex sequence, the discussion of physical barrier and practice. Neither Pat nor the authors of *Let's Talk Sex* indicate that the "sexual histories" the characters exchange are only rough beginnings, in need of mutual work and mutual revision, as well as simple reiteration. Telling the "histories" over to one another more than once would increase the chance for ambiguities to be made visible. An astute "Pat" would be able to put together something much closer to "truth" if s/he can compare a number of primary accounts—more the way "history" actually develops, of course. Pat and Chris should realize, and the pamphlet reader should be taught, that the "personal sexual history" is a joint construction that cannot come together without active work on the part of both individuals. When it is complete it will not resemble traditional autobiography so much as a hybrid between (oral) autobiography and history—what I have called consensual autobiography or the shared sexual record.

Of course, the authors of *Let's Talk Sex* may plead lack of space, and certainly this aspect of pamphlet materiality will continue to prove problematic. But the fact remains that for whatever reason, they have fallen back on a dangerous set of assumptions, one that furthers their reader's traditional impression that "sexual histories" exist intact, somewhere inside each of us, and that once our partner has poured out this series of "real" chronological impressions, we may go on about our business. This issue becomes the more critical when we realize that the hostility and resistence that "Pat" has been taught (by pamphlets) to expect over the use of condoms could be much greater when the two are arguing instead over events to which "Chris" may very well feel that s/he has exclusive rights, because, after all, *s/he was there*, not Pat.

Toward a More Effective Pamphlet Literature

Anyone familiar with the pamphlet literature on HIV transmission and AIDS knows that the authors of these documents have accomplished an astonishing amount of the work that originally lay before them. The documents are easy to read and understand; they are attractive, nongender specific, and nonthreatening; they teach in accessible formats, such as numbered steps, charts, and give-and-take dialogues; and finally, they make a stringent attempt to avoid the moralizing strain that persists in much of the political rhetoric surrounding the AIDS issue. Still, the authors of these documents have left in place a somewhat dangerous set of assumptions regarding the exchange of sexual information as an autobiographical practice.

At those junctures in pamphlet literature when authors wish only to touch upon the process of communication between partners, small changes could stress that negotiation must accompany the exchange of sexual information as well as the decisions concerning physical barriers and acts. Consider the following:

> Encourage your partner to exchange sexual information with you, but remember that such information can truly emerge only through several talks, not one. Your goal should be to know each other, not to proceed prematurely to the next sexual step. Make sure that what your partner says makes sense to you—don't be afraid to clarify things. Remember that both of you are supplying half of what will be a *joint history* should you decide to have sex. As with a contract, make sure you are both comfortable with the wording beforehand.

The stress here is on an ongoing mutuality, the unfolding of a conarrative that demands two active participants.

Further, while *Making Sex Safer* gives a brief warning that deception is possible between partners, general treatments of communication should not stress this aspect. To repeat the key point quoted above from *Equivocal Communication,* "Given the choice, people will not lie but equivocate truthfully."[14] General treatments need to put across this idea, primarily to rid readers of the notion that there are "honest" and "dishonest" lovers in the world, but also to reinforce the idea that good intentions are not enough in communication—hard work is required as well. "Truthful equivocation" might be handled with a set of lines such as the following:

> You may feel that your partner is an honest person, and he or she most probably *is* well-meaning and trustworthy. But true communication is still difficult for sensitive, honest people—they worry that the truth may harm the relationship. They won't lie, but they may fall back on vague phrasing to lessen tension. You may, too. Be sure to watch for such moments during your talks, and have the courage to address them.

The U.C. Irvine pamphlet *Let's Talk Sex* does an excellent job of preparing readers to negotiate the discussion of sexual experiences as well as condom use. In particular, its list of topics to be covered during sexual negotiation is invaluable (it provides the only such list that I know of). I suggest here only another step in the negotiations between Pat and Chris, a few exchanges demonstrating the evolving nature of the shared sexual record:

> PAT: This is really tough to talk about, but I'm glad we're doing it. Don't get upset, but you said you used condoms most of the time. Were the times you didn't with people you knew well? Were there only a few times you didn't wear one?
> CHRIS: Well, I guess I used one mostly with people I didn't know well. The times I didn't use one were when I had been going out with someone for a year or so. We'd just decide to stop using them, sort of.
> PAT: That makes me feel a little better. Do you mind if we talk about this again, later, or another day? I really feel like I see you a lot more clearly, and I'd like that to keep happening before we get to the really hard decisions.

Readers need to be familiarized with verbal negotiation even at the level of another's oral autobiographical narrative. Such a skill seems to ask no more of them than the backbone required to push for the talk in the first place; the only reason that continued negotiation seems a harder step is that most of us retain the idea that our "past" is factual and is, even in this time of HIV threat, private.

Conclusion

The lingering concept of a "personal sexual history" stems from misguided nostalgia. HIV, and the logic of the retrovirus, has done a great deal to relieve us of our sexual privacy and our essentially puritanical reticence, a reticence likely at the root of our outward national mania for sexual conquest. We have been forced to communicate with one another about sex, not just with regard to the present, but about sexual decisions made as much as a decade ago. Every bit as important as the threatened unseating of a condom is the common impulse in this day and age to see one's life as less sexually irresponsible than it has been, to remember one's past behavior as stricter, sounder, more given to restraint and probity. Boswell's caveat, "But you must take my character from myself," can only strike us as horribly naive and wrongheaded from the perspective of post-AIDS America.

Implicit in the sort of interpersonal narrative I have suggested is a new picture of the individual and a new sense of ethical responsibility evolving outward from it. In the recent book *Situating the Self: Gender, Community and Postmodernism in Contemporary Ethics*, Seyla Benhabib argues persuasively for an ethical and political model in which the "human infant becomes a 'self,' a being capable of speech and action, only by learning to interact in a human community. . . . The identity of the self is constituted by a narrative unity, which integrates what 'I' can do, have done and will accomplish with what you expect of 'me,' interpret my acts and intentions to mean, wish for me in the future, etc."[15] Such a "participationist" community model ties individuals to one another through the harmonizing of competing narratives ("yours," "mine," juridical, economic, domestic), and in this way stands in opposition to an "integrationist" model, which seeks to reactivate a single, often reactionary, narrative. One of the key ways of accomplishing this harmonizing is to encourage "nonexclusive principles of membership" among different sociopolitical spheres; for example, in the traditional paradox of motherhood and female career aspirations, affordable child care aids in the "reduction of contradiction" (p. 78). The participationist approach is the more difficult, of course, but the only one that can preserve "the values of autonomy, pluralism, reflexivity and tolerance in modern societies" (p. 11).

Such a reformulated community model—for all of its difficulties—brings with it distinct advantages, prominent among them its more positive approach to gender and the position of women. As Benhabib notes, "The 'privacy' of the private sphere, which has always included the relations of the male head of the household to his spouse and children, has been an opaque glass rendering women and their traditional spheres of activity invisible and inaudible" (pp. 12–13). Shared-narrative community would contribute to the breakdown of rigid public/private oppositions and the gender-based modes of repression that have traditionally accompanied them.[16] And women, both more used to dealing closely with "concrete individuals, with their needs, endowments, wants and abilities, dreams as well as failures" and "in their capacities as primary caregivers," would be less likely to fall back on notions of a "generalized other" (one of the bases of political repression) and more experienced in facilitating discourse "from the standpoint of the concrete other" (p. 14).

The "community of two" that I have been presupposing thus far in this essay assumes a similar agenda on the part of both individuals: a willingness to perform relatively difficult narrative work and to scale back traditional levels of privacy in ways that protect the safety of the community as a whole, rather than one component member or gender. It is not such a radical step in generic terms, as Marilyn Chandler's recent work on autobiography and AIDS suggests: "All autobiography ultimately can be seen as a call to community, a reminder that we are in this generation, on this planet, in this human condition together and have lessons and gifts for one another."[17]

The notion of distinct sexual histories, like that of the "one-night stand," must be given up. Any "stand" will last a decade or more, in terms of effective biological possibilities. Sex *is* commitment now, it *is* relationship, of a certain visceral sort. Hence the stress throughout this essay on dialogic rather than monologic narrative construction between partners, whether they see themselves as monogamous, lifelong partners or not. Constructing a sexual record with someone will continue to mean negotiating actively and assertively with his or her invisible past. As I have tried to suggest, this necessity need not be seen bitterly, with a sense of repining, loss, repulsion. It can also be seen as an opportunity to communicate more fully and honestly, without many of the self-protective (or gender-protective) baffles previously natural-ized in Western society. It can spur us to be the sorts of couples—and, at the largest level of interaction, "participationist" citizens—we have never yet been forced to be.

Notes

1. James Boswell, *Boswell's London Journal: 1762–1763,* ed. Frederick Pottle (New York: McGraw-Hill, 1950), 113. Parenthetical page citations refer to this text until otherwise stated. The argument in the first pages of this essay—comparing the discursive and social practices surrounding syphilis and AIDS—has been made in a slightly differ-ent context by Sander L. Gilman in "AIDS and Syphilis: The Iconography of Disease," in *AIDS: Cultural Analysis, Cultural Activism,* ed. Douglas Crimp (Cambridge: MIT Press, 1987), 87–108. Gilman carefully traces the means by which representations of both epidemics have been used to isolate target groups, women in the case of syphilis and gay men in the case of AIDS.

2. Jean-François Lyotard, *The Postmodern Condition: A Report on Knowledge,* trans. G. Bennington and B. Massumi (Minneapolis: University of Minnesota Press, 1984), 15. Throughout this paragraph I summarize from this particular page of the text.

3. Janet Beavin Bavelas, Alex Black, Nicole Chovil, and Jennifer Mullett, *Equivocal Communication* (London: Sage, 1990), 177.

4. Here I should make clear my own working assumption that oral self-narrative may be seen as autobiographical, even as serial autobiography is more fruitfully viewed as a subgrouping of autobiography. Although Lejeune, for one, insists on "prose narra-tive" as the fundamental fabric of the autobiographical, it seems to me obvious that one might orally "tell" an autobiography with every element of the genre present (ex-cept, for Lejeune, the title page—but in this case certainly the verbal self-assertion of the narrator would be enough). See Philippe Lejeune, *On Autobiography,* ed. Paul John Eakin, trans. Katherine Leary (Minneapolis: University of Minnesota Press, 1989), 4. According to this logic—that there is more to be gained by applying autobiographical theory to oral self-narrative than is to be lost—I will hereafter use the larger generic term in this inclusive fashion. Page numbers for further citations to *On Autobiography* appear in text.

5. Nancy K. Miller, "Facts, Pacts, Acts," in *Profession* (New York: MLA, 1992), 10.

6. Georges Gusdorf, "Conditions and Limits of Autobiography," in *Autobiography: Essays Theoretical and Critical,* ed. James Olney (Princeton, N.J.: Princeton University Press, 1980), 45.

7. Here I am thinking of a number of canonical autobiographies, among them *The Education of Henry Adams,* sent out to numerous friends in manuscript, and the *Auto-biography of Benjamin Franklin,* in which Franklin insists that the work has been essen-tially commissioned by a group of friends for the use of their sons. In this way, the author conveys the impression that he or she is at least theoretically subject to the cor-rectional impulses of the surrounding community.

8. Elizabeth A. Meese, "The Languages of Oral Testimony and Women's Litera-ture," in *Women's Personal Narratives: Essays in Criticism and Pedagogy,* ed. Leonore Hoffman and Margo Culley (New York: MLA, 1985), 24.

9. The relationship here is similar to that between ghostwriter and celebrity auto-biographer. *Lady Sings the Blues,* for instance, owes almost as much to William Dufty's sharp prose and artful structuring as it does to Billie Holiday's tragic life—a state of af-

fairs signaled by Dufty's billing on the book's cover. In the case of ghostwriting, we think in terms of professional competence meeting raw material; the sexual self-record, however, is a collaboration between equal parties exhibiting ordinary skills, and in this way it should be seen as fundamentally different from other "amenuensis-aided" autobiographies (such as the *Book of Margery Kempe*).

10. Numerous studies have shown that the interview continues to be the first line of defense, and often the only line: "Interviews with heterosexual college students revealed that the 'most popular prophylactic' was the selection of a noninfected partner." See Sandra Metts and Mary Anne Fitzpatrick, "Thinking about Safer Sex: The Risky Business of 'Know Your Partner' Advice," in *AIDS: A Communication Perspective,* ed. Timothy Edgar (Hillsdale, N.J.: Lawrence Erlbaum, 1992), 1.

11. It is interesting to note that despite consulting the libraries of information available at Planned Parenthood, Family Planning, and the University of California, Irvine, including the campus Women's Resource Center and Health Education Center, I was unable to find one instructional manual (or even a chapter in a more general instructional manual) on exchanging personal histories. Even *The New Our Bodies, Ourselves* (New York: Simon & Schuster, 1992) proved disappointing in this regard.

12. Metts and Fitzpatrick, "Thinking about Safer Sex," 8.

13. The idea that couples often split on the safe-sex issue and oppose one another in subtle ways is not a new one to communication theorists concerned with the AIDS issue. Kymber N. Williams, for one, has traced "compliance-resistance" as it applies to the practice of "safe-sex" condom usage in "Interpersonal Communication between Partners: Addressing the Issues of Safe Sex Practices," paper presented at the annual meeting of the Eastern Communication Association, Philadelphia, 19–22 April 1990. Williams discusses power scenarios and the best way to model avoidance of such conflicts. Her communication theories take into account the fact that interpersonal communication requires a complex set of usable strategies, and thus a set of dialogue models, as opposed to a single-message, "magic bullet" theory of communication. This emphasis on complex dialogic models applies equally well to the negotiation of the "sexual history."

14. Bavelas et al., *Equivocal Communication,* 177.

15. Seyla Benhabib, *Situating the Self: Gender, Community and Postmodernism in Contemporary Ethics* (Cambridge: Polity, 1992), 5. Page numbers for further references to this text appear in the text in parentheses. The contrast to the Althusserian model should be apparent: whereas Althusser stresses a political hegemony (or ideological state apparatus) sustained by human language, among other material rituals, Benhabib sees language as part of a given community identity, an essentially constructive rather than repressive agency. Particularly relevant for my purpose is the way in which Benhabib's "narrative unity" asserts control over "what 'I' have done," that is, over referential experience. In this way, "history" becomes more openly community inscribed, deterring single groups or individuals from attempting to control the process. For more information concerning the intersections of AIDS public policy, the individual, and the community, I would also suggest the collection edited by Frederic G. Reamer titled *AIDS and Ethics* (New York: Columbia University Press, 1991).

16. In my view of Benhabib's model, "private" is a means of asserting power distinctions, as in "private" property, or the privacy of a home. Whereas certain forms of privacy would remain intact, other realms would be "publicized" and open to shared community inscription. Benhabib's notion of "participationist communitarianism" parallels a number of other similar concepts in poststructuralist thought, such as the "unsutured [political] identity" proposed by Ernesto Laclau and Chantal Mouffe in *Hegemony and*

Socialist Practice: Toward a Radical Democratic Politics (London: Verso, 1985), 166. Laclau and Mouffe work to theorize a new "political imaginary," in which a plurality of such malleable identities can effectively combat a hegemony bent on suppressing them, determining their political reality for them (p. 152). In each of these cases something of a utopian nature persists; it is difficult to imagine truly discordant ideologies being harmonized merely through the dialogue/coalition models that each suggests.

17. Marilyn Chandler, "Voices from the Front: AIDS in Autobiography," *a/b: Auto/Biography Studies* 6 (Spring 1991): 63.

9 / Survivor Discourse: Transgression or Recuperation?

Linda Martín Alcoff and Laura Gray-Rosendale

Michel Foucault argues that speech is not a medium or tool through which power struggles occur, but is itself an important site and object of conflict.[1] He also claims that bringing things into the realm of discourse, as the confessional structures of the church brought bodily pleasures into discourse and thus "created" sexuality, is not always or even generally a progressive or liberatory strategy; indeed, it can contribute to our own subordination.

These claims are at odds with each other, or at least point in different directions. The first suggests that movements of social change should focus on the arena of speech as a central locus of power. The act of speaking out in and of itself transforms power relations and subjectivities, or the very way in which we experience and define ourselves. But the second claim warns that bringing things into the realm of discourse works also to inscribe them into hegemonic structures and to produce docile, self-monitoring bodies who willingly submit themselves to (and thus help to create and legitimate) the authority of experts. In particular, discourses about sex, Foucault warns, are far from liberatory. These discourses developed from a punitive structure within Catholicism (the confession of sins for penance and absolution) into an evaluative structure within psychotherapy (the confession of trauma for diagnosis and treatment). In both cases the speaker discloses her innermost experiences to an expert mediator who then reinterprets those experiences back to her using the dominant discourse's codes of "normality."[2] In this way the speaker is inscribed into dominant structures of subjectivity: her interior life is made to conform to prevailing dogmas. Thus, Foucault's description of the confessional depicts it as an effective mechanism for enhancing the power of its administering experts, subsuming subjectivities under an increasingly hegemonic discourse, and diminishing the possibilities for transgression or intervention by individuals within its domain.

It is within the contradictory space of these two claims—speech as an important object of conflict and disclosures as increasing domination—that we would like to initiate a discussion of the discourse of those who have survived rape, incest, and sexual assault. This discourse is relatively new, yet now in the United States it is accessible every day on television talk shows, on talk radio, and in popular books and magazine articles. What is the political effect of this speech? What are its effects on the construction of women's subjectivities? Is this proliferation and dissemination of survivor discourse having a subversive effect on patriarchal violence? Or is it being co-opted, taken up and used but in a manner that diminishes its subversive impact? Our motivation to reflect on these issues emerges from our need to reflect on our own practices. We are two women who share three traits: we are survivors, we have been active in the movement of survivors for justice and empowerment, and we also work within (and sometimes against) postmodernist theories. We have also been affected by the distancing and dissonance institutions enforce between (what gets thought of as) "theory" and "personal life," which splits the individual along parallel paths that can never meet. This essay is an attempt to rethink and repair this dissonance and to begin weaving together these paths—and their commitments, interests, and experiences.

The principal tactic adopted by the survivors' movement has been to encourage and make possible survivors' disclosures of our traumas, whether in relatively private or in public contexts.[3] This strategic metaphor of "breaking the silence" is virtually ubiquitous throughout the movement: survivor demonstrations are called "speak-outs," the name of the largest national network of survivors of childhood sexual abuse is VOICES, and the metaphor figures prominently in such book titles as *I Never Told Anyone, Voices in the Night, Speaking Out, Fighting Back,* and *No More Secrets.*[4] Speaking out serves to educate the society at large about the dimensions of sexual violence and misogyny; to reposition the problem from the individual psyche to the social sphere, where it rightfully belongs; and to empower victims to act constructively on our own behalf and thus make the transition from passive victim to active survivor.[5] As one book on the subject of incest puts it, "We believe that there is not a taboo against incest, merely against speaking about it. And the reason for this taboo, once examined, is clear: if we begin to speak of incest, we may realize its place as a training ground for female children to regard themselves as inferior objects to be used by men. . . . By beginning to speak about it, we begin to threaten its continued, unacknowledged presence."[6] Furthermore, survivors who often have been silent because they feared retaliation or increased humiliation, and who have been carrying around the burden of a hidden agony for months, years, and even decades, report the experience of speaking out as transformative as well as a sheer relief. As Nancy Ziegenmeyer—the woman who made history by allowing the *Des Moines Register* to use her name in recounting the story of her rape—puts it, "One of the most important things I've learned is that I found my sanity when I found my voice."[7]

On the other hand, the speaking out of survivors has been sensationalized and exploited by the mass media, in fictional dramatizations as well as "journalistic" formats such as the television talk shows hosted by Geraldo Rivera and Phil Donahue.[8] The media often use the presence of survivors for shock value and to pander to a sadistic voyeurism among viewers, focusing on the details of the violations, with close-ups of survivors' anguished expressions.[9] They often eroticize the depictions of survivors and of sexual violence to titillate and expand their audiences.[10] Survivor discourse has also been used in some cases by the psychiatric establishment to construct victim- and woman-blaming explanatory theories, such as the argument that some people have a "victim personality."[11] These discursively constituted subjectivities are then made dependent upon expert advice and help. In short, survivor discourse has paradoxically appeared to have empowering effects even while it has in some cases unwittingly facilitated the recuperation of dominant discourses.

This double effect coincides in an interesting way with Foucault's disparate claims about speech. Foucault suggests that confessional speech is not liberatory but a powerful instrument of domination. Yet he has demonstrated (along with others)[12] that speech is an important site of struggle in which domination and resistance are played out. For this reason, Foucault's analyses offer a useful frame for our considerations of survivor discourse; they help us to reflect on and to evaluate the dynamics of speaking out as a political tactic. Foucault will not, however, be the focus of this essay, nor will his accounts sit in judgment over our discussion. Rather, we will set ourselves up as the "experts": fallible, partial, and momentary, but capable of judgment nonetheless without outside expert mediation. We do not want simply to assume a traditional expert role for ourselves, but instead to reconfigure the practices and meanings of expertise, toward legitimating survivor discourse.[13]

Within a general account of speech and discourse we will explore the transgressive character of survivors' speech. Then we will discuss Foucault's account of how the confessional mode of speech participates in the construction of domination. Through specific examples, we will subsequently consider the multiple and subtle mechanisms by which dominant discourses have co-opted our collective speech and whether this tendency toward co-optation can be effectively resisted. One of our central concerns will be how the tendency of the confessional structure to disempower the confessor can be overcome. Finally, we will offer some constructive and reconstructive suggestions concerning the use of speaking out as a political tactic.

Speech and Discourse

According to Foucault, "Speech is no mere verbalization of conflicts and systems of domination. . . . it is the very object of man's conflicts."[14] Speech is the site of political conflict because speech itself is that over which there is struggle. Philosophers have often relegated themselves to an analysis of the content of speech, distilling the lived reality of speech into a set of propositions that could be analyzed through logical and empirical procedures.[15] More recently, however, many philosophers (on both sides of the analytic/continental divide) have pointed out that there are other features of speech that deserve more than sociological or stylistic analysis. Speech is an event involving an arrangement of speakers and hearers; it is an act in which relations get constituted and experience and subjectivities are mediated.[16] These facts bear on the propositional content of speech, but they also suggest that an analysis of propositional content alone can provide only an inadequate account of the full meaning of any speech act. In order to assess the diverse variables that are involved in any particular

202 / *Linda Martín Alcoff and Laura Gray-Rosendale*

discursive situation we must avoid reducing speech to a collection of propositions and recognize it as a temporally and spatially specific event.

In any given discursive event there will be a normative arrangement in which some participants are designated speakers and others are designated hearers. In many speaking situations some participants are accorded the authoritative status of interpreters and others are constructed as "naive transmitters of raw experience." Such situations reveal clearly that speech not only contains sense and reference but sets up roles for participants and determines relationships between these roles. Consider the arrangements of speaking in a classroom, in a courtroom, in a psychiatrist's office, or in a child's bedroom. Moreover, the *roles* particular participants are assigned to play affect our internal experience of ourselves as well as our construction of what it means to be a self. What happens to your speech and sense of self as you move from the role of professor in a classroom to the role of daughter or son when visiting your parents should not be construed as superficial to your "true" self that lies submerged beneath the influence of such changes. Your true self simply is that changing self. This is part of what it means to say that the structures of speech acts mediate our subjectivity and experiences.

The arrangements of speaking will affect the subjectivity and experience of survivors in both political and metaphysical ways. Our power relationships to those with whom we are speaking and our sense and knowledge of ourselves and of our experiences will both be changed by the structural arrangements of the discursive event.

Foucault introduces the concept of discourse as distinct from speech or a collection of speech acts. The term *discourse* for Foucault denotes a particular configuration of possibilities for speech acts. Through rules of exclusion and classificatory divisions that operate as unconscious background assumptions, a discourse can be said to set out not what is true and what is false but what can have a truth value at all—in other words, what is statable. Discourses structure what it is possible to say through systems of exclusion such as the prohibition of certain words, the division of mad and sane speech, and the (historically contingent) disjunction between true and false. In any given context there may exist more than one discourse, although discourses will exist in hierarchical relations with one another.

Foucault's account of discourses refuses to attribute their ultimate

features to the conscious intentions of speakers. The structural regu-
larities of a given discourse should be understood in relationship to the
interchange between discursive elements, not by reference to a level of
manipulation and intentionality conceptualized as existing somewhere
"behind" the discourse. Just as conversations have a dynamic all their
own that can seem to carry speakers along, so discursive events—
whether written or spoken—are guided, constrained, and organized
by rules "never formulated in their own right."[17]

This analysis can usefully be applied to survivor speech.[18] The
speech of survivors involving reports of their assaults has been excluded speech, constrained by rules more often implicit than explicit
but nonetheless powerful. At various times and in different locations it
has been absolutely prohibited, categorized as mad or untrue, or rendered inconceivable: presuming objects (such as a rapist father) that
were not statable and therefore could not exist within the dominant
discourses. The speech of incest survivors has been especially restricted
on the grounds that it is too disgusting and disturbing to the listeners'
constructed sensibilities, which often continue to receive deferential
preference. Incest survivors have also been construed as mad: "hysterical" women who are unable to distinguish reality from their own
imaginations. Truddi Chase recounts how her father kept her silent by
telling her, "No one is ever going to believe a word that you say, so my
best advice to you is don't say anything."[19] Dominant discourses have
assisted such silencing strategies through formation rules that invali-
date "rapist father" or "rapist boyfriend" as an object of discussion or
analysis; one's boyfriend or father could not simultaneously be one's
rapist.

A variety of discursive strategies have operated to preempt or to dismiss the speech of women and children generally and survivors in particular.[20] Within the arena of legal discourse, much of survivor speech
continues to be excluded in most states because husbands cannot be
charged with rape and because children are generally considered incapable of giving credible testimony.[21] Women who are accusing boyfriends, women with histories involving any criminal or drug-related
activity, and women who wait too long to report (so that examinations for physical evidence cannot be performed) are usually excluded
from speaking in courtrooms. Within more informal discursive arenas,
women and children historically have been prohibited from speaking
in any public place; this is now changing for women, but not for chil-

dren. Homophobia operates to intimidate male survivors from speaking out, although as one authority on the topic puts it, "A child molester is neither heterosexual nor homosexual. He is a *child* molester."[22] The ideology of machismo also shames male survivors to such an extent that they are less likely than females to tell anyone. For survivors generally, incest accounts and reports of acquaintance rape have had less credibility than accounts of stranger rape. But even reports of stranger rape have been discounted unless the survivors looked and acted in certain ways. Older women and women who are not conventionally attractive often have a harder time getting acceptance for their accounts. Then again, women who are considered "too sexy" and women who are prostitutes are either not believed about rape or held responsible for it. Women from oppressed races who have been raped by white men are much less likely to be believed than white women reporting rapes by men of oppressed races. Lesbian survivors may be believed, but their rapes are more often discounted as less important (and may be seen as therapeutic!). Survivors of multiple incidents of sexual violence are not believed. Survivors of especially heinous ritualized sexual abuse are not believed.[23] The pattern that emerges from these disparate responses is that if survivor speech is not silenced before it is uttered, it is categorized within the mad, the untrue, or the incredible.

Foucault's concept of discourse helps to explain why feminist renaming of sexual violence has incurred so much resistance from the dominant discourses. Given that each discourse has what Foucault calls its own "positivity" that sets rules for the formation of objects and concepts, new and anomalous objects and concepts will implicitly challenge existing positivities. Discourses must be understood holistically as interconnecting elements. In Foucault's view, the rules for formation of concepts and objects do not exist prior to or apart from the system of statements but emerge from the configurations of the speech acts and their interrelations.[24] Given this, a change in statements alone or the emergence of new statements that do not cohere with the whole will have a disruptive effect on discursive formation rules.[25]

Survivor speech involves multiple such effects. It is transgressive first of all in simply challenging conventional speaking arrangements, arrangements in which women and children are not authoritative, where they are often denied the space to speak or be heard, and where their ability to interpret men's speech and to speak against men—to contradict or accuse men—has been severely restricted to a few very specific types of cases (for example, in U.S. dominant culture, a white woman may speak against, may even be encouraged to speak against, an African American man or a Latino). The case of Anita Hill demonstrates this transgressive quality of survivor speech. Despite all of Hill's extensive personal and professional credentials, her sexual harassment allegations against Clarence Thomas in the fall of 1991 elicited fantastic hypotheses about her psychological and emotional motivations from U.S. senators and members of the press and were not allowed to thwart his nomination to the U.S. Supreme Court.

Survivor speech is also transgressive to the extent that it presumes objects antithetical to the dominant discourse. Given that the term *husband* has historically been defined as the man to whom a woman has given unconditional sexual access, the term *husband rapist* will necessarily transform our previous understandings of the terms *husband* and *rapist,* which in turn will affect how we understand *wife, woman, sexuality, heterosexuality,* and even *man.* The formation rules that determine the generation of statements and that tell speakers how and in what circumstances they can meaningfully form and utter specific statements about sexual violence will also be affected. The simple use of the term *husband rapist* will therefore have the effect of calling into question rules of the dominant discourse for forming statements about whether a rape has occurred and how to distinguish rape from sex.

To the extent that survivor speech acts cannot be subsumed within a given discourse, they will be disruptive of its positivity and at least point to the possibility of a different set of formation rules. The tendency, however, will always be for the dominant discourse to silence such speech or, failing this, to channel it into nonthreatening outlets. Silencing works by physically denying certain individuals a speaking role—for example, through institutionalization, denial of access to listeners or readers, or the controlled administration of drugs. But dominant discourses can recuperate their hegemonic position even when disruptive speech is not silenced by subsuming it within the framework of the discourse in such a way that it is disempowered and no longer disruptive. Strategies of recuperation include categorizing survivor speech as mad, as evidence of women's or children's hysterical or mendacious tendencies, or even as testimony to women's essential nature as helpless victims in need of patriarchal protection. The feminist movement has helped to reduce the effectiveness of silencing techniques by creating forums where survivors can speak—in magazines, newsletters, journals, support groups, and demonstrations. As a result, the dominant discourse has shifted its emphasis from strategies of silencing to the development of strategies of recuperation.

Our conclusions at this point must remain cautious. Given the structured nature of discourses, survivor speech has great transgressive potential to disrupt the maintenance and reproduction of dominant discourses as well as to curtail their sphere of influence. Dominant discourses can also, however, subsume survivor speech in such a way as to disempower it and diminish its disruptive potential. These discourses should not be conceptualized as static, unchanging, or monolithic entities but as fluid, flexible, and capable of transforming to accommodate survivors' speech while not significantly changing the underlying systems of dominance. Certainly some have argued that this is occurring in major U.S. media, where previously excluded survivor speech is now included in ways that do not seriously threaten patriarchy.[26] We will consider specific examples of recuperation to determine whether and how the disruptive potential of speaking out can be actualized. First, however, we will look at the effects of a very specific discursive arrangement, the one that most often frames survivor speech: the confessional.

The Confessional

According to Foucault, the confessional structure achieved a central role in the civil and religious practices of Western societies from the time of the codification of the sacrament of penance by the Lateran Council in 1215.[27] The confessional constituted an imperative to speak those acts that contravened the law, God, or societal norms. In speaking these acts, the agents of the actions would ostensibly be transformed. The confessional would realign the speaker's desires from the illegitimate to the legitimate, and thus change the speaker's very subjectivity from bad to good, from outside law and truth to inside. In this way, the confessional became "one of the main rituals relied on for the production of truth."[28]

The relationship between the expert mediator, or the person to whom one confessed, and the confessor was one of domination and submission. The expert had the power to demand that the confession be made and to decide what was to follow it, thereby constituting a "discourse of truth based on its decipherment."[29] The confessor's status, identity, and value were all determined by the expert mediator through the process of interpreting and evaluating the confessor's discourse. Thus the confessor was by definition dependent on the expert's interpretation of the real truth of her actions, experiences, and thoughts. Much later, confession proliferated beyond the church principally into the domains of psychiatry and criminal psychology, and thus these spheres became organized partially by and through relations of discursive subordination.[30]

Given Foucault's analysis, although confessional modes of discourse may appear to grant survivors an empowering "permission to speak," they give the expert mediator the power to determine the legitimacy of survivor discourse. It is the expert rather than the survivor who will determine under what conditions the survivor speaks and whether the survivor's speech is true or acceptable within the dominant discourse's codes of normality. The confessional discursive structure produces an "institutional incitement to speak,"[31] or an imperative to speak, based on the presumption (encoded in Christian church dogma through the pastoral and the penance) that the "sinner" has something to "confess."[32] The imperative to speak comes in the form of a command or prescription from a dominant figure—priest, psychiatrist, or judge (usually a dominant male)—to a subordinate figure—sinner, "neurotic," "pervert," or criminal (subordinate male, or woman or child).

At the same time that speech is incited, a "policing of statements" occurs whereby the expert sifts through the raw data of the confessor's speech for signs of sin or pathology.[33] The expert will interpret the speech according to dominant cultural codes and on the basis of his interpretation "punish, give console, or reconcile" and determine whether the confessor can have absolution.[34] The confessional is always implicated in (both constituting of and constituted by) an unequal, nonreciprocal relation of power. And the explicit goal of the process of confession is always the normalization of the speaking subject and thus the elimination of any transgressive potential that might exist. The sexual energy of the confessor is funneled into a process that produces anxiety, confusion, guilt, and subservience to an indisputable authority.

Foucault also argues that the confessional mapped the space in which discourses on truth and sexuality might be joined, noting its genealogy from a religious ritual designed primarily around the organization of sexual practices and imbued with belief in intrinsic connections among the body, sin, and truth. The confessional's demand for a transformation of "sex into discourse" resulted in the "dissemination . . . of heterogeneous sexualities" aligned with heterogeneous subjectivities.[35] Through the confessional the parameters of normal and/or moral sexual functioning could be "discovered" or constituted and the forbidden could be articulated.[36] From the early Christian dogma of the thirteenth century through to a more contemporary manifestation of the confessional in Freud's work, we find the argument that an individual's sexual history represents the "deep truth" about her moral and/or psychological character.

Moreover, in Foucault's view, the production of sex as a discourse of truth was always predicated on desire and pleasure. The confessor's disclosure was always pleasurable to hear because it paralleled the "entire painstaking review of the sexual act in its very unfolding."[37] The sexual act itself, understood as requiring a full disclosure of mind and body, was repeated in the confessional process that demanded everything be told, be laid bare. And the pleasure produced by the confession was enhanced by the very difficulty of extracting the disclosure. This economy of pleasure therefore had an interest in constructing the confession as a difficult and arduous extraction so as to invest it with more meaning and power and to intensify its pleasure. This required that the confession occur in a privatized space, intended to reinforce the perceived link between sexuality and the "deep, hidden truth" of subjectivity, revealed by the expert mediator as an "individual secret." Given a situation in which sexuality is said to represent the core truth of one's identity as a person but can be revealed only in a private space by a designated interpreter, the power of the expert over the confessor can indeed become enormous.

In the past decade this private confessional space has gone public. First-person accounts of sexual assaults have made headlines and been featured prominently on TV talk shows, reaching an audience of millions. The very act of speaking out has become used as performance and spectacle. The growth of this phenomenon raises questions: Has it simply replayed confessional modes that recuperate dominant patriarchal discourses without subversive effect, or has it been able to create new spaces within these discourses and to begin to develop an autonomous counterdiscourse, one capable of empowering survivors? Given that power operates not simply or primarily through exclusion and repression but through the very production and proliferation of discourses, should we not be more than a little wary of contributing to the recent proliferation of survivor discourse? Answering these questions will involve paying close attention to the structural features of the discursive arrangements, as we have tried to show in the preceding two sections.

Scenes from Television

In fall of 1990, ABC's *The Home Show* invited two student activists from our university to discuss rape on college campuses. Our university was chosen because it had recently gained national notoriety for the high number of rapes reported by its students and because one of the recent rapes occurred on the chancellor's lawn. The program's producers contacted a student group founded for the express purpose of discussing and preventing such rapes and asked specifically for survivors who would appear on the show. They also said that they would prefer recent survivors and survivors of rapes that occurred on the campus itself. The students in the group discussed this, and one survivor volunteered to do the show, along with another member of the group.

When the segment began, the camera zoomed in for a close-up on Tracy (the survivor) as Gary Collins and Dana Fleming, the cohosts of the show, asked her to tell the audience "what happened." Tracy proceeded to outline her acquaintance rape, focusing on the normality of the situation prior to the assault. Her goal was to say something useful for other women who may be struggling with the aftermath of an assault and feeling as uncertain about what to do as she had felt.[38] Fleming, however, wanted to focus on the violent act itself; she asked Tracy to explain to the audience whether she had done "anything that in any way could have provoked him [the rapist]." Fleming prefaced her question by saying, "You have to understand that we are on your side but I think the question has to be asked," implying that the audience may not comprehend Tracy's behavior. This, of course, made assumptions about the audience, positioning it as unfriendly or skeptical, perhaps displacing Fleming's own reaction onto the audience.

Thus it was not Collins but his female cohost who put Tracy in the position of having to defend herself. Tracy tried bravely to respond by shifting to the issue of why the assumption is usually made that the woman is responsible. Lindy Crescitelli, the other student on the show, also made an effort to shift the focus from women's actions to men's responsibility for rape, but neither his nor Tracy's points were taken up for discussion. Collins asked instead what parents could do in preparing their daughters for college to reduce the risk of rape. An "expert on rape prevention counseling" then proceeded to discuss the ways in which women in our society have difficulty in communicating their sexual desires and how sex can be more pleasurable for men when it is done with a willing partner.

What did this show do? It produced an emotional moment of a survivor's self-disclosure to get audience attention, it focused a discussion of rape on women's behavior, and it created or re-created a scenario in which older women are skeptical and judgmental of younger women and older men take the role of paternalistic protectors. Tracy became an object of analysis and evaluation for experts and media-appointed representatives of the masses (Collins and Fleming) to discuss. The camera insistently cut to Tracy's face even when others were speaking, as if to display the "example" being discussed. The students' attempt to focus on the institutional and cultural ways in which rape is excused or is blamed on the victim was effectively circumvented when the show's hosts put Tracy in the position of having to defend her own actions and when they directed the discussion to the ways in which women should change their behavior to prevent rape and how their (paternalistic) parents could educate them toward this end. The contribution of the "expert" was to reiterate the hosts' focus on women's behavior and parental protection. When she was asked to say something about men, she discussed the enhancement of their sexual pleasure. The entire show was characterized by an objectification of survivors, a reaction to survivor accounts that mixed pity and skepticism, and a deflection away from men's responsibility for rape. And the repeated invocation of the idea that "our daughters" leave "a protected environment" when they leave home for college reinforced the myth that rapes most often happen away from home, when the reverse is the case. The notion that the "home" signals safety and protection is a claim that is not only wrong but complicitous with sexual violence.[39]

Numerous episodes of *The Phil Donahue Show, Geraldo,* and *Sally Jessy Raphael*—and, to a lesser extent, *The Oprah Winfrey Show*—have produced similar effects. These shows display the emotions of survivors for public consumption and unfailingly mediate the survivors' discourse through expert analysis and interpretation. Usually the format follows this pattern: at the start of the show survivors are shown in close-up, "telling their stories."[40] The host of the show makes sure to ask questions that are sufficiently probing to get the survivors to cry on-screen (this can be accomplished by discovering their most vulnerable issues in a preshow interview and then keying in on those when cameras are rolling).[41] After a few minutes of this, the host usually says "wow" or something comparable and breaks to a commercial. The show resumes with a period of audience questions; then (or sometimes beforehand) the inevitable expert shows up, almost invariably a white man or woman with a middle-class and professional appearance, who, with a sympathetic but dispassionate air, explains to the audience the nature, symptoms, and possible therapies for such crimes of violence. The survivors are reduced to victims, represented as pathetic objects who can only recount their experiences as if these are transparent, and who offer pitiable instantiations of the universal truths the experts reveal. These shows especially like to get victims with "disorders," such as multiple personalities, because this can expand opportunities for sensationalism and widen the emotional distance between the audience and the survivors, making it easier to objectify them as victims. Geraldo Rivera consistently heightens the drama of his shows by including participants who contradict the stories of the survivors. His shows are often organized around survivors, rather than perpetrators, having to explain and defend themselves.[42]

In a culture where audience sensations are dulled by graphic depictions of violence (both real and fictional) on television and in which mass sensibilities have atrophied under conditions of late capitalism, these shows provide a moment in which real, raw, and intense feelings can be observed, and in some cases remembered. This emotional "shock value" is their use value as a media commodity. It appears, however, that the goal of producing disturbing feelings for the audience must be tempered with a dose of moderation: too few feelings will make for a boring show, but too many may frighten and alienate viewers and induce them to change the channel. The mediation of a coolly disposed expert can serve as a mechanism for displacing identification with the victims to reduce the emotional power of the survivor presence.

The preceding account may appear to be an excessively pessimistic reading of these programs; certainly it is a one-sided analysis. The media moguls, producers, and show hosts do not have absolute control over audience reactions to their products. In a discursive regime in which survivor stories constitute excluded speech, hearing these stories can be very powerful for survivors in the audience. This has at least the potential to help these survivors name and validate their experience and to bring the trauma out of the privacy of their psyches and into the public arena. And the visual image of the survivor, although it can be used to objectify, has the potential to explode stereotypes about who survivors are as well as to counter an invisibility that in the long run serves only to hide the true nature of patriarchy, which condones and promotes sexual violence.

But recuperation occurs when the public arena does not take up the survivor's discourse except as a way to experience a sensational moment of confession. And the transgressive potential of the discourse is lost when the victim is reified as pure object, in need of expert interpretation, psychiatric help, and audience sympathy. The most transgressive moments have occurred on TV talk shows when the splits between victim and audience and between recorder of experience and interpreter of experience are obstructed. This has occurred not surprisingly on *The Oprah Winfrey Show* when Winfrey has referred to her own history as a survivor and thus subverted her ability to be an objective and dispassionate observer of the victims on the stage. Because of her own identification with survivors, Winfrey rarely allows them to be put in the position of having to defend the truth of their stories or their own actions. And when the focus is on child sexual abuse, Winfrey does not always defer to experts but presents herself as a survivor/expert, still working through and theorizing her own experience.

One particularly transgressive segment of *The Oprah Winfrey Show* stands out: nearly (or possibly all) the entire audience of about two hundred women was made up of survivors, and a wide-ranging "horizontal" group discussion took place, with little deferral to the designated expert.[43] This show had considerable power to thwart the efforts to contain and recuperate the disruptive potential of survivor discourse precisely because it could not be contained or segregated within a separate, less threatening realm: there was too much of it for any one expert to handle effectively, and the victim-expert split could not be maintained. Without a segregated discursive arrangement, victims of sexual violence could speak as experts on sexual violence. For at least one brief moment on television, survivors were the subjects of their own lives.

Dangers of the Confessional

Survivor discourse and the tactic of speaking out may often involve a confessional mode of speech including personal disclosure, autobiographical narrative, and the expression of feelings and emotions. This mode of speech, as we have discussed, is fraught with dangers, which we shall summarize here.

As in the television examples above, one of the dangers of the confessional discourse structure is that the survivor speech becomes a media commodity that has a use value based on its sensationalism and drama and that circulates within the relations of media competition to boost ratings and wake up viewers. In this way, a goal or effect probably not intended by the survivors is made the organizing principle for how the show gets arranged, produced, and edited. The results of this process may well have no positive effect on the production/reproduction of practices of sexual violence.[44]

Another drawback of the confessional mode is that it often focuses attention on the victim and her psychological state and deflects it from the perpetrator. Although a rule of exclusion is broken when a survivor names and describes her experience, the move from privatization to a public or social arena does not occur if the survivor's speech gets constructed as a transmission of her "inner" feelings and emotions, which are discussed separately from their relationship to the perpetrator's actions and the society's rules of discourse. The discussion of the survivor's "inner" self and feelings replaces rather than leads to a discussion of links to the "exterior" and ways to transform it.

Given its historical trajectory through religious ritual to institutional therapy, the confessional mode can also invite or appear to necessitate the invocation of a dispassionate mediator. If there is someone playing the role of the confessor, historical precedence and the logic of the confessional's discursive structure dictates the need for someone to be confessed to—someone who has the role of the absolver, interpreter, and/or judge. This strips the survivor of her authority and agency. Such an effect can be mitigated if the one being confessed to is also a survivor, for example, within a survivors' support group. Disclosing to another survivor works to undermine the assumption that a mediator must be neutral and objective and must derive her authority not from "personal experience" but from "abstract knowledge."

The confessional mode also reproduces the notion of "raw experience" and sets up binary structures between experience and theory, feelings and knowledge, subjective and objective, and mind and body. These binaries are instantiated in the discursive arrangement of the confessional, which splits speaking roles on the basis of these divisions. Such a split is not only possible but considered necessary for the development of a credible theory because of the internal structure of the binary, which subordinates one term to the other. The first part of the binary—experience, feelings, emotional pain—provides the raw data needed to produce theory and knowledge. But these "subjective" entities will be obstacles to the production of theory unless they are made sharply subordinate to and are contained and controlled by the theory, knowledge, and "objective" assessments of the second half of the binary structure. The confessional constructs a notion of theory as necessarily other than, split from, and dominant over experience. And it creates a situation in which the survivor—because of her experience and feelings on the issue—is paradoxically the person least capable of serving as the authority or expert. The survivor's views on sexual violence often enjoy less credence than anyone else's.[45] The female witnesses who testified before the U.S. Senate on behalf of Anita Hill were each asked before giving testimony whether they had been victims of sexual harassment. If they had been, they would have been disqualified as incapable of providing "objective" and therefore credible testimony.[46]

There is one final danger survivors face in confessional discourse. When breaking the silence is taken up as the necessary route to recovery or as a privileged political tactic, it becomes a coercive imperative on survivors to confess, to recount our assaults, to give details, and even to do so publicly. Our refusal to comply might then be read as weakness of will or as reenacted victimization. But it may be that survival itself sometimes necessitates a refusal to recount or even a refusal to disclose and deal with the assault or abuse, given the emotional, financial, and physical difficulties that such disclosures can create. Many survivors are put in risk of physical retaliation by disclosure and may also face difficulties on their jobs, negative repercussions for their supportive relationships or the welfare of their children, and debilitating emotional trauma. Disclosures can elicit horrifying flashbacks, insomnia, eating disorders, depression, back pain, suicidal thoughts, and other assorted problems, which the survivor often has to hide from coworkers and cope with alone. Therapy is extremely expensive, and few survivors can easily afford all of the therapeutic assistance they might need to work through these problems. The coercive stance that one must tell, must join a support group, must go into therapy, is justly deserving of the critique Foucault offers of the way in which the demand to speak involves dominating power and an imperialist theoretical structure. This is, of course, doubly the case when it is an expert, therapist, or "well-meaning" outsider who demands of the survivor that she speak.

Although we want to stress here the tremendous difficulties survivors face, it is equally important to avoid viewing survivors as dysfunctional or as emotionally defective, which essentializes and reifies survivors. All survivors face debilitating trauma, and there is no "cure" that can take the pain away or remove all the effects of sexual violence, but we are not objects with attributes ("syndromes" or "disorders"). We are fluid, constantly changing beings who can achieve great clarity and emotional insight even from within the depths of pain.

Our summary of these dangers is not meant as an argument that speaking about one's experiences on TV or in any public arena will inevitably be recuperative rather than transgressive. The nature of the discursive landscape involves enough indeterminacy and instability to resist absolute predictability or monodimensional effects. Nevertheless, in evaluating the likely political effects of various speaking events, the structural arrangements of the speakers and hearers will be key determinants, and the dangers listed above are significant even if not inevitable. In our final section we want to turn to a more constructive question: How can we maximize the transgressive potential of survivor discourse in such a way that the autonomy and empowerment of the survivor who is speaking as well as of survivors elsewhere will be enhanced rather than undermined?

Subversive Speaking

Clearly, a primary disabling factor in the confessional structure is the role of the expert mediator. To alter the power relations between the discursive participants, we need to reconfigure or eliminate this role. This requires that the bifurcation between experience and analysis embodied in the confessional's structure be abolished. We need to transform arrangements of speaking to create spaces where survivors are

authorized to be both witnesses and experts, both reporters of experience and theorists of experience. Such transformations will alter existing subjectivities as well as structures of domination and relations of
power. In such a scenario, survivors might, in bell hooks's words, "use
confession and memory as tools of intervention" rather than as instruments for recuperation.[47] In her essay "Feminist Politicization: A
Comment," hooks suggests how the production of personal narratives
can effect political transformations instead of increasing the privatization and individualization of political phenomena.[48] In part, this discussion connects to the ongoing debate among feminists about the political effects of consciousness-raising (CR) groups. Critics of CR have
argued that it moves politics into the realm of the personal and the individual and emphasizes individual transformation at the expense of
struggle in larger social spaces.[49] In our view, this critique correctly
perceives the recuperative strategy of the therapeutic establishment at
work in CR—which tends to promote a solution of private therapy
geared toward social functioning rather than political action geared
toward social change. But the critique errs in offering a one-sided account of CR's political effects and once again presupposing a per-
sonal/political split. Individual empowerment through therapy or CR
is itself a political action with social consequences (unless the therapy
is not designed to empower but to shut the person up, which has until
recently been the purpose of most therapies designed for women).[50]

Another, more current, critique of the production of personal narratives has been that they essentialize experience and often identity as
well. This happens when individual narratives are related as if they are
not narratives but simple reports, thus obscuring the way in which all
experience is itself discursively mediated. In hooks's view, the realm of
the personal can become politically efficacious and transformative,
and need not obscure the conditions of the production of experience, if
women do not merely "name" their experiences but also "place that
experience within a theoretical context."[51] In this case, "story-telling
becomes a process of historization. It does not remove women from
history but enables us to see ourselves as part of history."[52] If the narration of experience is not bifurcated from theory, then, as hooks suggests, the act of speaking out can become a way for women to come to
power.[53] One already existing example of this is the self-facilitated
survivor support group, in which a survivor speaks out among other
survivors and participates in a collective process of analysis and evalu-

ation of experience. Such a collective process may enhance a survivor's individual ability to act as the theorist of her own experience.

We need new ways to analyze the personal and the political as well as new ways to conceptualize these terms. Experience is not "pretheoretical," nor is theory separate or separable from experience, and both are always already political. A project of social change, therefore, does not need to "get beyond" the personal narrative or the confessional to become political but rather needs to analyze the various effects of the confessional in different contexts and struggle to create discursive spaces in which we can maximize its disruptive effects.

A nonbifurcating ontology of experience and theory requires us to relinquish the idea that in reporting our experiences we are merely reporting internal events without interpretation. To become the theorists of our own experience, we must become aware of how our subjectivity will be constituted by our discourses and aware of the danger that even in our own confessionals within autonomous spaces we can construct ourselves as reified victims or as responsible for our own victimization.

This recognition that no experience is pretheoretical does not entail a complete relativizing of experience or of the effects of sexual violence. It does mean that there are multiple (not infinite) ways to experience sexual violence, for example: as deserved or not deserved, as humiliating to the victim or as humiliating to the perpetrator, as an inevitable feature of women's lot or as a socially sanctioned but eradicable evil. And this more adequately reflects the experience most of us have had of "coming to" our anger and even our hurt only after we have adopted the political and theoretical position that we did not deserve such treatment, nor did we bring it on ourselves.

Our analysis suggests that the formulation of the primary political tactic for survivors should not be a simple incitement to speak out, as this formulation leaves unanalyzed the conditions of speaking and thus makes us too vulnerable to recuperative discursive arrangements. Before we speak, we need to look at where the incitement to speak originates, what relations of power and domination may exist between those who incite and those who are asked to speak, as well as to whom the disclosure is directed. We must also struggle to maintain autonomy over the conditions of our speaking out if we are to develop its subversive potential. An important aspect of this autonomy is the disenfranchisement of outside expert authority over our discourse, obstructing the ability of "experts" to "police our statements," to put us in a defensive posture, or to determine the focus and framework of our discourse.

We are not arguing that (nonsurvivor) experts cannot contribute to the empowerment and recovery of survivors. This contradicts our own experience and those of nearly every survivor we know. Our point is that, as we begin to break our silences, we must be wary of helping to create a public discursive arena that confers an a priori advantage on the expert's analysis and credibility over the survivor's. We may be able to use expert help in individual therapy and even sometimes in group therapy situations, but we do not need authoritative mediation of our experience for public consumption or for experiential validation. Nor will we submit our experience uncritically to the judgment of outsiders' theories: we ourselves will determine which theories have validity and usefulness, or we will construct our own.

Thus our argument here is not directed against theory or therapy per se, but against theories and therapeutic practices that position themselves as dominant over a survivor discourse conceptualized as "nontheoretical." Our intent is to redefine theory and reconceptualize its relationship to experience and then to claim it for ourselves. Both the psychiatric theories and Foucault's theories of speech and sexuality (and anyone else's, for that matter) can then be submitted to an interrogation on our terms, rather than allowed to pass judgment on us as if from a more "theoretically advanced" position.

How, then, can survivors attain autonomy over the conditions of our speaking out in a way that will unleash its disruptive potential while minimizing its adverse effects on our safety and well-being? One recent approach has been the method of anonymous accusation. In fall 1990, students at Brown University began listing the names of rapists on the walls of women's bathrooms on campus.[54] By not signing such lists and by choosing relatively secluded places in which to write, the women could minimize their own exposure to recrimination, although more than a few survivors declined to participate even in this anonymous action for fear that perpetrators would guess or surmise who had written their names. But the bathroom list represents an interesting and innovative attempt to make survivor discourse public in such a way as to minimize the dangers of speaking out for survivors yet maximize the disruptive potential of survivor outrage.

This incident created tremendous disruption: great consternation for the named perpetrators and frantic responses by administrators unable to "contain" the discourse about sexual assault on their campus. Although custodians were instructed (in some cases against their wishes) to erase the lists as soon as they appeared, the lists kept reappearing and grew from ten names to about thirty. The *Brown Alumni Monthly* reported that the university was in the midst of a "thorough examination of its policies relating to sexual assault" when the lists began to appear. In other words, an officially organized and sanctioned discursive arrangement for speaking about sexual violence on campus already existed when the students decided to create their own discursive space on the bathroom walls. Their belief that the official avenues for survivor discourse were ineffective was clearly the motivation behind the graffiti, as evidenced by what the women wrote. Here is a sample:

> [X] is a rapist.
> Report the animal.
> If you think "reporting the animal" will do any good at all, you have a lot to learn about the judiciary system.
> Let's start naming names. If we don't take care of each other, no one will.
> Who erased all the names?
> Don't let this get washed away. Fight!
> [Y] is a rapist. Nothing can get him off this campus. He's been tried, went home for a week for "psychiatric evaluation." Rich white boys can do whatever they want on this campus.
> You have erased our list, but that doesn't erase their crimes. We, the survivors, are still here.

University administrators were so incensed by their loss of discursive control that they publicly accused the list writers of libel, harassment, and "striking against the heart of the American judicial system." They also wrote to the men named on the lists offering to help them file complaints. The bathroom lists ultimately resulted, however, in an increased commitment by the university to strengthen and improve procedures for dealing with crimes of sexual violence and in the creation of two new administrative positions to deal with women's issues.

This suggests again that Foucault is correct to argue that speech itself—the very words, their discursive context, and the conditions in which they are spoken—is a critical site and object of conflict. We conclude that survivor strategy must continue to develop and explore ways in which we can gain autonomy within (not over) the conditions of our discourse. The disruptive potential of this strategy must override a concern about "bringing sex into discourse"; certainly a strategy of discursive autonomy will resist the effort to inscribe this discourse into dominant codes. The applicability of Foucault's analysis to survivor discourse thus ends here: what we need to do is not retreat, as Foucault might suggest, from bringing sexual violence into discourse, but rather to create new discursive forms and spaces in which to gain autonomy within this process. What we need is not to *confess,* but to *witness,* which Ziegenmeyer defines as "to speak out, to name the unnameable, to turn and face it down."[55] A witness is not someone who confesses, but someone who knows the truth and has the courage to tell it. In a poem titled "157 Ways to Tell My Incest Story," Emily Levy encourages us to give witness to sexual violence in ways that cannot be contained, recuperated, or ignored.[56]

Notes

We would like to offer our gratitude to the following people for their generous help with this essay: Dympna Callahan, Susan Jeffords, Tracy Lawrence, Ingeborg Majer O'Sickey, and Robyn Wiegman. This chapter is a shortened version of an article that appeared in *Signs* 18 (Winter 1993): 260–90.

1. Michel Foucault, "The Discourse on Language," in *The Archaeology of Knowledge and the Discourse on Language,* trans. A. M. Sheridan Smith (New York: Pantheon, 1972), 216.

2. Michel Foucault, *The History of Sexuality,* vol. 1, *An Introduction,* trans. Robert Hurley (New York: Pantheon, 1978), 67.

3. Ellen Bass and Louise Thornton, eds., *I Never Told Anyone: Writings by Women Survivors of Child Sexual Abuse* (New York: HarperCollins, 1991), 260.

4. VOICES can be reached at VOICES in Action, Inc., P.O. Box 148309, Chicago, IL 60614, (312) 327–1500; Bass and Thornton, *I Never Told Anyone;* Toni A. H. McNaron and Yarrow Morgan, eds., *Voices in the Night: Women Speaking about Incest* (Minneapolis: Cleis, 1982); Vera Gallagher with William F. Dodds, *Speaking Out, Fighting Back: Personal Experiences of Women Who Survived Child Sexual Abuse in the Home* (Seattle: Madrona [P.O. Box 22667, Seattle, WA 98122], 1985). The metaphor of "unsilencing" what has been made secret is also found in these titles: Anna Clark, *Women's Silence, Men's Violence: Sexual Assault in England, 1770–1845* (New York: Pandora, 1987); Diana E. H. Russell, *The Secret Trauma: Incest in the Lives of Girls and Women* (New York: Basic Books, 1986); Sandra Butler, *Conspiracy of Silence* (San Francisco: Volcano, 1985); Caren Adams and Jennifer Fay, *No More Secrets: Protecting Your Child from Sexual Assault* (San Luis Obispo: Impact, 1981); KCRR Staff and Jennifer Fay, *He Told Me Not to Tell: A Parent's Guide for Talking to Your Child about Sexual Assault* (Renton, Wash.: King County Rape Relief [305 S. 43rd, Renton, WA 98055], 1979); Linda Tschirhart Sanford, *The Silent Children: A Parent's Guide to the Prevention of Child Sexual Abuse* (New York: McGraw-Hill, 1980); Karen Johnson, *The Trouble with Secrets* (Seattle: Parenting Press, 1986); Carolyn Polese, *Promise Not to Tell* (New York: Human Sciences Press, 1985); Elly Danica, *Don't: A Woman's Word*

(Pittsburgh: Cleis, 1988); Florence Rush, *The Best Kept Secret: Sexual Abuse of Children* (New York: McGraw-Hill, 1980).

5. See the chapter "Breaking Silence," in Ellen Bass and Laura Davis, *The Courage to Heal: A Guide for Women Survivors of Child Sexual Abuse* (New York: Harper & Row, 1988), 92–103, esp. 95. More recently it has been suggested that we can even go beyond surviving; see, e.g., Christine Dinsmore, *From Surviving to Thriving: Incest, Feminism, and Recovery* (Albany: State University of New York Press, 1991).

6. McNaron and Morgan, *Voices in the Night*, 15.

7. Nancy Ziegenmeyer and Larkin Warren, *Taking Back My Life* (New York: Simon & Schuster, 1992), 218. See also Liz Kelly, *Surviving Sexual Violence* (Minneapolis: University of Minnesota Press, 1988), 13.

8. We offer support for this claim in the section below headed "Scenes from Television."

9. One of the authors of this chapter was interviewed for a local television news show about sexual violence. In a half hour of video-taping, she said three sentences with information about her own experience; the rest of the time, she offered political analysis. In the aired version of the interview, all three sentences about personal experience were used and only two other sentences of analysis made it past the editing process.

10. There is a market among pornographers for survivors; for example, *Penthouse* magazine paid Jessica Hahn—a rape survivor from a highly publicized case involving television evangelist Jim Bakker—large sums of money to pose, and has tried to entice other publicly known survivors to appear in the magazine as well.

11. Scores of "self-help" books maintain what Richard Carlson says in his title, *You Can Be Happy No Matter What* (San Rafael, Calif.: New World Library, 1992). If the source of happiness lies within, no matter what one's circumstances, there is only one person to blame for one's misery. Susan Faludi offers a useful discussion of the "masochistic personality disorder" created by the American Psychiatric Association in 1985 and included in the powerful *Diagnostic and Statistical Manual of Mental Disorders*. See her *Backlash: The Undeclared War against American Women* (New York: Crown, 1991), 356–62. The APA panel that introduced this "disorder" suggested that masochists (read: women) choose "people who 'disappoint' or 'mistreat' them" and choose to remain "in relationships in which others exploit, abuse, or take advantage." See also Phyllis Chesler, *Women and Madness* (New York: Doubleday, 1972).

12. See, e.g., Jean-François Lyotard, *The Postmodern Condition: A Report on Knowledge,* trans. G. Bennington and B. Massumi (Minneapolis: University of Minnesota Press, 1984); Jürgen Habermas, *The Theory of Communicative Action,* trans. Thomas McCarthy, 2 vols. (Boston: Beacon, 1981).

13. We realize that part of Foucault's project as well is to criticize the authority of experts; this is one of the features we find useful in his work. Our concern is with the way in which Foucault's texts are sometimes used as an authoritative source to repudiate certain kinds of voices, despite his own repudiation of that role.

14. Foucault, "The Discourse on Language," 216.

15. Michel Foucault, *The Archaeology of Knowledge* (New York: Pantheon, 1972), 231.

16. The concept of mediation comes from a Hegelian tradition that opposes the notion that experience or the self exists in a pure, uninterpreted, directly apprehensible state. For Karl Marx, labor or practical activity provides the mediator between human beings and nature, whereas for Foucault, discourses and epistemes would seem to play this role. But the critical point here is that no entity such as "human being," "nature," or "experience" can be described or apprehended prior to its mediation. See "Media-

tion" in Tom Bottomore, ed., *A Dictionary of Marxist Thought* (Cambridge: Harvard University Press, 1983), 329–30.

17. Michel Foucault, *The Order of Things* (New York: Random House, 1970), xi–xiv; see also Foucault, *The Birth of the Clinic* (New York: Random House, 1973), xvii.

18. The analysis in this essay is primarily applicable to the experiences of survivors who are female. We wish to stress that this is not because we do not recognize the existence and special difficulties of male survivors. The significant majority of sexual violence occurs between perpetrators who are male and victims who are women or children (because so many sexual assaults go unreported, all statistics are provisional, but the portion of sexual violence that fits this model ranges between 80 and 90 percent). Our focus on female victims is not based solely on numbers, however. The strategies by which survivors are silenced vary by the gender of the survivor. The violations and silencing of women and children are intrinsically connected to the system of male dominance and to ancient structures of asymmetrical discursive relationships. To some extent, children occupy the same position vis-à-vis dominant male power regardless of their gender. But there are unique differences in the relationship females have with the dominant discursive structures. For example, where a young girl may not be believed or may be called crazy when she discloses incest, a young boy is more likely to be silenced through homophobia. We regret that we do not have the space available here to explore adequately the specific silencing strategies imposed on adult male survivors, but it is likely that we would not be the best theorists for that issue in any case.

19. Truddi Chase, *When Rabbit Howls* (New York: Dutton, 1987).

20. See, e.g., Lee Madigan and Nancy Gamble, *The Second Rape: Society's Continued Betrayal of the Victim* (New York: Macmillan, 1991); Susan Brownmiller, *Against Our Will: Men, Women, and Rape* (New York: Simon & Schuster, 1975); Angela Davis, *Women, Race and Class* (New York: Vintage, 1983); Rush, *The Best Kept Secret;* Frederique Delacoste and Priscilla Alexander, *Sex Work: Writings by Women in the Sex Industry* (Pittsburgh: Cleis, 1987); Susan Estrich, *Real Rape* (Cambridge: Harvard University Press, 1987); Robin Warshaw, *I Never Called It Rape* (New York: Harper & Row, 1988).

21. Many prosecutors still routinely refuse to put forward cases that involve a child's testimony against a male adult's, unless there is "corroboration" by physical evidence or by an adult witness. And many prosecutors will defend such decisions by arguing that although they themselves believe the child, it is extremely difficult to get juries to convict solely on the basis of a child's testimony.

22. Sanford, *The Silent Children*. Most perpetrators against boys younger than twelve also assault girls; see Rush, *The Best Kept Secret*.

23. For example, Sandi Gallant, a police officer and investigator with the San Francisco Police Department, says of ritual sexual abuse cases, "The reason so few of these cases are successfully prosecuted is that the information is so unpleasant that no one wants to believe it. The investigators hear these stories and they say to themselves, 'No, this can't be true,' and so they don't write it down, they don't document it. . . . The most unfortunate thing is that the victims are so often accused of making all this up. The victims end up being the suspects, and the suspects end up being the victims." See Bass and Davis, *The Courage to Heal*, 420–21.

24. Foucault, *The Archaeology of Knowledge*, 79.

25. Liz Kelly offers an insightful discussion of the ways in which the dominant categories of sexual violence and conceptualizations of sex offenders in the literature of psychology and sociology function to minimize the acknowledged harms to victims and deflect responsibility from the perpetrator. Thus, they function in general as an attempt to

minimize the disruptive potential of survivor reports on dominant discourses and practices. See her *Surviving Sexual Violence.*

26. See, e.g., Louise Armstrong, "The Personal Is Apolitical," *Women's Review of Books,* March 1990.

27. Foucault, *The History of Sexuality,* 58.

28. Ibid.

29. Ibid, 67.

30. We do not mean to suggest that discursive subordination operates only in the spheres of psychiatry and criminal psychology, thus leaving out economic, sexual, and social subordination. Rather, discursive subordination, as we understand it, is also inseparable from, inclusive of, transformed by, and subject to these other oppressive relations.

31. Foucault, *The History of Sexuality,* 18.

32. Foucault traces the Western evolution of the confessional from early in the thirteenth century through to our present day. Although once bound exclusively to the Christian church, at present the confessional structure has been disseminated, often working outside contemporary Christian doctrines. Yet this confessional structure still produces similar discursive arrangements. Historically within the Christian tradition, Foucault states, the disclosure of sexual acts was the "privileged theme of confession"; *The Archaeology of Knowledge,* 61. In this specific ritual of discourse, both within and outside Christian dogma, the one who speaks the confession is always also the subject of that speech. It is this ritual of confession that continues to unfold "within a power relationship, for one does not confess without the presence (or the virtual presence) of a partner who is not simply an interlocutor but the authority who requires the confession, prescribes it, and appreciates it"; ibid.

33. Ibid., 18.

34. Ibid., 61–62.

35. Ibid.

36. According to Foucault, the Christian pastoral prescribed the imperative that Christians must confess all acts and thus transform their every desire into discourse; *The Archaeology of Knowledge,* 21. The confessional was the space in which those vocabularies censored elsewhere were demanded to be spoken. As Foucault elucidates, this "duty to confess" prescribed earliest by the Christian church also effectively rendered such speech "morally acceptable, and technically useful."

37. Ibid., 19.

38. Personal communication, December 1990.

39. It is complicitous because it makes it more difficult for women and children to name their fathers, brothers, uncles, and neighbors as their attackers and be believed. It also makes it more likely that, internalizing the ideology of "home," women and children will blame themselves when the romantic image is not fulfilled, rather than understanding the structural dangers inherent to a system that makes women and children vulnerable to and dependent on men.

40. There are numerous examples of this. Consider Raphael's typical opening remarks in a program that aired January 21, 1991: "Our first guests today say they never thought they would survive the hell their lives have become. Stephanie was walking through a park near her home when a man pulled a knife. He dragged her 100 yards and then viciously raped her. To make matters worse, Stephanie was three months pregnant at the time of the rape. Stephanie, take us back to that day and, fairly briefly, tell us about this."

41. Personal communication with Kristin Eaton-Pollard, May 1990, who has appeared on numerous talk shows, including *Geraldo.*

42. For example, on Rivera's November 14, 1989, show on "campus rape," one of the survivors was challenged by the vice provost for student life at her university; the program thus undermined the credibility of her disclosure and analysis by presenting the skeptical and contradictory views of an "authority," that is, someone higher up on the dominant discursive hierarchy. It also diverted the discussion from its earlier focus—on the problems of security and support procedures for survivors on college campuses—to a debate over whether a rape really occurred at all. When survivors agree to appear on such shows, they are often unaware of who the other guests will be; Nancy Ziegenmeyer relates how she felt "sandbagged" when she walked onto *Sally Jessy Raphael* because she had not been told that a guest hostile to her story had also been invited; see *Taking Back My Life*, 214.

43. This show aired April 14, 1988, on ABC.

44. This point as well as others are corroborated by a recent study undertaken by sociologist Joel Best to explore the cultural representations of child abuse in the United States over the past thirty years. Best demonstrates that the structure of news shows is such that they tend to describe the problem rather than explain it or consider solutions, and that their descriptions are usually misleading—for example, in characterizing most cases of child sexual abuse as involving strangers rather than family members and as caused by individual deviance rather than social forces. He also shows that "the press is most likely to repeat . . . claims that are constructed so that . . . there seems to be a consensus among knowledgeable, interested parties, and *the explanations and solutions offered are consistent with existing institutionalized authority*. Of course, radical demands for social change cannot meet the latter two criteria, and it is not then surprising that radical claims rarely surface on the network news" (emphasis added). See his *Threatened Children: Rhetoric and Concern about Child-Victims* (Chicago: University of Chicago Press, 1990), 110.

45. Valerie Heller explains this point, in terms of child sexual abuse, as follows: "The myth is that adults who were sexually abused see sexual abuse everywhere . . . that they are 'too sensitive' because of what happened to them. . . . The result is that . . . the survivor's reality is seen as fantasy. The truth is not that sexual abuse survivors are 'too sensitive.' It simply is that we know what abuse looks like, what it feels like, and what effect it will have on the abused." See her excellent article "Sexual Liberalism and Survivors of Sexual Abuse," in *The Sexual Liberals and the Attack on Feminism*, ed. Dorchen Leidholt and Janice G. Raymond (New York: Pergamon, 1990), 157–61; the preceding quote appears on p. 159. Madigan and Gamble also discuss a case in which a defense attorney tried to discredit the testimony of a rape survivor on the grounds that she was molested as a child; *The Second Rape*, 51. This notion, that survivors are less credible on issues of sexual violence than anyone else, has affected nearly every survivor we know, as well as each of us. In response to her whistle-blowing on a sexual harassment case, one of the authors of this essay has been rumored to be "overly sensitive" because of her childhood experience and because she is Hispanic. Here, racist images of Latinas as "overemotional" collude conveniently with the discrediting of survivors on the same grounds.

46. It is also interesting to note that the witnesses in support of Clarence Thomas were allowed to testify even though they had histories of harassment (which some of them did), whereas the witnesses in support of Anita Hill could not. The logic here is that if women who have experienced harassment previously—and thus were certain to be overly sensitive to it now—did not see Thomas as a harasser, this provided a strong case for his innocence. In other words, a biased perspective could serve the purposes of the case for Thomas, but not the case against him. The assumption at work here is that

women who have experienced sexual harassment previously cannot provide an objective judgment but will err on the side of the accuser. Our thanks to Lynne Arnault for pointing this out.

47. bell hooks, "Feminist Politicization: A Comment," in *Talking Back: Thinking Feminist, Thinking Black* (Boston: South End, 1989), 110.

48. For an example of the discussion concerning personal narratives and whether or not they are political, see Armstrong, "The Personal Is Apolitical." Armstrong criticizes self-help books and "I-story" collections for channeling survivor discourse toward a nonthreatening outlet. See also the ensuing heated debate in the letters column of the following issue of the *Women's Review of Books,* April 1990.

49. See, e.g., Jo Freeman, *The Politics of Women's Liberation* (New York: Longman, 1975); Hester Eisenstein, *Contemporary Feminist Thought* (Boston: Hall, 1983).

50. See Chesler, *Women and Madness.*

51. hooks, "Feminist Politicization," 110.

52. Ibid.

53. Ibid., 129.

54. This incident is described in *People* magazine, December 17, 1990, 102, and in the *Brown Alumni Monthly,* December 1990, 13–15. It was also the topic of *The Phil Donahue Show* on December 4, 1990.

55. Ziegenmeyer, *Taking Back My Life,* 218.

56. The complete version of this poem can be found in Bass and Davis, *The Courage to Heal,* 101–3.

10 / Taking It to a Limit One More Time: Autobiography and Autism

Sidonie Smith

Perhaps the world resists being reduced to mere resource because it is—not mother/matter/mutter—but coyote, a figure for the always problematic, always potent tie of meaning and bodies.

DONNA K. HARAWAY, *Simians, Cyborgs, and Women*[1]

Transgression . . . is not related to the limit as black to white, the prohibited to the lawful, the outside to the inside, or as the open area of a building to its enclosed spaces. Rather, their relationship takes the form of a spiral which no simple infraction can exhaust.

MICHEL FOUCAULT, "A Preface to Transgression"[2]

Part of the complexity of the everyday is that it represents conflicting registers and assumptions at one and the same time; it charts a fault-line between the conscious and unconscious, between determining powers people can see and those they cannot, between theories that seek change and those that enmesh their subjects in determinism. It marks a site of conflict that makes consensus—about "our" shared sense of lived experience as well as ideas about such everyday experience's transformative potential in culture—difficult if not impossible. The everyday becomes a crucial category because its consolidations and deconstructions touch directly on the subject's relation to ideology and culture.

LAURIE LANGBAUER,
"Cultural Studies and the Politics of the Everyday"[3]

The data of our everyday lives travel around the community, the nation, and the globe in unfathomably split seconds, far faster than our

226

consciousness can register our own transformations. But it might be arresting to slow down, to pause and consider the everyday impediments to autobiographical storytelling—that is, to go to the limits of everyday autobiography, if only provisionally, in order to ascertain the extent of limits on our narrative "lives."

As I thought about this notion of "limit" lives, I began to list for myself diverse circumstances that impose some kind of limits to autobiographical telling in everyday situations.

A suicide note can mark the drastic limit. Or, when the attempt fails, it can measure the hunger for reaching and passing a boundary, for irreversibility.

But narratives by persons who have near-death experiences tell stories of returns from that conclusive limit.

People suffering from Alzheimer's disease are gradually evacuated of their everyday lives.

Autistic persons may never get their everyday "lives" outside of themselves, may remain forever silent, private, incommunicative.

Persons in witness protection programs are assigned new identities overnight and then scramble to get lives that scramble their old lives.

Some people live two entirely separate lives, a duplicity often discovered only upon their deaths by their duplicate spouses.

People whom we describe as compulsive liars habitually and concretely get another life.

Persons with multiple personalities change identities and experiential histories by the day or the hour.

Some people go through life with the conviction that somebody else, somebody more real, lies inside them just waiting to get out: the "thin" person waiting to get out of the "fat" person; the daring and dashing person waiting to get out of the body of the uptight drudge.

On a daily basis people make arduous efforts to pass themselves off as someone/something else.

Some people undergo radical reidentification, such as sex-change operations.

Twins separated at birth reunite only to discover they have spouses with the same names or that they surround themselves with the same kinds of objects, colors, professions.

And now, thanks to Dr. Jerry Hall, scientists have the capability of splitting human embryos in order to make duplicate copies of genetically identical persons, thereby turning an oxymoronic phrase, mass-produced individuality, into a commonplace autobiographical possibility.

If this list conjoins an eclectic array of eccentric and not-so-eccentric circumstances, it seems suggestive nonetheless.

The limits here intensify as they confuse the relationship between making a life narrative and believing oneself to be a certain kind of subject. "To make people believe is to make them act," suggests Michel de Certeau. Yet, he continues, "by a curious circularity, the ability to make people act—to write and to machine bodies—is precisely what makes people believe."[4] In their different ways these limits are profoundly disorienting, for they pressure our notions of the subject and its determinations, of the relationships of persons to experiential history, and of the integrities of life storytelling. I look here at one of them, the circumstance of the person diagnosed as autistic.

I remain fascinated by the questions raised at each of these limits, but frustrated by the proliferation of questions generated and their heterogeneous implications. This essay has refused to settle into some conventionally tidy shape; it has taken me to parts of the library I've never visited, beamed me into Library of Congress numbers that never come up on the screens I normally peruse. This change in venue has required some intellectual hopscotch. I do not present myself as an "expert" on the clinical, neurochemical, and psychobiological aspects of the limit taken up here. Yet the medicalization of conditions of everyday lives should neither prevent nor inhibit our engagement of them as part of our everyday discourse. Their very organization within "abnormality" discursively marks off what is not knowable to, not discussable by, everyday subjects. At the heart of medical and clinical science are issues of human subjectivity about which clinicians and researchers consequentially theorize. The theoretical bases of research, diagnosis, and treatment invite continual examination and critique, and one obvious point of departure for such an examination becomes the everyday uses of autobiography. Postmodern understandings of the subject, of autobiographical narrative, and of the contexts of enunciation bear on these limits, of which autism is a striking instance.

An Autistic Subject—Selved and/or Unselved?

Clinical psychologists have delineated a repertoire of physical and linguistic behaviors they now gather together under the diagnosis of "autistic." Autistic persons have difficulty with spoken language; they often echo the words of others; they respond erratically to sensory stimuli; they display repetitive behaviors that can become obsessive; they fixate on objects for long periods of time; they become emotionally and physically unsettled with unexpected changes in environment; they retreat into a private "inner" world distant from "the social world"; they have difficulty relating emotionally to other people.[5] These behaviors are symptoms, visible to the world, that in the gaze of the clinician are read off the body as signs of "abnormal" development. Behaviors thus become the descriptive and predictive script of an "autistic," who becomes the signified to which these signifiers point. "Autism" is a system of signs pointing to a condition of difference. In a sense, then, the person diagnosed as autistic is assigned an autistic subjectivity and with it is provided an autobiographical, or more precisely a biographical, script.

The gathering of this system of behavioral markers under the diagnostic sign "autism," rather than their dissipation in a larger field of heterogeneous markers termed "mental illness" or "mental retardation," took place only in the mid-twentieth century, when Leo Kanner and Hans Asberger independently coined the term *autism* in the early 1940s. Since the identification of this specific condition and the consolidation of its discourse within clinical psychology, several generations of clinicians have attempted to locate the "cause" or "origin" of these effects by probing further into the recesses of the autistic subject.[6] This search for an etiology of "abnormality" has been driven by the bourgeois logic of Western medicine, which situates the unknown or unintelligible within the individual.[7]

In the 1950s, clinicians proceeded to theorize the observational data on the basis of a "widespread belief in the psychogenic origin of childhood behavior disorders,"[8] a belief generated through a particular understanding of the relationship of the visible to the invisible. The behavioral, linguistic, and emotional differences of an autistic subject could be accounted for only in the unconscious nested deep within the subject. Because "the reflexive, dialectical connection between the subject and the world, between consciousness and the unconscious, was explained by the concept of the linear development of the psyche, where conscious life was caused by the subconscious,"[9] they sited the etiology of "autism" through the explanatory and deterministic model provided by the discourses of psychoanalysis and developmental psychology: an autistic subject developed an autistic condition, that is, became an autistic, because of psychic trauma. Thus the unintelligible condition of the autistic was explained (or rationalized) through a psychoanalytic frame of knowledge that traced dysfunctional conditions back to dysfunctional family relationships. But more particularly, the dysfunctional relationship was identified as the relationship of the child to an "unnatural" mother who refused to hold and nurture the infant adequately. The autistic subject was a subject of an inadequate pre-Oedipal relationship. The failure of nurturant motherhood disrupted the developmental process whereby the infant successfully made his or her entry into language. Parents, but particularly mothers, were assigned blame for the failure of the autistic to develop a normal everyday life as well as to develop the means to narrate a "life."

This explanation of origins, produced through the powerful cultural metaphor of psychoanalysis, has gradually been displaced by another explanatory model, one that emerged in what Donna K. Haraway describes as a "post-Second World War period characterized by the translation of Western scientific and political languages of nature from those based on work, localization, and the marked body to those based on codes, dispersal and networking, and the fragmented postmodern subject."[10] Out of the research of neurophysiologists a consensus has emerged in the clinical community that biochemical and neuroanatomical abnormalities in brain development cause persons diagnosed as autistic to be "oblivious to many of the social cues and to the constant stream of cause-and-effect sequences that give coherence and meaning to normal experience"; finding it difficult to process the information pressing upon them from the world, they experience life "as an incoherent series of unconnected events."[11] Neurons do not fire properly, and so the network does not transmit information in an effective form to an appropriate destination. Interruptions in internal processing units at the cellular level generate interruptions in the processing of exterior information at the level of consciousness. The brain, a complex processing unit, becomes dysfunctional. With this explanation, researchers press even further into the recesses of the individual, now the cellular and subcellular recesses, and even further within the genetic coding of the double helix. The differences of the autistic person are the differences of genetic coding.[12]

This explanatory model constructs an everyday autistic subject along the following lines. The subjectivity of the autistic becomes a condition of surfeit, what we might call the surfeit of aporia: information processing units cannot find the right way out for the transmission of messages. Everywhere there are excessive gaps in continuities and meanings. As a result, the very materiality of the body, the materiality at the end of nerves and in the neurochemistry of the brain, the materiality that generates a processing system, interrupts an autistic person's efforts to assemble meaning through narratives. In effect, the neurophysiological model consigns the autistic to an unautobiographical life. Multiple gaps in message transmissions force a limit to everyday autobiography, frustrating efforts to get a narrative based on memory fragments together at all, or to manipulate the story and its meanings in coherent and recitable narratives. Perhaps, then, autistics remain outside the linguistic, narrative, and communal circuits of autobiographical telling, unautobiographical subjects who cannot get the message into the narrative "life" in our everyday sense of the term. Biology/physiology would seem to outprocess, or unprocess, autobiography in a communication landscape traversed by processing units that run amok.

"Narrowing in" on the microcellular causes of autism has been facilitated by the increasingly sophisticated processes through which researchers use computers to map localized response centers in the brain.[13] In this way, a new technology generates a new metaphor through which the unintelligibilities of an autistic subject can be comprehended, can be known in order to be treated, can be bio-graphed. The geneto-biography gets written in cellular and subcellular codings. And bioengineering rather than psychotherapy becomes the strategy for intervention and cure.

Yet it may be that as research technologies and methodologies become more and more complex and precisely targeted, precise causal explanations become more and more difficult to specify,[14] for however sophisticated the mappings of the brain as a composite of localized response centers might become, what exactly constitutes consciousness, in this case autistic consciousness, has thus far eluded the experts. The consciousness of the autistic subject remains a matter of speculation among clinicians. In this sense it is what some contemporary philosophers call "secondness"—"the materiality that persists *beyond* any attempt to conceptualize it."[15] At this limit of the elusive and unknowable the discourses of science can only invoke metaphor. An autistic subject can be conceived or known only through representations.

So "autism" is itself a metaphor through which the differences of an unknowable subjectivity, in getting a (clinical) name, become culturally intelligible—and intelligible in historically precise ways within historically situated institutional settings. "Autism" becomes a metaphor through which experts can construct everyday "biographies" of different subjects with the hope or pretense of making them over into "normal" subjects.

Mapping the Humanist Self onto Autistic Subjects

Strangely, it took me four more years to realize that normal children refer to themselves as "I."

DONNA WILLIAMS, *Nobody Nowhere: The Extraordinary Autobiography of an Autistic*[16]

Persons diagnosed with severe autism often neither construct nor communicate accounts of their experiential histories. In this way they do not appear to get together an "I" and a "you" through which to develop a concept of a narrative subject and a narrative life. Autistics, then, in all their differences, throw out of kilter everyday expectations that people assume themselves to be "I"s and situate themselves in various locations through their personal storytelling. They remain subjects for whom autobiographical narrating does not become an everyday practice. This silence that displaces personal storytelling disrupts the everyday activities through which people engage in the building of families and communities. And in this lack of speaking, as well as emotional bonding, lies so much of the profound pain and suffering experienced in real lives around them.

Without minimizing the real suffering of autistic persons, I would like to consider certain clinical strategies for intervention in this silence. William Chaloupka notes in chapter 16 of this volume that constituting people as autobiographical subjects has become "an important practice in the tactical—and, because tactical, also contingent—field of power." Effectively, the silences of persons diagnosed as autistic frustrate therapeutic institutions, whose restoration of persons to healthy normality through various modes of observation, assessment, and reorientation or behavior modification, all based on a concept of coherent and autonomous selfhood, has become so much a part of contemporary life. Excessive silences about personal lives, about feelings, values, memories, and so on, become obdurate signs of unintelligibility, of unknowable differences, that in their persistence invite intervention.

One controversial strategy for intervention in the everyday silences and unautobiographically marked existences of autistics has been known as "facilitative communication." It is designed to turn inscrutable, unvoiced, and apparently unselved persons into autobiographical subjects, into persons who speak and express their "inner selves." It is designed, that is, to transform an autistic subject into a "humanist" subject. Facilitative communication pairs a trained volunteer with an autistic person. The volunteer, supporting the autistic's hand, helps the autistic communicate through an electronic device. Through this collaborative approach, the autistic spells out and thereby produces the text of his or her "life."

This interventionist strategy has its roots in the history of clinical psychology and its foundational belief in the efficacy of the talking cure and in its various post-Freudian manifestations. Although this strategy may derive from a belief in the therapeutic value of piecing together and articulating the "real" story and the self-empowering effects of coming to voice as a communicative act, it also reveals the degree to which autistics who remain silent, withdrawn, and incommunicative trouble those who identify themselves as normal. That is, they trouble the belief in humanist selfhood. In addition to being a condition in need of an explanation, autism becomes a more general problem in need of a solution—in this case a silence in need of a story. Autistics' obdurate silences, their frustrating and eruptive mimeses, thwart all efforts to conform them to modernist notions of a unified, autonomous, and free self. They seem to remain the unselved out of whom clinicians would release, or create, communicative autobiographical "selves."

There is, of course, bitter controversy within the clinical community about the results of facilitative communication. Its supporters insist on its success in enabling autistics to communicate with loved ones and caregivers, on its restoration of hope in family and friends. The detractors of facilitative communication argue that the narratives autistic persons get/give through these electronic devices may not be their own experientially based stories. In reviewing videotapes of the process, critics note that autistic persons often do not look at the keyboard as they move fingers to letter after letter. This failure to look becomes a critical issue. If they are not looking at the keys, then whose narrative is coming out of the machine? In whose hands does the "life" lie? Whose fingers are doing the talking?

The consequences of this confusion of fingers and "lives" have been glimpsed in a recent *Frontline* documentary on facilitative communi-cation.[17] In a significantly larger percentage of cases than are found in the general population, the narratives that have come through the fin-gers and keys are ones of child sexual abuse. Not surprisingly, charges have been brought, families broken up, autistic children placed in fos-ter or protective care, fathers criminalized. Adjudicating criminal charges, courts have enlisted other clinicians to comment on the likeli-hood that the narrative came from the autistic person. And sometimes the third party, after spending time with the autistic person alone and with the autistic and the facilitator, has argued persuasively to the courts that the narrative could not have come from the autistic person.

We see here how the "autobiographical narrative" of the autistic person circulates in complex ways through various institutions—through the family, the clinic, the penal system, the law, social service agencies—all of which deploy, if only implicitly, theories of autism and theories of autobiographical personhood as they make and unmake truth claims with consequences. For persons who understand the ori-gins of autism to be psychogenic, the story of childhood sexual abuse makes powerful sense; for those who understand autism through neu-rophysiological explanations, the story may make less sense as other factors, such as the direction of the gaze of the autistic person, take on more significance. This particular instance of autobiographical enunci-ation seems to reverberate through society in contradictory ways as a particular kind of story is singled out as problematic.

Think, for instance, of the possible auto/biographical sources: the re-pressed experiential history of the autistic, the fantasies of the facilita-tor, the repressed experiential history of the facilitator. Every possibil-ity multiplies our questions. Say, for instance, that the story emerges out of the crusaderly commitment of volunteers who want to liberate autistics from whatever horrible past (psychogenic trauma) keeps them locked in the silence of nonnarrative. It becomes the facilitator's fan-tasy biography of the autistic, a biography already written through cul-tural expectations of the relationship of silence to repression of trau-matic events. In this case the everyday life becomes a first-person biography. Suppose it is the facilitator's own unspeakable "life" that is coming through finger and machine. Then it functions as a screen au-tobiography through which the facilitator simultaneously reveals and conceals the trauma of his or her own experiential history. Suppose it is both at once, some amalgam of repression and projection—biography and autobiographical utterance. In this limit case we find ourselves at the fine line between an everyday use of biography and autobiography, a fragile and fluid limit between one "life" and another. Or suppose the narrative comes from the autistic. Given what has been described as an autistic's penchant for miming other persons' words, where might the narrative have come from? Might it be a mimic narrative? And in what senses? Or, if it is the narrative of an experientially based history, how might the differences of an autistic subject affect the meanings assigned to that story? How can an autistic subject get a life differently? Can that difference be registered through the hand of the facilitator?

It is not within my purview in this essay to review in depth the controversy surrounding facilitative communication—though I would note here that, in an increasingly skeptical environment, the practice no longer garners the support it did in the early 1990s. It has been my purpose to consider some of the implications of pursuing this collaborative form of intervention.

Here we are taken to the limits of the knowable and unknowable several more times.

Autistic Technologies

If autistics remain forever silent of speech, or become only occasionally communicative through mimetic utterances, then they might in one sense be said to remain subjects outside discourse, subjects culturally uninscribed. From one point of view, an autistic subject seems to navigate through life in the midst of an acultural space, in which there is little to no subjection to/in language and discourse. Uninscribed by the subjectivities provided to persons through the everyday operations of power/knowledge, autistics seem to inhabit an elsewhere beyond the limit. But, of course, we cannot know them to be or not to be such subjects, because as such subjects they do not speak. We cannot know whether or not the scrambling of the means of perception of the world scrambles the technologies of selfhood surrounding the autistic subject.

What we are told by high-functioning autistics who have been able to speak reflexively and to communicate with the world is that they in part imitate life through a kind of mechanical or rote mimesis of "scripts." "Mirroring, as with the matching of objects," reflects Donna Williams in *Nobody Nowhere,* "was my way of saying: 'Look, I can relate. I can make that noise, too'" (209). But the mimicry goes beyond words as autistics watch others for markers of appropriate performances of selfhood, developing scripts for everyday living through personal glossaries of appropriate responses. In a recent interview of Temple Grandin, whose narrative *Emergence: Labeled Autistic* I will discuss below, Oliver Sacks reports that Grandin explained to him that "she had built up a vast library of experiences over the years. . . . They were like a library of videotapes, which she could play in her mind and inspect at any time—'videos' of how people behaved in different circumstances. She would play these over and over again and learn, by degrees, to correlate what she saw, so that she could then predict how people in similar circumstances might act. She had complemented her experience by constant reading, . . . all of which enlarged her knowledge of the species."[18] High-functioning or recovering autistics apparently learn by rote the technologies of selfhood—the self-identifications, the narratives, the behaviors, the emotional scripts—through which people in their cultures make sense of the world and themselves. They learn to program themselves to "perform" as "normal" human beings, the kind of human beings their cultures expect them to be.

But if they perform as human beings, what does that performance reveal about the dynamics of autistic consciousness? What must be performed because it is not felt or experienced? This slight disalignment of performance and experiential history both reveals and conceals a particular kind of difference. And it points to the gap between believing oneself to be a culturally intelligible subject and recognizing that identities are performative in a most dramatic sense. And to what extent and degree is this performance the same as or different from the performance of selfhood generated unconsciously in childhood? Are we not then brought to another limit, the technologies of technologies of selfhood? Yet the narratives of Temple Grandin and Donna Williams also explore the ways in which they are subjects of discourse.

Getting Named: One

Not surprisingly, in the recall of such events, I referred to myself as "you." This was because "you" logically captured my relationship to myself. One develops an "I" in interaction with "the world." Donna didn't interact; the characters did. . . . I reverted to using "I" in a conforming effort to avoid [the therapist's] pedantic emphasis on the pronouns I was using. Her efforts to get me to refer to these incidents in a personal manner overlooked the fact that my use of "you" captured the impersonal way in which I had experienced the incidents at the time they happened. She probably felt that she had to help me to overcome my depersonalization, as though this were some recently developed defense reaction. I don't think she realized that I had actually experienced life this way since the creation of Willie and Carol, and my subsequent ability to communicate through them, thirteen years before.

DONNA WILLIAMS, Nobody Nowhere (103)

Throughout her autobiographical exploration of autistic selfhood titled *Nobody Nowhere,* Donna Williams emphasizes that autistic persons are often identified and treated as "crazy," loony, strange, unhinged; and they are often identified as violent crazy, because their frustrations often materialize in physically violent behavior. Because the experiential history of the autistic person troubles the limits of conventional understanding of autobiographical subjectivity, the strangeness of this difference is neutralized by reincorporation in conventional and reassuring identifications, identifications inflected with various discourses of otherness, of gendered madness, class-based madness, racialized madness among them. In other words, the differences of autistic behaviors are not "visible" to "normal" people except against the horizon of discourse defining madness or mental retardation in their various guises. And that horizon, Williams acknowledges, can become an internalized landscape of autistic identity. "I am both insane and retarded," she announces. "I would add to this deaf, dumb, and blind; for, although the accuracy of this is being constantly disproved by what I am able to perceive or express, this was often the way I perceived myself to be, and behaved accordingly" (199). She perceived herself to be mad because the people with whom she negotiated everyday life constructed her as mad, or insane, or crazy and strange. Through her negotiations of a "world" that perceived her as mad, Williams learned to "be" a mad person.

Being diagnosed as autistic, learning that she is an "autistic subject" rather than a mad subject, provides Williams with a shape-shifting opportunity. Assembling her narrative life as the life of an autistic, she reframes the diverse and disconnected memories, assigning them a "place within the scheme of things" (163), and reinterprets the patterns of her personal relationships, her experiences as a subject in/out of the world, and her relationship to her own body. As she becomes "somebody somewhere,"[19] she establishes an emotional and intersubjective basis for her conception of selfhood.

Williams understands her narrative project as a process through which she forges what she calls a "real self" out of her "alters"— "Carol" and "Willie." Carol and Willie are "depersonalized, communicative, worldly versions of myself that were able to sound out people and environments for a self that could not cope with things of such complexity" (134); she developed these alters as strategic means to survive everyday living. She works to understand how they function as specialized versions of herself, taking up bits and pieces of consciousness as if in isolation.[20] Isolated specialists, these versions of self take on the attributes of rigidly organized personalities, unified around a set of repetitive postures, behaviors, emotions, autobiographical scripts. In this everyday fragmentation of identities, the "host" subject—"Donna"—cannot consciously take responsibility for herself in the world, cannot assemble an experiential history, even an experiential history that organizes itself around multiplicity. The versions cannot integrate into a coherent narrative the experiential history from which they are divided. She further understands her project as a process of reinhabiting a body from which she has disassociated: "I began to find some sort of a rhythm and permanence within my own body, and this has helped in my acceptance of my body as belonging to me rather than something with a mind of its own, constantly driving me crazy" (202).

By bringing the disconnected and dissociated versions of herself that she turns to the world into alignment with a new definition of herself as a provisionally unified subject, separate from but mutually interdependent upon "the world," Williams, in fact, gets a life. As James Glass suggests about the struggle of persons with multiple personalities to integrate them, "the unity need not be monolithic, but it may be a unity representing a plurality of interests within the self, interests understood as emotions and moods."[21] Carol and Willie disappear, externalized and depersonalized multiplicities replaced by internalized multiplicities.

Through the very writing of her narrative Williams extracts herself from the subject position of the crazy child/young woman and claims for herself the subject position of the "autistic." In turn, this understanding of herself as an autistic subject enables her to change her perceptions and her experiences of her "madness." In reconstructing herself as an "autistic," Williams begins to find a place in the world and "a clear awareness of an 'I'" (190), that point of departure from which to engage the world. She becomes, that is, an autobiographical subject. But this description of the process does an injustice to the massive effort a concept of selfhood requires. Just how profound a change in consciousness this represents is suggested by Williams's comment about herself at age six: "Strangely, it took me four more years to realize that normal children refer to themselves as 'I'" (23).

Williams attributes the shift from an undiagnosed "crazy" person to an autistic subject to several interrelated processes: diagnostic labeling, the confessional enunciation of an "I," and the assemblage of a "coherent" narrative of her experiential history. Yet, in a spiraling action redolent of Foucault's notion of the limit, Williams paradoxically becomes what she is not. In the very process of constituting herself as an autistic subject, she moves beyond its restricted otherness. That is, in the process of defining herself as autistic, she exceeds the definition of an autistic subject, and she exceeds the definition through the very processes of confessional and assemblage. The autistic/recovering autistic subject becomes an autobiographical subject. In this way she situates herself both within and without the diagnostic label.

Getting Named: Two

How does a child, labeled autistic, emerge into the real world?
TEMPLE GRANDIN, *Emergence: Labeled Autistic*[22]

The different experiential histories of Grandin and Williams suggest ways in which clinical diagnosis can be differentially available to people depending upon their socioeconomic locations. Williams comes from a relatively poor family. Her parents and later the educational system responded to her as a difficult and disruptive child and crazy adolescent. She had, in fact, to find her own way to diagnosis in young adulthood. With relatively wealthy and educated parents, Temple Grandin was diagnosed at a very early age because of her parents' willingness to call on experts to help understand her abnormality.

Thus if Williams uses her narrative life to constitute herself as an autistic subject, Grandin uses hers to engage in a quarrel with the experts about the definition of the autistic subject. Grandin tells the reader early in her narrative that she was "labeled autistic" from a very early age (not too many years after the term was coined in the

1940s). If the label of autistic gave her an identity and gave her abnormalities an interpretive framework, it also served to fix her as a particular kind of dysfunctional subject with limited opportunities for leading a "normal" life. Autism, clinically understood, became the means through which her difference was named and known. In contesting this clinical "knowledge," Grandin structures her history as a history of negotiations with changing constructions of the autistic subject generated in the discourses of science and clinical therapy. Her narrative engages the ways in which the autistic is read—and misread—by the experts because it is "the autistic subject" whom they see, and not the person with variable and changing characteristics associated with autism. In effect, Grandin invokes an everyday autobiography of her own to displace the everyday biography of autistic subjects written by the experts.

She recalls, for instance, a particularly difficult period in her childhood when she was sent home from a summer camp for constantly talking about parts of her body and for masturbating. Because of the understanding of the etiology of autism at the time, she was directed to a psychiatrist, whose job it was to extract childhood secrets and repressed fantasies from her. But she presents herself as giving him nothing of what he wanted, except frustration at her recalcitrance. She remembers how she refused to become the kind of subject he required her to be. By incorporating her mother's letters to the psychiatrist (written at the time) within her text, Grandin introduces the voice of a concerned parent who reads her behavior differently from the "experts" and yet a parent who is influenced by the "authority" of the "experts," the authority that maintains its power of interpretation over the observable behaviors. In this way she counters the expertise of the clinicians with whom her parents worked; introduces the counterauthority of her "nonexpert" mother, whom she represents as supportive of her resistances; and critiques the blindness of the "enlightened" psychiatrists and the larger institution of medical science.

In this context, it is interesting to recall Grandin's comment to Oliver Sacks, reported in his *New Yorker* essay, about the absence of the unconscious in the autistic subject:

> There are no files in my memory that are repressed. You have files that are blocked. I have none so painful that they're blocked. There are no secrets, no locked doors—nothing is hidden. I can

infer that there are hidden areas in other people, so that they can't bear to talk of certain things. The amygdala locks the files of the hippocampus. In me, the amygdala doesn't generate enough emotion to lock the files of the hippocampus. (122)

In joining the discourses of computer technology (of files and storage and access and circuit breakdown) to that of physiology, Grandin invokes a more contemporary scientific discourse to call into question the certitudes of an earlier psychoanalytic discourse. She thereby disputes and displaces the earlier construction of the autistic subject that sent her to the psychiatrist's office as a young girl. Whatever her psyche or physiology, she here constitutes a self out of polarization, an argumentative self that is perhaps the most salient characteristic of the bourgeois "individual." In doing so, she confuses the grounds of sameness and difference.

This quarrel with the experts continues throughout her narrative. She challenges the scales of measurement they devise to calibrate degrees of autism and thereby control the identification of persons as autistic or not autistic. She persistently argues for the efficacy of her "squeeze machine" as a means to provide touching comfort to autistics who find human contact unbearable. Here again she provides a history of her confrontations with experts who discourage her fixation and reliance upon this mechanical device for adjusting pressure upon the body, and who succeed in encouraging her to internalize guilt about her dependency. She continually interrupts her narrative to introduce information about research findings on autism. In fact, the narrative ends with a three-line note to a recent finding—perhaps an addition made as the book went to press. In this way, she captures the ongoing construction and reframing of autism and emphasizes its unfixedness against the fixedness of diagnostic labeling and the fixedness of theories promoted by certain experts.

Always, Grandin emphasizes that autistic people are constantly changing subjects-in-process, by this means effectively de-essentializing the autistic subject and destabilizing the ground of diagnosis and treatment. But elsewhere, she goes even further. In the interview with Oliver Sacks, she argues for the depathologization of autism. "If science eliminated these genes," she suggests, invoking the discourses of genetic determination, "maybe the whole world would be taken over by accountants."[23] In other words, she challenges an underlying motivation for scientific research that is designed to discover the secrets of the "self" in order to intervene and make all people over into "normal" human beings. This drive to know the body and its pathologies might lead to genetic intervention to eliminate "dysfunctional genes," those differences in processing, that experts claim cause autism. For Grandin, the world might become a nightmare if everyone were to be remade as "normal" through techniques of bioengineering. And in her own resisting stance, she implies that we would all do better in a world in which people experience diverse normalities.

As she contests the meanings of the label, Grandin positions herself as an "authority" on autism. She claims that "authority" on two grounds: she is a trained scientist who, having kept abreast of the latest research on autism, can speak about it in highly technical terms; and she is an autistic subject herself. Therefore she speaks as one who knows—from experience and from training. In getting this narrative life, then, Grandin draws upon the authority of her experience as well as intimate clinical tutoring and cedes this to autobiographical forms of testimony. In so doing, she wrests the everyday experiences of autistics from the medical experts and researchers who would speak for autistics and normalize their difference through the medicalization of symptoms and psychologization of treatment. She thereby affirms what Haraway calls "situated knowledge." The autistic subject contests the expertise of clinicians and thereby educates clinicians and laypeople about the differential effects of the materiality of the body.

Like Donna Williams's narrative, Grandin's autobiographical performance spirals inexhaustibly. Grandin both relies upon and resists medical authorities in her effort to diagnose, understand, and gain control over her "self"; relies upon them and resists them in her assertion of her own "authority" over life, text, and audience. But her experiential self always exceeds the medical diagnosis of the "autistic" self. And this excessive subjectivity assumes its own authority, an authority paradoxically alterior to her representations of herself as an autistic self and as an expert on autism, both of which representations are caught up in discourses of selfhood.

Getting (out of) a "Life"

Mirroring, as with the matching of objects, was my way of saying: "Look, I can relate. I can make that noise, too."
DONNA WILLIAMS, *Nobody Nowhere* (209)

Of course, the very gesture of getting a life narrative generates another interesting question. Are these women still autistic subjects, or are they recovered/recovering autistics efficiently performing one or another version of a "life"? Bernard Rimland, a pioneering expert in the field of autism, calls Grandin "a recovered autistic individual" in his introduction to her autobiographical narrative (7), thus implying that the ability to compose a life narrative signals the transformation of an autistic into a nonautistic, or "normal" person. From this point of view, getting a life narrative is tantamount to getting out of autistic subjectivity. Does this mean that a person cannot be an autistic and an autobiographical subject simultaneously? Or that the very framing of an autobiographical narrative does the cultural work of transforming the unknowable and different subject into a knowable subject? Perhaps, and perhaps because this is a certain metamorphosis, a change of the morphos of the structure of being itself, we can never know. The ground or subject of our knowing may be obliterated in the creation of an autobiographical subject.

Afterword

In their narratives, Grandin and Williams simultaneously constitute themselves as autistic subjects and critique the everyday constructions of autistic subjects by laypersons and experts alike. Through their narrative efforts they resist identities attached to their behaviors and redefine themselves as different and not crazy, different and not doomed to remain fixed in their "dysfunction." Unfixing the categories of the mad, even of the autistic, they depathologize and provisionally de-essentialize the autistic subject. At the same time, they suggest that the autistic subject receives, perceives, and conceives the world from a usefully "situated" position of knowing. They make no claims for the universality of their knowledge of themselves or of their autistic subjectivity. Theirs are what Haraway aptly describes as "partial, locatable, critical knowledges sustaining . . . shared conversations in epistemology."[24] And their knowledge comes from specific and changing embodiments. These are limited knowledges, in a responsible sense, and, as such, views from autistic subjects that contribute to a construction of "objectivity as positioned rationality."[25]

Through such narratives of everyday lives, the body becomes an active agent for the knowing of the world and for the knowing of the subjective world differently. And so both of them turn the lens of dif-

244 / *Sidonie Smith*

ference—considered "abnormal" or "dysfunctional"—upon everyday normality. Against the experts' view of genes as a resource for cracking the code of human beingness, Grandin makes the matter of genes an agent (in the sense suggested by Haraway)[26] for creativity in the world. Williams recontextualizes the bodily strategies of the autistic, even their silences, as possible sources of sanity in the world and reasonably recontextualizes normality as a form of pathology: "I do not believe that being sane or intelligent is superior to being insane or retarded. Many times the insane person has turned his or her back on the often alienating normality that most people become conditioned to believe is a real and desirable goal" (199). She also proposes that an alternative language exists through which persons diagnosed as autistic communicate, a language constructed out of things and their sequences that has as yet gone untranslated.

For me this limit case provides a glimpse, at the remove of representation, into the conditions of the eccentrically embodied. Intriguingly, the secondness of the person diagnosed as autistic confuses the limits of the subject because it intimates another register of being, perhaps another register of embodied mind, to which the nonautistic person has no access except through these exceptional representations. Perhaps these representations of autistic personhood hint at a different subjectivity, only a portion of which is uneasily recuperable in culturally intelligible scripts even as those cultural scripts overwrite them.

Henri Lefebvre defines "the everyday" as "the *unrecognized*" or the "practically untellable."[27] In this consideration of the autistic subject I have tried to engage the tellable and untellable, the recognizable and unrecognizable limits of the everyday spiral of biographical and autobiographical acts, of prohibited and lawful selves as they promote and limit our understandings of autistic subjects. But I can engage these issues only after representation—representations of experts and specific autistics.[28] In this sense the everyday continues to elude, to remain elsewhere than in our interpretations. "Perhaps," as Haraway concludes in her consideration of situated knowledges, "the world resists being reduced to mere resource because it is—not mother/matter/mutter—but coyote, a figure for the always problematic, always potent tie of meaning and bodies."[29]

These two voices speak in very telling ways to the researchers and clinicians to whom the knowledge and the treatment of persons diagnosed as autistic is entrusted. And those clinicians and researchers, as well as literary critics like myself, can learn from them just how diverse and excessive subjectivity is and how different it can be from any monolithic notion of a "sane" or "normal" modernist self.

Notes

I wish to thank Kay Schaffer and Gregory Grieco for their exacting readings of earlier drafts of this essay.

1. Donna K. Haraway, *Simians, Cyborgs, and Women* (London: Free Association, 1991), 201.

2. Michel Foucault, "A Preface to Transgression," in *Language, Counter-Memory, Practice: Selected Essays and Interviews*, ed. Donald F. Bouchard, trans. Donald F. Bouchard and Sherry Simon (Ithaca, N.Y.: Cornell University Press, 1977), 34–35.

3. Laurie Langbauer, "Cultural Studies and the Politics of the Everyday," *diacritics* 22 (Spring 1992): 52.

4. Michel de Certeau, *The Practice of Everyday Life,* trans. Steven F. Rendall (Berkeley: University of California Press, 1984), 148.

5. I use the term *autistic subject* as a shortened referent to "a person diagnosed as autistic." Of course, there is no one unified autistic subject, but many persons diagnosed with varying degrees of autism. And so there are tremendous variations in the behavioral manifestations and differential capabilities of those persons diagnosed as autistic. There are those who remain permanently institutionalized, rocking back and forth, unable to make any sustained human contact; there are those identified as "autistic savants"—persons with remarkable powers in specific areas, such as the person upon whom Dustin Hoffman's character in *Rain Man* was modeled; and there are those identified with Asperger's syndrome, who are high functioning and are sometimes described as "recovered" or "recovering" autistics, persons who, having learned to adjust their behaviors, become active participants in society. The exact configurations of autistic behaviors/markers and their effects are individually specific.

There is also the intriguing statistic that autism seems to affect far more males than females—the ratio estimated at 3:1—which raises challenging questions about the etiology of the condition. In a recent newspaper article about autism, David Newnham suggests that "many of autism's manifestations—obsessiveness, a facility with rote learning, an inability to see the wood for the trees—echo types of behaviour with which we are all familiar in a certain type of 'normal' male" (*Guardian Weekend,* March 25, 1995, 27). What might be the relationship between autism and normative versions of masculinity?

6. For a discussion of the emergence of modern medicine and the modes through which it constituted the normal and the pathological subject, see Michel Foucault, *The Birth of the Clinic: An Archaeology of Medical Perception,* trans. A. M. Sheridan (London: Routledge, 1973).

7. See Donald M. Lowe, *History of Bourgeois Perception* (Chicago: University of Chicago Press, 1982).

8. Bernard Rimland, *Infantile Autism: The Syndrome and Its Implications for a Neural Theory of Behavior* (London: Methuen, 1965), 19.

9. See Lowe, *History of Bourgeois Perception*, 22–23, 105–8, for a discussion of the historical emergence of the concept of the unconscious as internal to the bourgeois individual as opposed to an unconscious whose source was extraindividual: "The unconscious within must assume the burden of accounting for that determinism. The concept of the linear development of the human psyche was the appropriate symbolization of the new bourgeois fate" (23).

10. Haraway, *Simians, Cyborgs, and Women,* 211.

11. Lawrence Bartak, "Introduction," in Donna Williams, *Nobody Nowhere: The Extraordinary Autobiography of an Autistic* (New York: Times Books, 1992), x–xi.

12. There are, of course, many factors affecting the ways in which scientific and clinical research gets done, some of which are the sources of funding, the institutions in which research takes place and the forms of knowledge they promote, and the development of research technologies.

13. It has also been facilitated by the large amounts of funding provided by pharmaceutical companies with their own interests in supporting explanatory theories that lead to biologically based intervention strategies.

14. Robert Barrett, in "Nineteenth Century Formulations of Schizophrenia: Degeneration and the Split Person," a paper delivered at the University of Adelaide, April 5, 1994, makes this point about the inverse relationship between the certitudes of explanation and the technological sophistication of the research into schizophrenia.

15. Drucilla Cornell, *The Philosophy of the Limit* (New York: Routledge, 1992), 1. Cornell reviews Charles Peirce's formulation of secondness and relates it to Jacques Derrida's deconstructive practice.

16. Donna Williams, *Nobody Nowhere: The Extraordinary Autobiography of an Autistic* (New York: Times Books, 1992), 23. Page references for all further citations of this work are included in the text in parentheses. I should note here that Williams grew up in Australia and is now living in England. Because of the limited number of everyday lives available to draw on for this discussion, I have decided to include her narrative despite this collection's focus on everyday life in the United States.

17. See "Prisoners of Silence," produced by John Palfreman for *Frontline* and aired on the Public Broadcasting System in Binghamton, New York, October 19, 1993.

18. Oliver Sacks, "An Anthropologist on Mars," *New Yorker,* December 27, 1993–January 3, 1994, 112.

19. This is the title of her second book, published recently. See Donna Williams, *Somebody Somewhere: Breaking Free from the World of Autism* (Sydney: Doubleday, 1994).

20. For further discussions of multiple personalities and their relationship to the host subject, see E. L. Bliss, *Multiple Personality, Allied Disorders, and Hypnosis* (New York: Oxford University Press, 1986), 133; James M. Glass, "Multiplicity, Identity and the Horrors of Selfhood: Failures in the Postmodern Position," *Political Psychology* 14 (1993): 255–78.

21. Glass, "Multiplicity, Identity," 268.

22. Temple Grandin and Margaret M. Scarriano, *Emergence: Labeled Autistic* (Novato, Calif.: Arena, 1986), 13. Page references for all subsequent citations of this work are included in the text in parentheses.

23. Sacks, "An Anthropologist on Mars," 124.

24. Haraway, *Simians, Cyborgs, and Women,* 191.

25. Ibid., 196.

26. Ibid., 200.

27. Henri Lefebvre, "Toward a Leftist Cultural Politics: Remarks Occasioned by the Centenary of Marx's Death," trans. David Reifman, in *Marxism and the Interpretation of Culture,* ed. Cary Nelson and Lawrence Grossberg (Chicago: University of Chicago Press, 1988), 78; Lefebvre, *Critique of Everyday Life,* trans. John Moore (New York: Verso, 1991), 24. Both quoted in Langbauer, "Cultural Studies," 49.

28. See Langbauer, "Cultural Studies," 48–52.

29. Haraway, *Simians, Cyborgs, and Women,* 201.

Part IV

Family Portraits

During certain hours, at certain years in our lives, we see ourselves as remnants from the earlier generations that were destroyed. So our job becomes to keep peace with enemy camps, eliminate the chaos at the end of Jacobean tragedies, and with "the mercy of distance" write the histories.

MICHAEL ONDAATJE, *Running in the Family*
(New York: Random House, [1982] 1993), 179

Is there any sense any longer in the question Who are you? Isn't it hopelessly antiquated, outstripped by the cross-examiner's question: What have you done?, which provokes in you the weak counter-question: What did they make me do? The sense of being accountable, worn thin by the things for which there is no accounting, which stop the flow of the narrative.

CHRISTA WOLF, *Patterns of Childhood,* trans. Ursule Molinaro
(New York: Farrar, Straus & Giroux, 1980), 350

11 / "What Kind of Life Have I Got?" Gender in the Life Story of an "Ordinary" Woman

Susan Ostrov Weisser

It got so to a point I said, "What kind of life have I got?"

MRS. F.

The Pragmatics of Everyday Self-Representation

I would like to begin by stating very directly that this essay is not about a particular woman's "real life," but about that life as a text, a text that takes on a life of its own in retellings. Recent autobiographical theory has opened up the definition of the genre of self-telling considerably beyond the once-sacrosanct precincts of literary autobiography to include fiction, memoirs, ethnographic portraits, and episodic texts such as letters, journals, and diaries. This essay is an attempt to apply the critical perspectives of contemporary autobiographical and feminist theory to a type of personal narrative only recently subjected to textual analysis: the oral life story of a woman—I shall call her Mrs. F.—who is "ordinary," in the sense that no specific claim about the specialness of her life is made by her or by me to justify her status as autobiographer.[1]

Even her typicality has no special claim: Mrs. F.'s recorded life is not a *testimonio,* neither meant to bear witness nor to exemplify—to represent or speak for any ethnic, religious, racial, or national group, or period of history, particular experience, age, generation, or occupation.[2] Though in this essay her text does indeed stand in metonymic relation to her gender, she, the living author of this text, was not asked to relate her story *for that purpose.* Yet as a feminist listener, sharply aware of issues of gender, I quite literally found myself constructing a different narrative—a different "woman," if you will—from the materials of Mrs. F.'s story.

Feminist theory in general has had a special relation to the field of autobiography: feminism, as the critic Rita Felski has pointed out, focuses on the "dual directions" of autobiography and politics, examining and reexamining a specifically female subjectivity, which then "acquires a representative status" in order to be liberating.[3] If, as Felski implies, any feminist critic must acknowledge the political agenda inherent in a hermeneutic reading of a life, to begin with, there is surely a special dilemma in confronting the everyday life of an "ordinary" woman. I refer to a dark corner of academic feminism that frequently goes unexplored, namely, that the feminist researcher's identification with her subject as a "woman" may prove more problematic than she, the researcher, would wish.

In 1986, Dr. Jerome Bruner, whose work has recently centered on the role of narrative in thinking, directed a project funded by the Spencer Foundation to study the question, What narrative rules and structures govern a self-made text about one's own life? Our small research group (more or less stable, eventually settling down to four women, including myself, and two men, including Dr. Bruner) examined how the act of constructing an identity takes place through narration, and further, how the text produced serves as a set of instructions to the audience on how to read it.[4]

In this project, the intention mapped out for our subjects was purposely kept as vague as possible: they were told only that we were doing an unnamed research project and needed to hear some life stories. When the subjects arrived for their interviews, they were given a disconcertingly bare minimum of instructions, namely, tell the story of your life. This section of the interview, which we called the "spontaneous" part, was followed by a second section consisting of a loose set of questions designed to elicit material about each subject's sense of agency, of causality, and other aspects of his or her theory of selfhood.

After the initial series of interviews, which I conducted alone over a year-long period, our task as researchers was to produce still other texts, specifically textual analyses of the concepts, values, judgments, perspectives, and, above all, rhetorical strategies embedded in each narrative. Our goal was to determine by (we hoped) sensible yet sensitive group discussion, what the life story meant to the one who lived it—as opposed to what the life itself meant.[5] These discussions were very stimulating, and as a group member not professionally trained as a psychologist, I often admired the insights of my research colleagues. But as a literary analyst, I was also aware that the purpose of our analyses was no less than to *retell* each subject's already told version of selfhood, as if it were somehow rendered more truthful, or more real, in our version.

In the West, autobiographical stories have frequently been seen as providing occasions for illuminating for others the seemingly unique and coherent configurations of intention, act, and meaning that we call autobiographical experience. The present research asserted a radically different premise about selfhood and "everyday life," which the group did not wish to approach either from the classic interpretive stance of the social sciences or from the traditional literary/critical stance entailing presumptions about aesthetic values. Our premise of the problematic relation of life narrative to factual truth led directly to several procedural paths: first, recognizing that the "life" is an intersubjective construction, we wished, unlike traditional interpreters of autobiographical narrative, to be painfully self-conscious about acting as players in the "cognitive game" that is discourse.[6] Moreover, we were emphatically *not* interested in verifiable facts—whether Subject A told the "truth" about his alcoholic father, or where Subject B was actually born.[7] Still less did we set out to make clinical interpretations, to describe the interestingly "atypical" in the spirit of psychoanalytic case history, or to look for pathology (though it seemed to look for us in one or two cases.)

Instead, we explored the possibilities of investigating the text of a "life" without continually referring back to the facts of the "real" life. We did not presume the "real" to be present and accessible as an objective, quantifiable, or verifiable entity. On the contrary, each "life" would be, *for our purposes,* temporarily presumed to exist only in language, which is to say, to exist outside of history. In "actual life" an autobiographical identity materializes through nonverbal practices in addition to (though not unrelated to) language, such as actions, gestures, encounters with others, and so on, in a temporal frame. In our study, the speaker's life history was whatever he or she said it was.

The self-narrative I will turn to, that of Mrs. F., will, I hope, engage an issue that became over the last two years of this project of great interest to me: how gender affects both the construction and the reading of a life story and, by extension, of texts and of "lives" as well. I want to emphasize again that this was a special interest of my own, as no identity categories such as class, region, and ethnicity were meant to be given particular emphasis in the group. Rather, what I observed is that the collective reading of gender emerged from obscured premises in the group discourse. Articulating these premises then forced me to examine those in my own interpretive framework.

Specifically, Mrs. F.'s story helped me reformulate ideas about how the life stories of "ordinary" women allow them to operate politically within a context whose structure affords them few direct expressions of power. In doing so, I was also forced to revise my received notions about the practice of everyday living and its general relation to theory in autobiography. In the next section, I hope to show that the way in which Mrs. F.'s narrative was read by our group points to the process by which gender, which is to say both the narrator's *and* the reader's idea of it, can constitute one of the major strategies for representing *and* reading selfhood in everyday life.[8]

An "Ordinary" Woman: Mrs. F.'s Story

Mrs. F., a sixty-year-old Italian American "housewife," mother of four grown children, and part-time worker in her husband's small business, indicated on the phone to me that she was afraid she would not do the right thing in the interview. As the unknown professional academic, I surely must have represented the public world to Mrs. F.: the critical view, the demand that she speak and perform. For my part, I had inevitably formed a certain impression of her before our first meeting from her family's references to her in their interviews. I thought of her, more or less consciously, as someone conservative, "narrow" in her focus, and marginal both within the structure of her family (whose members seemed to speak of her with amused condescension) and within that part of society that exists to get things *done*.[9]

I had already "gotten her life," which is to say, I had begun to frame my interpretation of her based on the disparity between us I anticipated before meeting her, especially the differences in our political and social values. I expected that she was going to be a conservator of traditional female roles, an emissary from the same sort of working-class Italian-Irish Brooklyn neighborhood I hoped to have left behind after an early marriage of my own. Mrs. F. was no feminist exemplar or working-class heroine; this was a traditional woman, bound by convention, and worse yet, not *aware* of being bound by convention. Clearly, she needed her consciousness raised. Yet as her interviewer, sworn to keep my opinions in my pocket, I was not going to be the one to do it.

Mrs. F. proceeded to produce the family's shortest spontaneous text, a mere two and a half pages, in contrast to the forty or so pages each produced by her son and daughter. Eschewing a sequence of events in narrative time, Mrs. F. jumped in with an evaluation:

> I'll start at the beginning, but roughly, childhood was half and half. I would have preferred a better childhood, a happier one . . .

No further description or explanation of this judgment followed, but the very next half line engaged me at once:

> but with God's influence, I prayed hard enough for a good husband and He answered me.

The entire group of educated, skeptical, professional readers found this line particularly striking, because it seemed to mark Mrs. F. as a certain kind of *character,* one with the attribute of naive piety. That is, she seemed to present herself from the very beginning as a passive, resigned, submissive receiver of benefits (or, by implication, curses) from an omniscient God. Interestingly, however, she allowed for active mediation through prescribed forms (i.e., "praying hard enough").

What followed this opening was not the traditional linear plot or model of maturational development paradigmatic of much Western autobiography,[10] but rather brief associative clusters, consisting of comments, opinions, and tidbits of information, often about others: her husband's and children's characters, their "problems" and deficiencies, the possibility of "coping" with something called Trouble:

> I got a very good husband, a little stubborn at times, but I'll take the stubbornness for the goodness that he's got there.
>
> I had four nice children, a little, shall I say, spoiled [laughs], all spoiled because of my husband, he's very easy. If it was up to me I think I would have been a little bit more stricter, but I think on the whole they turned out with less problems than a lot of other people.
>
> The major part of that is not being on dope. I think I was

blessed that they weren't, blessed in a way because I had a nephew, two nephews on either side and I had two brother-in-laws that were on dope. They are all off it now, thank God, and all doing well, but I am blessed that my kids didn't start it.

Other problems with them, you can't let that go and have them perfect.

Health-wise, up until the time I was 53, I had terrible health. After that I had a woman's operation, which I think helped me a lot, and I feel much better. I think I can cope better with things.

God bless my husband. He had a lot of patience with me, and my family. We had everything thrown at us because of my family. His family, he was the only boy and he had everything from the time he was seven years old. I think the life we both had as children, I think we both wanted something different when we got married. . . . His mother was very ill. His father was a drinker. He wasn't very fond of his stepmother, he never lived with her.

But I think what he went through, and what I went through, we built a better marriage on it. To a point I think we try to make our children not have too much of [the troubles] we had. I think we spoil them sometimes for the outside world. And I think that's what spoiled our two oldest children, their marriages.

My daughter is with a very nice man. I would have preferred someone else, but it's up to her.

My son, I'm still upset over him. It's six years that he is divorced and he just doesn't seem to pull out of it. He seems to compare other women to her, which isn't fair for him to do that, but I don't know. I really don't know, and I don't understand him now anymore. That's in general.

The only thing I can keep saying is I have a very good marriage, and hope and pray my kids will get the same type of a marriage that I had.

Outside of that, I don't know. I'm happy. I'd like to be in better health now, as my husband and I are getting older, especially him, but I'll take whatever God has given me.

And that's about it. Forty years of it [marriage] and it's all in there. . . . That's it.

If there is a unifying theme in this brief ramble around Mrs. F.'s "life," it is that marriage has been her lifelong work of construction, its "happiness" her safety net, its aim the carving out of a private haven in a problematic world. A dark past of difficult times is hinted at for herself, but only in the most general and opaque terms ("what I went through"; "the life we [she and Mr. F.] both had as children"; "we had everything thrown at us because of my family"). Her husband's troubles are more specifically delineated than her own: he is said to have had "everything thrown at him" from precisely the age of seven, and an ill mother, alcoholic father, and difficulties with a stepmother are expressly named. His "story," one might say, seems more present here than her own.

"Who Is She Kidding?" Versions of Mrs. F.'s Story

Our response to this narrative as professional readers/interpreters was to engage an issue that seemed to "explain" the effects we saw in Mrs. F.'s text, even as it rendered a new telling of it—our own. I am speaking of the issue of gender. Though as her interviewer, I was the only one of our research group to have met her, our collective ideas of Mrs. F. *as a woman,* partly derived from representations of her by her family, were inextricably implicated in our perception of her intention as a narrator.

It was our method in group discussions to take ourselves as Average Reader, positioning ourselves as a collective audience responding freshly, if self-consciously, to each text in order to see what reactions were evoked. When we assembled to discuss Mrs. F.'s life story, three characteristics of Mrs. F.'s first section were readily agreed upon by all: in comparison with the other five texts of her family, it was unusually brief, it was the least event oriented or sequentially organized, and it had the fewest number of statements directly describing the self in proportion to statements about others. Comparing her spontaneous narrative to those of her husband or her children, the group concluded that her text conveyed a sense of an "effaced" self (to use one researcher's word), or at least a selfhood defined almost completely through others in a very closely bound circle of family. This relational selfhood was not necessarily *articulated* as "feminine" at first, but for me the nuances were gendered even as I participated (at this point) in the general consensus.

Discussion continued: all the readers in our research group were in fact struck by the limited scope of the topics in Mrs. F.'s narrative, by the way in which the narrative's relative lack of structure emphasized present states at the expense of "story," and by her unusual lack of introspection, leading to the submergence of individual character traits in the group portrait of the family. The result was that her narrative was judged by several in the group to be not "well constructed." Whom, we might paraphrase the group response, was she kidding? What or where was she hiding? What kind of life *was* this, anyway?

The researchers in the project commented in different ways on a perceived gap between what the text *said* and what we as readers felt we *knew* about Mrs. F. as author of the text. Over the weeks of analysis, two different and quite opposite views of narrative selfhood in Mrs. F.'s text emerged to explain this gap. The first explained the above effects through a formal theory: the artlessness of the text derived from Mrs. F.'s apparent lack of knowledge of the narrative rules for autobiography. Thus, one research group member commented, "Mrs. F. *unwittingly* tells us a great deal about herself." Significantly, descriptions such as "restricted," "closed off," "ladylike," and "conventionally female" were mentioned by the proponents of this interpretation in connection with the narrator's supposed "naïveté." However, I was troubled by this interpretive stance, because a whole politics of reading was implicated in its conclusions. That is, Mrs. F.'s supposed withholding or suppression of a fuller narrative was experienced by so-called Average Reader as constitutively feminine (i.e., "ladylike").

What disturbed me about this interpretation was that it accepted so readily the social conditions of everyday living for women, especially those women who identify themselves with family and home. Thus Average Reader seemed to agree with Mr. F. himself, who spoke of his wife in his own text as not *there* in the real world in the same way he is:

> Uh my home life is pretty good. Uh with my wife and I—I don't think my wife was as educated as I would like her to be, although she graduated from high school. But she seems to be very bent on different things. She's too compliant; *she doesn't know the real world, the way things are.* (my emphasis)

Because the public world is defined as what is "real," the female subject who does not participate in or "know" its rules seems a kind of lacuna in the world, just as the selfhood of the female subject seems a kind of lacuna in the (expected) autobiographical text to Average Reader. It was here that Average Reader revealed himself or herself to be our very own historically situated, culturally biased, eager little group of text examiners, steeped in our own social conventions of reading gender.

At this point the second interpretation emerged, provoked by one reader's comment that Mrs. F.'s stance was only *"seemingly* passive." In this second version, her apparent naïveté about autobiographical conventions reflected a kind of "wily shyness," a subtle and sly way of achieving ego impulses while using (and, by implication, abusing) personal relations in a hierarchy of family politics. Mrs. F., in this version, would like to *appear* naive in order to protect her domain of power in the family. The implication was that the identity of Mrs. F. was not so much absent as *suspiciously present* in its deliberate absence, hovering in the wings, waiting to pounce on the unsuspecting audience.

This second interpretation, which implies that the narrator *knows* the narrative rules and deliberately manipulates or misreads them for artful effect, relies for evidence on the shifting and inconsistent disclaimers of agency in such key terms as "blessings" and *"if* it was up to me." In this view, the reader *suspects* the sparsity of events in the text and reads the "absences" as outward signs of a kind of perversion of intentionality. What was Mrs. F. leaving out and why? What does it reveal about her, for example, that a self-described "nervous breakdown" when her children were very young appears only later, under questioning? Thus Mrs. F., in this reading, is seen as manipulative, slipping in and out of active and passive roles when convenient for herself and the image she would like to project. Here Average Reader takes up the position of interrogator, policing the narrative for clues to bad faith and/or half-conscious motives of narcissism and self-aggrandizing power seeking.

If the first interpretation of protected naïveté idealizes (as it patronizes) the wife and mother roles, the second interpretive version implying Mrs. F.'s subtle domination invokes fears of the controlling, nagging, tyrannical woman that are always available in our shared cultural script. The import for understanding the everyday lives of "ordinary" women is that these two versions seemed to represent the only two possibilities for interpretation, inviting diminishment on the one hand (absence, unimportance, narrowness) or an inflated attribution of agency and power on the other (control, manipulation, domination).

Over time, neither of these descriptions seemed adequate to me when applied to Mrs. F. and the "kind of life she has got." As I pored over the lengthy text of Mrs. F.'s interview, I too felt an odd disparity or incongruity buried within it, but I did not locate the gap between what was said and my response in the same locutions. Rather than interpret this disparity as evidence of either simple naïveté *or* shrewd manipulation, I developed a third interpretive version that has greater explanatory power for me. In particular, it is my concern to see gender as neither a social determinant without individual variations nor a construct of specific personality traits, but as a strategic feature of the story.

For Mrs. F., who is not what the world would call "special" (least of all in her own eyes), the specific material and psychological conditions of what she considers her life's work, as well as her own conception of what constitutes womanhood, must be considered as compelling in her construction of her "life." I hope to show that the *form* of Mrs. F.'s story is structured so as to accommodate both the boundaries of her gendered position and the wish to break with these confines. The art of Mrs. F.'s narrative is the way in which it allows her to deny either position when necessary. In Mrs. F.'s case, that need for a different form is partially satisfied by the sharp demarcation in our interview method between the responsibility for having to "tell it yourself" in the first part and the release from the appearance of self-assertion in the imposed structure that followed (during which she was, after all, just answering questions). Simply put, the "Mrs. F." whose story appears so "self-effacing" in the spontaneously constructed narrative at the beginning is a very different "woman" when she is answering a set of specific questions in the second, more directed section of the interview, which constitutes by far the greater part of the text.

The Rhetoric of Mediation: "But," "So," and "Just"

As I read Mrs. F.'s text over and over, my interest increasingly centered on this gap. No other subject demonstrated such a striking difference in the portrait of the self as it is consecutively invoked in the first and second sections. If the emphasis in Mrs. F.'s first, "spontaneous" section is on self *through* others, that is, connected to or in association with others through the expressions of her caretaking in the text, in the question-and-answer part Mrs. F. presents herself as an individual, a self as *differentiated from* others.

Thus, the first, spontaneous part of the narrative is fueled by the constant awareness of the *possibility of trouble,* and the form the text takes is an inventory of troubles, with Mrs. F. as a kind of archivist of problems. Mrs. F.'s stance toward these troubles is implicated in her status as a knowledgeable authority on (family) Trouble. In this part of the text, knowledge for Mrs. F. appears as almost entirely *implied* rather than as an explicit topic.[11] The only knowledge she describes explicitly is negative: what she *doesn't* understand is her son's behavior. Yet she implies that she once did understand even him: "I don't understand him now *anymore."*

On the one hand, her area of knowledge, she says, is extremely confined: "Outside of that [her marriage], I don't know." But *within* that circumscribed area, Mrs. F. speaks as if her knowledge—the knowledge of intimacy—is so deep that it does not need to be articulated: it consists almost entirely of the unspoken but potent presence of the ordinary and the conventional, against which Mrs. F. leans her weight: "I think on the whole they turned out with less problems than a lot of other people." Mrs. F. goes on about her family and their concerns as if no explanation about context or history were necessary, as though she assumes we *know already* (e.g., what "turning out well" means to her). There is comparatively little interpretation, perhaps because her reliance on known and familiar ritual makes reflectiveness unnecessary. Indeed (one speculates), introspection may perhaps be seen as wasteful, even risky, in that it does not serve Mrs. F.'s need to preserve a certain definition of female self as *for* others.

Perhaps it is because so much in her world *is* given that very little in Mrs. F.'s first section *happens*. The textual strategy of the opening is balance and mediation, taking up disturbing or threatening elements only to find a way to justify, soften, soothe, or sigh them away. The essential argument of the first eight sentences may be diagrammed as follows:

(1) I'll start at the beginning	but	childhood was half and half
(2) I would have preferred a better childhood . . .	but	I prayed hard enough for a good husband and He answered me
(3) I got a very good husband, a little stubborn at times	but	I'll take the stubbornness for the goodness he's got

(4) I had four nice children, all spoiled because of my husband . . .	but	they turned out with less problems than other people. (6) The major part of that is not being on dope. (7) I was blessed
because I had [relatives] that were on dope . . .	but	I am blessed my kids didn't start it.

The significant conjunction "but" is used to override Trouble even as it is being pointed out. The negative element usually precedes the "but," which then is followed by the exception to the rule, the positive or optimistic side of the question, or the resigned acceptance of its inevitability. This stance subtly positions Mrs. F. as active negotiator in (and with) her family and her life, whereas her resignation signals her readiness to abjure agency when the die is already cast.

Yet in the second, question-and-answer, part of the interview, the Self that is initially constituted by *not telling* of itself or its origin then becomes, through questioning, a subject engaging with events through active agency. She also acquires a linear history, an explanatory past and a supposable future:

> Q: Did you feel understood as a child?
> A: No. No way. It was their way. In fact it was my father's way or no way at all. You didn't have a say if you wanted this, like school. I loved office work, wanted to go into that. He said no, it had to be a trade. He wanted me as a seamstress. I couldn't even sew a straight line. So I went in for beauty culture, but *I wasn't satisfied. So when I was 17, I quit school and went to work.* (emphasis mine)

This second self relies on assertion, followed by action in the world; "so" replaces "but" as the marker of this stance. The second "layer" also emerges in her double answer to the question, "What sort of child were you?" Mrs. F.'s first answer was "dependable," the type of child who did what was expected, who "had to" take care of her sister while her parents worked. This is the voice of the female roles of daughter-wife-mother, in which there is little room for individuation or choice (with one important exception, to which we shall come). The chief hallmarks of this expected behavior are the following: submitting to authority to purchase (male) protection; fulfilling obligation at the cost of individual choice; skillfully learning to field events "thrown at you" as an object, in order to negate the possibility of being a Trouble-making subject; being "ordinary" to avoid competing; and being silent to avoid saying the wrong or dangerous thing. The rewards of this gender role seem very clearly demarcated: it brings security, stability, protectedness, and love of a very particular sort.

While answering this question, however, Mrs. F. suddenly volun-teered that she was also "fresh," "kinda nasty with my mouth," a trait that she laughingly admitted "usually got [her] what she wanted." Here, to this listener's surprise, was a different self, as well as the dilemma: how to combine obedience to the boundary rules of her gen-dered role with "getting what you want," the assertion of an individ-ual desire and intention. Here the privileges stand in opposition to the rewards of feminine behavior. They include mastery; independence; being valued in the ways in which the public, so-called real world val-ues individuals; owning one's selfhood; owning up to one's choices and decisions; and having a "character" rather than fulfilling a role. If the problem in the spontaneous first part of Mrs. F.'s text is how to steer a safe course in the Sea of Troubles, the issue of the second is whether to risk *being* a Trouble to oneself. Again, the problem of being an "ordinary" woman in everyday life is the circumscribed na-ture of strategic choices: one may renounce agency and self-assertion as a defensive measure, or one may try to "get what one wants" and be seen as a troublesome rebel.

At home is a sort of female heroism: that of ordinary life, with its small sacrifices (risking marital disagreement over a daughter's wish for independence in her own apartment) and small dreams (a new par-lor), its hardly noticed self-suppressions and self-expressions. By con-trast, the "outside," largely male world (beginning with her husband's construction business) is the "real" world, defined as an arena of pub-lic activity with tools, products, earnings, and wide consequences in the public domain. The mediation between the two worlds is largely accomplished by the connection with men. Pleasing a male—whether father, husband, or God the Father—is one important way of using the secrets of the "inside" world to contain or obtain the given troubles/

blessings that are experienced as "just" imposed by the outside, namely, by fate or the physical world.

Courtship and Romance: "Just" One of Those Things

Mrs. F. speaks of courtship, and in particular of one moment of courtship, as the high point of drama in her life, the moment that, by its very atypicality, serves as a trope for what she *could be,* her possible self. The scenario of her courtship is clearly seen by her as *her* domain of interpretive authority. This was confirmed for us by the family interview, in which we saw that Mrs. F.'s version (as opposed to her husband's) was the one accepted by the children: she had taught them not merely what happened, but *how to tell it.*[12]

In this telling, Mrs. F.'s life was "predestinated" by her parents' and friends' and culture's expectations for her: "I was pressured into doing the first engagement, because all the other girls were doing that." As an engaged young woman, she was out with a girlfriend when Mr. F., her future husband, came in the door, and "the first time I put my eyes on him I said to myself, that's the one I'm going to marry." Later in the text Mrs. F. says she turned to her friend and said, " 'Jenny, I'm going home with that man tonight and I'm going to marry him,' " at the same time taking her engagement ring from her finger. In the same way, she asserts that they decided to marry when they did " 'cause I wanted to be with him"; later she adds, "it was *just—I* wanted to be with him and *that was it*" (my emphases). Mr. F., interestingly, tells something of a different story on this point. He says:

> And then I met my wife and we got married. And I think I should have waited a little longer to get married. . . . I thought I wasn't secure enough in a job. . . . I think I got married because there was pressure from her family, 'cause she was engaged to someone else when she met me.

Whereas Mr. F. concentrates on familial, practical, and economic circumstances, Mrs. F. focuses on the linguistic moment: though he never asked her to marry him "in so many words," she assumed that if he did not want to marry when she did,

> when I set the date I think he would have said, "Let's wait awhile." I think he would have said that.

He did not ask her *not* to set the date, and so she took the active role in the matter. She relates that when he mentioned getting engaged in a year's time, she replied, " 'By next New Year's Eve we will be married.' " "He never argued with me," she adds.

Clearly, within the realm of love and courtship, Mrs. F. experiences herself as being entitled to and having enjoyed a good deal of *legitimate* power, as opposed to the sort of self-assertion contained in "being nasty with your mouth." Indeed, her role of influencing behind the scenes, shaping opinion, directing talk (such as "letting" children have their say at the dinner table), and maintaining personal relations at home and in the neighborhood all seem to be extensions from that early high point of power. Because being in charge of love and marriage is an empowerment that to Mrs. F. is wholly normative and "ordinary" in a woman's life, it serves as a legitimating force in her entire history: there is, Mrs. F. says near the end of her transcript, "no greater *triumph*" than "finding someone" to share your life with.

The forcefulness and activity that Mrs. F. claims for herself at this special moment are, however, of a very particular kind. Her assertion of selfhood is conveyed through a pronouncement—"we will be married"—that has a certain force, but this linguistic power is strictly confined to and usable only in the private domain. As a result, it is aligned with the mystical in that it is defined as not "real" life (unlike salaried work, higher education, or forays into the public world), so that by its nature it remains limited and constrained.

Seizing this moment, one might say, is a domestic version of the counsel Mrs. F. says she gave her youngest daughter when the latter was in college: "You have to fight for what you want." Because this advice applies for Mrs. F. only within the parameters of institutionalized male-female relations, however, it reinforces those very boundaries against which her daughter Debbie will fight. Further, by defining this power as privileged by an extraordinary moment, she reaffirms the illegitimacy of power and rebellion in *ordinary* moments. And last, defining the authentic power as purely private and individual, this wisdom perpetuates discontinuity between those public and private worlds that form its limits.

Elsewhere, Mrs. F. connects shyness to the inability to talk or say the right thing outside the family:

> I died every time I went in his class. The minute I'd get up I'd know the answer but couldn't bring it out.

> I think I'm more outward now, because if I was younger I never would be doing this interview.

Verbal expression is associated with mastery—"fighting for what you want," "sticking to your guns," and so on—but this power and activity are legitimated by denying that the source of language is a subject who possesses agency. The strategic word is "just":

> No, it wasn't love, I *just* turned around to my girlfriend and said, "Jenny, I'm going home with that man tonight and I'm going to marry him."

> It was *just* one of those things, I don't know why . . .

> I don't know [what made her decide to get married when she did] it was *just*—I wanted to be with him and that was it.

> I think from the minute we met . . . I think it was *just* one of those things that we knew.

"Just" is as linguistically significant as "but" in Mrs. F.'s text: this small word takes on the weighty role of mediator between divisions, in this case between private assertion and public expectations of gender roles. In the passages above it serves as a disclaimer of agency in the midst of the most dramatic claim for Mrs. F.'s selfhood as founded on intentionality ("*I wanted* to be with him"). "Just" as a linguistic device is thus a fluid means for expressing Mrs. F.'s duality of feminine self-abnegation on the one hand and triumphant assertion of will on the other.

The romantic scenario *is* the drama of a woman being chosen (by a man, or by Fate) because *she* is special (or blessed) and/or the *moment* is special, entitling the protagonist to a temporally finite but seemingly unbounded freedom to choose for herself. "I can't blame my mother because the women were taught the man is everything and that's it," she later states. Earlier, she had referred to the Law of her father's word: "It was his way or no way at all," "You didn't have a say about what you wanted or liked to do." Romance is a way of stealing the language from the father, of having one's say, though at the price of limiting access to other, more public-oriented constructions of selfhood.

Yet here we must return to the apparent *withholding* of story in the first section, and especially to the repeated disclaimers of knowledge throughout, both of which led the research group to perceive a lack of verisimilitude in the text. Mrs. F. frequently remarks that she "doesn't know" or "has no idea," even remarking this when not asked, as if anticipating and defending against explanation. One might speculate that this cultivated lack of causality preserves the mysterious transcendence of "ordinary" women's affairs necessary to inform Mrs. F.'s life with meaning. Within this structure, events are "predestinated" and love itself is seen as an "outside" force, an unaccounted-for blessing: she and her husband would fight, for example, but "there's always something that draws us back . . . what it is *I don't know*." Similarly, when she fell in love with her husband, she describes herself as "very surprised" ("I couldn't understand why I picked him"); again, when she broke off her engagement to a previous fiancé, she felt no guilt, convinced she was doing the right thing: "I haven't got the slightest idea [why]."

Most revealingly, she states that when she and her husband became engaged, they did not use words to express emotion because "it was *just one of those things that we knew*." Although language can create romance and give shape to a life, at the most special times language itself (perhaps through its identification for Mrs. F. with masculine acts of assertion) can interfere with the acting out of the romantic fantasy, intruding on the space of imaginative truth, where things "just *are*." Though Mrs. F. says she would be described by her husband as "nosy," wishing to inquire and speak about the affairs of others, she also protects an extremely private core of the unspeakable, whether it is a deeply affecting and painful incident involving her father observed at age six, which she declined to describe; the personal affairs of her children, about which she says she "doesn't want to know"; or transcendent romantic feeling, which would be diminished by being expressed in words.

It is all the more interesting, then, that Mrs. F. chose to relate as a moment of autonomous will her decision to go "back to work" at age fifty-seven, after her daughter Nina, newly divorced and living at home again with a small baby, had attempted to cast Mrs. F. in the role of chief child rearer once more. For once, Mrs. F.'s reasons for her decision are clearly stated—there is very little demurral in the name of blessings, curses, or mysterious knowledge—and all point to her refusal of a gendered role of ordinariness, selflessness, and invisibility:

I felt that everyone was doing something worthwhile and I wasn't doing anything that was worthwhile.

It got so to a point I said, "*What kind of life have I got?*" I raised my kids and I'm raising another family again.

The ability to ask this crucial question, "What kind of life have I got?" represents the clearest expression of self-consciousness in Mrs. F.'s text, the point at which her representation of her "life" is open to reevaluation, articulated, and therefore changeable, rather than a given that is "just understood." Such questioning is particularly significant because the possibility of agency implies meaningful action, leading to a linear sequencing of events: If my life is not satisfactory, what has caused it to be so? And what then am I going to do about it? *What now*? This challenge to received beliefs and her implied consciousness of the relationship between belief and action was the narrative "hook," I will admit, that allowed me to share and collaborate with her in a different (re)construction of her story.

Conclusion: What Kind of Life?

In this reconstruction of Mrs. F.'s narrative as a gendered story, her text both enables *and* is the means of evading ownership of a female, narrativized "self" as that is ordinarily understood in our culture. Positioned outside the "real" (public) world, yet not permitted a sense of private self in the realm she supposedly "rules," Mrs. F. adopts a strategy for being a woman that is *textual*. This strategy requires a kind of double telling, presenting herself as an agent only in the private domain and as an absence in the public sector. Telling her life history, I would argue, requires such active strategizing; we might say that her prescribed gender role as self-effacing "ordinary" woman comes directly into conflict with her prescribed role as active creator in the genre of autobiography.

Similarly, the romance of idealized marriage and family is the informing myth of her text, yet the price of maintaining it is acting out a well-defined role, albeit in a comfortably familiar traditional script. In this way she avoids a fixed position. The theme and technique of this self-narration come together in the oscillations between what we might call the verbal assertiveness and verbal retreats of the text, as well as in the assertions, gaps, and silences of the narrative itself, as we see in the following pairs of closely associated textual moments:

Assertions	*Retreats*
"nosy"	not wanting to know
open family, talking	forgetting/escaping

nasty mouth/putting foot down	shy in classroom
stubborn, sticking to your guns	shy in public, in interview
getting what you want	fearfulness
assertiveness with husband—engagement	obeying father
assertiveness with husband over Nina's independence	nervous breakdown— paralysis
taking job	doing "what's expected"
asking: "What kind of life?"	doing the "predestinated"

In the end, Mrs. F. does seem to have gotten "what she wanted," as she said of her girlhood self: living out her own myth, she has a traditional marriage *but* has moved out into the world, though this move is qualified by her husband's being her boss, which seems an extension of the traditional script after all. Though, as Sidonie Smith claims, female autobiographers must "approach the autobiographical territory from their position as speakers at the margins of discourse,"[13] we may say that she has found a language that actively *works* the margin. Mrs. F. skirts the shoals of presence, just as she has learned to maneuver her way through absence, like a brave and "stubborn" craft in troubled waters.

As the first audience for Mrs. F.'s text, and later one of her reader-interpreters, I came to stand before it not with an authority over its interpretation that would foreclose or exhaust its multiple meanings, but with a certain humility, admiration, and, eventually, sympathy. For me the ingenuity (*not* ingenuousness or disingenuousness) of Mrs. F.'s narrative is the way in which it allows for, but also contains, a multiplicity of positions that are contradictory, yet also permits a certain fluidity of identity within the constraints of her gender, ethnicity, and class.

Having abjured the comforts of any claims to certainty and precision within social research, I was continually forced to confront the disturbing subjectivity of our collective interpretations, and to recognize the act of listening/reading/interpreting or criticizing as (another) *re*constructive act: not a recuperation of what is already there, hidden behind a more or less transparent screen of words, but an always secondary (or tertiary) act of *retelling,* a revision of what is already a continuously edited process, the telling of one's self to a "self" (one's own or other) constituted by previous tellings. I submit this interpretation, therefore, not as the authoritative one, but as still another version of what is already a version of selfhood—Mrs. F.'s representation of herself as a text. When the interpretation is gendered, Mrs. F.'s text appears to be a different story.

Mrs. F.'s life history was a disturbance to us as a research group partly because the enterprise and structure of her "everyday" life contradict the standard notion of autobiography, as rooted in an originary impulse of reflectiveness. In attempting to resolve this contradiction, the group, male and female members alike, turned to value judgments about the narrator and to familiar expectations of gendered asymmetry, rather than probing more deeply into the engagement among gender, selfhood, and the narrative act itself.

This particular interview was additionally a field of struggle for me because I see consciousness as the key to my own endeavors, both personal and professional, as well as the foundational force behind my belief in feminism. It was extremely difficult to avoid positioning myself as superior in my role as audience to this very "ordinary" woman telling the story of her everyday life. Thus Mrs. F.'s lack of introspection initially seemed tied to her status as a "traditional woman," while her reliance on the mythos of romance touched a nerve by recalling aspects of my own life. In coming to terms with Mrs. F.'s stratagem of telling, I was coming to terms with a disowned "Mrs. F." in myself, with a troublesome version of my life, in effect.

Yet in both the personal and political senses, seeing from the inside out what Mrs. F.'s story means to her in her own interpretation is one way out of the theoretical impasse of feminist confrontations with the so-called conventional or traditional woman. If the story of Mrs. F.'s text illustrates a collective act of constructing life history as a narrative of identity, my deliberate collaboration (to use a double-edged word) with Mrs. F.'s own view of the world is an attempt to make a particular use of this understanding. We might say that, as in all interpretive versions, I found what I went about looking for, in this case a feminist retelling based on my own construction of gender in everyday life.

Notes

1. Texts derived from oral performances have a special relation to issues of gender. See Carole Boyce Davies, "Collaboration and the Ordering Imperative in Life Story Production," in *De/Colonizing the Subject:The Politics of Gender in Women's Autobiography*, ed. Sidonie Smith and Julia Watson (Minneapolis: University of Minnesota Press, 1992).

2. I do not mean to deny that she occupies a specific place in each of these categories, or that any or all of these could be used as a window to the construction of her "identity" in another kind of work. See the discussion of this point in the Personal Narratives Group, *Interpreting Women's Lives: Feminist Theory and Personal Narratives* (Bloomington: Indiana University Press, 1989), 19.

3. Rita Felski, *Beyond Feminist Aesthetics: Feminist Literature and Social Change* (Cambridge: Harvard University Press, 1989), 83.

4. Several publications have resulted from this research, among them Jerome Bruner, "Life as Narrative," *Social Research* 54 (1987): 11–32; and his *Acts of Meaning*, (Cambridge: Harvard University Press, 1990), especially the chapter titled "Autobiography and Self." See also Jerome Bruner and Susan Weisser, "The Invention of Self: Autobiography and Its Forms," in *Literacy and Orality*, ed. D. Olsen and S. Torrence (New York: Cambridge University Press, 1991). I am indebted to the mentorship of Dr. Bruner during this project as well as afterward, and gratefully acknowledge his contribution. I also wish to acknowledge the unpublished work of my fellow research associates on this project, particularly Joyce Greenberg and Jamie Walkup.

5. I am thinking here of the ethnographic formulations of Clifford Geertz in *The Interpretation of Cultures: Selected Essays* (New York: Basic Books, 1973) and especially his introduction to *Local Knowledge: Further Essays in Interpretive Anthropology* (New York: Basic Books, 1983). See also James Clifford and George E. Marcus, eds., *Writing Culture: The Poetics and Politics of Ethnography* (Berkeley: University of California Press, 1986).

6. The impulse to do so comes mainly from reader-response theory and from feminist social science. See Helen Roberts, ed., *Doing Feminist Research* (London: Routledge & Kegan Paul, 1981), especially Ann Oakley's influential essay, "Interviewing Women: A Contradiction in Terms"; and Maria Mies's "Towards a Methodology for Feminist Research," in *Theories of Women's Studies*, ed. Gloria Bowles and Renate D. Klein (London: Routledge & Kegan Paul, 1983); Catherine K. Riessman, "When Gender Is Not Enough: Women Interviewing Women," *Gender and Society* 1 (1987): 172–207; Marjorie DeVault, "Talking and Listening from Women's Standpoint: Feminist Strategies for Interviewing and Analysis," *Social Problems* 37 (1990): 96–116; Personal Narratives Group, *Interpreting Women's Lives;* Sherna B. Gluck and Daphne Patai, eds., *Women's Words: The Feminist Practice of Oral History* (London: Routledge & Kegan Paul, 1991); Sandra Harding, ed., *Feminism and Methodology* (Bloomington: Indiana University Press, 1987). See also the work of Elliot G. Mishler, especially "The Analysis of Interview-Narratives," in *Narrative Psychology: The Storied Nature of Human Conduct,* ed. Theodore Sarbin (New York: Praeger, 1986), and his *Research Interviewing: Context and Narrative* (Albany: State University of New York Press, 1988).

7. See the special issue titled "The 'Vexingly Unverifiable': Truth in Autobiography," *Studies in the Literary Imagination* 23 (Fall 1990).

8. In separating gender from other categories, I am going against the grain of some trends in interpretation, as well as the theoretical stance of my research group. For the relation between "practice" and "theory" in autobiography, see the illuminating discus-

sion by Shari Benstock in her introduction to *The Private Self: Theory and Practice of Women's Autobiographical Writing*, ed. Shari Benstock (Chapel Hill: University of North Carolina Press, 1988).

9. The inherent discomforts and difficulties of doing research among groups whose social power differs from that of the researchers is taken up in Gluck and Patai, *Women's Words*, particularly in Karen Olsen and Linda Shopes's chapter, "Crossing Boundaries, Building Bridges: Doing Oral History among Working-Class Women and Men," 189–204.

10. For the relation of gender to traditional definitions of autobiography, see Carolyn Heilbrun, *Writing a Woman's Life* (New York: Norton, 1988); Susan Stanford Friedman, "Women's Autobiographical Selves: Theory and Practice," in *The Private Self: Theory and Practice of Women's Autobiographical Writing*, ed. Shari Benstock (Chapel Hill: University of North Carolina Press, 1988), 34–62; Regenia Gagnier, "The Literary Standard, Working-Class Autobiography, and Gender," in *Revealing Lives: Autobiography, Biography, and Gender*, ed. Susan Groag Bell and Marilyn Yalom (Albany: State University of New York Press, 1990). The ways in which the female life cycle is reconceptualized in fiction is the subject of Elizabeth Abel, Marianne Hirsch, and Elizabeth Langland, eds., *The Voyage In: Fictions of Female Development* (Hanover: University Press of New England, 1983).

11. I am in part deriving this distinction from Mary F. Belenky, Blythe M. Clinchy, Nancy R. Goldberger, and Jill M. Tarule, *Women's Ways of Knowing: The Development of Self, Voice, and Mind* (New York: Basic Books, 1986).

12. For feminist analyses of women and romance narrative, see Janice Radway, *Reading the Romance: Women, Patriarchy and Popular Literature* (Chapel Hill: University of North Carolina Press, 1984); Tania Modleski's criticism of Radway in her *Feminism without Women: Culture and Criticism in a "Postfeminist" Age* (London: Routledge & Kegan Paul, 1991), 40–45; and Laurie Langbauer, *Women and Romance: The Consolations of Gender in the English Novel* (Ithaca, N.Y.: Cornell University Press, 1990).

13. Sidonie Smith, *A Poetics of Women's Autobiography: Marginality and the Fictions of Self-Representation* (Bloomington: Indiana University Press, 1987), 44.

12 / Race/Identity/Culture/Kin: Constructions of African American Identity in Transracial Adoption

Sandra Patton

One of the problems is where do you put a multiethnic kid? It was harder the older I got. It's easier to place a 2-year-old than an 8-year-old who's been put through the ringer, or a 10-year-old who has a firm grip on rejection. . . . When my parents adopted me, I just wanted to be a little white girl with blond hair and blue eyes. I knew I was a black child and people didn't want me because of that.

> SANDI ILILONGA, adopted at age 12 by a white couple after living in ten foster homes and two orphanages, current spokesperson for the National Coalition to End Racism in America's Child Care System, *Los Angeles Times*, November 3, 1993[1]

I have a concern about white families. . . . We have a racist society. Many white families do deny the child's African American heritage. They say, "He's a human being. It doesn't matter." Any black person will tell you that's laughable.

> ZENA OGLESBY, executive director of the Institute for Black Parenting, *Los Angeles Times*, November 3, 1993[2]

[A] black child raised white will sooner than later be confronted with racism by virtue of the color of his/her skin. At that point, that young person must either deny his/her blackness or be forced to *feel* black while being culturally white. This is the stuff of identity conflict.

> TREVOR W. PURCELL, *Anthropology Newsletter*, February 1993[3]

Questions of racial identity have been at the center of public dialogues concerning transracial adoption since it first emerged as a controversial issue in the late 1960s and early 1970s. This heated cultural debate has focused on the transmission of African American cultural identity to black children adopted into white middle-class families.[4] The central question regarding the appropriateness of this social practice is whether or not white parents are capable of teaching their children African American culture and history, and enculturating them with the skills necessary for blacks to survive in this racially unequal society. Concerns over the transmission of identity have shaped public policies regarding racial matching between children and parents for more than two decades. Indeed, critiques of transracial adoption, articulated most prominently by the National Association of Black Social Workers (NABSW), are commonly cited as the primary cause of dramatic decline in such placements after the early 1970s.[5]

In the contested racial politics of the 1990s, transracial adoption has once again become the subject of fierce public debate. Although arguments against this practice continue to focus on racial identity, the political context in which this perspective is articulated has shifted since the 1970s. The contemporary discourse has been dominated by arguments against racial matching policies and by characterizations of the members of the National Association of Black Social Workers as the "new racists." The dominant narrative that has emerged begins by citing the increasing numbers of children of color in foster care and bemoans the inadequate numbers of black families able to adopt. The tension in this story emerges through the information that there are plenty of white families willing to adopt black children, but, in this narrative, "what keeps many children and parents apart is not the old-fangled segregation created by whites who oppose racial mixing. It's the new-fangled segregation now supported by a small but powerful group of black Americans who support 'racial matching.'"[6] The story continues with the explanation that racial matching policies and practices keep African American children waiting in long-term "foster limbo" while social workers search for black parents.[7] The narrative concludes with an argument in favor of transracial adoption, supported by reference to the "empirical evidence" demonstrating how well-adjusted transracial adoptees are.

Two key elements in this narrative require scrutiny. The representation of members of the National Association of Black Social Workers as the villains of the story—as the "new racists"—is fundamentally problematic. They have continued, since 1972, to oppose transracial adoption, but this stance is only one small piece of their much broader critique of the social welfare system's failure to serve the needs of black children and families. The other element that calls out for a deeper reading is the continual reliance on the findings of one longitudinal study of transracially adoptive families as evidence in favor of transracial adoptions. Although there are a number of speakers in this public dialogue, the argument has been presented as a polarized debate between two positions that have come to be represented by the National Association of Black Social Workers on one side and academic researchers Rita J. Simon and Howard Altstein on the other.[8] Underlying these divergent perspectives are conflicting definitions of race, differentially legitimated through the particular discursive practices operating in the realms of social work and public policy.

Although this view has dominated contemporary discourse, there are other, less prominent, readings of the issue, as well as a range of potential responses, that have not yet been articulated publicly. Some of the "facts" presented in this narrative are "true"; others are misleading or only partially correct. I would like to suggest that a facile acceptance of this argument against racial matching in adoption is problematic. My purpose is not to critique the dominant interpretation point by point, but rather to consider how it has been constructed in the context of racial politics in the postwar United States, how this construction of knowledge is an agent of power, and how it may affect the lives of black children.

The Social Construction of Identity: Adoption, Race, and the Policy Debate

Racial identity is the contested terrain in this social dialogue; thus, a consideration of identity and race as socially constructed is a useful entry point in understanding how this social issue has developed and how such questions are connected to the contemporary debate over racial matching policies. My interest in this topic began with my own experiences as an adoptee. I first began considering questions of identity and adoption in light of the racial and ethnic "match" between myself and my white parents. When I was adopted in the mid-1960s there were still enough white infants available for agencies to match children and parents closely enough to create the desired illusion of birth ties between them. Yet the invisibility of adoption and difference that this process was meant to ensure did not preclude struggles with identity issues. In a society that defines "real" families through biological ties, those of us with origin narratives beginning in a public agency rather than a human body cannot help but struggle with questions of who we "really" are, who we might have been, and how our identities have been constructed.

From a cultural studies perspective, all human identities are socially constructed; this understanding is often an assumption among adoptees as well. Adoption is the *literal* social construction of families and, thus, of identities. Those of us who were adopted into our families— whether across or within racial categories—often move through our everyday lives with an acute understanding that our identities have been constituted by outside forces, that who we are is not "natural." Not only are adoptees often aware that we would have been fundamentally different people had we been raised by our birth rather than adoptive parents, but this sense of identity as constructed, yet somehow arbitrary, is heightened by the feeling that there are other lives we could have lived, other people we could have been, had some small circumstance of our births or adoptions been different. Any sense of "natural"—born into—identity is easily displaced by the knowledge that the choice of which family is allowed to adopt which child is made by a social worker according to the policies and practices guiding a particular agency. The range of possible selves a child may become is dramatically multiplied when the social construction of identity begins in the files of the U.S. child welfare system.

The genealogy of an adoptee's identity, then, must move beyond the family tree, to the discursive roots of racial meaning embedded in the values, beliefs, policies, and practices of the institution governing this practice of social reproduction. Sociologists Omi and Winant argue that "through *policies* which are explicitly or implicitly racial, state institutions organize and enforce the racial politics of everyday life" (1986, 76). In the case of transracial adoption, racial matching policies directly organize racial identities by legislating which families—black or white—children are placed with. This determination significantly shapes which cultural meanings of race will be available to black children in constructing their identities. The construction of subjectivity happens at the phenomenological level, yet the range of cultural meanings of race available to individuals is structured systemically through racial matching policies and practices, as well as those child welfare policies that are not *explicitly* racial, but nonetheless, in practice, serve to track black and white children through different channels of the adoption/foster care system. In this context the social construction of identity is located at both the macro and micro levels, pointing toward inquiries into both structural factors at the level of policy and cultural influences at the level of individual meaning.

The state organization of racial identities is in transition.[9] The real stakes in this dialogue concern the institutionalization of racial meanings in policy that will continue for many years to shape the lives and identities of black children entering the child welfare system. The debate centers on a tension between the belief that black children should be raised by African American parents and the concern over large numbers of black children for whom no same-race placements have been found. It is broadly accepted that black children raised in African American families are typically taught—both overtly and by example—necessary methods for surviving in the racially stratified United States. This understanding underlies attempts to place children with parents of the same race. The tension stems from a recent increase in the number of children of color in foster care, which exceeds the numbers of African American parents selected to adopt.[10] The issue is framed by questions concerning how long agencies should search for black families for African American children before allowing adoption by white parents.[11] Thus, the salience of concerns over racial identity and survival skills is fundamental to contemporary policy debates, and such questions are inseparable from the racial politics of the 1990s.

In the contemporary United States, cultural meanings of race are available to individuals and groups differentially as well, based on where they are located in the social landscape of racial identity. Historian Evelyn Brooks Higginbotham argues that "we must recognize race as providing sites of dialogic exchange and contestation, since race has constituted a discursive tool for both oppression and liberation."[12] Thus, whereas all contemporary "subjects" must construct a sense of self amid a broad range of available meanings of race and identity, this task is significantly complicated for individuals growing up in multiracial families.

Their social location as black children raised by white parents in a racially stratified society provides transracial adoptees with access to a variety of often conflictual systems of cultural meaning regarding race and African American identity in the contemporary United States. Black children of white parents will be exposed to a different range of racial meanings and narratives of self than will black children raised by African American parents. Demographic and cultural factors such as the racial composition of the neighborhood and community and the racial assumptions of parents and other family members fundamentally shape the range of cultural systems of racial meaning that are made available to these children.

In the public discourse concerning transracial adoption, the identities of adoptees are often discussed in monolithic terms, as if they will develop *either* a white cultural identity *or* a black cultural identity. Judy Turner, a white foster parent who struggled to adopt a black toddler, and eventually succeeded, explains the primary argument against transracial placements that she and her husband faced: The private adoption agency "steadfastly maintained that if Jordan were raised by us, he would grow to hate both whites and blacks—presumably because he'd feel he didn't fit in with either race."[13] The human construction of a meaningful sense of self is rarely played out in such simple, neatly divided categories. Cultural anthropology provides a useful framework for considering how individuals in particular social contexts construct their identities through the cultural meaning systems available to them. Approaching culture as anthropologist John L. Caughey defines it, as "a conceptual system of beliefs, rules, and values that lies behind different ways of behaving,"[14] allows us to consider all human beings as multicultural; that is, all humans are exposed to and in turn utilize a broad range of cultural meaning systems in negotiating everyday life. From this perspective the central question concerning the formation of racial identity in transracial adoptees is not *which* culture—black or white—the adoptee belongs to, but rather *how* the individual's identity is informed by the particular versions of African American and white/hegemonic cultural meaning systems he or she encounters.

The focus on survival skills in the discourse concerning transracial adoption suggests that African American culture has developed particular *cognitive strategies* of survival and resistance for members of an oppressed group in a racist society. Damon Hersh, a twenty-five-year-old African American who was adopted by white parents at the age of three, explains: "The biggest thing would be to tell a black adopted child there's nothing wrong with being black, that in fact it's a very good thing, though society is going to tell the child otherwise."[15] Hersh's statement pinpoints a central issue in concerns over survival skills: the negative ideological messages black children growing up in the United States receive about themselves through such channels as popular culture, educational materials, and social interactions. Mastery of methods for deconstructing and delegitimating racial stereotypes and racist treatment is a necessity for African Americans in the racially stratified United States.

Survival skills can involve cultural knowledge as well as particular ways of seeing; indeed, the sense of a "double-consciousness" theorized by W. E. B. Du Bois is still socially relevant nearly a century later.[16] Sociologist Howard Winant explains: "Today we can see that dual consciousness is an immensely significant phenomenon. It can be theorized as resistance and subversion, as ambivalence, as standpoint and critique."[17] From the perspective of cultural anthropology, survival skills are part of a system of cultural meaning—a mental map that individuals use in navigating through their lives. The crucial question for transracial adoptees is whether white parents, whose (unmarked) racial identity is continually reinforced as the social norm, are capable of teaching their black children how to resist and undercut potentially devastating ubiquitous racial stereotypes.

Transracial adoptees are indeed multiply defined, multicultural selves. The pressing questions concern how racial matching policies structure racial identity by determining the social location from which an adoptee encounters cultural meanings of race. In this context the institutional definitions of race underlying child welfare policies and the debates concerning such policies must be considered critically.

Reproducing "the Family": Children, Race, and the State

There are two fundamental questions regarding race in the contemporary discourse concerning transracial adoption. The first question pertains to the construction of an adoptee's sense of racial identity, but also at issue are the racially defined relationships children and parents have to the adoption agency system.

The contemporary tension surrounding the increasing numbers of children of color, older children, and children with health problems and/or disabilities in the foster care system and the concomitant demand for healthy white infants on the U.S. mainstream and underground adoption markets has roots in the cultural, economic, political, and institutional construction of the adoption system in the post-World War II era. Although cultural mythology may still present visions of an adoption system dedicated to "the best interests of the child," in actuality, as Joyce Ladner's important and insightful qualitative sociological study demonstrates, the social practice of adoption was largely institutionalized following World War II in response to an unprecedented increase in adoption requests for healthy white infants from infertile white, middle-class, heterosexual, married couples, and "adoption policies and practices were formulated and functioned in behalf of this small clientele."[18] Not all children available for adoption were placed in adoptive families, and decisions about which children were placed in foster or group care, which children were adopted, and which children were placed with which families were made primarily along racial lines.

The postwar increase in demand for healthy white infants occurred in the context of cultural changes in the meaning of family. A narrowly drawn white, middle-class, Christian, suburban, nuclear family came to be seen as the most ideal and "legitimate" construction of family.[19] This suburban family ideal was not only a cultural formation, but also fundamentally rooted in economic access to homeownership, the means to acquire a wide range of consumer products, and the ability of a man to support his wife and family financially. Clearly, this middle-class view of the family was not equally accessible to whites and blacks; the discrimination in the U.S. labor force that African Americans have historically endured typically limited black men to low-wage jobs and required large numbers of black women to participate in the labor market in order to sustain their families.

This ideological, race-specific definition of the family defined other cultural forms as deviant, marginalizing the historically diverse kinship patterns and experiences of racial-ethnic groups and working-class cultures, as well as the broad range of family forms among and within European American groups. This narrow view of the ideal family became embedded in the policies and practices of an adoption agency structure that systematically disregarded children of color, those beyond infancy, and children with health problems and/or disabilities.[20] It also discouraged and discriminated against most prospective adoptive parents who were not able-bodied, married, white, heterosexual, and middle-class. Adoptive parents were typically required to own a home with a separate bedroom for the child, to demonstrate their ability to provide an education for the child, and to have a modest amount of savings; the family was required to meet these financial criteria through one person's paycheck—adoptive mothers were not allowed to be employed (Ladner 1977, 57).

Dawn Day's work demonstrates that the screening policies employed by most adoption agencies through the early 1970s enforced criteria that were inappropriate for most black families.[21] Large numbers of prospective black adopters were turned away from agencies for failing to meet such requirements as economic stability, homeownership (with a separate bedroom for the child), and a full-time wife and mother. Additionally, Day found that large numbers of black couples withdrew from the adoption screening process at each stage of evaluation in response to numerous forms of institutional discrimination and a sense of social distance from predominantly white social workers. The resulting difficulties in placing children of color, older children, and those with disabilities in adoptive homes led these groups of children to be labeled "unadoptable," and thus agency resources focused on placing what were commonly referred to as "blue-ribbon babies"— healthy white infants.

Whereas white infants were the most desired commodity in the adoption market, children of color were seen as an administrative and financial strain on the system. Historian Rickie Solinger's important study of out-of-wedlock pregnancy before the legalization of abortion demonstrates that social resources for young pregnant women were largely determined by race and class, and these factors intertwined with those determining the life courses of their children.[22] The social support services available for single pregnant women were completely different for white women and women of color. Solinger demonstrates that "the meaning assigned to the child's existence shaped public policies that distinguished between unwed mothers by race, as socially productive or socially unproductive breeders" (39–40). White women produced children who, upon adoptive placement, reproduced a "normal," white, middle-class, nuclear family by transforming an infertile —and thus "deviant"—couple into a hegemonically defined "legitimate" family. Thus, for white birth parents, infants, and adoptive parents the stigma of "illegitimacy" and infertility was made invisible through social policies and practices such as all-white maternity homes and the "matching" of physical characteristics and ethnic origins between adoptive parents and children. Conversely, the needs of black birth mothers and their children fell outside the purview of such social services; indeed, Day found in her research that some adoption agencies actually had regulations *against* black adoptions. Because these institutions were not designed with the needs of black children in mind and there was virtually no "market" for them, unmarried pregnant black women were frequently turned away from adoption agencies and pushed toward welfare agencies.

In the late 1950s and early 1960s, a growing awareness began among social workers, as well as among the broader public, as to the urgent need for adoptive homes for children of color. Transracial and transcultural adoptions began in the 1950s and first involved Korean and Native American children.[23] The civil rights movement raised public awareness of the large numbers of African American children relegated to foster homes, and the integrationist spirit of the movement made transracial adoption a new consideration for many social workers and prospective white parents.

Subsequently, several agencies and organizations were formed toward the end of the 1950s with the intent of promoting the adoption of those children who, because of the enormous demand for healthy white infants, had previously been classified as "unadoptable"— particularly children of color, older children, and those with health problems and disabilities.[24] Although some agencies began actively recruiting white couples willing to adopt children of color, other agencies began making transracial placements only when an increasing number of white applicants expressed interest in adopting "hard-to-place" children.[25] It was often when faced with waiting periods of several years that white couples first considered adopting children of color. The introduction of birth control pills in 1960, changing cultural patterns of white teenage sexuality in the 1960s and 1970s, changing social attitudes regarding single parenting, and, eventually, the legalization of abortion in 1973 contributed to the decline in the numbers of white infants surrendered for adoption. These factors contributed to an increase in transracial placements in the late 1960s and early 1970s.

The contemporary situation, in which there are more children of color waiting in foster care than there are African American families who qualify for adoption, has developed as a result of the state's valorization of white, middle-class, nuclear families, the inscription of this ideological definition of the family in public policies, and the subsequent marginalization of racial-ethnic minority families and children. Although there have been reforms in the system since the 1960s and 1970s, the fates of black and white children are still determined differently by the state. Indeed, the question of how the state defines and uses racial categories of identity remains one of the most salient and contentious issues in the current policy debate.

Contested Meanings: Race, Identity, Culture, and Kin

As the number of black children adopted by whites increased in the late 1960s, transracial adoption became an "issue" at levels of public discourse, including social welfare journals, newspapers, and popular magazines. Ladner summarizes the two contending positions on transracial adoption:

> Transracial adoption became a social problem when, on the one hand, adoptive parents and adoption agencies and, on the other, black social workers and black nationalists enunciated two fundamentally different sets of values. The values in conflict are racial integration, espoused by the adoptive families, and black autonomy, a preliminary step to the development of cultural pluralism, advocated by black social workers and their allies. (1977, 73)

The questions at the heart of the debate between those for and those against transracial adoptions concern the importance of maintaining African American cultural identity and the capacity to transmit survival skills for children of color in a racially oppressive society. Underlying these perspectives are conflicting definitions of race.

Ladner's 1977 sociological study of transracially adoptive families indicates that parental motivations are often related to a liberal, integrationist view of the future: "They acknowledge that, although transracial adoption will have but a small impact on creating their idealized integrated society, it is, nevertheless, an expression of their commitment to the philosophy of the 'brotherhood of man'" (92). In attempting to teach the values of a society where people are judged on "merit" rather than skin color, their interaction with their children often translates to language and behaviors that downplay the importance of race. Indeed, McRoy and Zurcher found that 60 percent of their sample of transracially adoptive parents said they approached the issue of race from a "color-blind" perspective.[26]

This construction of race is not as innocuous as it may appear. The cultural discourse of "color blindness" is informed by a liberal humanist stance in its construction of race as a characteristic added on to an essential human sameness. In her recent book, Ruth Frankenberg explores the dangers of this tendency:

> The sharp cutting edge of color-blindness is revealed here: within this discursive repertoire, people of color are "good" only insofar as their "coloredness" can be bracketed and ignored, and this bracketing is contingent on the ability or the decision—in fact, the virtue—of a "noncolored"—or white—self. Color-blindness, despite the best intentions of its adherents, in this sense preserves the power structure inherent in essentialist racism.[27]

This view of race is rife with contradictions. Although color blindness has frequently been embraced as an antiracist perspective, it has also been played out as an *evasion* of race that situates whiteness as the "norm" and denies the salience of racial difference.

Although many white parents saw this approach to race as a positive way of affirming their children's identities, this perspective on raising black children was not shared by the most vocal among African American communities.[28] In an influential article, Edmond D. Jones, assistant director of Family and Children's Services in the city of Baltimore, states:

> My basic premise, in opposing placement of black children in white homes, is that being black in the United States is a special state of being. At a time of intense racial polarity, recognition of this fact is crucial to survival. I question the ability of white parents—no matter how deeply imbued with good will—to grasp the totality of the problem of being black in this society. I question their ability to create what I believe is crucial in these youngsters—a black identity. I suggest that creation of a black identity is a problem for many black parents also; the difference, perhaps, is one of degree.[29]

At issue here are questions of identity and survival; indeed, Jones defines "black identity" as a phenomenological state of *being* that, by definition, white parents cannot have experienced and thus cannnot convey to their children. The National Association of Black Social Workers, which has taken center stage in fighting against transracial adoption, argues that white parents are incapable of providing a child with a positive sense of African American cultural identity or the survival skills necessary in this society to confront the racism that the child will inevitably encounter. The NABSW argues that to have positive individual and community identities, children must learn "their own" cultural traditions and histories. A 1972 NABSW position paper states:

> Black children should be placed only with Black families whether in foster care or for adoption. Black children belong physically, psychologically, culturally in Black families in order that they receive the total sense of themselves and develop a sound projection of their future. Human beings are products of their environment and develop their sense of values, attitudes and self concept within their family structures. Black children in white homes are cut off from the healthy development of themselves as Black people.[30]

Along with the concern over African American identity, some black nationalists have labeled the adoption of black children by whites an act of cultural genocide. Clearly, the stakes in these dialogues concern more than the well-being of particular children; these arguments are grounded in integrationist versus nationalist visions of the future.

The nationalist political perspective is rooted in a nation-based racial paradigm, which has historically understood racial dynamics as products of colonialism, and thus, in resistance, has emphasized "collective identity, community, and a sense of 'peoplehood'" (Omi and Winant 1986, 42). And although some defenders of transracial adoption have argued that separatist political ideologies should not stand in the way of serving "the best interests of the child," particularly in light of the generally positive findings in the research on transracial adoptees, the criticisms are rooted in the historical and present-day material reality of life for African Americans in a racially stratified society. The sharing of culture and survival skills in an oppressive system is tied to a particular tradition of parenting in African American families that developed historically in response to the systematic assault that African American families endured under the system of slavery.[31] Evelyn Brooks Higginbotham has shown how, "through a range of shifting, even contradictory meanings and accentuations expressed at the level of individual and group consciousness, blacks fashioned race into a cultural identity that resisted white hegemonic discourses" (1992, 267).

Questions of cultural identity, as raised by black nationalists concerning transracially adopted individuals, are inseparable from power relations. Within this framework, the rearing of black children in white families is viewed as a form of colonization; conversely, raising black children with a strong sense of an African American identity and a sense of belonging to a people and a history is seen as a process of resistance to hegemonic racial meanings.

Although the research shows that, overall, most transracial adoptees have adjusted positively, the literature also suggests that the concerns raised regarding the construction of a "double consciousness," considered necessary for the cultural survival of African Americans, are well-founded. Central to the question of cultural survival for African Americans is "the ambiguity and marginality of living simultaneously in two worlds—the world of the Black community and the world of mainstream society, a phenomenon unique to Blacks."[32] In a comparative study of blacks adopted into European American families and blacks adopted into African American families, McRoy and Zurcher concluded that the "major distinction" between the two populations of adolescent adoptees "stemmed from their socialization concerning ethnicity"(1983, 138). The transracial adoptees tended to be more white-identified. The differences were attributed to the "social psychological contexts" in which their racial identities were constructed. Most of the black transracial adoptees studied (87 percent) were raised in predominantly white communities and subsequently had limited social contact with African Americans. The researchers found that while these adoptees acknowledged "their racial group memberships," they tended to develop "negative or indifferent" attitudes regarding their classification as African Americans, a preference for white friends and dates, and a "problematic ambiguity about racial identity" (140). Yet differences in a sense of African American identity were found between those transracial adoptees raised in predominantly white communities and those raised in integrated areas: "Adolescent adoptees who had the opportunity to relate to blacks and whites tended to internalize the duality of character, or functional cultural paranoia that so often is necessary for survival in a racist society" (140).

Despite many white adoptive parents' professed beliefs in an integrated future, McRoy and Zurcher found that "only a few of the white adoptive families behaviorally responded to the necessity of equipping the child to become bicultural and to realistically perceive the historical and current black-white relations in American society" (1983, 140). Simon and Altstein found that 78 percent of the families they studied lived in all-white neighborhoods, 4 percent lived in predominantly black neighborhoods, and only 18 percent lived in integrated communities (1987, 31).

This social debate must be understood in the context of a broader political discourse concerning the cultural construction of racial meanings—specifically, contested definitions of African American cultural identity following World War II. The emergence of movements for change in the postwar era are themselves evidence of the contested nature of race (as well as gender) as a category of social identity. Higginbotham explains: "Black nationalism itself has been a heteroglot conception, categorized variously as revolutionary, bourgeois reformist, cultural, religious, economic, or emigrationist. Race as the sign of cultural identity has been neither a coherent nor static concept among African-Americans" (1992, 270).

The politics of the civil rights and black nationalist movements were not only concerned with legislative and structural changes in U.S. society, but also addressed questions of *identity*. Indeed, Omi and Winant argue that a defining feature of the "new" social movements following World War II was a "politics of identity" that spilled over into arenas not traditionally defined as "political" (1986, 146). The cultural debate regarding the appropriateness of transracial adoption represents a political contestation of African American cultural identity rooted in integrationist versus nationalist paradigms of racial meaning.

Science, Race, and Social Work

In the 1990s, adoption policies and laws vary from state to state, but "there is general agreement among agency policymakers that children should be placed on a same-race basis if possible, and transracially only as a last resort."[33] Whereas the critiques of this practice in the 1970s contributed to a sharp decline in transracial placements, the swelling numbers of children in foster care in the 1990s have led to a reconsideration of racial matching practices. The Multiethnic Placement Act of 1994 raises questions about how racial meaning is inscribed in federal policy, and thus how foster children's lives will hereafter be constructed by the state. The arguments in favor of transracial adoption draw their support primarily from the results of one longitudinal study of transracial families. This study, conducted by Rita J. Simon and Howard

Altstein, is consistently and unproblematically cited by opponents of racial matching policies,[34] and, indeed, Simon and Altstein themselves have been active speakers in this debate.[35] Their work has been credited with helping to sway the Texas Legislature toward the 1993 passage of the "first law in the country that forbids using race as a criterion for placing adoptive children."[36] Children's lives and identities are directly affected by child welfare policy decisions, thus this unquestioned reliance on this research should be considered critically.

From a Foucauldian perspective, an exploration of adoptees' identities must consider the discourses of power/knowledge drawn on in implementing the policies and practices of the social agency that constitutes and legitimates adoptive families. This social constructionist perspective is grounded in feminist and race relations scholarship as well: "Both begin with assumptions that families are social products and then proceed to study their interrelationships with other social structures."[37] In adoption agencies, families and selves are *literally* socially constructed; yet, in more subtle ways, this is true of *all* families in the United States. Differing family formations between racial-ethnic groups in U.S. society are not only rooted in diverse cultural traditions and histories, but also develop in response to different socioeconomic locations, as well as different relationships to social institutions defined and determined by racial categories. Historically, African Americans, European Americans, Mexican Americans, Native Americans, and Asian Americans, among others, have occupied different places in the socioeconomic structure in relation to such social institutions as labor markets, educational institutions, and government policies and laws.[38] These institutions have actively defined social meanings of race, class, and gender.[39] Feminist sociologist Bonnie Thornton Dill explains, "From the founding of the United States, and throughout its history, race has been a fundamental criterion determining the kind of work people do, the wages they receive, and the kind of legal, economic, political, and social support provided for their families."[40]

As discussed previously, racial categories have historically been used as the primary determinant of how a child is treated by the social welfare system. In this context, the question of *how race is defined* becomes weighty. In the contemporary dialogue the research of Simon and Altstein is typically drawn on to support a "color-blind," integrationist perspective in favor of transracial placements; thus the question of how this "objective" research defines racial categories points toward inquiries into the role of power in the construction of knowledge regarding adoption, race, and identity. Sociologists Omi and Winant offer an analytic framework for the study of race that encompasses the range of social sites permeated by and emanating racial meanings. They argue that race needs to be understood as *"an unstable and 'decentered' complex of social meanings constantly being transformed by political struggle"* (1986, 68). They note:

> Our theory of *racial formation* emphasizes the social nature of race, the absence of any essential racial characteristics, the historical flexibility of racial meanings and categories, the conflictual character of race at both the "micro-" and "macro-social" levels, and the irreducible political aspect of racial dynamics. (4)

Clearly, definitions of race have been highly contested in the discourse surrounding transracial adoption, and, indeed, the questions raised concerning the ability of white parents to instill survival skills and a sense of African American identity in their black children indicate that the central questions in this conflictual dialogue concern *how* transracially adopted individuals define a sense of racial identity for themselves. Yet these questions are not directly addressed in the research.

The major studies of transracially adopted individuals and their families do not address questions of how race is defined; rather, the disciplinary and methodological boundaries of the field of social work rely on positivistic assumptions that translate into research practices that approach race as a "natural" fact of identity. Adoptees are unproblematically considered to "be" black or white. Thus, rather than being seen as an "objective" framework for gathering "facts," the assumptions of positivism can be seen as an ideology that mystifies the power relations through which hegemonic definitions of race are constructed and maintained. The "scientific" methodology employed by Simon and Altstein encodes racial categories in static and immutable ways; linguistically, race is "assigned 'object' nature,"[41] bearing out Omi and Winant's assertion: "Although abstractly acknowledged to be a sociohistorical construct, race *in practice* is often treated as an objective fact: one simply *is* one's race; in the contemporary U.S., if we discard euphemisms, we have five color-based racial categories: black, white, brown, yellow, or red."[42]

In keeping with the child welfare practice of racial classification of adoptive children, in social work scholarship on transracial adoption, adoptees are racially classified based on the race of their *biological* parents. The word choice here is significant: the term *birth parent* has been in common use in adoption communities for many years, thus it is significant that the word *biological* is chosen over *birth* in reference to the child's race. *Birth* focuses on the event; *biological* emphasizes physiological, genetic ties. The scientific discourse of genetics and biology serves as an ideological template of legitimacy here; familial connections are normatively defined through biology and genetics in Western societies. Within this framework race is objectively encoded as biological, and thus "natural."

In the context of its history the use of race as a fixed category in the research on transracial adoption is highly problematic. Since World War II the concept of race has undergone significant transformation in the academy. It has been firmly established through the work of physical anthropologists that "race" is a physiologically meaningless category,[43] and a social constructionist perspective that views race as culturally and historically defined has been broadly accepted in the humanities and social sciences. "Chromosome research reveals the fallacy of race as an accurate measure of genotypic or phenotypic difference between human beings" (Higginbotham 1992, 253). Biological anthropologist Fatimah Jackson explains, "In a socially complex and highly mobile species such as ours, race, as a subspecific taxonomic category, becomes more of a construct of our imaginations and a convenient tool than a true and independent biological reality."[44]

Although race is no longer considered a legitimate biological category, it is a *socially constructed reality* at both the phenomenological level of identity and the institutional level of social organization.[45] Despite this move beyond biological determinism in scholarship, "natural" and "biological" views of race still permeate social discourse and institutional practices. "The recognition of racial distinctions emanates from and adapts to multiple uses of power in society" (Higginbotham 1992, 253–54). Thus, the question of institutional and ideological power emerges in considerations of how race is defined in the academic knowledge produced regarding transracial adoption.

In Simon and Altstein's *Transracial Adoptees and Their Families: A Study of Identity and Commitment* (1987), the perspectives of the National Association of Black Social Workers are cast as "political" and "passionate," in contrast to the authors' own "scientific," "objective," and thus, the assumption is, apolitical research. The NABSW's position is a political one, but, despite a veneer of positivist objectivity, so too is the work of researchers in the field of social work. The NABSW argues through a nation-based racial paradigm—an explicitly political perspective. The social work literature is legitimated through a positivist paradigm—a framework constructed on assumptions defining the "political" as oppositional to an "objective" scientific view, a view that denies the political construction of its own position. Within this framework the political nature of social work literature is unmarked, whereas the concerns of black nationalist social workers are marked as political and, thus, delegitimated. The research becomes the most "legitimate" knowledge in the public debate, in that, "logically," according to the discursive assumptions of the field, the results of the research become the standard reference for policy and legal decisions.

The methodology employed by researchers in the field of social work defines the scope of research in a way that avoids the issues raised by critics of transracial adoption. The NABSW is concerned with the transmission of *culture,* and the questions raised by these concerns do not fit into the frame of inquiry defined by positivist approaches to research. Indeed, considerations of culture are outside the purview of such studies, because these studies approach identity unproblematically as bounded at the individual level. Simon and Altstein do attempt to address questions of racial identity; the problem is a matter of methodology. For example, they, like other researchers in this field, "measured" racial identity with the "Twenty Statements Test." Adoptees were asked to answer the question "Who am I?" twenty times. Simon and Altstein note, "The results reported by McRoy and Zurcher are consistent with ours, insofar as they also found that the transracial adoptees were more likely than the inracial adoptees (their White siblings) to refer to race in their self-descriptions" (1987, 68).

I do not take issue with this finding; rather, I question what it tells us. Simon and Altstein conclude that it "demonstrates the greater salience of race among minority group respondents" (68). I am certain this is true, yet it says nothing about how a black child raised by white parents constructs a sense of racial identity. A second example is the following question, which they asked their respondents:

Which of the following statements fit how you really feel:

(a) I am proud to be (select one): black, brown Indian, Korean, white, other. Or,
(b) I do not mind what color I am. Or,
(c) I would prefer to be _____. (68)

There are several problems here. The formulation of this question does not allow any room for adoptees to express in their own words, from their own perspectives, who they are and how they define their racial identities; in providing the language through which respondents may express their views, the researchers impose static racial categories and deny any linguistic space for redefinition. The specific language chosen is highly problematic as well. Transracial adoptees transcend and confound the categories of racial identity through which contemporary society defines people, yet here the researchers enforce social categories of identity that deny the legitimacy of multiply defined selves. Indeed, by instructing respondents to "select one" of the categories presented, Simon and Altstein compel adoptees who do not fit neatly within the "black, brown Indian, Korean, or white" boundaries to define themselves as "other." A study that is sensitive to the issues of racial identity and survival skills would be designed to explore *how* African American children raised by white parents *define* a sense of racial meaning *for themselves.*

The concerns of the members of the NABSW—African American cultural identity and survival skills—are consistent with a cultural approach to the construction of race. In this view identity, cultural knowledge, and survival are inseparable. In contrast, Simon and Altstein and other researchers enforce a biologically immutable definition of race as a category of identity. Thus, whereas one group speaks in a language framed by "culture," the other speaks through language guided by objectivist constructions of fixed "biological" categories of race. This polarized debate plays out a false dichotomy. I argue that, although racial meanings are certainly culturally constructed, they are also structurally defined. Indeed, the history of transracial adoption in the post–World War II United States demonstrates the profound impact institutional definitions of race have had on black children's lives.

Conclusion

The issue of trans-racial adoption has always been a topic of great
controversy and never fails to provoke intense debate. Debate
which is heartfelt and thrusts to the very core of what we are, where
we came from and where we will go in the future. It is a debate for
which one answer, one "right" answer, satisfying all the participants, will not be easily found.

THE REVEREND JESSE L. JACKSON, statement to a
U.S. Senate subcommittee[46]

The social practice of adoption, viewed here as a system of legitima-
tion and reproduction, creates particular kinds of families, and thus
particular "subjects"—adoptees—according to racialized hegemonic
definitions of legitimate social identities. As the unequal history of
transracial adoption illustrates, the unproblematic use of static racial
categories by the child welfare system has profound implications for
black and mixed-race children in the adoption/foster care system. This
practice raises fundamental questions regarding the inscription of ideology in social policy and the differential impacts such policies have on
children and families in a diverse range of racial-ethnic groups.

I am not arguing "for" or "against" transracial adoption. Rather, I
would like to suggest a reframing of this debate. In my own view,
these issues cannot be easily resolved, but the following four points
may facilitate a more carefully considered discussion that is sensitive
to the needs of the children involved. First, a structural critique of the
adoption/foster care system is a necessary component of any analysis
of transracial adoption. Attempts to solve a crisis in the foster care
system that focus almost exclusively on the individual/familial level
by encouraging whites to adopt black foster children and do not address systemic inequalities built into the structure of the U.S. child
welfare system are simply cosmetic. They do nothing to alleviate the
circumstances that lead more black children than white children into
the social welfare system. Second, an understanding of this issue depends on a recognition that each constituent in the practice of transracial adoption—children, birth parents, and adoptive parents—has
had a different history and a different relationship to the social institution of adoption, and these differences should be made apparent
and respected.

Third, in light of the ways in which the use of racial categories has
created varied histories of interaction with the child welfare system, it

is crucial to recognize that race is not a static, immutable concept, and thus has had vastly different meanings for people in a range of racial-ethnic groups. We must consider critically the dominant meanings of race drawn on in the determination of the life courses of black and white children if we are to reveal how such definitions maintain and legitimate inequalities in the dissemination of social services for children and their caretakers.

Finally, if those involved in this debate are truly interested in serving "the best interests of the child," they must listen to the voices of the children who have been through this system. In the mid-1990s the largest cohort of transracial adoptees is made up of adults quite capable of speaking to the profound questions concerning racial identity and survival skills that have been central to this social issue. *How* these black children raised by white parents construct a sense of racial identity is the very issue that should be considered; at a fundamental level, this involves moving beyond essentialist racial categories and learning to hear the multiply defined voices of people whose life experiences have placed them on the boundaries between the typically polarized cultures and communities we call black and white.

Transracial adoption, with its history of contested racial politics, offers an arena of dialogue where the shifting meanings of race may be explored in all their contradictions. Although the debate concerns a particular population of adoptees, the questions raised concerning identity and race, family and community, assimilation and resistance, culture and social structure, as well as societal responsibility for *all* children speak beyond the specific circumstances of these adoptees' lives. Indeed, transracial adoption has reemerged as a controversial issue precisely at a moment of renegotiation of the social meanings of race, identity, culture, and family in public discourse in the United States.

Notes

This essay is part of a larger interdisciplinary ethnographic study of transracial adoption. A version of this chaper was first presented at the 1993 convention of the American Studies Association in Boston. I am grateful to the following people for their engagement in thoughtful, challenging discussions of these issues and for critical readings of this essay: John L. Caughey, Bonnie Thornton Dill, Lillie S. Ransom, Deborah S. Rosenfelt, and Dabrina Taylor.

    1. Lynn Smith, "Salvation or Last Resort?" *Los Angeles Times*, November 3, 1993, E5.

his play would not run forever. Sitting amid other prisoners, perhaps held briefly at Hood River before being moved to more serious prisons, he must have known how small (perhaps even selfish) his gesture was. But in a classic reversal of terms, his small, temporary gesture reminds us how impossible it is for all prisoners to escape a deeper, systematic anonymity. How does one develop an identity amid such powerful forces of displacement? To rephrase Jacobo Timmerman, it is not only prisoners of overtly inhumane detention systems who are nameless; every modern subject of incarceration is a prisoner without a name, in a cell without a number.

How few prisoners we remember by name—as prisoners, not as holdovers from their theatrical trials. There are political prisoners, such as Timmerman or Nelson Mandela, publicized by Amnesty International or in the context of political struggles. Martin Luther King, Jr., Gandhi, Gramsci, and other famous prisoners appropriated the jail as a stage, but even they seldom publicized and named their cell mates in any lasting way. Much the same is true of former prisoners, such as Malcolm X, who move into other political contexts. A few prisoners are picked up by the publicity machines—Bob Dylan's Hurricane Carter, *The Thin Blue Line*'s Randall Adams, and of course Willie Horton. It is an oddity in itself that as a country we can have so many prisoners, and can be adding so many more, and still can remember so few names.[36]

This is no "failure to communicate," as suggested in the story of one famous movie prisoner; it is a triumph of discipline and the manipulation of prisoner identity. Hood River John Doe's expressive silence—his temporary escape from identity—briefly illuminates how power now works, how successfully it captures and rearranges the seemingly simple, unproblematic fact of having an identity and expressing it. The mode of analysis invented by Foucault and amplified by Deleuze carries with it a potential response to those new modes of power. Finding new and odd examples, we evoke the possibility of a politics attentive to domination and matched to circumstances in which freedom might still be practiced. Such a postmodernism would not carry the rejection of politics—it would signal its reemergence.

Notes

1. Gilles Deleuze, *Foucault,* trans. Sean Hand (Minneapolis: University of Minnesota Press, 1988), 30.

2. Michel Foucault, "Clarifications on the Question of Power: Interview Conducted by Pasquale Pasquino," trans. John Johnston, in *Foucault Live: Interviews, 1966–1984*, ed. Sylvére Lotringer (New York: Semiotext[e], 1989), 187.

3. Ibid., 188.

4. Ibid. See also Deleuze, *Foucault,* 75.

5. Michel Foucault, "The Dangerous Individual," in *Michel Foucault: Politics, Philosophy, Culture: Interviews and Other Writings, 1977–1984,* ed. Lawrence D. Kritzman, trans. Alan Sheridan et al. (New York: Routledge, 1988), 151.

6. Michael Rollins, "Doesn't Anybody Know Who Nobody Is?" *Oregonian,* 12 July 1989, C-1, C-10.

7. Ibid., C-1.

8. Ibid.

9. Ibid.

10. The specific way prisoners know themselves has not always been hidden or obvious. Indeed, earlier in U.S. history it was a focus of public discussion, perhaps even forming an alternate site for the moral formation of American culture. See Thomas L. Dumm, *Democracy and Punishment* (Madison: University of Wisconsin Press, 1987).

11. The other buffer, of course, is racism. On scope, see Marc Mauer, *Young Black Men and the Criminal Justice System: A Growing National Problem* (Washington, D.C.: Sentencing Project, 1990). On method, see Robert Gooding-Williams, *Reading Rodney King: Reading Urban Uprising* (New York: Routledge, 1993).

12. Rollins, "Doesn't Anybody Know Who Nobody Is?" C-10.

13. Ibid.

14. Foucault, "The Dangerous Individual," 126.

15. Ibid., 138.

16. Ibid., 142.

17. Rollins, "Doesn't Anybody Know Who Nobody Is?" C-10.

18. Murray Edelman explains: "As if to paper over their inattention to daily life, the media devote considerable attention to one kind of public event that they present as a private one: the human interest story. . . . Human interest stories are political events because they reinforce the view that individual action is crucial: that biography is the paramount component of historical accounts." *Constructing the Political Spectacle* (Chicago: University of Chicago Press, 1988), 99.

19. Louis Althusser, *The Future Lasts Forever: A Memoir* (New York: New Press, 1993), especially chap. 2. Althusser notes Pierre's case and discusses several of Foucault's themes.

20. Michel Foucault, ed., *I, Pierre Rivière, having slaughtered my mother, my sister, and my brother . . . A Case of Parricide in the 19th Century,* trans. Frank Jellinek (Lincoln: University of Nebraska Press, 1982), 21. Further quotations from this text will be cited by page numbers in the body of the chapter.

21. James Miller, *The Passion of Michel Foucault* (New York: Simon & Schuster, 1993), makes just this mistake, as Miller is unable to get beyond issues of transgressive psychology. In the case of Pierre, Miller seems consumed with intrigue about the criminal character: "What a character to be captivated by!" (225). And Miller *is* captivated. Foucault, on the other hand, repeatedly poses the issue as the "coexistence of [a criminal's] madness and [the] rationality" of social systems (*I, Pierre,* 273). This is not the same thing as the internal struggle, within the self, between madness and rationality. For Foucault, "The theoretical (as well as political) stake at issue [is] whether and in what way rationality could be criminal and how it all, crime and knowledge, could be 'borne' by what was called the 'social order'" (*I, Pierre,* 273). Miller is so captivated by Pierre

that he misses that political point, exclaiming that Foucault calls him "a 'tragic' hero" and italicizing his protest that Foucault thinks that Pierre's *"crime ends up not existing anymore"* (228). But Foucault's entire argument involves the many disappearances Pierre was subjected to by a legal process in transition. Foucault is clear and emphatic; Pierre's case is interesting precisely because such a notable case disappeared—not from its victims or their friends, but from history and public view.

22. Foucault, "The Anxiety of Judging," in *Foucault Live: Interviews, 1966–1984*, ed. Sylvére Lotringer (New York: Semiotext[e], 1989), 173–74.

23. Michel Foucault, "Truth, Power, Self: An Interview with Michel Foucault, conducted by Rux Martin," in *Technologies of the Self: A Seminar with Michel Foucault*, ed. Luther H. Martin, Huck Gutman, and Patrick H. Hutton (Amherst: University of Massachusetts Press, 1988), 11.

24. Jean Baudrillard, *Forget Foucault* (New York: Semiotext[e], 1987), 9–10.

25. Deleuze, *Foucault*, 28. Baudrillard's commentary on Foucault may not be entirely incompatible with Deleuze's. Baudrillard did locate Foucault's excessive clarity, but he can also be read as presenting an alternate reading strategy. His critique could be ironic; Foucault's "meticulous outpourings," his scene of "flawless writing" finally—perhaps only too late—reminds us that "truth" is not at stake. Indeed, Baudrillard explicitly grants Foucault this: "Foucault's discourse is no truer than any other. No, its strength [is] in the analysis which unwinds the subtle meanderings of its object, describing it with a tactile and tactical exactness, where seduction feeds analytical force and where language itself gives birth to the operation of new powers." Baudrillard, *Forget Foucault*, 10. See Calvin Thomas, "Baudrillard's Seduction of Foucault," in *Jean Baudrillard: The Disappearance of Art and Politics,* ed. William Stearns and William Chaloupka (New York: St. Martin's, 1992), 131–45.

26. Deleuze, *Foucault*, 14.

27. Ibid., 14. The spatial tropes Deleuze and Foucault use have a specific importance: "Multiplicity is neither axiomatic nor typological, but topological" (14). Foucault's move—which Deleuze identifies as the "most decisive step yet taken in the theory-practice of multiplicities"—becomes more obvious when Deleuze moves it into the even more familiar discourse of the "global," "local," and "diffused" (14). Deleuze summarizes: "'Local' has two very different meanings: power is local because it is never global, but it is not . . . localized because it is diffuse. . . . Foucault's functionalism throws up a new topology which no longer locates the origin of power in a privileged place, and can no longer accept a limited localization (this conception of social space . . . is as new as that of contemporary physics and mathematics)" (26). Deleuze's chapter "Foldings, or the Inside of Thought" convincingly applies the topological even to Foucault's epistemology, at the very center of his project (94–123). As Paul Bové notes in his introduction to Deleuze's book, this Foucault—Deleuze's Foucault—"is entirely different from Jameson's or Taylor's" (xxvi). On multiplicity and language, see Michel Foucault, "Maurice Blanchot: The Thought from Outside," in *Foucault/Blanchot,* trans. Brian Massumi and Jeffrey Mehlman (New York: Zone, 1987), 53–58.

28. See Dan Baum, "The Drug War on Civil Liberties," *The Nation*, 29 June 1992, 886–88.

29. Don Delillo, *Libra* (New York: Penguin, 1988), 18.

30. Michael Rollins and Jeanie Senior, "John Doe Unable to Hide Identity from Father," *Oregonian*, 14 July 1989, A-1, A-12.

31. Deleuze, *Foucault*, 47.

32. See Edelman, *Constructing the Political Spectacle*, especially chaps. 1, 2, and 7.

33. Michel Foucault, "An Ethics of Pleasure: Interview Conducted by Stephen Rig-

gins," in *Foucault Live: Interviews, 1966–1984*, ed. Sylvére Lotringer (New York: Semi-otext[e], 1989), 264.

34. Deleuze writes harshly of those who deny the possibility for such a politics: "Three centuries ago certain fools were astonished because Spinoza wished to see the liberation of man, even though he did not believe in his liberty. . . . Today new fools, or even the same ones reincarnated, are astonished because the Foucault who had spoken of the death of man took part in political struggle. . . . This is not the first time an idea has been called eternal in order to mask the fact that it is actually weak or summary." *Foucault*, 90.

35. "Mystery Man from Seattle Is Released on Probation," *Seattle Post-Intelligencer*, 24 July 1989, B3. A search of newspaper databases for 1989–92 found no further mentions of Slattengren in the Seattle or Portland newspapers.

36. A telling counterexample is the prison (and postprison) autobiography of Nathan McCall, *Makes Me Wanna Holler: A Young Black Man in America* (New York: Random House, 1994). One reviewer, Adam Hochschild ("A Furious Man," *New York Times Book Review*, 27 February 1994, 11–12), wished McCall "had waited a bit longer to write," as if the experience of crime and imprisonment could not be enough of a basis for autobiographical treatment.

Epilogue: Pieces of My Heart

Julia Watson

At an advanced stage of preparing the essays for *Getting a Life*—when I felt more like it was taking my life—one day my wallet was stolen. Because we have somewhat mobile, disorderly lives, it wasn't the first time something had disappeared. But this time I noted with interest how the loss of identity cards undermined me—not my sense of identity, but my practice of it in everyday situations.

A day and a half on the phone shutting down credit cards and getting annoyed because the Touch-Tone system asks for a card number to process the call. Identity is recursive. Calls to 800 numbers for the car and health insurance companies. Rifling through drawers for an expired driver's license and old ID cards, souvenirs of past lives. Pleased when I found my birth certificate, more legit than anything else I now had. But I couldn't cash checks with it—no photo. Identity is recursive. The worst was trying to remember what else was in the wallet. Had I cashed the reimbursement check? Left anything at the cleaner? What pieces of my life would be on hold for months because I had forgotten they were there? Identity is recursive.

For weeks there were times when I would suddenly stop and remember another missing piece of myself. Public library cards. A kindergarten photo of my son. A few times I reached for the card requested—a frequent flier number, a gas credit card—only to realize with embarrassment that it wasn't there. It made me feel strange—like being in a foreign country where people stare at you because, no matter how you try to fit in, little gestures give you away. Passing for a citizen, but you're not quite right.

How do they know who I am till they see what my cards say?

I read an article on "Customer Impersonation." The news is that someone who has stolen a driver's license or social security card can have store accounts set up to buy things—Buy Now, Pay Later—in the name on the cards. When the purchases go unpaid, central credit bureaus get a bad report on the card owner—unpaid debts, loans, ripoffs. This impersonation can extend years into the future and can wreck the credit of the customer. The article concludes that little can be done other than to complain to credit agencies that the cards are not "you." If somebody has your identity—they have the fun, you pay the bills. Like a double in a Poe story.

How do they know it's not me when they see the cards? Even if they do, who cares when a quick sale is at stake? The impersonator in the article bore little resemblance to the picture on the driver's license and misspelled the name when she signed for a diamond ring. How much of identity is having it in hand?

Or in someone else's hand. In Detroit, the home of innovative crime, it has happened: "Stella Sproule's family can't accept that she was killed only for her good name. Police say Annie Lee Cole wanted Sproule dead in order to steal her identity and put her own troubled past, including bad-check charges and a parole violation, behind her" (*Missoulian*, June 2, 1994, A-10). Cole, who had Sproule killed in order to use her credit cards, posed as the victim's sister to arrange her cremation. Police intervened—that time. The plot of a dime-store detective novel, updated nineties style—identity-jacking.

The postmodern fantasy—becoming someone else. Identity in motion. AKA.

Contributors

Linda Martín Alcoff teaches philosophy and women's studies at Syracuse University. She is coeditor, with Elizabeth Potter, of *Feminist Epistemologies* (1993), and her *Real Knowing* is due out in 1996. Her essays on epistemology, Foucault, and subjectivity have appeared in *Signs, Cultural Critique, Philosophical Forum, Hypatia,* and other journals. For several years she has also been active in the movement to decrease sexual violence.

Philip E. Baruth is assistant professor of English at the University of Vermont. His work on biography and autobiography has appeared in *Modern Language Quarterly, Biography,* and *The Age of Johnson.*

H-Dirksen L. Bauman is a visiting faculty member in the English Department at the National Technical Institute of the Deaf at the Rochester Institute of Technology. He is currently writing his dissertation on American Sign Language literature at Binghamton University (SUNY).

Michael Blitz is associate professor of English at John Jay College, City University of New York. With Louise Krasniewicz, he has published and/or presented a number of projects on cyborgs, dreams, e-mail, narrative, and posthumanity. He has also collaborated with C. Mark Hurlbert on a book, *Composition and Resistance,* and on many articles and chapters dealing with culture, higher education, and academic rhetoric. He is the author of three books of poetry, most recently *Five Days in the Electric Chair*. He is currently living in Brooklyn, New York, and is, to his ongoing wonder and delight, the father of Daina and Cory, the two greatest children ever born since the beginning of time.

Traci Carroll is assistant professor of English at Rhodes College. She received her Ph.D. from Northwestern University in 1992. She has written on Pauline Hopkins and Harriet Jacobs, and her work in progress includes an exploration of the literary intersections between queer theory and African American theory. She is currently completing a book-length manuscript on race, gender, taste, and consumer culture in the late nineteenth century titled "Subjects of Consumption: Race and the Discourse of Taste in Nineteenth-Century America."

William Chaloupka teaches political science at the University of Montana. His *Knowing Nukes: The Politics and Culture of the Atom* and *In the Nature of Things: Language, Politics, and the Environment* (coedited with Jane Bennett) have been published by the University of Minnesota Press. With Williams Stearns, he coedited *Jean Baudrillard: The Disappearance of Art and Politics*. His articles have appeared in *International Studies Quarterly*, *Policy Studies Journal*, *Environmental Ethics*, and elsewhere. He is currently at work on a study of cynicism in American politics.

Salome Chasnoff has recently completed her Ph.D. in performance studies with a certificate in women's studies at Northwestern University. Her dissertation on the performance of birthing was itself autobiographically inspired and informed. She is a performer, video maker, educator, and political activist who works with Women in the Director's Chair, an alternative media arts organization based in Chicago.

Kay K. Cook is associate professor of English and associate department chair of language and literature at Southern Utah University. She has published articles and frequently gives presentations on issues of women's health, specifically breast cancer. Her other areas of research and publication are nineteenth-century British romanticism and autobiography studies. She is also a playwright.

Martin A. Danahay's identities include, but are not limited to, nonpatriarchal father of two children, associate professor of English at Emory University, straight-but-not-narrow male, British subject, and baseball fanatic. His name appears on the title page of a book published in 1993 called *A Community of One: Masculine Autobiography and Autonomy in Nineteenth-Century Britain.* Copies of his C.V. are available upon request.

Laura Gray-Rosendale is a doctoral student in the Humanities Department at Syracuse University and a teacher of rhetorical studies and composition theory. She is also a cofounder of a campus support group for survivors of sexual abuse and is committed to the project of producing theoretical work that is valuable and accessible to a variety of audiences.

Linda S. Kauffman is professor of English at the University of Maryland, College Park. She is the author of *Discourses of Desire: Gender, Genre, and Epistolary Fictions* (1986) and *Special Delivery: Epistolary Modes in Modern Fiction* (1992) and editor of *Gender and Theory, Feminism and Institutions* (both 1989), and *American Feminist Thought at Century's End* (1993). Her contribution to this volume is part of a forthcoming book, *Bad Girls and Sick Boys: A Secret History of Sex in Fiction, Film, Performance.*

Louise Krasniewicz has a Ph.D. in anthropology and an M.A. in media and technology. Her research focuses on conflict and identity in American culture, and on the relationships among bodies, the cinema, and new technologies. With Michael Blitz, she is writing a book and designing a CD-ROM about cultural responses to Arnold Schwarzenegger. She is also exploring alternative multimedia forms for presenting academic research to general audiences, and is currently exhibiting works in photography, digital imagery, and digital video. She resides in Santa Monica, California, and is the delighted mother of the best son ever created, Drew Robert.

Helena Michie is Professor of English at Rice University and is the author of *The Flesh Made Word: Female Figures, Women's Bodies* (1987) and *Sororophobia: Differences between Women in Literature and Culture* (1993). She is currently at work, with Naomi R. Cahn, on a book on the policing of the reproductive body. She has written frequently on Victorian studies, feminist theory, and contemporary popular culture and is interested in the Brontës, the Judds, ice-skating, and bathroom doors.

Sandra Patton is a doctoral candidate in American Studies and the recipient of a graduate certificate in women's studies at the University of Maryland, College Park. She served as the assistant director of the Curriculum Transformation Project's Faculty Summer Institute for three years at UMCP, where she has taught both women's studies and Afro-American studies. She is coauthor, with Bonnie Thornton Dill and Maxine Baca Zinn, of "Feminism, Race, and the Politics of Family Values" (*Report from the Institute for Philosophy and Public Policy*, Fall 1993). Her dissertation is an interdisciplinary ethnography of transracial adoption. She is a 1995-96 recipient of an American Fellowship from the American Association of University Women.

Janice Peck is associate professor in the School of Journalism and Mass Communication at the University of Colorado in Boulder. A cultural critic who explores the ways social and political issues are embodied in mediated popular culture forms, she is the author of *The Gods of Televangelism: The Crisis of Meaning and the Appeal of Religious Television*. Her work on religious programming and television talk shows has appeared in *Journal of Communication Inquiry*, *Cultural Critique*, and *Communication Theory*.

Sidonie Smith is professor of English and comparative literature at Binghamton University. She is the author of *Where I'm Bound: Patterns of Slavery and Freedom in Black American Autobiography* (1974), *A Poetics of Women's Autobiography: Marginality and the Fictions of Self-Representation* (1987), and *Subjectivity, Identity, and the Body: Women's Autobiographical Practices in the Twentieth Century* (1993); coeditor, with Julia Watson, of *De/Colonizing the Subject: The Politics of Gender in Women's Autobiography* (University of Minnesota Press, 1992); and coeditor, with Gisela Brinker-Gabler, of *Writing New Identities: Gender, National, and Immigration in Contemporary Europe* (University of Minnesota Press, forthcoming). She is currently completing a book on women's travel narratives titled *Unbecoming Women: Mobility, Modernity, Mechanics*.

Robyn R. Warhol is professor and director of women's studies at the University of Vermont. She is the author of *Gendered Interventions: Narrative Discourse in the Victorian Novel* (1989) and coeditor of *Feminisms: An Anthology of Literary Theory and Criticism*, with Diane Price Herndl (1991), and *Women's Work: An Anthology of American Literature*, with Barbara and George Perkins (1994). She has published essays on feminist narratology in *Style, Novel*, and *PMLA*, among other journals. Her current project is to develop a poetics of serial narrative.

Julia Watson is professor of liberal studies and director of women's studies at the University of Montana. She is coeditor, with Sidonie Smith, of *De/Colonizing the Subject: The Politics of Gender in Women's Autobiography* (University of Minnesota Press, 1992). Her essays on women's autobiography, theory of autobiography, and Montaigne have appeared in collections as well as in *a/b:Auto/Biography Studies* and other journals. She is currently working on a study of self-decolonization in women's autobiographical writing and experimenting with personal narrative.

Susan Ostrov Weisser is associate professor of English at Adelphi University. She is coeditor, with Jennifer Fleischner, of *Feminist Nightmares: Women at Odds* (1994) and of *Craving Vacancy: Women and Sexual Love in the British Novel, 1740-1880* (forthcoming).

Index

Compiled by Suzanne Sherman Aboulfadl

402 / *Index*

Part V

Institutionalized Lives

Far from being grounded in mere "recovery" of the past, which is waiting to be found, and which when found, will secure our sense of ourselves into eternity, identities are the names we give to the different ways we are positioned by, and position ourselves within, the narratives of the past.

> STUART HALL, "Cultural Identity and Diaspora," in *Colonial Discourse and Postcolonial Theory*, ed. Patrick Williams and Laura Chrisman (New York: Columbia University Press, 1994), 394.

A revolution takes place when and only when . . . people can no longer lead their everyday lives.

> HENRI LEFEBVRE, *Everyday Life in the Modern World*, trans. Philip Wander (New Brunswick, N.J.: Transaction, 1984), 32.

Of course, I tell myself, "file" is an anagram for "life"!

> ANDREI CODRESCU, "Adding to My Life," in *Autobiography and Postmodernism*, ed. Kathleen Ashley, Leigh Gilmore, and Gerald Peters (Amherst: University of Massachusetts Press, 1994), 24.

14 / Twelve-Step Teleology: Narratives of Recovery/Recovery as Narrative

Robyn R. Warhol and Helena Michie

The Recovery Story as Coherence System

"Our stories disclose in a general way what we used to be like, what happened, and what we are like now." Drawn from the chapter titled "How It Works" in the "Big Book," *Alcoholics Anonymous* (originally published in 1939),[1] this formula describes the storytelling that forms the backbone of Twelve-Step recovery programs. Every sober alcoholic in A.A. has a "story," a chronological narrative of substance abuse, epiphany, and recovery. Although most persons entering A.A. carry with them an aggregation of recollections they would call their life stories, few recovering alcoholics could have predicted, at the time they "put down the drink," how closely their own life stories would come to resemble those that they hear in their first meetings.

The A.A. "story," as a discursive form, is an example of what Charlotte Linde defines as the subject of her book *Life Stories:*

> A life story is an oral unit that is told over many occasions. Conventionally, it includes certain kinds of landmark events, such as choice of profession, marriage, divorce, and religious or ideological conversion if any. Both in its content (the items that it includes and excludes) and in its form (the structures that are used to make it coherent), it is the product of a member of a particular culture. . . . Indeed, the notion of a "life story" itself is not universal, but is the product of a particular culture.[2]

Linde explains that oral life stories display coherence, which bears no particular relation to the "facts" of a person's life, but is rather "a property of texts; it derives from the relation that the parts of a text bear to one another and to the whole text, and that the text bears to other texts of its type."[3] Life stories follow "coherence systems," or "systems of assumptions about the world that speakers use to make events and evaluations coherent."[4] This essay examines the way Twelve-Step programs function as a "coherence system" in the life stories of their members and raises questions about the implications and repercussions of that system for Alcoholics Anonymous as a subculture and—by implication—for U. S. culture at large.

A.A. etiquette (grounded in what the Big Book says about the experience of the founding members) requires that public recitals of one's story disclose life experience primarily "in a general way," although each story necessarily carries its own individual set of details. Nevertheless, those details are selected and shaped according to a governing teleology determined by the "Twelve Steps" themselves.[5] The plural pronoun of the formula—"*our* stories disclose"—carries a force beyond the merely referential. A powerful master narrative shapes the life story of each recovering alcoholic, an autobiography-in-common that comes to constitute a collective identity for sober persons. Ostensibly cutting across lines of gender, sexual preference, ethnicity, race, social class, religion, and nationality, the narrative of recovery elides social and cultural differences to construct a diverse yet unified speaking position: "we, the men and women of Alcoholics Anonymous."[6] Put in its simplest terms, the master narrative is that the recovering person admitted to addiction, gained a faith that a "higher power" could provide relief if the addict were to take certain actions, and reaped the spiritual and material benefits of taking those actions within the A.A. program.

If there were no such thing as life stories, there could be no Twelve-Step programs. The oral autobiographical act is central at each stage of recovery as the programs conceive it. Indeed, the structure of individual stories relies on oral-formulaic practices within the group, providing individual storytellers with formulas that aid in the composition and recall of their stories of recovery. These stories are repeatedly rehearsed: most prominently, the individual alcoholic's story is the featured attraction at most A.A. "speaker meetings," where recovering persons gather to listen to one or more individuals tell, for anywhere from ten minutes to an hour, "what it was like, what happened, and what it's like today." Speakers "qualify," as it is sometimes called, extemporaneously: very few A.A. members speak from notes, and those who cannot resist planning their talks in advance generally rely on no more than a mental outline. Although spontaneity is the ostensible ethic, the master narrative functions mnemonically to provide the speaker with a structure for shaping the individual story's details. Paradoxically, the oral formula serves both to signal and to reinforce the internalization of the master narrative of recovery. The result is an innumerable set of autobiographies, as similar in their plots as they are different in their details.

Meetings are not the only setting in which recovering alcoholics are called upon to tell their stories. When a sober alcoholic pays a "twelfth-step call" upon an alcoholic who may be considering A.A. (Step 12 states, "We tried to carry this message to alcoholics"), he or she follows the examples set in the Big Book by telling his or her own story to the new recruit. After a new member has taken the first three of the Twelve Steps, the fourth step involves making a "searching and fearless moral inventory of ourselves," often in the form of a written autobiography that focuses on drinking-related behavior. In the fifth step, the recovering alcoholic orally recounts that autobiography to a disinterested auditor, probably his or her A.A. "sponsor" (a person who, having accumulated more of A.A.'s chief capital—time in sobriety—advises the A.A. member and is usually the audience for the fifth-step recitation).

Speakers who tell their stories at large meetings receive thanks and hugs from many who listen; speakers whose stories stray too far from the approved narrative (those who, for example, express doubts that they are "really an alcoholic" or who state that they do not need to attend meetings or to "work the program" to stay sober) are advised—sometimes privately, sometimes in public responses to the talk—to "keep coming back." The implication is that the more one "comes back," the more one hears and internalizes the structure of the master narrative in the infinite iterations that get played out in every speaker meeting, the more one will be able to reconceive one's own story to fit that narrative. "Don't compare. Identify," is what the newcomer is told to do in weighing the details of his or her own life story against those that are being told. For those who can manage to do it, this formulaic revision of their life stories can play a part in changing their lives.

The actual stories told at A.A. speaker meetings follow a fairly strict format consisting of two parts, which David Rudy has identified as the "drunkologue," or narrative of the experiences the speaker has had while drinking, and the "sobriety story," or account of how things have changed since the decision to stop drinking. As one A.A. member explained to Rudy (in a version of the Big Book formula that begins this essay), speaker meetings are for speakers' "telling what it was like when [speakers] were drinking," "explaining how they found out about A.A.," and "telling how good it is now."[7] Like all conversion narratives, whether of religious awakening or lesbian and gay coming out, these stories are retrospective narratives designed to reinterpret the past in the light of a more enlightened present identity.

A recent letter signed "Grateful in the United States" that appeared in the syndicated "Ann Landers" advice column took the form of a testimonial to A.A; it provides an encapsulated version of the two-part A.A. narrative of recovery:

> Dear Ann Landers:
>   I'm writing to you about a disease for which there is no cure. It is a baffling and powerful sickness called alcoholism. I am now 35 years old, and I've had it since I picked up my first drink when I was 12.
>   This disease caused me to lie, cheat, steal and drive when I was drunk. I was arrested so many times I can't count them. My life was miserable. But today I am sober and happy, only because I found Alcoholics Anonymous.
>   A.A.'s simple 12-step program works one day at a time. It has given me back my life. I now own a home, have a good job and am married to a fine woman, and we have a beautiful son. I never could have had any of the wonderful things in my life had I not found A.A.[8]

A close reading of this A.A. story in miniature shows that it follows the master narrative laid out sequentially by the first two of the Twelve Steps. Step 1 is "We admitted we were powerless over alcohol [and] that our lives had become unmanageable." To call alcoholism a "disease," as Grateful does, is to admit to being powerless over alcohol; this principle follows the same line of reasoning as acceptance of any fatal disease, such as cancer or AIDS. The person with the disease has no personal power to exert over that disease: he or she cannot will a cure. The second part of the first step—"admitted . . . that our lives had become unmanageable"—usually forms the bulk of a drunkologue, as it does in Grateful's story. Many recovering alcoholics' life stories, once they have been filtered through the "inventory taking" of the fourth step and the "admitting [the exact nature of our wrongs] to another human being" of the fifth, parallel Grateful's account of his activities: "This disease caused me to lie, cheat, steal and drive when I was drunk." In outline form, this is what recovering alcoholics mean by an "unmanageable" life. Although not every recovering alcoholic can identify with the statement about having been arrested many times, all could say, "My life was miserable." Attributing this misery to alcoholism is the "first step" in following the master narrative.

The second step is "[We] came to believe that a Power greater than ourselves could restore us to sanity." Grateful's story does not recount the process of "coming to believe," as many oral A.A. narratives do, but the results of that process are evident in the statement: "But today I am sober and happy, *only* because I found Alcoholics Anonymous" (emphasis added). A reader familiar with Twelve-Step programs would recognize the elision here of A.A. with "a Power greater than ourselves": many A.A. members express the belief that they never would have encountered an awareness of a higher power had they never entered the program. Grateful's narrative suggests that in the program the recovering alcoholic found the power that he himself could not exert over the unmanageability of his life. "I never could have had any of the wonderful things in my life had I not found A.A." Implicit in the denouement of Grateful's story is a promise of material and emotional prosperity that A.A. literature avoids making explicit.[9]

As Carole Cain points out in her analysis of A.A. personal stories, A.A. members actively learn to tell their stories according to the two-part structure outlined above. One can also, according to Cain, predict the extent of individuals' identification with A.A., as an organization and as a way of life, by looking at how far their personal stories deviate from a structure she identifies as the A.A. model story.[10] We are less interested in producing or refining such a model than in outlining its institutional and identity-conferring power. We find the master narrative of recovery manifested in individual accounts of alcoholism (personal stories), A.A. pamphlets and other official publications of the General Service Office of Alcoholics Anonymous, and public stories about alcoholics' recoveries in the mainstream media.

In reading these different cultural representations of the A.A. master narrative, we will point to signs of a struggle in contemporary U.S. culture over the question of identity itself, and over the relation of the individual recovering subject to community, difference, and publicity. First, we will examine the community-based model of identity that arises in sanctioned A.A. discourse, focusing especially on what we will call the "collective protagonist" of A.A.'s master narrative. Next, we will raise the issue of difference, questioning the place of individualism and diversity in that narrative. Finally, we will examine what happens when the identity of the recovering subject gets publicized and spectacularized in *People* magazine, reflecting on the contradictions that arise when the recovery story meets that other hegemonic cultural narrative, the marriage plot. Our goal is to identify the teleology of the Twelve Steps, and—pointing to its traces in mainstream culture—to consider what it says to and about the culture's need to uphold the fiction of the unified subject.

The Collective Protagonist of Twelve-Step Stories

At first glance, the Twelve Steps might not appear to follow a narrative structure, but part of "getting sober" in A.A. is learning to interpret the steps as a chronological sequence. The subject-verb structure of each of the steps suggests a chronological, past-tense story having a collective protagonist: "We admitted," "came to believe," "made a decision," "made a . . . moral inventory," "admitted," "were entirely ready," "humbly asked," "made a list," "made direct amends," "continued taking . . . inventory," "sought . . . to improve," and "tried to carry this message . . . and to practice these principles." The insistent repetition of past-tense verbs places the newcomer to A.A. in a peculiar position with regard to the steps. The sentences' verb tense denotes that the speaking subject ("we") has already completed these actions. Someone encountering the steps for the first time is positioned as auditor or interlocutor: "we" tell the newcomer what "we" have done. Frequently, newcomers are asked to read the steps aloud as part of the ritual that begins meetings. Asking them to read is one way of involving new members in the group; as they articulate this series of past-tense actions, however, they find themselves giving voice to a speaking subject with which they do not yet identify, until they have "worked the steps." Reading the steps aloud in a meeting is one of the many ways A.A. members learn to internalize the narrative the steps represent.

Many sponsors in A.A. insist that recovering alcoholics must "work the steps" in order, which means focusing on each step in turn until the material or spiritual task it describes has been accomplished. The first nine steps outline a sequence of quite specific actions, described in some detail in the Big Book and elaborated in a volume titled *Twelve Steps and Twelve Traditions* (the "Twelve and Twelve," in A.A. slang).[11]

To "take" these steps is to embark on a standard set of actions: first, to experience the conversion described in the "two-part" story; next (in Step 3), to commit oneself to the care of a "higher power," thus embarking on what many A.A. members call "the God stuff" or "the spiritual part" of the program. Having decided to believe that a higher power, not the individual person, has ultimate control over what will happen in that person's life, the recovering alcoholic then writes the fourth-step autobiography (the "moral inventory") and recounts it, in the fifth step, to another person, most likely the sponsor. Steps 6 and 7 require "attitude adjustment" (many people jocularly interpret "A.A." to signify this phrase), as the recovering person works on becoming "entirely willing to have God remove all our defects of character" (as inventoried in the fourth step and expressed in the fifth) and "humbly asks Him to remove our shortcomings." Step 8 requires another action, making a list "of all persons we had harmed, and becom[ing] willing to make amends to them all"; Step 9 requires making such amends, which may take such forms as apology, repayment of debts, or a determined effort to behave better in general to the persons who have been harmed by the alcoholic's previous way of living. The past-tense form of the steps underlines the idea that they are a narrative of the actions of the founding members, and a description, from their point of view, of "how it works."[12]

Steps 10, 11, and 12 are also phrased in the past tense, but are interpreted in A.A. as ongoing actions. They involve a continuous critique of one's actions in relation to other people, a concerted practice of prayer and meditation (in whatever form the recovering person and his or her sponsor find appropriate), and a purposeful outreach to other alcoholics, usually in the form of meetings, sponsorship, and "twelfth-step calls," where sober alcoholics go to "carry the message" to actively drinking alcoholics who may have reached their "bottom." The sequence of the steps suggests that these last three, continuous steps cannot be properly enacted before the other nine have been undertaken, and although some steps may overlap (making amends, for example, can take years, and not everyone completes it before working the last three steps), the steps are themselves a story of what every person recovering in A.A. is ultimately supposed to have experienced.

The collective protagonist of the steps' narrative—A.A.'s "we"—is crucial to the structuring of the autobiographical act within the program. The steps are usually read aloud at the beginning of each meeting, and are often posted in the rooms or the halls where meetings are held. Their continual, ritualized repetition functions as a structuring principle for each recovering person's understanding of his or her experience of sobriety. In giving individual testimony to the effectiveness of the program—at speaker meetings or at discussion meetings focusing on the steps or on other matters—most A.A. members are careful to specify that they speak only for themselves, because there is no officially sanctioned dogma within A.A., beyond the practice of tolerance: A.A. literature refers to the steps as "suggested," and individual members are free to interpret the written materials as they will.[13] But the narrative structure of the steps ensures that those who stay in the program will eventually frame their autobiographies to follow the experience outlined by the "we" who speak collectively through the steps. If the popular conception of Twelve-Step programs is that they foster egocentric self-absorption among their members, the reality of A.A. storytelling suggests quite another experience: the focus is a communal one, the story collective, rather than individualized; the "self" in A.A. is conceived as resembling and relating to others, rather than existing in isolated uniqueness. In this respect, the A.A. life story is antiautobiographical, in that it differs significantly from the dominant Western autobiographical tradition that Sidonie Smith has characterized as "the unfolding or the development, the reenactment or the discovery, of an individual's unique historical identity."[14]

The story told by the whole Twelve Steps differs significantly from the two-part narrative that makes its way into such public forums as the Ann Landers column. The biggest difference is the emphasis in the Twelve Steps on the "God stuff," a difficult passage for many newly sober alcoholics to traverse. As the Big Book and the Twelve and Twelve insist, many A.A. members describe themselves as agnostics or atheists upon entering the program. To tell one's life story as structured by all the Twelve Steps, however, is to attest to a belief in a "higher power," which the steps quite pointedly gender as masculine and name as "God." This aspect of Twelve-Step programs is the reason many alcoholics give for not being willing to "work the steps," and has, of course, been the impetus for the creation of such competing programs as Rational Recovery.

Most sober alcoholics in A.A. do refer to the Twelve Steps as a "spiritual program," and the oral and written discourse attributes the program's success to "a power greater than ourselves," as the second step puts it. This "power"—known in A.A. literature as "the God of our understanding," one's "higher power," or "God as we understand Him"—has as many definitions as there are members of A.A. Some think of the A.A. group ("Group Of Drunks," or GOD) as the power to which they "turn our will and our lives over," some conceive of a more abstract but personally formulated version of a power greater than themselves (a "life force," the "Goddess," the "Great Spirit," for example), some refer to "my higher power whom I choose to call God" (members seldom if ever say "my higher power whom I choose *not* to call god"), and many speak relatively unself-consciously about that power simply as "God." Given the discursive power centered in the master narrative of the Twelve Steps, however, one possible interpretation of that "higher power" might be that it is the master narrative, the coherence system—the "story"—itself.

Difference, Identification, and Identity

To reproduce the master narrative in recasting his or her life story, the recovering person constructs a new referent for the word *I:* "My name is Susan, and I am an alcoholic." As part of the process of constructing that referent, A.A. stories produce and rely on symptomatology that allows, for example, what might have been at the time experienced as "normal" drinking behavior to be reinterpreted retrospectively as signs of alcoholism. (For instance, "I only drank wine with dinner" might become "I was a daily drinker"; repeated assertions that "I can stop drinking any time I want to" can be reread as signs of defensiveness or anxiety over the compulsion to drink.) Nondrinking behaviors can also be read back as symptoms: these can include a sense of difference, of feeling alone, or of a seemingly free-floating or unspecified anxiety. The A.A. narrative offers a name for this familiar condition and a story that produces and reproduces that name.

The recourse to the symptom has both pathologizing and historicizing functions: it localizes a particular behavior in time and in relation to other behaviors of the same individual and compares them explicitly to the behaviors of those already designated as "alcoholics." At the same time, the label of "alcoholic" insists upon an essential difference between the person so labeled and the "normal" drinker or "social" drinker, who is imagined within the discourse of the program as someone indifferent to alcohol and immune to the feelings of isolation, alienation, and inadequacy that signal the "alcoholic" personality. The word *alcoholic* moves from noun to adjective as it gets attached to various behaviors and attitudes. "My alcoholic character defects," "alcoholic all-or-nothing thinking," and "an alcoholic family" are examples of this usage that may frequently be heard in meetings. The difference from normality that "alcoholic" signifies is figured as ineluctable and unchanging: that is why alcoholics in A.A. seldom refer to themselves as "recovered," more frequently saying they are "recovering," to signal an endless process.

At the same time that the recovering person adopts a sense of difference from nonalcoholics, he or she is encouraged to identify with the members of the group. Without identification there would be no A.A. program and, A.A. members might argue, few recovering alcoholics. The master narrative of alcoholism privileges the identity of "alcoholic" over other possible identities, making identifications across class, race, or gender—for example—possible, and indeed necessary. A.A. has published a series of pamphlets designed to appeal to various subcultures—"A.A. and the Gay/Lesbian Alcoholic," "A.A. for the Woman," and so on—but these pamphlets insist on the primacy of the alcoholic identity: "Although we are a gay and lesbian group, we don't lose sight of the fact that our primary purpose is to carry the message of recovery from alcoholism. In most respects we are no different than other A.A. groups."[15] Although "A.A. and the Gay/Lesbian Alcoholic" does begin with stories in the voices of lesbian and gay alcoholics, there is surprisingly little discussion of sexuality in the drunkologues with which they begin. Instead, the stories stress acceptance by A.A., figured as cross-category identification: "When Joe came by that night, my worst fears were confirmed. He was an older man, fiftyish, driving a station wagon and wearing a baseball cap. Though I was immediately persuaded that we had nothing in common, I soon found him so unassuming and so uncanny in his remarks about drinking that I found myself relaxing and even managed to add a few words to the conversation."[16]

Despite the existence of pamphlets targeted to particular subgroups, difference within A.A. is routinely contested. Nowhere is ambivalence about difference more clearly demonstrated than in the pamphlet "Do You Think You're Different?" The direct address of the title offers a simultaneously capacious and accusatory "you" whose potentially multiple subject positions are outlined in the table of contents of the pamphlet. The heading on the introduction, "Many of Us Thought We Were Special," is followed by a series of titles of individual stories followed by parenthetical adjectives linking the stories' protagonists to particular subgroups ("black," "Jewish," "high bottom," "movie star," "atheist"). Each story title follows the formula of introduction and identification with which speakers at meetings begin their remarks: "My name is George [Paul, Gloria], and I'm an alcoholic." The story titles build up on the left side of the table of contents; each name is followed by the designation "and I'm an alcoholic." It is only after this statement that the signal parenthetical other (previous?) identity appears. The repeated term *alcoholic,* then, is orthographically displayed as a primary identity, defining each individual and his or her relation to the others on the same page. "Alcoholic" cuts across lines of age, status, gender, and race, as it cuts across the black lines that provisionally separate one title in the table of contents from the others.

The table of contents (which does not appear in any of the other pamphlets addressed to subgroups) manages the difference it simultaneously invokes and undermines in both its title and—when we get to it—its substance. The opening paragraph of the pamphlet raises the specter of many possible differences:

> "A.A. won't work for me. I'm too far gone." "It's nice for those people, but I'm president of the P.T.A." I'm too old. Too young. Not religious enough. I'm gay. Or Jewish. A professional person. A member of the clergy. Too smart. Or too uneducated.[17]

The list of possible differences begins with two longish sentences in quotation marks, suggesting that these are comments by "real" individuals. Suddenly, however, by the third example, the quotation marks stop and what we can only call the narrative voice begins to enact an impersonation of differences. The implication of this shift seems to be that these disembodied voices of resistance have been heard before, that they do not belong to particular people but to some litany of perceived differences so familiar as almost not to count as difference at all. The narrative impersonation suggests not only reiteration of difference, but the ability of the A.A. master narrative to voice differences for other people, to represent and literally to advocate for all people, including those whose subject position would seem to distance them the most from A.A.

By the third paragraph, the pamphlet has banished all difference in the ecumenical "we" that so frequently marks the A.A. master narrative: "We in A.A. believe alcoholism is a disease that is no respecter of age, sex, creed, race, wealth, occupation, or education. It strikes at random. Our experience seems to show that *anyone* can be an alcoholic. And, beyond question, *anyone* who wants to stop drinking is welcome in A.A."[18] This paragraph moves smoothly from disease to cure; because the *disease* makes no distinctions, A.A. makes no distinctions either. Categories are supposed to collapse under the weight of a common humanity, a common body and soul under attack.

As the very existence of these pamphlets shows, the master narrative has had to contend with competing narratives of difference that establish—however tentatively—the category of the "woman alcoholic" or "gay/lesbian alcoholic" within the discourse of the organization.[19] The homogenizing master narrative cannot, however, absorb all difference, all contestation: over the past twenty years, other groups for recovering alcoholics have formed, sometimes explicitly in opposition to some foundational principles of A.A. Difference has been a foundational trope for some of these groups, such as Rational Recovery, formed in defiance of the first step, "We admitted we were powerless over alcohol." Many members of Rational Recovery, as well as other critics of A.A., see the first step as especially problematic for women, who, they argue, scarcely need yet another voice reminding them that they are powerless. In *A Passion for Friends,* Janice Raymond connects her analysis of A.A.'s disempowerment of women with a larger spiritual project of feminist reempowerment.[20] For some feminists, it is not so much A.A. itself as the extension of the Twelve Steps to other recovery efforts, especially those for incest survivors, that constitutes the problem in overlooking the historically specific relationship of women to power.[21]

While A.A. does acknowledge some differences in the cultural history of alcoholism—for example, that women alcoholics may tend to drink in private, and for that reason might have a harder time acknowledging their alcoholism and beginning the process of recovery—

the sense of difference ends with the entry of the differently marked "woman alcoholic" into A.A. Although nearly two-thirds of the forty-two stories in the Big Book are narrated by white men, twelve are told by white women, three by men of color, and one by a black woman. The title of the fourth story to appear—the first with a female narrator—is "Women Suffer Too." The explicit message is gender inclusiveness, but the insistent leaning on similarity that the "too" carries may denote a defensiveness about the disruptive potential of difference. There is no official discourse of race or gender difference persisting as the newcomer becomes involved in the program; there is no structural difference, for example, in the way A.A. literature represents women's or African Americans' relation to the Twelve Steps. The stories in the Big Book are also very careful to depict protagonists from a broad range of socioeconomic classes, from a "titled lady," to a "psychiatrist and surgeon," to a "tough prisoner," to a "waitress by day, barfly by night."[22] The only distinctions between individuals that persist in A.A. discourse are conceived in terms of the disease, such as "high bottom drunk" and "low bottom drunk," referring to how desperate a person's external circumstances had become at the time he or she entered A.A. The master narrative insists, however, that even these distinctions are ultimately immaterial, and that "we are all just alcoholics," suffering from the same disease.

The imbrication of disease and universalism is important for another way in which difference is managed within A.A. The discourse of the master narrative not only erases difference but pathologizes it as the need to be different becomes itself a sign of an "alcoholic personality." The disease of difference, like the disease of alcoholism itself, is perceived as fatal: some A.A. members use the phrase "terminal uniqueness" to designate a repeated insistence on specialness. Alcoholics, the master narrative maintains, all think they are different or special; this form of egoism, although perhaps not unique to alcoholics, is nonetheless a characteristic of the disease. "Uniqueness" is figured in A.A. discourse as a form of denial, in that it can interfere with an alcoholic's recovery by preventing the unique individual from taking on the collective identity imposed by the Twelve Steps as necessary for recovery.

The master narrative of A.A. is also, of course, a master narrative of identity, for which the word *alcoholic* is a convenient and resonant shorthand. "As the A.A. member learns the A.A. story model, and learns to place the events and experiences of his own life into the model, he learns to tell and to understand his own life as an A.A. life, and himself as an A.A. alcoholic. The personal story is a cultural vehicle for identity acquisition," as Cain puts it.[23] Identity is, of course, deeply imbricated in the notion of identification: the A.A. master-narrative is capacious enough to allow many different people to hear the story of their own lives in other people's highly detailed autobiographical accounts. ("You told my story" is a common way to express this experience.)

In his book *Treating Alcoholism*, sociologist Norman Denzin defines "self" in an A.A. context: "That process that unifies the stream of thoughts and experiences the person has about himself or herself around a single pole or point of reference; not a thing, but a process. . . . The self is not in consciousness, but in the world of social interaction. It haunts the subject."[24] If, in A.A., "self" is a process, not an entity, and if it exists in social interaction, not consciousness, then the A.A. master narrative does not merely shape or influence the identity of the recovering alcoholic. The acquisition and continual retelling of the story becomes the very process that constitutes the alcoholic's self. Paradoxically, the recovering alcoholic adopts a new identity, but the identity is a deindividualized or "anonymous" one: the "self" that exists in the world of social interaction within A.A. has no distinguishing appellation, no surname beyond the occasional initial: "I'm Bill W., and I'm an alcoholic."

Among A.A.'s twelve traditions—policies established by the General Service Office to "keep groups united around the world"—the principle of anonymity comes up twice: "Our public relations policy is based on attraction rather than promotion; we need always maintain personal anonymity at the level of press, radio, and films" is Tradition 11, and Tradition 12 is "Anonymity is the spiritual foundation of all our traditions, ever reminding us to place principles before personalities." The Twelve and Twelve explains that anonymity within groups is necessary for confidentiality's sake, especially for newcomers who worry that others outside the group (at their jobs or schools, for instance) will learn that they have declared themselves to be alcoholics. For this reason, few people at A.A. meetings use their surnames in introducing themselves, and groups typically distinguish among members with the same given name by specifying a last initial ("Karen T." and "Karen W.") or assigning unofficial nicknames ("big John," "wild Bill," "Mary the nurse"). In keeping with the practice of voicing the master narrative and speaking for the collective "we," given names allow a certain degree of specificity to each speaker, but not as much as full names would carry in the world outside the program. Each member is granted a modicum of individuality, but only so much.

Anonymity "at the level of press, radio, and films" is mandated less in the interest of personal confidentiality than to avoid individual aggrandizement among members, to keep any one person from embodying the A.A. identity in the public eye. According to the Twelve and Twelve, "this tradition is a constant and practical reminder that personal ambition has no place in A.A."[25] Tradition 12 elaborates:

> We simply couldn't afford to take the chance of letting self-appointed members present themselves as messiahs representing A.A. before the whole public. The promoter instinct in us might be our undoing. If even one publicly got drunk, or was lured into using A.A.'s name for his own purposes, the damage might be irreparable. At this altitude (press, radio, films, and television), anonymity—100 percent anonymity—was the only possible answer. Here principles would have to come before personalities, without exception.[26]

A.A. literature states that the program relies upon the press's understanding of this principle to keep surnames of members out of the public view. To do so is to insist that "alcoholic" is the operative identity and identification for every member, and that one's family/professional/married name is irrelevant to one's status as a recovering person.

Going Public: The Recovery Story as Spectacle

Some A.A. members conform to the tradition of anonymity, and some do not. In the case of Nan Robertson, a journalist who wrote *Getting Better: Inside Alcoholics Anonymous* to explain the workings of the program to persons outside it, the decision to "break anonymity" was a self-conscious one. Robertson tells of a visit she paid to Lois Wilson, the widow of the program's founder, to explain her project. Mrs. Wilson asked her if she planned to break her anonymity as an alcoholic, and Robertson "blushed and said, 'I don't know. I'm a reporter as well as an alcoholic; I don't think I should cheat the reader by not being completely honest.' I told her that I thought the book would be much more authentic and believable if I revealed that I was in A.A."[27] For

Robertson, the identities of "journalist" and "alcoholic" are not mutually exclusive: she ends her study with a detailed version of her own A.A. story, structured to follow the master narrative. At the same time, her departure from the tradition of anonymity brings her authority for speaking about A.A. into question, from the program's perspective. Her subtitle, *Inside Alcoholics Anonymous,* takes on a double valence: to speak publicly about the inside of A.A. is to position oneself as outside A.A.'s sanctioned discourse.

When celebrities speak to *People* magazine about their recoveries, they cannot rely—as the General Service Office evidently hopes—upon the reporters' adherence to the principle of anonymity in A.A. Some celebrities seem to be as sensitive to the issue as Robertson's blush implies she was: John Larroquette, for instance, whose current situation comedy casts him in the role of a recovering alcoholic attending A.A. meetings, was featured in *People* in 1985 as an alcoholic in recovery, but has never been mentioned in that magazine as a member of A.A.[28] In a detailed 1989 *People* story telling of his drunkologue, conversion experience, and current happiness, another celebrity does not speak directly of A.A. membership, but communicates his affiliation with the program in a code that other members would recognize:[29] like Grateful, Ann Landers's correspondent, he refers to alcohol as "very cunning and baffling," an echo of the Big Book's caution, "Remember that we deal with alcohol—cunning, baffling, powerful!"[30] Like many of A.A.'s "slogans" ("One day at a time," "Take it easy," "First things first"), this oft-repeated phrase is one of the oral formulas that frequently make their way into A.A. members' stories. Without promoting himself as a program member, this celebrity manages to communicate his affiliation through this coded phrase and through the structure of his self-account.

Not every celebrity has so thoroughly internalized the principle of anonymity. In a 1990 cover story in *People,* Drew Barrymore mentions attending A.A. meetings, and even reveals the name of her A.A. sponsor.[31] From the perspective of the Twelve Traditions, her doing so arrogates the A.A. identity to herself; she risks jeopardizing her own spiritual condition by allowing herself to be "special" in the media's view, and she risks A.A.'s reputation if, as has happened before, she "slips" and fails in her recovery. Her story in *People* conforms to the A.A. master narrative in its overarching structure, but this public rendition of Barrymore's story becomes a metonymy for the A.A. story itself. *People*'s characteristically arch treatment of Barrymore's experience tends to trivialize it (the magazine renders her "bottom" thus: "The next day, while waiting to be picked up for a Fourth of July barbecue, she heard that some friends were mad at her. It was a minor blow, but enough to send Drew over the edge"),[32] and hence to trivialize the master narrative her story follows.

The public story of recovery as it appears in the mainstream media is, then, a deeply paradoxical genre. For those celebrities who are working on their sobriety through A.A., the story of recovery is always entangled in a tension between the anonymity on which the program depends and the publicity that must attend them as stars. Because A.A. sees the breaking of anonymity as imperiling both individual sobriety and the integrity of the group, the public recovery story can be read from one point of view as celebration of achievement and from another as a symptom of a particularly vulnerable or false sobriety (sometimes called a "dry drunk"). Some celebrities, as we have seen, resist talking about their recovery, even in the context of articles celebrating their passage from drugs or alcohol to sobriety. In a story about actor Michael Des Barres titled "From Rock to Roles: With the fog of drugs lifted, former glam-rocker Michael Des Barres may be the busiest actor on television," Des Barres is described as hitting bottom one day and attending an A.A. meeting that night: "Michael went to an Alcoholics Anonymous meeting, stopped drinking and drugging, and has been clean and sober since."[33] After this highly condensed rendition of the A.A. master narrative, the article goes on to say that Des Barres "doesn't like to talk about it," and quotes him as saying "recovering celebrities are sober for a month, and they think they can do anything."[34] Although Des Barres has broken his anonymity, at least to the extent of mentioning A.A. at all, his comment provides a moment of resistance to the genre of the public recovery story. His resistance is nonetheless absorbed into a characteristic *People* story based on what Nancy K. Miller has defined in another context as a "euphoric" narrative, in which the protagonist moves from a position of danger and social marginality to one of triumph.[35]

The prototypical euphoric narrative in *People* has much in common with the master narrative of recovery we have discussed above. The very publicity of the narrative, however, radically changes the master narrative's assumptions about the individual and community. Over the years, the *People* narrative of recovery has been accommodated by and has accommodated itself to new subgenres within the magazine. The past four years have seen the development of a new category of story that appears in many issues: titled "Sequel," this category includes follow-up stories to articles in previous issues as well as stories of the "where are they now" type. "Sequel" is, of course, hospitable to stories of recovery, which depend on an actual or assumed account of a crisis that can be followed up by a happy ending. Typical "Sequel" recovery stories—like "A Camelot Comeback: *Naked Gun*'s Robert Goulet has a reunited family and a recharged career" or "*Shindig*'s Star Frugs Again: After years of chaos, '60s rock show host Jimmy O'Neill finds a new groove"—depend not only on a notion of progress but of recovery in which a successful past is recaptured and improved upon after intervening years of trial. This sense of repetition with a difference is dictated, of course, by the fact that the subject of the "Sequel" story was already a celebrity when the substance abuse became a problem. "Sequel" stories, like other celebrity recovery stories, then, embed the teleology associated with the A.A. master narrative in a cyclical structure of return and, as O'Neill puts it in the story about him, "reincarnation."

The public recovery story is also typically embedded in another important cultural master narrative: the marriage and reproduction plot, which depicts maturity, sanity, and normalcy as coterminous with marriage and parenthood. Like nineteenth-century marriage-plot novels, these stories frequently end with marriage and/or the birth of a child. The structure and teleology of the marriage plot is activated in these stories of recovery even—or perhaps especially—in a magazine such as *People,* which repeatedly chronicles divorces, breakups, and child custody battles.

Nowhere is the interrelation among narration, happy endings, marriage, and recovery more complexly set out in *People* than in the series of stories about actors Melanie Griffith and Don Johnson. The cyclical structure of public recovery is amplified by the fact that in the past fifteen years Johnson and Griffith have been a couple twice: they were married when Griffith was fourteen and Johnson twenty-one, divorced soon thereafter, and, after lengthy involvements with other people (including Patti D'Arbanville, who figures in the story as Johnson's partner between his unions with Griffith), became a public couple again around 1988. The final story in the series features Griffith and Johnson having a baby in 1989.

The story of the Johnson-Griffith relationship is consciously set out against the euphoric narrative structure of the public recovery story. "*Miami Vice* and a Good Woman Save Bad Boy Don Johnson" is quite explicit about the master narrative within which it is being written:

> Drugs and drink and compulsive sex and suicidal spending sprees: They are so integral a part of the cliched Hollywood life that it seems de rigueur, if you are an actor, to pass through a lost-soul phase on the way to stardom—if only to amass your own war stories and join your confreres when they graduate to Sobriety Deluxe. The most popular scenario involves indulging in a series of drugged and drunken scrapes, failing at love, hitting bottom and being rescued by a woman who inspires you to grow up. Under her gentle guidance you seek professional help, dose yourself with yogurt, embrace monogamy and dump the coke down the john. You rejoice when your madonna ex machina conceives a child and herald its birth as a metaphor of your own deliverance. . . . Meet Don Johnson of *Miami Vice*.[36]

The direct address of this opening paragraph, with its insistence on the personal pronoun "you," suggests that this template for the master narrative is being authored by the recovering subject. The narrative it invokes is not the story in *People* but the story that inspires the story in *People*: the story the celebrity tells (him)self, his friends, and the public. *People*'s acquiescence to and amplification of this narrative remain unthematized, although its symptoms persist in the title and the body of the piece. The "good woman" who saves Don Johnson is not Melanie Griffith but Patti D'Arbanville, the *People* piece a celebration of their monogamy and parenthood. As the story title that appears in the index—"Family Virtues Now Come First for *Miami Vice*'s Reformed Don Johnson"—suggests, this is a story of temporal and spiritual progress told from the safe haven of a precariously achieved but triumphant domesticity.

The crisis in this euphoric narrative is explicitly framed as a crisis in conjugal life told from the subject position of an achieved domesticity. As the baby "gurgles happily," Johnson tells the story of his hitting bottom:

> I walked into the breakfast room one morning . . . and the sun was shining and the birds were singing, and Patti was feeding the baby. I came staggering in and sat down and looked at them, and

she looked at me and I knew that if I didn't do something she was going to leave.[37]

This story depends on a double gaze: Johnson's desiring and guilty taking in of this blissful scene of domesticity and D'Arbanville's diagnostic return look, influenced in its understanding of the situation by her own experiences with and recovery from addiction. The scene of domesticity becomes, through baby Jesse's gurgle in the present tense, a scene that can be revisited and reclaimed.

This story of recovery is, like the diagnostic gaze itself, curiously and crucially double. D'Arbanville's own history makes her aware of "what was ahead for Don"; she brings him to his first A.A. meeting and makes possible his recovery. As Johnson explains, "You ask for a higher power to help you. . . . I got down on my knees and humbled myself and said 'I can't do this alone.'"[38] Whatever Johnson's construction of his "higher power" may be, the higher power at work in the structure of the *People* narrative is Patti. She is the "good woman" who "saves the bad boy." Johnson's "I can't do this alone" can be read back against the marriage plot of the piece as a reference to Patti; the "madonna ex machina" literally becomes the higher power.

A.A.'s own position on the relation of recovery and marriage is typically cautious. Although the Big Book suggests that many people's domestic lives improve as a result of recovery, this is deliberately not made the focus or the goal of sobriety in A.A. literature. A.A.'s notion of a group relation with the higher power puts husbands, wives, and other partners—usually figured in the Big Book explicitly as wives—in an ambiguous relation to the process of recovery.[39] Certainly, A.A. argues that no one else can be responsible for another person's recovery; A.A. does not promote the notion of familial interventions, of forcing someone into the program and into recovery before the person has hit bottom.

In *People*, however, euphoric marriage and professional successes structure and give meaning to recovery. Professional progress is of course the sine qua non of inclusion in *People*, but marriage and reproduction serve as both signs and guarantors of recovery. This is even, and perhaps especially, so given *People*'s constant chronicling of breakups and divorce. In the case of the D'Arbanville-Johnson relationship, the conflation of conjugality and recovery—the happy ending to the marriage plot—is of course not an ending at all. Johnson and

D'Arbanville again split up, despite their denials of rumors to this effect in a *People* story somewhat open-endedly titled "America's Favorite Vice: The ex-druggie is now a devoted dad, but there's still an irresistible aura of danger about *Miami Vice*'s Don Johnson."[40] Johnson goes on to become involved once again with Melanie Griffith, whom he has significantly, along the way, "helped" to "conquer addictions." The story—up to this point—ends with another baby on the way. "A Baby for Don and Melanie" reinserts Johnson into a marriage and reproductive plot, but this time with another woman, the woman to whom he had been married before. Once again, the teleology of reproduction structures the story; as Melanie's mother puts it, "'[The baby] is something Melanie has wanted for a very long time, since she first met Don.'" Johnson's view is even more explicitly teleological: "This is God's plan," he is reported as saying to Melanie.[41]

From the narrative perspective of the final article, Johnson's relationship to D'Arbanville serves only as an interruption to the marriage plot that finally brings Johnson and Griffith together. At each moment in the larger story, God's plan—for recovery, for marriage, for reproduction—shifts along a continuum of individual "final" moments or gestures. The story of recovery, implicated as it is in the story of marriage, is likewise haunted by the possibility of slipping, changing, drinking. *People,* however, seems unfazed by these possibilities; its faith in the euphoric plot remains untouched. Indeed, there is something about the act of repetition itself, at least in the marriage plot, that acts to consolidate rather than to challenge its own master narrative. For instance, *People*'s obsession with the marriages of Elizabeth Taylor—themselves of course entwined in a narrative of recovery from substance abuse—displays the capaciousness of the euphoric plot as it relates to both marriage and addiction.

The narratives of recovery in *People* magazine and those in A.A. literature and meetings differ, then. The magazine's coherence system is intertwined with assumptions inherited from the marriage plot and from the traditional Western autobiography's emphasis upon individual achievement. By contrast, the Twelve-Step program's teleology borrows more heavily from the conversion narrative tradition, where individual self-knowledge is conceived in terms of one's relation to a community and a higher power. In *People*'s narratives of recovery, the individual is emphasized and glorified; in A.A.'s, the individual is absorbed into the group. Neither of these coherence systems offers much in the way of an interestingly complicated concept of the self-in-recovery: the alternatives offered seem to be the triumphant individual and the anonymous nonentity.

What the two narratives have in common is a reliance upon a relatively uncomplicated model of a unitary self, though the two posit that self differently. Both the spectacularized public stories of *People* and the anonymously reiterated master narrative of A.A. present the self as coherent, in spite of abundant internal evidence to the contrary: that evidence is implicit in A.A.'s defensiveness about difference and its emphasis on the dangers of slipping; it is explicit in *People*'s blithe obliviousness to the fact that the stories it recounts are far from coherent, taken collectively as biographical representations of a unified self (as, for instance, when Don Johnson finds "final" happiness with two completely different—yet, for the purposes of the story, interchangeable—women). Difficult as it may be for these narratives to accommodate the differences *between* persons that "diversity" signifies, it is impossible for them to take into account difference *within,* or split subjectivity. As Barbara Johnson puts it, "The search for wholeness, oneness, universality, and totalization can . . . never be put to rest. However rich, healthy, or lucid fragmentation and division may be, narrative seems to have trouble resting content with it, as though a story could not recognize its own end as anything other than a moment of totalization."[42]

Telling one's story in conformity with the teleology of Twelve-Step programs, one embraces that totalization. The end of every Twelve-Step story is the moment of its telling or its writing: the act of telling is itself the evidence of sobriety. The "I" who tells the story participates fully in the fiction of a unified self. To resist that fiction is not necessarily to reject the potential benefits that A.A.'s institutional conferral of identity provides, however. Reflecting on the interplay of identity and anonymity, difference and identification within Twelve-Step discourse can make it possible for a recovering person to stand both inside and outside A.A., to be at once part of it and apart from it. To conceive of the recovering subject's identity in this double way would be to enact the split subjectivity that the master narratives suppress, but that analysis of the master narratives brings forward.

The story of recovery is, after all, "only" a story. Like all compelling narratives, however, the story holds emotional power for those who "willingly" suspend their disbelief. Seen from the perspective of our analysis, recovery and narrative are indistinguishable. "Living sober," in A.A.'s terms, means continuously telling, retelling, hearing, and revising the story of recovery, a recovery that can exist only in and through the power of narrative.

Notes

1. *Alcoholics Anonymous: The Story of How Many Thousands of Men and Women Have Recovered from Alcoholism*, 3rd ed. (New York: Alcoholics Anonymous World Services, 1976), 58.

2. Charlotte Linde, *Life Stories: The Creation of Coherence* (New York: Oxford University Press, 1993), 11.

3. Ibid., 220.

4. Ibid., 221.

5. In this essay, we distinguish between two versions of the recovery narrative, one following the teleology of the entire twelve steps, the other—a more abbreviated version typically found in mass-media accounts of the narrative of recovery—focusing on just the first two of those twelve steps.

6. The foreword to *Alcoholics Anonymous* identifies the text's speaking subject as "We, of Alcoholics Anonymous . . . more than one hundred men and women who have recovered from a seemingly hopeless state of mind and body" (xiii).

7. David R. Rudy, *Becoming Alcoholic: Alcoholics Anonymous and the Reality of Alcoholism* (Carbondale: Southern Illinois University Press, 1986), 12.

8. "Ann Landers," *Burlington Free Press*, 14 July 1993, Living section.

9. Some A.A. speakers' stories are structured around "the promises," a series of predictions in the Big Book that bear upon emotional and spiritual—but not material—advantages to be gained from sobriety. One of the promises is, for example, that "fear of people and of economic insecurity will leave us" (*Alcoholics Anonymous*, 84); economic prosperity itself, however, is not promised.

10. Carole Cain, "Personal Stories: Identity Acquisition and Self-Understanding in Alcoholics Anonymous," *Ethos* 19 (March 1991): 210–46.

11. *Twelve Steps and Twelve Traditions* (New York: Alcoholics Anonymous World Services, 1982), 21–87.

12. "How It Works" is the title of chapter 5 of *Alcoholics Anonymous*, 58–71. This book and the "Twelve and Twelve" were originally drafted by Bill Wilson, the co-founder of A.A., according to *"Pass It On": The Story of Bill Wilson and How the A.A. Message Reached the World* (New York: Alcoholics Anonymous World Services, 1984). The author's name does not appear in either book, in keeping with A.A.'s principle of anonymity and in concert with the collective identity of the books' speaking subjects.

13. For instance, "Here are the steps we took, which are suggested as a program of recovery." *Alcoholics Anonymous*, 59.

14. Sidonie Smith, *A Poetics of Women's Autobiography: Marginality and the Fictions of Self-Representation* (Bloomington: Indiana University Press, 1987), 21.

15. "AA and the Gay/Lesbian Alcoholic" (pamphlet). (New York: Alcoholics Anonymous World Services, 1989), 10.

16. Ibid., 8.

17. "Do You Think You're Different?" (pamphlet). (New York: Alcoholics Anonymous World Services, 1976), 7.

18. Ibid.

19. See, for instance, "A.A. for the Woman" (pamphlet). (New York: Alcoholics Anonymous World Services, 1976).

20. Janice Raymond, *A Passion for Friends: Toward a Philosophy of Female Affection* (Boston: Beacon, 1986).

21. For a well-argued recent example, see Ellen Driscoll, "The Politics of Recovery," in *Consuming Passions: Feminist Approaches to Weight Preoccupation and Eating Disorders,* ed. Catrina Brown and Karin Jasper (Toronto: Second Story, 1993), 251–73.

22. *Alcoholics Anonymous,* vi–x.

23. Cain, "Personal Stories," 215.

24. Norman K. Denzin, *Treating Alcoholism: An Alcoholics Anonymous Approach* (Newbury Park, Calif.: Sage, 1987), 140.

25. *Twelve Steps and Twelve Traditions,* 183.

26. Ibid., 187.

27. Nan Robertson, *Getting Better: Inside Alcoholics Anonymous* (New York: William Morrow, 1988), 18.

28. "After a Bout with Booze, John Larroquette Hauls in a *Night Court* Emmy," *People,* 9 December 1985, 109–13.

29. "Once and Forever the Lovable . . . ," *People,* 28 August 1989, 68.

30. *Alcoholics Anonymous,* 58–59.

31. "Falling Down . . . and Getting Back Up Again," *People,* 29 January 1990, 56–61.

32. Ibid., 58.

33. "From Rock to Roles," *People,* 9 December 1991, 88.

34. Ibid., 88–89.

35. Nancy K. Miller, *The Heroine's Text: Readings in the French and English Novel, 1722–1782* (New York: Columbia University Press, 1980), 82.

36. "Family Virtues Now Come First for *Miami Vice*'s Don Johnson," *People,* 3 December 1984, 124.

37. Ibid., 126.

38. Ibid.

39. *Alcoholics Anonymous* addresses one of its early explanatory chapters "To Wives," 104–21.

40. "America's Favorite Vice," *People,* 7 October 1985, 106–11.

41. "A Baby for Don and Melanie," *People,* 27 February 1989, 84.

42. Barbara Johnson, *A World of Difference* (Baltimore: Johns Hopkins University Press, 1987), 164.

15 / Professional Subjects: Prepackaging the Academic C.V.

Martin A. Danahay

Academics are institutionalized. Although it may be uncomfortable for academic professionals to acknowledge this, the structure of the academic curriculum vitae (C.V.) replicates at the level of the subject the power of the university as an institution. Sidonie Smith and Julia Watson argue in the introduction to this collection that "only certain kinds of stories become intelligible as they fit the managed framework, the imposed system. The recitation is, in effect, prepackaged, prerecited." The power of the university to "pre-package" job candidates is exemplified in the uniformity of C.V.s. All C.V.s look alike, and in their uniformity confirm that "recitations of personal narrative . . . attest to and verify [individuals'] participation in corporate culture." In the case of the C.V., the "corporate culture" affirmed is that of the university.

In registering the power of the university as a regulatory body, academics like myself occupy a position similar to that of other professionals; doctors, for instance, have review and certification boards that maintain "professional" standards and police the behavior of their members. However, doctors as professionals can choose either to situate themselves in the corporate structure of an HMO or turn themselves into independent businesses. Doctors' means of social control tend to be more diffuse than those exercised by hiring committees, promotion and tenure committees, and review boards within universities. Because academic professionals have to sign up with universities if they want to practice their trade, they are far more deeply embroiled in the structure of institutions than are other professionals. Academics, whether they like it or not, would not have a profession without the institution of the university. As I will demonstrate, the concept of an academic "career" reproduced by the structure of the C.V. is enabled by the existence of the university as an institution; the C.V. as the narrative of a career confirms the power of the university to elicit a prepackaged narrative in terms that ensure the reproduction of existing power relations within the institution.

This structural difference between the academic professional and the position of other professionals such as doctors, lawyers, and engineers accounts for the major differences between the C.V. and the résumé. The résumé is far less clearly defined as an autobiographical narrative than the C.V. Books offering advice on résumés frequently give two or three examples of possible forms that the subject can present to a prospective employer.[1] Frequently the emphasis is upon defining a set of "skills" that relate directly to the performance of a particular job within the company structure. The academic C.V. never mentions "skills" as a possible category because it is assumed there is only one possible job available for the candidate, that of professor. It would be redundant to recite the skills acquired in this case because it is assumed that somebody who applies for the position in the first place will have completed a long socialization process, known as graduate school, and therefore will be equipped with the necessary skills.

The differences between résumés and C.V.s should not be exaggerated, however. In both cases the power of the corporation is confirmed by the very act of the subject submitting his or her résumé or C.V. The major difference between the C.V. and the résumé is the way in which the idea of professional "skills" is clear in one and mystified in the other. In the résumé it is acknowledged that the subject is selling his or her labor, and that the employer is most interested in the person as a worker. The C.V. is also the résumé of a prospective worker, but academics are uncomfortable about naming what they do "work" or, even more disturbingly, "labor," and this mystification is carried over into the C.V., where the idea of "skills" is completely absent. It would be useful and enlightening for academics to think of what they do as demanding skills, and would help them talk to students about what they could do with their lives after graduation, but to do so would mean deconstructing some of the ideologies that undergird academic daily practice.[2] It is my modest aim in this essay to initiate a discussion of the way in which the practice of constructing and disseminating C.V.s reinforces ideologies that mystify the relationship between the academic professional and the university as a corporate structure.

This is a field of inquiry that Richard Ohmann has pursued in both *English in America* and *The Politics of Letters.*[3] Ohmann provides an illuminating critique of the operation of literary criticism as a "profession" and of the professional organization that represents those who work in English and foreign-language departments, the Modern Language Association (MLA). The MLA is the professional organization with which I am most familiar, and so my analysis will focus on this body. The MLA operates in the same way as the American Historical Association (AHA) in history and the American Anthropological Association (AAA) in anthropology. I have attended the annual meetings of both these groups, and they operate on the same principles as the MLA. Each reinforces the definition of its discipline as a "profession" and helps define "professional standards." The standards are uniform across the disciplines because all disciplines are housed in universities. Although the subject matter at each conference is different, the structures are the same, and the organizations and their annual meetings all serve the same function. Thus, although my analysis targets the MLA specifically, it is applicable to other professional organizations that gather academics into large groups.

Proponents of what has come to be called "cultural criticism" frequently argue that analysis should take into account the political and ideological battles that inform texts. Jonathan Dollimore, under the rubric of "cultural materialism," has called for a critique of texts that also accounts for the interpreters' own social contexts.[4] Similarly, Pierre Bourdieu has carried out a sociological critique of French academia that parallels Ohmann's critique of the profession. Bourdieu argues that sociologists should turn their analysis back upon themselves and "undertake a sociological critique of sociological reasoning." He asserts that "one cannot avoid having to objectify the objectifying subject" if one wishes "to gain a theoretical control over his own structures and inclinations as well as over the determinants whose products they are."[5] Bourdieu then proceeds to analyze the structure of the French university system of which he is a part, although he himself, surprisingly, does not appear as a subject of study in his book.[6] Bourdieu and Dollimore both call for the kind of "backyard ethnography" that Smith and Watson name in the introduction to this collection.

A collection of backyard ethnographies such as this, which focuses deliberately on the micropolitical implications of everyday uses of autobiography, provides a useful corrective to the kind of abstract sociological critique mounted by Bourdieu, but also underlines the limitations of an approach based upon personal experience. Defining autobiography as a genre distinguishable from other forms of writing privileges the anecdotal and parochial over the kind of large-scale system that Bourdieu represents in *Homo Academicus*. As I am not a sociologist, I will be presenting in this chapter a critique of academia based upon personal experience and textual analysis. Although this allows me to make observations about the ideals that inform academia, and the ideological contradictions they efface, I was aware in writing this essay of the limitations of my point of view. I can only gesture at what I know of the informal, oral culture of academia within which everyday practices take place.[7] As a male, I cannot speak directly to the experience of being female, or for that matter of being a "minority" in academia. As a white male, I can draw upon the experiences of such colleagues as bell hooks only indirectly. However, I will suggest in my conclusion how the experiences of both women and minorities mobilized in personal narratives help destabilize the regime of the C.V. and the professional standards it validates.

Bourdieu's *Homo Academicus* suggests that analysis should and can be profitably turned back on itself. If Michel de Certeau's assertion in *The Practice of Everyday Life* that we are now *all* "marginalized" as consumers in a commodity culture is correct, however, then academics should view themselves as victims of hegemony as much as the peoples they study.[8] Rather than take an imaginary position outside the system, academic analysis should include the writing subject him- or herself. Thus, although my own experience is limited by my position as a white male academic, I hope that the following analysis may nonetheless illuminate ways in which cultural criticism and postmodern theory might usefully be employed in our own backyard, and academics become the subjects of their own formidable powers of analysis.

The primary source for my remarks on the structure of academic C.V.s is the MLA's own publication *A Career Guide for PhDs and PhD Candidates in English and Foreign Languages*. The *Career Guide* is most helpful, like most job-hunting guides of this sort, not in what it says, but in the examples it provides in its appendices. Appendix C contains "sample letters and forms" for a fictional job candidate. The appendices provide models for the way in which the prospective academic should fabricate his or her life, and thus these models carry important ideological messages for job candidates. The *Career Guide* warns that "these sample résumés and letters are intended only to suggest possible formats and styles," not as a hard-and-fast template.[9] Although the introduction to Appendix C suggests that diversity is possible in the land of résumés, this benevolent pluralism is subverted by the fact that there is only *one* example of each type of C.V. The model C.V.s serve as templates within which the apprentice professional should fit his or her life. The C.V.s included in the MLA's job guide indicate to the subject how he or she should "prepackage" the autobiography in order to make it acceptable to university and college hiring committees. The *Career Guide* tacitly validates the power of the university as an institution that imposes narrative structures on those wishing to enter its hierarchy in a manner reminiscent of the forms that must be filled out by those seeking entrance to a hospital or by those applying for welfare.

The dominance of the C.V. format presented in the *Career Guide* is supported by its uncanny resemblance to my own C.V. I did not have the benefit of reading the *Career Guide* either before or during my own job search. Nonetheless, the C.V. I sent out was exactly the same as the *Career Guide* sample "Curriculum Vitae: Four-Year College or University,"[10] using the same headings and the same chronological format. I learned about the C.V. from the English department where I earned my Ph.D. All prospective job candidates were given the C.V. of the person who the year before had landed the "best" job. The implicit message was that this was a model we should follow if we too wanted to obtain employment.

The C.V. thus reproduces itself through emulation; other people I have spoken to on this topic have related similar tales of being given someone else's C.V. and then modeling their own on that example. The C.V. is part of the folklore that is passed down by oral tradition within departments, but despite the informality of the socialization process at work, it is remarkably uniform across institutions. As in other professions, conventions such as the C.V. are "learned through observation of the experience of other members and through the communications of experiences, ideals, myths and hopes among other members of the group."[11] Rather than pass on a self-conscious theory about the C.V. and its function, such methods rely upon imitation and informal socialization to transmit values. It is precisely at these moments of "common sense" and unexamined practice that a theoretical perspective becomes most crucial. Although literary critics are happy to deconstruct the texts of others, they are resistant to the sort of backyard ethnography called for in this collection; analyzing the C.V. as autobiography, using the tools of cultural criticism, however, reveals the ideological messages encoded in the C.V.'s structure.

Academics are encouraged to identify themselves with their C.V.s; C.V.s are the emissaries that go out in applications for jobs, grants, and awards. If asked, most academics would probably assent to the idea that their C.V.s are their professional autobiographies, and that in them they fashion themselves for presentation to the rest of the academic community. The C.V. takes on a different meaning, however, if we consider it in the context of the Althusserian paradigm of "interpellation." In Althusser's model, ideological state apparatuses (ISAs) "interpellate" their subjects, imposing upon them their own particular images, images that help reproduce existing power relations.[12] The power of the university as an ISA is immediately apparent in the first two areas of the C.V.: the institutional address at the top of the page and the "educational background" section.

Institutional Address: Interpellation and the Power of Letterhead

Given the academic class system, the institutional address at the top of the C.V. endows those affiliated with elite universities with an immediate advantage over those who work at other institutions. In an informal poll, my colleagues, when asked what they looked at first on a C.V., answered "the institutional address" and then "the place the Ph.D. was awarded." One colleague volunteered the information that having an institutional affiliation is vitally important. One has only to consider briefly the status of independent scholars, those without jobs currently, or the ambiguous category of "adjunct" faculty to realize how important having the letterhead of an institution can be. The institutional power of universities is nowhere more apparent than in the issue of who does, or does not, get to use the university's letterhead and name on his or her correspondence. Along with the letterhead come a mailbox and a telephone number; someone without these resources is in a situation analogous to a homeless person trying to compete for jobs against those who have houses with mailboxes and telephones. The ability to use letterhead and to give an institutional address at the top of the C.V. indicates access to resources that are crucial in finding and landing a job.

Like most Americans, academics in this country would like to believe they are autonomous individuals. When any changes are proposed in academic practice, such as changes in language usage in the profession, those who do not favor change cite a threat to academic autonomy and freedom. For instance, Francine Wattman Frank and Paula A. Treichler, in the introduction to their volume *Language, Gender and Professional Writing,* quote a letter in which an outraged member of the MLA complained that the organization's statement titled "Nonsexist Usage in Scholarly Writing" has "the totalitarian scent of . . . *stylistic* bigotry" that is inimical to "true academic freedom."[13] Attempts to recognize the role of ideology or power in the daily practices of the profession are resisted as attacks on academic "freedom," a word that posits an image of the academic as an unattached and freelance intellect.[14] Like most ideals of this type, it depends on the myth of a time when academic discourse was "free" from any constraints. Such sentiments rely upon an image of "freedom" as a state in which the subject is not interpellated by any external institutional forces. This appeal to academic "freedom" is belied by the "educational background" section in my C.V. and the C.V.s of others.

Educational Background: The Bureaucratized Life Course

Marlis Buchmann argues that the elaboration of a state-sponsored educational system in Western industrialized nations has entailed the "bureaucratization" of the life history. The C.V. itself encodes this "bureaucratization" of the life history in its "educational background" section. This section relies upon a model of education in which the subject passes through a series of stages in which credentials are conferred by sponsoring educational institutions that function, in Althusser's terms, whether they are private or state funded, as ISAs. The institutionalization of an academic "career" is based upon these ISAs' increasing control over the life cycle of its citizens, so that the organization of the C.V. is attuned to a chronologically based series of steps that reveal the power of the state as embodied in the bureaucratized life course:

The state is increasingly involved in defining and enforcing the rules pertaining to the social structuring of the life course. The mode of the social organization of life thus follows the logic of state intervention. . . . the state produces a formalized, standardized, and bureaucratized life course. The more the state regulates individuals' progression through organizationally and functionally differentiated institutional domains, the more the life course assumes a bureaucratic structure. State regulation turns these [private] aspects of life into "public" life events and "public" life stages from which the noninstitutionalized elements (i.e. the "private" life course) are isolated.[15]

Buchmann's analysis corroborates Althusser's model of "interpellation" in the way that it emphasizes the subject's voluntary alignment of his or her life history within a chronological paradigm sponsored by the state. Such a view undermines the conventional distinction between "private" and "public" in both political and personal terms. The C.V. as autobiography turns the subject into a "public" artifact who has already been prepackaged in such a way as to be acceptable to a prospective employer. Far from being free, an academic has been molded by a long period of education that helps inculcate a particular set of attitudes and orientations. Academic freedom is in fact created by and dependent on the institutional power of the university. Only if one ignores the power of the institution can one view academics as free and unattached intellectuals.

The single most important aspect of this formation is the way it is standardized and bureaucratized according to a chronological model. The educational system in the United States, as in most other Western industrialized nations, is based upon chronological age. There is pressure to push students through the system based upon their age as long as they fulfill minimum skill requirements, although of course some students may be "held back." The C.V. mimics this organization both in microcosm in its "educational background" section and in its overall chronological arrangement. The chronological format of the C.V. indicates the extent to which the subject has internalized a bureaucratized image of the life course.

The *Career Guide* assumes that a C.V. is based on chronology, not upon skills. Rather than present him- or herself as having mastered certain crucial skills, the academic subject presents a chronological narrative that privileges longevity and continuity over skill. "Gaps" in employment in education are going to be glaringly obvious in the C.V., given its format.[16] This is precisely the point of its organization.

The chronological format not only helps enforce an "ideal" career trajectory against which job applicants are measured, it also creates a hierarchy based upon biological age. The chronological format helps "manage" competition within the profession by ensuring that only applicants whose careers are at a certain level will compete against one another.

Chronology in the C.V.: Education as Managed Competition

The chronological arrangement of the C.V. helps reinforce the model of an "ideal" career trajectory. In a mirror image of primary and secondary education, higher education imposes a chronological model on the progress of subjects in the educational system, and retards or speeds progress in order to conform to this model. It is possible, for instance, for a subject to finish a Ph.D. program "too fast" or "too slowly" as measured against a loosely defined conventional period of time. Either instance would cause suspicion on the part of a hiring committee, even if this suspicion has no grounding in any other criterion than that of relative speed. It also ensures that chronological structure of the profession is maintained even beyond the granting of the Ph.D.[17]

Those who are in a position to hire others therefore reinforce the existing structure of the profession by enforcing a timetable based primarily on chronology. They reinforce the importance of chronology by using it as the primary yardstick by which to measure a candidate's progress through the educational system; thus, as Smith and Watson put it in their introduction to this volume, "those acting on behalf of the institution promote an official reading of the life to fit their institutional parameters."

The notion of a "career" itself, which undergirds the chronological arrangement of the C.V. and its list of educational institutions and professional positions held, depends upon the existence of the university as an institution. Harrison C. White points out that "professionalism . . . presupposes a corporate institution or some other tangible social grounding" without which the idea of a "career" makes no sense.[18] In other words, the existence of colleges or universities authorizes the idea of a "career" by providing an institutional context for the ambitions of the subject of the C.V. The list of educational institutions attended and positions held therefore validates both the subject's career progress and the authority of those institutions listed as the appropriate site for the development of a career.

The chronological basis of the C.V. ultimately reflects the management of competition within the profession. The imposition of a chronological structure helps manage the universal competition among its members that the profession itself stimulates. The profession promotes "permanent competition" among its members for its resources, but structures that competition along lines expressed in chronological terms.[19] The MLA's annual convention itself is an embodiment of this "permanent competition." The graduate student who attends the MLA convention knows that he or she is potentially in competition with every other graduate at the meeting. He or she is not, however, in competition with the associate or full professors because of the system of "temporal distances" and the awards dispensed based upon this distance.[20] The refusal to consider untenured applicants for senior or endowed positions also helps maintain a chronological hierarchy and discourages competition among those at different "levels" in the career trajectory.

To structure one's C.V. according to chronology is, therefore, to align oneself with this strategy of managing competition among the members of the profession. Constructing one's C.V. and one's subject position in this way indicates that one is willing to enter the profession on its terms and to play the game according to the chronological allocation of resources.[21] It also makes it easy for those who receive the C.V. to decode it according to their expectations and to lay it alongside the other hundreds of similar documents they read as members of admissions committees. If I were to decide to arrange my C.V. idiosyncratically, by following, say, Roland Barthes's model of a roughly alphabetical autobiographical narrative, I would expect my application to be rejected.[22] It would simply take too much effort for the reader to reconstruct the narrative embedded in the C.V. along chronological lines, and the extra effort involved would negate any advantage I might gain by implicitly demonstrating my originality by disregarding professional conventions. In doing so, I would in any case have drawn attention to myself as someone who might not accept the established hierarchy.

The subject who adopts the chronological format of the C.V. signals a willing internalization of the demands of the profession and of the university. The C.V. indicates one's status as a "good" subject and one's identification with the norms of the institution. To violate the chronological structure would be to position oneself as what Michel Pecheux terms a "bad" subject and to express disidentification with and resistance to the norms of the profession.[23] Although academics praise resistance in others, Richard Ohmann's analysis of the MLA indicates that dissidence within the profession's own ranks and criticism of its daily practices is labeled "unprofessional."[24]

The C.V. and the Class System

It is unsettling in the context of the C.V. and academia to invoke hierarchy. Education in the United States is often viewed as promoting the meritocracy, so that busing or other ways of mixing students in schools are proposed as ways of eradicating, or at least ameliorating, class differences. Hierarchies reintroduce the class differences that we professional educators are all supposed to be busily replacing with merit and hard work. However, the educational system is not exempt from the wider power relations of society, and in fact reproduces them in its practices, as Bourdieu and Passeron have argued.[25] From their perspective, education actually reproduces the conditions under which existing power relations can continue to exist, thus radically overturning the image of education as breaking down class or race barriers.

The *Career Guide* reconstructs the educational hierarchy by the way in which it contrasts the C.V. appropriate for four-year colleges, that appropriate for community or junior colleges, and the business résumé.[26] The C.V. for four-year universities has a category for "dissertation" but does not have a category for "other work experience." The assumption is that four-year colleges will be interested primarily in a candidate's research, but not interested in any nonacademic work experience. I internalized this ethic when I put together my own C.V., and made no mention of my brief career as a technical writer. This had no "relevance" to the jobs for which I was applying.

The assumption governing the community college model is a mirror image of that governing the four-year college C.V. It is assumed that research will be irrelevant, the person's time being taken up primarily with teaching, whereas work experience will be an asset. The community or junior college C.V. gives only the dissertation title and no description of its content. These assumptions rely partly upon judgments about the students at these institutions; students at four-year universities tend to be relatively free, or at least until recently felt themselves free, of vocational considerations and can consider themselves to be buying a "liberal education" that does not align them with any particular form of work. Students at community colleges, it is assumed, need to be given skills that translate immediately into job-related demands.

Larson, in her analysis of the professions, suggests that "the socio-economic status of the client . . . influences the professionals' *own* status and ranking."[27] This innocuous-sounding proposition turns the internal ranking of universities and colleges by the profession on its head. Although within the profession the standing of a university or college is presented as an effect of the productivity and fame of its faculty and the corresponding approbation of colleagues, this standing actually derives from the socioeconomic status of the students in the subject's institution. The *clients* of those who teach them establish the teachers' social status, rather than the informal ranking system of the profession itself.

The distinction in the C.V. between community colleges and four-year colleges and universities underscores the way in which academic professionals are themselves interpellated by the class system. If one teaches students from wealthy backgrounds, one's own "professional" standing will be increased. Professional status derives, therefore, not from some internal system of reward but directly from the class structure of American society. This class structure is dutifully reproduced by hiring committees as they allocate jobs based upon the professional prestige of applicants' sponsoring institutions.

Like doctors, professors encourage a mystique that distances them from their clients as sources of revenue and frame their labor in terms of a higher spiritual calling. Professions are colleague oriented rather than client oriented,[28] but this focus on colleagues rather than clients is at odds with the actual basis for academic prestige. If the real basis for a faculty's prestige were recognized, the current vaunting of research over teaching would have to be reversed, but to emphasize teaching would of course be in conflict with the image of professors as free-floating intellects, beholden to no particular institution or group of clients for their income.

Academic professionals simply follow other professionals in their strategies for controlling the terms of their own labor. It is much more palatable for all concerned to appear to be responding to demands for one's work generated by the profession rather than by students as clients. This strategy is mirrored in the academic C.V., where a great deal of attention is paid to publications, presentations, and professional activities, and relatively little to teaching. The focus when hiring candidates for university positions is almost exclusively on a job candidate's "promise" as a potential publisher of scholarly articles and books. The "publications" section of the C.V. thus becomes the most important aspect of the C.V. for four-year colleges and universities.

Publications: Individualism and Scholarly Production in the C.V.

A number of recent articles on literary criticism as a "profession" have analyzed insightfully the tension within English departments over theory and its place within critical practice. The debate over theory has been generated by the contradiction between a humanist commitment to a general, nonspecialized image of the literary critic performing work that is accessible and understandable to some fictional general public and an image of the literary critic as a professionalized worker in a distinctly defined area of expertise. Whatever the terms of the debate, Paul Lauter's acerbic summary of the current situation underlines the ways in which such debates promote the careers of individuals and maintain the status of literary criticism as a profession:

> The practice of literary theory in no sense challenges the individualistic, production-oriented forms of the American academy; like other forms of critical production, the work of theorists can easily be measured (so many articles, books, or citations in other works) and displayed to appropriate authorities. And it helps maintain a hierarchical relationship between the privileged discourse of the academy and practical criticism, mainly carried out in the classroom.[29]

Although this summary is overly cynical in its reduction of the motives of those who profess theory to self-interested career goals, it is a salutary corrective to the detachment that characterizes most academic debates. Books, articles, and papers are not just items on a C.V., but also tokens that can be redeemed at one's own institution, or a competing institution, for more salary and benefits, more travel and equipment money, or, ideally, all four at once. This frame is never acknowledged overtly in the presentation of papers at conferences or in articles on literary theory and other topics.

Lauter notes in passing the individualist basis of assessment in the academy. This individualism is nowhere more apparent than in the "publications" section of the C.V. Lisa Ede and Andrea Lunsford, in the introduction to their book *Singular Texts/Plural Authors,* relate the difficulty they experienced in trying to convince their colleagues that they should receive credit on their C.V.s for having cowritten a text.[30] True to its nineteenth-century origins, the ideology that governs autobiography defines writing as a form of individual property right that gives an individual sole claim to a text.[31] When a text has more than one author, as in Ede and Lunsford's case, it belongs to nobody. Texts in the C.V. can be owned only by one person in an approach to literary texts that, as George Landow points out, "emphasizes individuality, separation and uniqueness."[32] This ideology bears no resemblance to how texts are actually written. Scholarship is in fact a collaborative enterprise, but it is represented in the C.V. as the product of individual minds working in isolation.

The C.V. represses not only collaborative labor, but also the class, racial, or gender status that has contributed to a particular subject's positioning within the profession. The C.V. represses the body and encourages the complete identification of the subject with "pure" intellect as embodied in the "publications" section. The *Career Guide* indicates, however, that biology threatens to erupt into the C.V. whether the profession likes it or not.

Professional versus Private: Ideological Conflict in the C.V.

As the *Career Guide* makes clear, biology once played a crucial role in determining how one's C.V. was received:

> Information on age, marital status, number of children, health, ethnic or national origin, and religious affiliation is sometimes found on a vita. It is inappropriate, and indeed in most instances illegal, for potential employers to ask candidates for such information. It is not illegal for the candidate to volunteer it. . . . Obviously, however if most candidates provide such information as a matter of course, the purpose of the policies and laws—to prevent unfair discrimination—will be frustrated.[33]

This carefully balanced rhetoric, couched almost entirely in the passive voice, signals one site of ideological conflict in the C.V. On the one hand there is the model of the "free" candidate, volunteering information to a prospective employer on his or her initiative. On the other hand there is the tacit acknowledgment that employees are relatively powerless compared with employers. Although information such as the gender of the applicant has been used by employers to discriminate against women, it is difficult for job applicants to withhold information or to know how such information is going to be used.

The *Career Guide* comes down on the side of repressing information on one's marital status, number of children, ethnic origin, health, and religious beliefs. This catalog of possible identities is revealing, however, in the way it makes explicit those identities excluded from the narrative constructed in the C.V. Bruce Robbins has argued perceptively that "while exercising our profession, we simultaneously occupy overlapping and conflicting institutions, and these institutions (families, classes, churches, political parties, and so on) generate conflicting and overlapping values that make conflicting and perhaps 'unprofessional' claims on us."[34] The crucial word here is "conflicting": these other identities conflict with the "professional" subject constructed in the C.V. and threaten to destabilize its categories.

To return to my opening statement, academics are "institutionalized." Academics are not, however, inmates of a single institution. Like other subjects, they participate in many institutional identities simultaneously. As "professionals," academics repress many of these identities as irrelevant to their daily practices. Robbins's analysis suggests that if one mobilizes these other "unprofessional" identities, then one may highlight areas of ideological conflict in the C.V. and in the profession itself.

A recent example of how personal narrative can be mobilized to highlight ideological conflicts within the profession is bell hooks's *Talking Back: Thinking Feminist, Thinking Black*. In this autobiographical volume, hooks questions academic daily practice precisely because she speaks self-consciously from her perspective as both female and black.[35] She is led, for instance, to question why teachers with an avowedly radical agenda would teach in an authoritarian manner, and how following a liberatory pedagogy is perceived within the university "as threatening the maintenance of hierarchical status" by colleagues.[36] hooks's refusal to repress her biological, ethnic, and political positions generates the threat to hierarchy perceived by colleagues. The identities she mobilizes are "unprofessional" in the terms established by the MLA, but it is in the ideological conflict between "professional" and "private" identities that those who follow a liberatory agenda may find a way to question the hierarchies maintained by the current configuration of the academic C.V.

Notes

1. For instance, in Nancy Schuman and William Lewis, *Revising Your Resume: Career Blazers* (New York: John Wiley, 1987), the authors list the following options: a chronological résumé, a functional résumé, and a form that combines elements of both (3–5).

2. See Jim Merod, *The Political Responsibility of the Critic* (Ithaca, N.Y.: Cornell University Press, 1987), chap. 4. Merod calls for the articulation of the relationship between literary criticism as work and contemporary corporate structures, because "knowledge is a product of institutions, of institutionalized activities" (103). The C.V. is one of these "institutionalized activities."

3. Richard Ohmann, *English in America: A Radical View of the Profession* (New York: Oxford University Press, 1976); and *Politics of Letters* (Middletown, Conn.: Wesleyan University Press, 1987).

4. Jonathan Dollimore, *Political Shakespeare: New Essays in Cultural Materialism* (Ithaca, N.Y.: Cornell University Press, 1985), viii.

5. Pierre Bourdieu, *Homo Academicus,* trans. Peter Collier (Stanford, Calif.: Stanford University Press, 1988), xii.

6. Bourdieu represents others as the victims of ideology while implicitly situating himself outside of the system he is analyzing. As his syntax above implies, he views the subjects of his study as "products" of "determinants," not as agents. There seems little space in Bourdieu's analysis for a concept of resistance to determination by "structures" and "determinants," as Deborah Reed-Danahay argues in "The Kabyle and the French: Occidentalism in Pierre Bourdieu's Theory of Practice," in *Occidentalism,* ed. James G. Carrier (New York: Oxford University Press, 1995).

7. Michael Moffatt has carried out an ethnographic study of Rutgers University in *Coming of Age in New Jersey* (New Brunswick, N.J.: Rutgers University Press, 1989), but he focuses on undergraduate culture. Clifford Geertz, in *Local Knowledge: Further Essays in Interpretive Anthropology* (New York: Basic Books, 1983), calls for ethnographic study of academic practices. Geertz compares the career pattern in anthropology with the organization of the army and the Catholic Church. As Geertz says, "So far as I know, no one has investigated the consequences for thought of this peculiar pattern" in academic careers (159).

8. Michel de Certeau, *The Practice of Everyday Life* (Berkeley: University of California Press, 1984).

9. Modern Language Association of America, *A Career Guide for PhDs and PhD Candidates in English and Foreign Languages,* rev. English Showalter (New York: Modern Language Association of America, 1991), 79.

10. Ibid., 81.

11. Julius A. Roth, *Timetables: Structuring the Passage of Time in Hospital Treatment and Other Careers* (Indianapolis: Bobbs-Merrill, 1963), 100.

12. See Louis Althusser, *Lenin and Philosophy and Other Essays* (London: New Left,

1971). Terry Eagleton draws upon an Althusserian model when, in *Literary Theory: An Introduction* (Minneapolis: University of Minnesota Press, 1983), he says that "departments of literature in higher education, then, are part of the ideological apparatus of the modern state" (200).

13. Francine Wattman Frank and Paula A. Treichler, *Language, Gender and Professional Writing: Theoretical Approaches and Guidelines for Nonsexist Usage* (New York: Commission on the Status of Women in the Profession, Modern Language Association of America, 1989), 27.

14. Bruce Robbins, in his introduction to *Intellectuals: Aesthetics, Politics, Academics* (Minneapolis: University of Minnesota Press, 1990), notes caustically that "a discussion centered on the ideal of universality without ties, on intellectuals as unattached and disembodied . . . could easily appear to occupy a realm of male fantasy" (xvii–xviii). In this instance, the male fantasy is threatened by feminism.

15. Marlis Buchmann, *The Script of Life in Modern Society: Entry into Adulthood in a Changing World* (Chicago: University of Chicago Press, 1989), 17.

16. Schuman and Lewis emphasize that in the chronological format "data are highlighted and the writer must be aware of any obvious gaps in one's work history." *Revising Your Resume*, 4.

17. Bourdieu points out that "because of the fact that the accumulation of academic capital takes up time (which is evident from the fact that the capital held is closely linked with age), the distances . . . are measured in time, in temporal gaps, in age differences. It follows that the structure of the field is perceived by the agents in the form of an ideal career . . . against which all other trajectories are objectively measured. The agents tend to associate with each of the major stages of this itinerary, which is also an obstacle race and a competitive examination, a normal age of access, with reference to which one might appear young or old at any (biological) age." *Homo Academicus*, 87.

18. Harrison C. White, *Identity and Control: A Structural Theory of Social Action* (Princeton, N.J.: Princeton University Press, 1992), 22–23. Magali Sarfatti Larson, in *The Rise of Professionalism: A Sociological Analysis* (Berkeley: University of California Press, 1977), similarly suggests that the idea of a career "closely binds the projected self to organizations or to the institutions which ensure 'continuity' in status in a labor market" and that, "subjectively, career is a pattern of organization of the self" (229). Having a career thus binds one to the institutions listed on the C.V. and organizes the construction of self encoded in the C.V.'s categories.

19. Bourdieu notes that, thanks to the chronological structure of academic professions, "far from containing the threat of a permanent revolution, the struggle of each against all which this permanent competition stimulates among those who have entered the race, and who have the competitive dispositions both required and reinforced by the race, contributes its own logic to the reproduction of the order as a system of temporal distances." *Homo Academicus*, 87.

20. Adam Westoby, in "Mental Work, Education and the Division of Labor," in *Intellectuals, Universities and the State in Western Modern Societies*, ed. Ron Eyerman, Lennart G. Svensson, and Thomas Soderquist (Berkeley: University of California Press, 1987), links mental labor, bureaucratization, and temporal delay in his analysis of the division of labor within professions. He asserts that in a bureaucracy, "middle and lower functionaries are already equipped by initial education for the higher posts they aspire to. What separates them are those infuriating intangibles of time and experience. They are wedded by avocation to the worldview that rational bureaucratic organization can accomplish most things. . . . Yet their day-to-day experience is dominated by the showering down of irritants, problems and delays" (141). This is a perfect description of the experience of a graduate student in a Ph.D. program.

21. Bourdieu states pessimistically that "the very fact of competing implies and elicits recognition of the common objectives of the competition." *Homo Academicus,* 88. He apparently sees no way of avoiding interpellation by the profession as soon as one sets about constructing a C.V.

22. See Roland Barthes, *Roland Barthes by Roland Barthes,* trans. R. Howard (New York: Hill & Wang, 1975).

23. Michel Pecheux, *Language, Semantics and Ideology* (New York: St. Martin's, 1982).

24. Ohmann, *English in America* and *Politics of Letters.*

25. Pierre Bourdieu and Jean-Claude Passeron, *Reproduction in Education, Society and Culture,* 2d ed., trans. Richard Nice (London: Sage, 1990). Michael W. Apple, in *Ideology and Curriculum* (London: Routledge, 1979), has analyzed schooling "as part of a system of mechanisms for cultural and economic reproduction" (11).

26. MLA, *Career Guide,* 83, 87.

27. Larson, *The Rise of Professionalism,* 221.

28. Ibid., 226.

29. Paul Lauter, "The Two Criticisms: Structure, Lingo, and Power in the Discourse of Academic Humanists," in *Literature, Language and Politics,* ed. Betty Jean Craige (Athens: University of Georgia Press, 1989), 8

30. Lisa Ede and Andrea Lunsford, *Singular Texts/Plural Authors: Perspectives in Collaborative Writing* (Carbondale: Southern Illinois University Press, 1990), ix–x.

31. I give an account of this history in Martin A. Danahay, *A Community of One: Masculine Autobiography and Autonomy in Nineteenth Century Britain* (Albany: State University of New York Press, 1993).

32. George P. Landow, *Hypertext: The Convergence of Contemporary Critical Theory and Technology* (Baltimore: Johns Hopkins University Press, 1992), 90.

33. MLA, *Career Guide,* 17.

34. Robbins, *Intellectuals,* 3.

35. bell hooks, *Talking Back: Thinking Feminist, Thinking Black* (Boston: South End, 1989). Carolyn Steedman, in *Landscape for a Good Woman: A Story of Two Lives* (London: Virago, 1986), mobilizes her identities as an academic professional, working-class child, and feminist to critique class hegemony in Britain in much the same way hooks critiques racism in *Talking Back.*

36. hooks, *Talking Back,* 69.

16 / (For)getting a Life: Testimony, Identity, and Power

William Chaloupka

It is as if, finally, something new were emerging in the wake of
Marx. It is as if a complicity about the State were finally broken.
Foucault is not content to say that we must rethink certain notions;
he does not even say it; he just does it, and in this way proposes new
co-ordinates for praxis. In the background a battle begins to brew,
with its local tactics and overall strategies which advance not by to-
talizing but by relaying, connecting, converging and prolonging.

GILLES DELEUZE, *Foucault*[1]

One of the ways Michel Foucault broke the "complicity about the
State" was to emphasize the settings, purposes, and power associated
with our individual, everyday activities. One of the most important of
those activities, he suggested, is how we tell the stories that, in turn,
compose our "life." The varieties of testimony we offer to others and
to ourselves constituted an increasingly central role in Foucault's
analysis, eventually informing not only his groundbreaking description of the self, but also his discussion of contemporary power.

These issues of identity and power reshaped Foucault's entire project. Throughout the 1970s and until his death in 1984, he addressed
power as an issue, criticizing excessively general approaches. He studiously avoided theorizing a confrontation between "Power with a
capital P, a kind of lunar occurrence, extra-terrestrial," on one side,
and "the resistance of the unhappy ones who are obligated to bow before power" on the other. Such analyses, Foucault argued, were "com-

pletely false." Instead, "power is born out of a plurality of relation-ships which are grafted onto something else, born from something else, and permit the development of something else."[2]

Accordingly, Foucault shifted his attention from power as such to the practices onto which power relations were grafted. When *the practices of power* became the issue, Foucault's clarity emerged as a discursive strategy with a particular plot. If power acts broadly while still residing in marginal settings—if it extends through the social body and individual identities in unexpected ways—the most effective practices of power now take the form, "differing from time to time, of a series of clashes which constitute the social body."[3] Rather than hypothesizing a rational field within which we exercise tactics, Foucault came to understand power in terms of its diffuse and particular moments: "Power, then, is something like the stratification, the institutionalization, the definition of tactics, of implements and arms which are useful" in all the particular, often marginal, clashes that occur over the question of identity.[4]

Such odd lists dot Foucault's landscape. Their discontinuity reminds us that complicity is trickier to oppose than is a state, a class, or an abstract notion of power. Ever attentive to that "complicity about the State," as Deleuze called it, Foucault privileged the thick contingency imparted by events themselves. That move was precarious, opening Foucault to charges of political evasion. But there is no necessary evasion implied by Foucault's project, only an altered political map. The act of composing oneself as a self—the autobiographical impulse—is important on its own terms. But then that compositional practice sediments into other realms, into institutions and power relations. Testimony, for instance, becomes a feature of courts and police stations. Each site and act is in contingent relation to other sites and acts. At the end of the contingent sequence, the power of the state comes to rely on practices Foucault called tactical sedimentations or stratifications of successful, diffuse institutional acts.

Foucault's strategy was based on his judgment—then novel, now obvious—that such practices and relations are crucially important. Our acts of autobiographical telling spread, incorporating themselves throughout social life. There are many ways to understand this telling, but Foucault emphasized political readings. Power has shifted and now operates through the practices of autobiographical telling, even if we tellers never intended to invite power into our stories, practices, and lives. This mode of power is relatively new, as Foucault demonstrated through his genealogical studies. But despite this novelty, the relationship between telling and power is still hard to see. It has taken on the obviousness of a natural process.

Foucault's concern about this operation of power pervaded his historical studies, each of which aimed to make seemingly obvious practices appear as problematic moves, constructions that deserved a much more prominent role in social criticism. To make the ordinary seem newly strange, Foucault—perhaps more than any other great political thinker—relied not on the dominant events of the day, but on odd and marginal examples of social and institutional practices. He pursued these odd examples for an explicit reason: in these often strange case studies, the "pre-recited," "framed-up" quality of contemporary power (operating through practices of identity-production) might start to emerge.

In this essay, I consider an extended example that I think resonates with some of Foucault's themes. In the example, the state's power functions (with some brutality, because it is out of proportion) primarily to constitute a criminal subject (introduced in the first section). The second section connects my example to Foucault's attempts to write about power, identity, and modern subjects in one of his archival studies (*I, Pierre*). The third section and conclusion relate this discussion to issues of social analysis and the politics that now gathers around notions of identity.

Hood River John Doe

When a man comes before his judges with nothing but his crimes,
when he has nothing else to say but "this is what I have done,"
when he has nothing to say about himself, when he does not do the
tribunal the favor of confiding to them something like the secret of
his own being, then the judicial machine ceases to function.
          MICHEL FOUCAULT, "The Dangerous Individual"[5]

The story first appeared in the local section of a midsummer's weekday issue of Portland, Oregon's, daily newspaper.[6] The reporters and editors obviously felt they had a funny, screwball crime story. The subhead promised a "strange-but-true" case. The headline read "Doesn't Anybody Know Who Nobody Is?" The story began:

Later this month, as complete a nobody as Hood River County Sheriff Richard J. Kelly has ever run across in his 26 years of policing will be sentenced for stealing a car. The crime is almost incidental to the man's refusal to identify himself. And because police have been unable to identify him and establish a criminal history, John Doe could be a free man after a July 21 sentencing hearing.[7]

The story's lead divulges that a number of assumptions and prejudgments are already in play. It establishes the issue of identity (with the odd formulation, "as complete a nobody"), affirms the minor character of the "almost incidental" crime, and still fits the story fully within a genre we know, crime coverage, with recognizable police practices such as sentencing hearings and investigations into criminal histories.

"John Doe" had been arrested nearly three months before and had "politely challenged authorities to try to find his true identity, insisting that the efforts [would] be in vain." Sounding like a man whose official responsibilities were drawing him across uncharted turf, the jail commander said, "He's kind of a likable guy, except that he won't tell us anything."[8] Foucault could have explained to the commander, I suppose, why "likability" and "telling" might be related; he argued that the judicial system now functions by creating a certain kind of individual on which to operate. A prisoner who narrates his own story (to prosecutors, jailers, and, eventually, parole officers) provides material the system needs. In exchange, the system's operators can extend their appreciation; they like a guy who "cooperates," who joins them in operating the system.

The police at Hood River, a sailboarding resort and timber town on the Columbia River, had not taken this silence passively. It is not too much to say that they struggled against it. They circulated photographs to newspapers and fingerprints to the FBI and Royal Canadian Mounted Police. The chief suggested a failure of communication and surveillance practices might be the problem: "a lot of two-horse police departments" fail to fingerprint all arrestees. For his part, Doe communicated clearly enough, listing his address as the address of the Hood River County Courthouse on the requisite paperwork. The DA reported that the trial was unremarkable, except that they did not know whom they were trying.

[County Sheriff] Kelly said the irony of the situation is that Doe would probably have been out of jail already had he cooperated with authorities. Without a past, no one could determine if Doe was a risk to flee the area. . . . He was found guilty June 22, becoming the only unidentified person in the recent memory of law enforcement officials to actually be convicted as an unknown person.[9]

Already, we see that the *Oregonian* did not entirely grasp the story it was telling. Not quite close enough to the police, the newspaper thought Doe might "be a free man" soon *because* "police have been unable to identify him and establish a criminal history." Their own news story, however, quotes the sheriff admitting that Doe would probably be out already "had he cooperated." Something odd is afoot here, something that puts the reporters slightly off track.

We can speculate about the reason for their confusion. In the naive, commonsense version of the criminal justice system, all we would care about is the fairness of arrest, trial, verdict, sentence, and perhaps rehabilitative strategies. A concern about identity seems out of place. In the old westerns—some no doubt set near Hood River—the sheriff cares little what the drifter calls himself. The sheriff does not need that information to escort the rascal to the city limits and point to the horizon. But, as the westerns also tell us, times have changed. Now, if the suspect refuses to identify himself, the system cannot function as fully as its operatives believe it should. As Foucault helps us to understand (even if it seems to baffle the *Oregonian* reporters), Doe's reluctance prevents the criminal justice system from doing what it is supposed to do.

In short, the job of jailers is not only to incarcerate, but also—perhaps more so—to *know* prisoners, as an adjunct to the even more central requirement that prisoners know themselves. Setting subjects (suspects, selves) onto the project of knowing and controlling themselves has become a key site for the operations of power.[10] This is a development of no small consequence for both institutions and individuals, whose autobiographical impulse prepares them for and, sometimes, marks their entry into a disciplinary grid that promotes some constructions of self and discourages others. In a thoroughly humanist, professional, and modernist mode of operation, a huge governmental apparatus sets out to find (e.g., create) suspects, then

374 / William Chaloupka

track their identity, then implicate them into a courtroom drama, followed by yet more tracking through prison or parole. It may not be excessive to suggest that this elaborate dance of identity, testimony, surveillance, and behavior buffers us from a recognition of the astounding facts of the scope of this social intervention.[11]

In this case, Doe is not important because of his action (the car theft) so much as for his refusal to enter this process of creating himself as a prisoner. Hood River John Doe hooded himself, refusing to enter the game of identity and control. He could be remarkable only as an unknown, an effect of the case that the *Oregonian* writer did understand and report.

> There are no "John Does" in the entire federal prison system, except for those whose identities are being kept secret as part of the witness protection program. The state of Oregon also has no recent record of a true John Doe inmate. "I can't recall ever going completely through a trial with a John Doe," said [Portland area] District Attorney Mike Schrunk, who is now in . . . his 16th year as a prosecutor in the state's most populous county. [A] spokesman for the state Corrections Department said people have gone through court sentencing with multiple identifications but never as an unknown.[12]

Deprived of cooperation, the Hood River authorities were left to their own inept attempts to psychologize this odd offender. The DA guessed that Doe might be hiding from some facet of his personal life, or that "the guy has a little hangup on principle."[13] The DA's befuddlement is obvious. Whipping up a psychological explanation for a serious offender is now routine police practice. Doing the same for a car thief with no verifiable criminal record breaks that routine, however strangely. The testimony—the autobiography—essential to begin the criminal justice system's processes was missing, and its absence was notable.

Foucault understood that constituting prisoners as subjects had become an important practice in the tactical—and, because tactical, also contingent—field of power. A prisoner who would not explain himself was a special case, an exception that provides a glimpse of the tactical field. Accordingly, Foucault studied records of nineteenth-century criminals who would not or could not articulate their "reasons." In one instance, the accused responded to questions with steadfast silence, eventually leading a juror to exclaim, "For heaven's sake, defend yourself." The accused's silence was one of those revealing episodes that mapped the judicial system's most important mechanisms. "The accused evades a question which is essential in the eyes of a modern tribunal, but which would have had a strange ring to it 150 years ago: 'Who are you?'" As Foucault explained, the courtroom dialogue "shows that it is not enough for the accused to say in reply to that question, 'I am the author of the crimes before you, period. Judge since you must, condemn if you will.' Much more is expected of him. Beyond admission, there must be confession, self-examination, explanation of oneself, revelation of what one is."[14]

"Who am I?" "What am I doing here?"—these are autobiographical questions raised to the level of parody by Admiral James Bond Stockdale, Ross Perot's running mate in the 1992 presidential election. But these questions were not always so deeply entrenched that they could be parodied. Foucault's historical examples found recalcitrant trial subjects whose reluctance lets us see, in retrospect, that a new, detailed, and sophisticated rationality had begun to form. This new logic made some "inexplicable" crimes into treatable offenses and provided a basis for the adjustment of criminal law, which in turn further elaborated the new arrangements. Through practices associated with that new rationality, the unspeakable recedes and new patterns of thought become almost inescapable.

Recounting these events, Foucault noted the emergence of professional psychiatry but also pointed to broader political and institutional change. The prosecutors in Foucault's story "obstinately referred to the law: no *dementia*, no *furor*, no recognized evidence of derangement; on the contrary, perfectly organized acts; therefore, the law must be applied." The law—a literal and, until then, stable system—did not explicitly require that crimes be explained in terms of motivation. But it no longer seemed possible for the system to avoid the issue of where criminal behavior came from. "No matter how hard [the prosecutors] tried, they could not avoid the question of motivation, for they knew very well that from now on, in practice, the judges would link punishment, at least in part, to the determination of motives."[15]

As the modern criminal justice system was assembled—in this odd, often indirect, tactical and sedimentary way—prosecutors came to understand that they were now operating on a criminal "self." The institutional and cultural effects of this shift began to spread, under the sign of humanized, professional law enforcement. Police networks developed, as did closer surveillance of urban space, more efficient prosecution of minor delinquency, and a popular literature of criminology in newspapers and detective novels. A collective fear of—and fascination with—crime was inscribed on the body politic itself. That enchantment now pervades the politics, entertainment culture, styles of fashion, and other consumer choices of U.S. society, even in towns and neighborhoods where there is little objective reason to be so engaged.

In Foucault's genealogy of this system's emergence, the resistant prisoners offer unusual marks of progress. Unwilling to answer the "Who are you?" question, momentarily exposing the gathering practices of new power relations, these exceptional prisoners cause the judicial machine to cease functioning, if only momentarily. During that brief, awkward pause, these cases offer a glimpse of what unexpected and new kinds of cooperation that machine requires to keep going.[16] The system's primary enterprise is to monitor and mold offenders in a normalized, everyday manner. The system no longer works, as it once had, by reminding royal subjects of its sovereign monopoly on enforcement.

Even if only for a moment, Hood River John Doe caught the system off guard when he resisted the project of constituting himself. However silly his case, and however temporary the effect, Doe still confounded Hood River's judicial mechanism. Even the standard presentencing report posed problems. The contents of police records "are usually based in part on a family and criminal history profile of the offender," but those variables were unavailable in Doe's case.[17] To announce that a car thief had been apprehended and punished quite severely would have made for a very brief—and unprofessional—report.

Doe's was a "human interest" story, which is what we call news items that are somehow intriguing but lack serious connection to more legitimate news.[18] The implications of his actions were trivial, involving only a few news stories and an extra boarder in the Hood River jail. His crime was not mass murder, but car theft; the spectacle comes around this time as farce. Even in this entertaining diversion, however, the newspapers and police were compelled to issue a reminder: even trivial criminals must tell us who they are, becoming subjects who confess, testify, and examine reasons. They need to cooperate—to operate the system with their jailers, with whom they form a team that establishes identities for them as individuals who will participate in their re-constitution as parolees.

(By so thoroughly defining the system in terms of the management of "telling," the system also, inevitably, creates the opposite case as confirmation and reflection of its commitment. So, some suspects are pointedly prevented from telling, and this condition, too, carries special weights and impacts, as Louis Althusser has detailed at length in a commentary on his own situation.)[19]

As serious as all these components of disciplinary power—confession, testimony, cooperation with parole restrictions, and so on—are for the person subjected to them, this seriousness may not in itself vindicate Foucault's emphasis of such practices as the keys to contemporary power. Critics much more comfortable with moral denunciation of the traditional, sovereign power of the state have resisted Foucault's move, claiming that it diminishes our capacity for political response. Indeed, in his early work, Foucault himself had employed a broader, more polemical style in denouncing the old conception of the state. But that denunciation did not satisfactorily break the odd complicity around the state, which is how Deleuze describes the grid of obligations, privileges, practices, and constraints that supports the state and makes its task of governing easier than it otherwise would be. As satisfying and familiar as broad denunciation might be, it still failed.

Subsequently, Foucault increasingly emphasized archival studies, those odd genealogies of criminal testimony and other institutional practices. His intent in pursuing such studies was to move the analytic level toward specifics and examples, and away from abstract denunciation. For those readers he reaches, Foucault's approach provides a brief, glimmering glance into contemporary power's operations.

Still, even after Foucault has taught us to see the practices he emphasized, skeptical readers might resist his analysis of those practices. Crime is dangerous, such a skeptic might insist. And any calculus of the damage that disciplinary practices might cause, balanced against the dangers of crime, will favor the crimes. In Doe's case the offense is so trivial that it lets us bracket the danger, lets us set it aside to consider whether discipline can also be seen as independent of the crime that supposedly justifies it. At the same time, the example may also bring the complexity of autobiographical enterprises into sharper focus by reminding us that the act of autobiographical telling has roots and functions crucial to the operations of contemporary power.

The statistics on parole and prison are frightening, but those numbers stay at arm's length; they do not quite get through to us. An overt injustice (such as a death row inmate's almost being executed before someone else's confession absolves him) does draw attention to judgment and the character of penalties; but such episodes are sporadic and in the end may even help the system justify itself. Doe lets us see something else; this is what the prison system really wants. It *wants* Kafka's interminable trap of information and introspective self-creation. The system knows how to foster identities as a form of complicity with the state apparatus. This is no longer secret or guilty; it is what the enterprise is about, in a dull, boring, everyday way. Only something as marginal as the Doe case lets this important development surface, and then only fleetingly.

I, Pierre . . .

You claim to excuse your crimes by saying, which is absurd and impious, that they were ordered by God; confess rather that, being unluckily born with a ferocious character, you wished to steep yourself in the blood of your mother whom you had long abominated, whom you abominated above all after she had conceived the idea of obtaining a separation from your father's bed and board.
      examining judge's first interrogation of Pierre [20]

Foucault studied several instances of confession in criminal justice systems amid transition, constantly linking the juridical practices of testimony—of autobiographical telling—with the practices of identity-creation that would become so important to modern power. The overtly insistent question quoted here was posed by the first prosecutor in the case reported in Foucault's *I, Pierre Rivière, having slaughtered my mother, my sister, and my brother . . . A Case of Parricide in the 19th Century.* As in my (much less gruesome) example, this study involved a prisoner who would not confess in a form consistent with the practices of his time. Pierre's confessions trick the authorities and their explanations. The first prosecutor was obviously unwilling to accept the self-descriptions Pierre originally offered. For his part, Pierre has one more story left to tell.

Pierre continues to invoke God, but the examiner returns to his question. "So far you have tried to deceive the law, you have not given truth its due. . . . so tell us frankly . . . , what cause could have led you to murder your mother, your sister, and your brother." This time Pierre complies:

> I wish no longer to maintain the system of defense and the part which I have been acting. I shall tell the truth, I did it to help my father out of his difficulties. I wished to deliver him from an evil woman who had plagued him continually ever since she became his wife, who was ruining him, who was driving him to such despair that he was sometimes tempted to commit suicide. I killed my sister Victoire because she took my mother's part. I killed my brother by reason of his love for my mother and my sister. (pp. 23–24)

The examiner concludes his report abruptly: "Here the accused gives in an orderly and methodical manner a very detailed account which lasts for over two hours. . . . Rivière promises to communicate to us in writing what he has stated" (p. 24).

Pierre's written account forms the body of Foucault's book. The lucidity of Rivière's story only exacerbates the tensions generated by his instantaneous turnaround. The system had to explain both the lucidity and the transformation. The pretrial judge was openly surprised. Pierre's account was logical, written in a manner of which "he could certainly not have been supposed capable" (p. 44). The document contains "a sketch of the character of the accused . . . , drawn with a vigor which is simply astonishing and makes it most regrettable that Rivière has by an atrocious act rendered henceforth useless to Society the gifts so liberally imparted to him by nature" (p. 45). The judge went on to list those gifts: "a remarkable memory, a great aptitude for the sciences, a lively and strong imagination coupled with an eagerness for instruction and the achievement of glory" (p. 45). The prosecutor moved more quickly to simple declaration:

> Rivière is not a religious monomaniac as he tried to make out at first; nor is he an idiot, as some witnesses [supposed]; so that in the eyes of the law he can only be regarded as a cruel being who has followed the promptings of evil, because, like all heinous criminals, he stifled the voice of conscience and did not struggle hard enough to control the propensities of his evil character. (p. 40)

Foucault explained that he had spent so much time on the case because it seemed "unique among the printed documentation" (p. viii).
The case itself generated little interest; there were several cases of parricide yearly in that period. The case did not become a classic of criminal psychiatry, as others of the period did. Pierre's counsel, who was
later well known, seems not to have written about it. As Foucault
noted, there were good reasons to think that Pierre's case should have
received more attention in its own day. It was important enough to
document, and it occurred just as the debate over the use of psychiatry
in criminal justice was producing a discourse still recognizable to us
today. But instead of engendering further discussion and reinterpreta-
tion, the Rivière dossier found "an immediate and complete silence,"
prompting Foucault to ask, "What could have disconcerted the doctors and their knowledge after so strongly eliciting their attention?"
(p. ix).

Foucault's response to that question confirms Deleuze's reading of
Foucault's notion of contemporary power. The Rivière example is "a
case, an affair, an event that provided the intersection of discourses that
differed in origin, form, organization, and function" (p. x). The case
provides more opportunities for Foucault's strange lists, odd mis-
matches (and near matches) that carry the rhetorical force of his claims
about multiples. The case's many participants, with their many purposes, exemplify multiplicity. Each discourse addresses Pierre's act.
"But in their totality and their variety they form neither a composite
work nor an exemplary text, but rather a strange contest, a confrontation, a power relation, a battle among discourses and through discourses. And yet, it cannot simply be described as a single battle" (p. x).

Foucault's explanation is carefully posed. Several struggles and several modes of writing convene in the Rivière example, while still remaining distinct and specific. The case carries the multiplicity theme
well enough, but Foucault still found it necessary to remind contemporary readers how to read it so that its strangeness can emerge. Criminal psychology had developed as a practice at the time of the Rivière
case, even though, as Foucault explained, this practice is absent from
the case. By now, that psychological discourse is fully established; we
are so comfortable with "depth psychology" readings of criminal behavior that the odd silence Foucault carefully explained seems im-
probable, at best. But Foucault was not writing about psychology as
such, and was certainly not proposing a Dionysian fascination with

transgressive hatred as motive (either for himself or for Pierre). Such a reading of Foucault's project misses his point completely.[21]

Foucault was interested in explaining how the relations of identity and institutional practices emerge in the Rivière case. The very theatricality of the judicial process makes possible an exercise of power that might otherwise seem endangered by the "excuse" psychology can offer. At the end of a trial—"this great juridico-psychological liturgy"—the participants in the ritual can *act*. "The jurors finally accept this enormous thing: to punish with the feeling that they have accomplished an act of social security and public health, that one deals with 'evil' by sending a fellow to prison for five years. The incredible difficulty of punishing someone is dissolved into theatricality. It doesn't function badly at all."[22] The spectacle becomes central, not only as misdirection and publicity, but also as the sediment of power relations, their form. Only when these arrangements are put under stress—in the trivial Hood River case or the infinitely more grave Rodney King case—can we see how fully the scene has been arranged.

Technologies of Identity

I deal with obscure figures and processes for [a reason]. The political and social processes by which . . . societies were put in order are not very apparent, have been forgotten, or have become habitual. They are a part of our most familiar landscape, and we don't perceive them anymore. But most of them once scandalized people. It is one of my targets to show people that . . . things that are a part of their landscape—that people think are universal—are the result of some very precise historical changes. All my analyses are against the idea of universal necessities in human existence. They show the arbitrariness of institutions and show which space of freedom we can still enjoy and how many changes can still be made.
                    MICHEL FOUCAULT, "Truth, Power, Self"[23]

Foucault's attention to style in his writing and analysis has been much commented upon. In the Rivière book, Foucault repeatedly and eloquently (always eloquently) praised Pierre's lyricism, going so far as to suggest that his advanced seminar spent a year studying this obscure case for no better reason than "simply the beauty of Rivière's memoir" (p. x).

Responding to Foucault's lyricism, French sociologist Jean Baudrillard earned Foucault's lasting enmity with an essay Foucault read as backhanded praise. Baudrillard's transgression was to claim that

"Foucault's writing is perfect in that the very movement of the text gives an admirable account of what it proposes." That writing "flows, it invests and saturates, the entire space it opens. The smallest qualifiers find their way into the slightest interstices of meaning; clauses and chapters wind into spirals. . . . There's no vacuum here, no phantasm, no backfiring."[24] Baudrillard argued that Foucault's lyrical writing mystified both itself and its objects, shutting off the quest for a language that could actually dissolve itself—that could represent the change it also advocated.

Deleuze, on the other hand, reads Foucault's clarity as a strategic choice, a component in the effort to make a particularly subtle aspect of power visible. As Deleuze reminds us, Foucault continually used diverse and minor examples—amid the near epic ones—to underscore that point. "Far from operating in a general or appropriate sphere, the power-relation establishes itself wherever individual features, however tiny, are to be found."[25] In short, Foucault pursued marginal examples, then applied his lightning eloquence to them—and both moves were part of a specific and intentional writing strategy. The mismatch, then, was not a residue of Marxist praxis (Baudrillard's concern) or of liberal practice (Richard Rorty's opportunity). Instead, Foucault's strategic choices redirected his project, and did so for clear, explicitly stated reasons.

The Rivière case forms an odd and scrambled origin, a site of contestability that remained unspoken, not because it contained too simple a truth—a taboo—but because it contained multiple struggles around the issue of truth. Foucault's rehabilitation of Rivière struggles to reclaim the sense of surprise the case must have evoked in its own time. Power had been at work, since Pierre's day, bringing the autobiographical impulse (the confession, in this case) more fully into "the system." Testimony and confession—autobiographical impulses we now regard as utterly normal—became insinuated in a court system, also in a normal, everyday, habitual way. Court TV now makes just as much sense for evening viewing as sitcoms or ball games. Foucault's use of Rivière's story shows how that normalizing pattern relates to discipline and thus to crucial contemporary operations of power.

Deleuze emphasizes that this is not simply a matter of listening to one voice or another, or of choosing a prisoner's view over the collective wisdom sedimented in a court system. In other words, Foucault did not simply choose "the multiple" over "the one." Instead, he altered their relationship, allowing his reader to examine the regulatory logic of multiples in ways neither dialectical nor essentialist. In a move rife with implications for the current American debate about multiculturalism and identity politics, Foucault's work does not simply introduce multiplicity and contingency in order to pose "the problem of a subject who would think through this multiplicity, give it conditions, account for its origins, and so on."[26]

Instead of falling into such a domesticated view of the subject, Foucault showed how language continually reasserts ambiguity and indeterminacy, while simultaneously enabling the construction of seemingly stable identities. Foucault managed to write without granting undue privilege to either "one" (the analyzing self) or "multiple" (contingent events), in the sense that either would have "recourse to a consciousness that would be regulated by the one and developed by the other."[27] No regulatory principle solves such paradoxes in the long run, but the political struggles set off by identity and event remain lively and relevant. Indeed, they intensify in the absence of such a regulatory logic.

Foucault's account of the Rivière case exemplifies a kind of writing that recognizes this ambivalent quality of language while still maintaining a political edge. The Rivière book contains the entire criminal justice system, but in a multiple, contested, discursive way. This is the form of emergence Baudrillard often invokes. The case contains the whole system, metonymically, but still remains partial, evading a settled explanation, or rather bringing any such explanation into play. Foucault explains that he published the Rivière dossier "to draw a map, so to speak, of those combats, to reconstruct these confrontations and battles, to rediscover the interaction of those discourses as weapons of attack and defense in relations of power and knowledge" (p. xi). A metaphorical analysis—one that presents a model, a dynamic, a set of unified and characteristic practices—explains events too straightforwardly. Metonymy is not so clear; the judicial "system" itself, in this case, points to something other than a system, in the clearest structural or modernist sense. Foucault's example draws just such a map. Without making claims about human nature or consciousness or any general material condition, Foucault still locates a point of emergence for practices that now carry crucial power relations.

Foucault's approach helps untangle some binds operating in our political discourses about crime. Liberals fall into the trap of emphasizing the "causes" of crime, which means they reify the confession, insofar as it addresses origins. Thus, "cause" collapses into the application of power, the operations that inscribe the effects of power onto the criminal's self. Far from opening up the structural or socioeconomic aspects of crime, the liberal ends up inviting institutions to extend their power by normalizing its disciplinary techniques. Conservatives, on the other hand, can criticize the liberal bind as a weak excuse for intolerable criminal behavior. That criticism has been hugely successful, surely in part because it follows the discursive structure of the liberal position.

For their part, conservatives make a spectacle of long, mandatory prison sentences—terms that are "spectacular" precisely because they are now effectively disconnected from any hypothesis of treatment or moral rehabilitation. In doing so, conservatives reclaim an old impulse—their rage at the convict, an emotion Foucault thought had been permanently displaced by the humanistic reforms of the previous century. But this time the conservatives do not propose to draw and quarter; instead, they express their rage by producing exorbitant versions of incarceration and parole supervision, the "humanist" systems whose emergence Foucault's analyses expose. The humanist justifications have simply become less important now that there are other ways to manage the potential backlash that any given drive to power might generate. Political advantage finds less and less need to apologize or explain.

One consequence of recent discursive collaborations between the liberal and conservative positions is an ever more stable disconnection between crime and power. Mandatory sentences and sentencing guidelines deliver a criminal who was abused as a child into a penal and parole system at the same time that therapeutic discourses multiply around child abuse. Spectacular cases (the Menendez brothers case, for example) function to publicize abuse and generate new opportunities for power to act, without generally deterring the increasingly expensive and inhumane movement to "get tough" on crime by passing measures such as "three strikes" legislation.

If a crime involves drugs—in fact, even when it does not—the response prescribes surveillance (as in drug testing) or disciplinary techniques of drug avoidance. Circumventing the discretion of judges, new sentencing laws sometimes seem to mock the calibration of a crime's damage to the punishment levied against a convicted criminal—a calibration Foucault saw as central to the supposed humanization of the system. At the same time, a precise calibration is established in schools and workplaces, grading the progressively increasing seriousness of drinking, drunk driving, alcoholism, and drug use of each specific kind—concluding with the maliciously calibrated provisions of increasingly federalized drug laws.[28] In the case of crimes against women, typical responses emphasize the mythos or therapeutics of family—an abusive history absolves one suspect, a defensive urge to punish in the name of a victimized family sends another to jail. In neither case is the equality of women a response that satisfies the criminal justice system. No matter what the specific crime, a search for "cause," if unaccompanied by an interest in power, displaces our attention further into discipline and spectacle.

Even if it courts the eloquence Baudrillard criticizes, Foucault's odd and rigorous intervention transforms our understanding of the system. His approach remained tenaciously and studiously multiple—simultaneously local and diffuse, grand and trivial, serious and silly, said and situated. In such an analytic setting, the importance of the negotiations undertaken by Pierre and Doe begins to emerge. Pierre could negotiate the conditions (the timing, form, and medium) of his testimony. Our problem is related to his, but is more serious. To have a name is already to have been placed on a grid of education, record of imprisonment, good credit (or bad debts), military service, and health care treatments, mental or physical. Those steps onto the grid are simple and obvious.

Soon, the only imaginable resistance possible may be the (vain and futile, but perhaps notable) denial that one even has a name. Freedom shrinks one more time, finally swallowing anyone who claims it. The free are not absorbed in the violence of anarchy, this time. Instead, they implode, pursuing anonymity as freedom's last stand. But the nameless trickster has, at best, only fleeting effect, and perhaps ends up only reminding us of the anonymity of all the "named" prisoners. Still, the trickster sends out a message, in the short moment he has our attention. There is drama here. After all, the joker-to-be-named-later might turn out to be a terrorist, a spy, an artist; each is more free than the citizen. The free, in an astounding reversal, are the anonymous, the ones who might yet intervene in the process of their own naming or categorization.

The Rivière case reveals some connections between autobiographical telling and the institutional setting that was forming at the time. The diffusion of power—the contests surrounding it, composing it—become visible in Foucault's account. But Rivière's case faded from the literature of criminology, which sought to make each of its practices seem normal, obvious, and transparent. On the other hand, Hood River John Doe's intricate disappearing act surely comes to us near the conclusion of this project's trajectory through late modernity. Only profound, needless, and inarticulate silliness will even be notable, now that the pieces are all in place. In other words, there are serious (but not grim) reasons for these odd experiments in displaced and mal-practiced analytic rhetoric, for Baudrillard's giddiness or Foucault's lyricism.

"John Doe" Resolved

This is what we end up doing, he thought. Spying on ourselves. We are at the mercy of our own detachment.

DON DELILLO, *Libra* [29]

The Hood River John Doe case does have a conclusion, and it is just as farcical as Baudrillard might have predicted. Two days after the first story appeared, a follow-up reported that a wire service dispatch printed in Minneapolis had solved the police's problem. Doe's father—himself a judge and former DA—recognized his son from the photograph.[30] In a moment of minor triumph, the *Oregonian* ran Doe's mug shot again, this time with the name Brent Slattengren attached, under the headline, "John Doe Unable to Hide Identity from Father." The mystery man was actually a University of Washington graduate student in geology who had either faked his own death or failed at a suicide attempt ten days before his arrest. With (media) light speed, Slattengren had already been reunited with his wife of two years, a psychology student whose photograph appeared, in color, on the front page of the *Oregonian*.

The Slattengren example—hardly a case that would have been relevant to any previous social theory—illustrates a break. This is a new genre of the social absurd; hardly angst-ridden, the example instead seems flat, frivolous, or, in Baudrillard's term, giddy. But Slattengren's marginality helps make the point. Having heard that Doe has a name—that he fits on the grid—we relax. The drama has been generated by the tension of naming Doe, an action that places him fully within the system, accessible to sentence and treatment. Without the name, without a self at stake, the court could not judge; it adjudicates, sentences, and treats a self, not simply the perpetrator of an act. The court requires more than evidence to take action; it requires a sense of historical terrain and the individual's place on that map. Once named, Slattengren fits; a judgment can be rendered—by us, as well as the magistrate at Hood River.

Still, for a brief moment, Doe had been nameless *and* visible—beyond judgment, but still sending signals—a postmodern trickster. Slattengren marks the transition from Kafka or Camus to Wapner or Mason. His case works at the level of Foucault's serious examples, exposing patterns that link institutions as diverse as incarceration, education, and medicine. In his immaterial irrelevance, before he was named, Doe provided a start toward a genealogy of the cynical, hyperreal, public relations society that postmodern theorists take so seriously.

But Doe did not cause the system to cease functioning; in that sense Foucault overstated the effects a recalcitrant prisoner might have. Power relations quickly relearn how to function, even after the practices that compose these relations have met resistance; the political project can hardly aspire to decenter power any more than power has already learned to decenter itself, for its own purposes.

This explicitly political problem is closely related to the issues of sign and referent that contemporary literary criticism addresses. It is not only the flood of images that leads us toward the giddy, postsocial posture assumed by the postmodernists. The character of signs has changed, not only the number of these signs that pervade modern life. As Deleuze notes, the break at the center of Foucault's *Discipline and Punish*—the departure from the king's body as the central signified event in politics—initiates a process whereby the referent breaks free from any signified in the political world, in the functioning of power as it is experienced by citizens of contemporary societies.[31] The absence of the signified is possible to understand (and has its unique character) as a process where layers of sayability and visibility sediment, letting language function without ever producing a signified. At the end of the process, Murray Edelman has suggested, the process goes spectacular.[32] Social habits dissipate in spectacle and velocity, taking an unpredictably broad range of institutions out with them.

In such a situation, how one writes and tells about oneself—in autobiography, testimony, confession, and all other such practices—

becomes an unavoidably political issue. It was no fit of obliviousness that led Foucault to turn the analytics of liberty inside out, denying that liberty conceptualized as an essential force results in a *larger* field of freedom: "I do not think that there is anything that is functionally— by its very nature—absolutely liberating. Liberty is a practice." Projects remain, aiming to "modify some constraints, to loosen, or even to break them."[33] In fact, Foucault's work intensified such projects; only a perverse reading could conclude that his work disabled politics.[34] There is no reason to limit politics to the sphere of universal rights and legalisms, nor is it sensible simply to privilege the autobiographical enterprise without recognizing the ways power works through even the simplest expressions of identity.

Is Doe an exemplar of identity politics? No, of course not. His case opens possibilities for political inquiry, when viewed from the angle established by Foucault and others. Such analysis emphasizes the interaction of identity-creation and legal practice, fueling skepticism about the police and court institutions that have been regarded—by scholars as well as citizens—as generally professional, largely trustworthy guardians in an uncertain world. In a country that is inventing ever harsher penalties and ever more lavishly funded police squads, the complaint that Foucault's analysis implies the end of punishment sits blithely—no, smugly—by while we become a nation of prisoners and imprisoners, collapsing every political or social struggle into a demand for more jails, more discipline, and ever more studious (and absurd) inattention to power's actual effects and techniques.

Any politics that forms on the basis of such an analysis will be marked by its attention to contingent events, rather than by its certainty and confidence. In that sense, too, the Hood River case is illustrative, as was Pierre's. Soon after his name was discovered, Slattengren was sentenced to ninety days in jail and was promptly released on probation, as he had already served far more than ninety days. The judge also ordered Slattengren to pay $145 to the owner of the pickup truck in which he was found, to undergo a psychiatric evaluation, and to perform 150 hours of community service. Once incorporated back into the system, Slattengren again became invisible.[35]

Refusing to participate in his own identification, Slattengren placed himself, for just a short time, in a blank spot that intensifies the arguments, trends, and tendencies Foucault discusses. Slattengren's intervention is temporary; the middle-class son of a judge, he surely knew his play would not run forever. Sitting amid other prisoners, perhaps held briefly at Hood River before being moved to more serious prisons, he must have known how small (perhaps even selfish) his gesture was. But in a classic reversal of terms, his small, temporary gesture reminds us how impossible it is for all prisoners to escape a deeper, systematic anonymity. How does one develop an identity amid such powerful forces of displacement? To rephrase Jacobo Timmerman, it is not only prisoners of overtly inhumane detention systems who are nameless; every modern subject of incarceration is a prisoner without a name, in a cell without a number.

How few prisoners we remember by name—as prisoners, not as holdovers from their theatrical trials. There are political prisoners, such as Timmerman or Nelson Mandela, publicized by Amnesty International or in the context of political struggles. Martin Luther King, Jr., Gandhi, Gramsci, and other famous prisoners appropriated the jail as a stage, but even they seldom publicized and named their cell mates in any lasting way. Much the same is true of former prisoners, such as Malcolm X, who move into other political contexts. A few prisoners are picked up by the publicity machines—Bob Dylan's Hurricane Carter, *The Thin Blue Line*'s Randall Adams, and of course Willie Horton. It is an oddity in itself that as a country we can have so many prisoners, and can be adding so many more, and still can remember so few names.[36]

This is no "failure to communicate," as suggested in the story of one famous movie prisoner; it is a triumph of discipline and the manipulation of prisoner identity. Hood River John Doe's expressive silence—his temporary escape from identity—briefly illuminates how power now works, how successfully it captures and rearranges the seemingly simple, unproblematic fact of having an identity and expressing it. The mode of analysis invented by Foucault and amplified by Deleuze carries with it a potential response to those new modes of power. Finding new and odd examples, we evoke the possibility of a politics attentive to domination and matched to circumstances in which freedom might still be practiced. Such a postmodernism would not carry the rejection of politics—it would signal its reemergence.

Notes

1. Gilles Deleuze, *Foucault,* trans. Sean Hand (Minneapolis: University of Minnesota Press, 1988), 30.

390 / William Chaloupka

2. Michel Foucault, "Clarifications on the Question of Power: Interview Conducted by Pasquale Pasquino," trans. John Johnston, in *Foucault Live: Interviews, 1966–1984*, ed. Sylvére Lotringer (New York: Semiotext[e], 1989), 187.

3. Ibid., 188.

4. Ibid. See also Deleuze, *Foucault*, 75.

5. Michel Foucault, "The Dangerous Individual," in *Michel Foucault: Politics, Philosophy, Culture: Interviews and Other Writings, 1977–1984*, ed. Lawrence D. Kritzman, trans. Alan Sheridan et al. (New York: Routledge, 1988), 151.

6. Michael Rollins, "Doesn't Anybody Know Who Nobody Is?" *Oregonian*, 12 July 1989, C-1, C-10.

7. Ibid., C-1.

8. Ibid.

9. Ibid.

10. The specific way prisoners know themselves has not always been hidden or obvious. Indeed, earlier in U.S. history it was a focus of public discussion, perhaps even forming an alternate site for the moral formation of American culture. See Thomas L. Dumm, *Democracy and Punishment* (Madison: University of Wisconsin Press, 1987).

11. The other buffer, of course, is racism. On scope, see Marc Mauer, *Young Black Men and the Criminal Justice System: A Growing National Problem* (Washington, D.C.: Sentencing Project, 1990). On method, see Robert Gooding-Williams, *Reading Rodney King: Reading Urban Uprising* (New York: Routledge, 1993).

12. Rollins, "Doesn't Anybody Know Who Nobody Is?" C-10.

13. Ibid.

14. Foucault, "The Dangerous Individual," 126.

15. Ibid., 138.

16. Ibid., 142.

17. Rollins, "Doesn't Anybody Know Who Nobody Is?" C-10.

18. Murray Edelman explains: "As if to paper over their inattention to daily life, the media devote considerable attention to one kind of public event that they present as a private one: the human interest story. . . . Human interest stories are political events because they reinforce the view that individual action is crucial: that biography is the paramount component of historical accounts." *Constructing the Political Spectacle* (Chicago: University of Chicago Press, 1988), 99.

19. Louis Althusser, *The Future Lasts Forever: A Memoir* (New York: New Press, 1993), especially chap. 2. Althusser notes Pierre's case and discusses several of Foucault's themes.

20. Michel Foucault, ed., *I, Pierre Rivière, having slaughtered my mother, my sister, and my brother . . . A Case of Parricide in the 19th Century*, trans. Frank Jellinek (Lincoln: University of Nebraska Press, 1982), 21. Further quotations from this text will be cited by page numbers in the body of the chapter.

21. James Miller, *The Passion of Michel Foucault* (New York: Simon & Schuster, 1993), makes just this mistake, as Miller is unable to get beyond issues of transgressive psychology. In the case of Pierre, Miller seems consumed with intrigue about the criminal character: "What a character to be captivated by!" (225). And Miller *is* captivated. Foucault, on the other hand, repeatedly poses the issue as the "coexistence of [a criminal's] madness and [the] rationality" of social systems (*I, Pierre*, 273). This is not the same thing as the internal struggle, within the self, between madness and rationality. For Foucault, "The theoretical (as well as political) stake at issue [is] whether and in what way rationality could be criminal and how it all, crime and knowledge, could be 'borne' by what was called the 'social order'" (*I, Pierre*, 273). Miller is so captivated by Pierre

that he misses that political point, exclaiming that Foucault calls him "a 'tragic' hero" and italicizing his protest that Foucault thinks that Pierre's "*crime ends up not existing anymore*" (228). But Foucault's entire argument involves the many disappearances Pierre was subjected to by a legal process in transition. Foucault is clear and emphatic; Pierre's case is interesting precisely because such a notable case disappeared—not from its victims or their friends, but from history and public view.

22. Foucault, "The Anxiety of Judging," in *Foucault Live: Interviews, 1966–1984,* ed. Sylvére Lotringer (New York: Semiotext[e], 1989), 173–74.

23. Michel Foucault, "Truth, Power, Self: An Interview with Michel Foucault, conducted by Rux Martin," in *Technologies of the Self: A Seminar with Michel Foucault,* ed. Luther H. Martin, Huck Gutman, and Patrick H. Hutton (Amherst: University of Massachusetts Press, 1988), 11.

24. Jean Baudrillard, *Forget Foucault* (New York: Semiotext[e], 1987), 9–10.

25. Deleuze, *Foucault,* 28. Baudrillard's commentary on Foucault may not be entirely incompatible with Deleuze's. Baudrillard did locate Foucault's excessive clarity, but he can also be read as presenting an alternate reading strategy. His critique could be ironic; Foucault's "meticulous outpourings," his scene of "flawless writing" finally—perhaps only too late—reminds us that "truth" is not at stake. Indeed, Baudrillard explicitly grants Foucault this: "Foucault's discourse is no truer than any other. No, its strength [is] in the analysis which unwinds the subtle meanderings of its object, describing it with a tactile and tactical exactness, where seduction feeds analytical force and where language itself gives birth to the operation of new powers." Baudrillard, *Forget Foucault,* 10. See Calvin Thomas, "Baudrillard's Seduction of Foucault," in *Jean Baudrillard: The Disappearance of Art and Politics,* ed. William Stearns and William Chaloupka (New York: St. Martin's, 1992), 131–45.

26. Deleuze, *Foucault,* 14.

27. Ibid., 14. The spatial tropes Deleuze and Foucault use have a specific importance: "Multiplicity is neither axiomatic nor typological, but topological" (14). Foucault's move—which Deleuze identifies as the "most decisive step yet taken in the theory-practice of multiplicities"—becomes more obvious when Deleuze moves it into the even more familiar discourse of the "global," "local," and "diffused" (14). Deleuze summarizes: "'Local' has two very different meanings: power is local because it is never global, but it is not . . . localized because it is diffuse. . . . Foucault's functionalism throws up a new topology which no longer locates the origin of power in a privileged place, and can no longer accept a limited localization (this conception of social space . . . is as new as that of contemporary physics and mathematics)" (26). Deleuze's chapter "Foldings, or the Inside of Thought" convincingly applies the topological even to Foucault's epistemology, at the very center of his project (94–123). As Paul Bové notes in his introduction to Deleuze's book, this Foucault—Deleuze's Foucault—"is entirely different from Jameson's or Taylor's" (xxvi). On multiplicity and language, see Michel Foucault, "Maurice Blanchot: The Thought from Outside," in *Foucault/Blanchot,* trans. Brian Massumi and Jeffrey Mehlman (New York: Zone, 1987), 53–58.

28. See Dan Baum, "The Drug War on Civil Liberties," *The Nation,* 29 June 1992, 886–88.

29. Don Delillo, *Libra* (New York: Penguin, 1988), 18.

30. Michael Rollins and Jeanie Senior, "John Doe Unable to Hide Identity from Father," *Oregonian,* 14 July 1989, A-1, A-12.

31. Deleuze, *Foucault,* 47.

32. See Edelman, *Constructing the Political Spectacle,* especially chaps. 1, 2, and 7.

33. Michel Foucault, "An Ethics of Pleasure: Interview Conducted by Stephen Rig-

gins," in *Foucault Live: Interviews, 1966–1984*, ed. Sylvére Lotringer (New York: Semi-otext[e], 1989), 264.

34. Deleuze writes harshly of those who deny the possibility for such a politics: "Three centuries ago certain fools were astonished because Spinoza wished to see the liberation of man, even though he did not believe in his liberty. . . . Today new fools, or even the same ones reincarnated, are astonished because the Foucault who had spoken of the death of man took part in political struggle. . . . This is not the first time an idea has been called eternal in order to mask the fact that it is actually weak or summary." *Foucault*, 90.

35. "Mystery Man from Seattle Is Released on Probation," *Seattle Post-Intelligencer,* 24 July 1989, B3. A search of newspaper databases for 1989–92 found no further mentions of Slattengren in the Seattle or Portland newspapers.

36. A telling counterexample is the prison (and postprison) autobiography of Nathan McCall, *Makes Me Wanna Holler: A Young Black Man in America* (New York: Random House, 1994). One reviewer, Adam Hochschild ("A Furious Man," *New York Times Book Review*, 27 February 1994, 11–12), wished McCall "had waited a bit longer to write," as if the experience of crime and imprisonment could not be enough of a basis for autobiographical treatment.

Epilogue: Pieces of My Heart

Julia Watson

At an advanced stage of preparing the essays for *Getting a Life*—when I felt more like it was taking my life—one day my wallet was stolen. Because we have somewhat mobile, disorderly lives, it wasn't the first time something had disappeared. But this time I noted with interest how the loss of identity cards undermined me—not my sense of identity, but my practice of it in everyday situations.

A day and a half on the phone shutting down credit cards and getting annoyed because the Touch-Tone system asks for a card number to process the call. Identity is recursive. Calls to 800 numbers for the car and health insurance companies. Rifling through drawers for an expired driver's license and old ID cards, souvenirs of past lives. Pleased when I found my birth certificate, more legit than anything else I now had. But I couldn't cash checks with it—no photo. Identity is recursive. The worst was trying to remember what else was in the wallet. Had I cashed the reimbursement check? Left anything at the cleaner? What pieces of my life would be on hold for months because I had forgotten they were there? Identity is recursive.

For weeks there were times when I would suddenly stop and remember another missing piece of myself. Public library cards. A kindergarten photo of my son. A few times I reached for the card requested—a frequent flier number, a gas credit card—only to realize with embarrassment that it wasn't there. It made me feel strange—like being in a foreign country where people stare at you because, no matter how you try to fit in, little gestures give you away. Passing for a citizen, but you're not quite right.

How do they know who I am till they see what my cards say?

I read an article on "Customer Impersonation." The news is that someone who has stolen a driver's license or social security card can have store accounts set up to buy things—Buy Now, Pay Later—in the name on the cards. When the purchases go unpaid, central credit bureaus get a bad report on the card owner—unpaid debts, loans, ripoffs. This impersonation can extend years into the future and can wreck the credit of the customer. The article concludes that little can be done other than to complain to credit agencies that the cards are not "you." If somebody has your identity—they have the fun, you pay the bills. Like a double in a Poe story.

How do they know it's not me when they see the cards? Even if they do, who cares when a quick sale is at stake? The impersonator in the article bore little resemblance to the picture on the driver's license and misspelled the name when she signed for a diamond ring. How much of identity is having it in hand?

Or in someone else's hand. In Detroit, the home of innovative crime, it has happened: "Stella Sproule's family can't accept that she was killed only for her good name. Police say Annie Lee Cole wanted Sproule dead in order to steal her identity and put her own troubled past, including bad-check charges and a parole violation, behind her" (*Missoulian,* June 2, 1994, A-10). Cole, who had Sproule killed in order to use her credit cards, posed as the victim's sister to arrange her cremation. Police intervened—that time. The plot of a dime-store detective novel, updated nineties style—identity-jacking.

The postmodern fantasy—becoming someone else. Identity in motion. AKA.

Contributors

Linda Martín Alcoff teaches philosophy and women's studies at Syracuse University. She is coeditor, with Elizabeth Potter, of *Feminist Epistemologies* (1993), and her *Real Knowing* is due out in 1996. Her essays on epistemology, Foucault, and subjectivity have appeared in *Signs, Cultural Critique, Philosophical Forum, Hypatia,* and other journals. For several years she has also been active in the movement to decrease sexual violence.

Philip E. Baruth is assistant professor of English at the University of Vermont. His work on biography and autobiography has appeared in *Modern Language Quarterly, Biography,* and *The Age of Johnson.*

H-Dirksen L. Bauman is a visiting faculty member in the English Department at the National Technical Institute of the Deaf at the Rochester Institute of Technology. He is currently writing his dissertation on American Sign Language literature at Binghamton University (SUNY).

Michael Blitz is associate professor of English at John Jay College, City University of New York. With Louise Krasniewicz, he has published and/or presented a number of projects on cyborgs, dreams, e-mail, narrative, and posthumanity. He has also collaborated with C. Mark Hurlbert on a book, *Composition and Resistance,* and on many articles and chapters dealing with culture, higher education, and academic rhetoric. He is the author of three books of poetry, most recently *Five Days in the Electric Chair*. He is currently living in Brooklyn, New York, and is, to his ongoing wonder and delight, the father of Daina and Cory, the two greatest children ever born since the beginning of time.

Traci Carroll is assistant professor of English at Rhodes College. She received her Ph.D. from Northwestern University in 1992. She has written on Pauline Hopkins and Harriet Jacobs, and her work in progress includes an exploration of the literary intersections between queer theory and African American theory. She is currently completing a book-length manuscript on race, gender, taste, and consumer culture in the late nineteenth century titled "Subjects of Consumption: Race and the Discourse of Taste in Nineteenth-Century America."

William Chaloupka teaches political science at the University of Montana. His *Knowing Nukes: The Politics and Culture of the Atom* and *In the Nature of Things: Language, Politics, and the Environment* (coedited with Jane Bennett) have been published by the University of Minnesota Press. With Williams Stearns, he coedited *Jean Baudrillard: The Disappearance of Art and Politics*. His articles have appeared in *International Studies Quarterly, Policy Studies Journal, Environmental Ethics*, and elsewhere. He is currently at work on a study of cynicism in American politics.

Salome Chasnoff has recently completed her Ph.D. in performance studies with a certificate in women's studies at Northwestern University. Her dissertation on the performance of birthing was itself autobiographically inspired and informed. She is a performer, video maker, educator, and political activist who works with Women in the Director's Chair, an alternative media arts organization based in Chicago.

Kay K. Cook is associate professor of English and associate department chair of language and literature at Southern Utah University. She has published articles and frequently gives presentations on issues of women's health, specifically breast cancer. Her other areas of research and publication are nineteenth-century British romanticism and autobiography studies. She is also a playwright.

Martin A. Danahay's identities include, but are not limited to, nonpatriarchal father of two children, associate professor of English at Emory University, straight-but-not-narrow male, British subject, and baseball fanatic. His name appears on the title page of a book published in 1993 called *A Community of One: Masculine Autobiography and Autonomy in Nineteenth-Century Britain.* Copies of his C.V. are available upon request.

Laura Gray-Rosendale is a doctoral student in the Humanities Department at Syracuse University and a teacher of rhetorical studies and composition theory. She is also a cofounder of a campus support group for survivors of sexual abuse and is committed to the project of producing theoretical work that is valuable and accessible to a variety of audiences.

Linda S. Kauffman is professor of English at the University of Maryland, College Park. She is the author of *Discourses of Desire: Gender, Genre, and Epistolary Fictions* (1986) and *Special Delivery: Epistolary Modes in Modern Fiction* (1992) and editor of *Gender and Theory, Feminism and Institutions* (both 1989), and *American Feminist Thought at Century's End* (1993). Her contribution to this volume is part of a forthcoming book, *Bad Girls and Sick Boys: A Secret History of Sex in Fiction, Film, Performance.*

Louise Krasniewicz has a Ph.D. in anthropology and an M.A. in media and technology. Her research focuses on conflict and identity in American culture, and on the relationships among bodies, the cinema, and new technologies. With Michael Blitz, she is writing a book and designing a CD-ROM about cultural responses to Arnold Schwarzenegger. She is also exploring alternative multimedia forms for presenting academic research to general audiences, and is currently exhibiting works in photography, digital imagery, and digital video. She resides in Santa Monica, California, and is the delighted mother of the best son ever created, Drew Robert.

Helena Michie is Professor of English at Rice University and is the author of *The Flesh Made Word: Female Figures, Women's Bodies* (1987) and *Sororophobia: Differences between Women in Literature and Culture* (1993). She is currently at work, with Naomi R. Cahn, on a book on the policing of the reproductive body. She has written frequently on Victorian studies, feminist theory, and contemporary popular culture and is interested in the Brontës, the Judds, ice-skating, and bathroom doors.

Sandra Patton is a doctoral candidate in American Studies and the recipient of a graduate certificate in women's studies at the University of Maryland, College Park. She served as the assistant director of the Curriculum Transformation Project's Faculty Summer Institute for three years at UMCP, where she has taught both women's studies and Afro-American studies. She is coauthor, with Bonnie Thornton Dill and Maxine Baca Zinn, of "Feminism, Race, and the Politics of Family Values" (*Report from the Institute for Philosophy and Public Policy*, Fall 1993). Her dissertation is an interdisciplinary ethnography of transracial adoption. She is a 1995-96 recipient of an American Fellowship from the American Association of University Women.

Janice Peck is associate professor in the School of Journalism and Mass Communication at the University of Colorado in Boulder. A cultural critic who explores the ways social and political issues are embodied in mediated popular culture forms, she is the author of *The Gods of Televangelism: The Crisis of Meaning and the Appeal of Religious Television*. Her work on religious programming and television talk shows has appeared in *Journal of Communication Inquiry*, *Cultural Critique*, and *Communication Theory*.

Sidonie Smith is professor of English and comparative literature at Binghamton University. She is the author of *Where I'm Bound: Patterns of Slavery and Freedom in Black American Autobiography* (1974), *A Poetics of Women's Autobiography: Marginality and the Fictions of Self-Representation* (1987), and *Subjectivity, Identity, and the Body: Women's Autobiographical Practices in the Twentieth Century* (1993); coeditor, with Julia Watson, of *De/Colonizing the Subject: The Politics of Gender in Women's Autobiography* (University of Minnesota Press, 1992); and coeditor, with Gisela Brinker-Gabler, of *Writing New Identities: Gender, National, and Immigration in Contemporary Europe* (University of Minnesota Press, forthcoming). She is currently completing a book on women's travel narratives titled *Unbecoming Women: Mobility, Modernity, Mechanics*.

Robyn R. Warhol is professor and director of women's studies at the University of Vermont. She is the author of *Gendered Interventions: Narrative Discourse in the Victorian Novel* (1989) and coeditor of *Feminisms: An Anthology of Literary Theory and Criticism*, with Diane Price Herndl (1991), and *Women's Work: An Anthology of American Literature*, with Barbara and George Perkins (1994). She has published essays on feminist narratology in *Style, Novel,* and *PMLA,* among other journals. Her current project is to develop a poetics of serial narrative.

Julia Watson is professor of liberal studies and director of women's studies at the University of Montana. She is coeditor, with Sidonie Smith, of *De/Colonizing the Subject: The Politics of Gender in Women's Autobiography* (University of Minnesota Press, 1992). Her essays on women's autobiography, theory of autobiography, and Montaigne have appeared in collections as well as in *a/b:Auto/Biography Studies* and other journals. She is currently working on a study of self-decolonization in women's autobiographical writing and experimenting with personal narrative.

Susan Ostrov Weisser is associate professor of English at Adelphi University. She is coeditor, with Jennifer Fleischner, of *Feminist Nightmares: Women at Odds* (1994) and of *Craving Vacancy: Women and Sexual Love in the British Novel, 1740-1880* (forthcoming).

Index

Compiled by Suzanne Sherman Aboulfadl